MEDIEVALISM

Medievalism

THE MIDDLE AGES IN MODERN ENGLAND

MICHAEL ALEXANDER

YALE UNIVERSITY PRESS
NEW HAVEN AND LONDON

Published with assistance from the Annie Burr Lewis Fund.

For information about this and other Yale University Press publications, please contact:

U.S. Office: sales.press@yale.edu   www.yalebooks.com
Europe Office: sales@yaleup.co.uk   www.yalebooks.co.uk

Typeset in Minion Pro by IDSUK (DataConnection) Ltd
Printed in Great Britain by Hobbs the Printers Ltd, Totton, Hampshire

Library of Congress Cataloging-in-Publication Data

Alexander, Michael, 1941–
    Medievalism: the Middle Ages in modern England/Michael Alexander.
       p. cm.
    Includes bibliographical references and index.
    ISBN 0–300–11061–8 (alk. paper)
       1. Medievalism—Great Britain—History.   2. Great Britain—Intellectual life.
3. Gothic revival (Architecture)—Great Britain.   4. Civilization, Medieval, in art. 5. Civilization, Medieval, in literature.   I. Title.
    DA110.A44 2006
    942.01—dc22

ISBN 978-0-300-22730-7 (pbk)

A catalogue record for this book is available from the British Library.

10 9 8 7 6 5 4 3 2 1

For Mary

Contents

Illustrations

Preface

A new interest in medieval things surfaced in England in the 1760s and with it a revival of medieval forms, manifest in literature and in architecture. At first this modern medievalism was experimental and uncertain. A more serious attitude to the medieval past developed during the long war with Revolutionary and Napoleonic France. A longer historical perspective altered the ways in which the English – and perhaps the British – came to think of the evolution of their society and its political arrangements. In the 1830s this Medieval Revival affected religion, and produced major changes in architecture, and then painting and the decorative arts. The country's idea of its history, and of its identity, changed.

In 1960, the founding editor of Penguin Classics, Dr E.V. Rieu, received a proposal for a book of verse translations, to be called *The Earliest English Poems*. The proposal consisted of trial versions of two Old English elegies, 'The Ruin' and 'The Wanderer', with a list of other poems to be translated. Dr Rieu, who had sat Classical Moderations in Oxford in 1908, accepted the proposal, though the translations were in verse, not the 'readable modern English prose' which was his policy for the series. Over lunch at the Athenaeum, he offered his undergraduate guest a piece of traditional advice: 'You will find it a very good practice always to verify your references.'

Completing that book entailed the verification of many references, and the translator, my younger self, eventually took to teaching English literature, modern and medieval, to translating *Beowulf* and the Exeter Book *Riddles*, making glossed editions of *Beowulf* and of Chaucer, and writing about modern poetry.

In the 1980s, British universities were told by British governments to reward research, not teaching. One of the evil consequences of this directive was that the common inheritance of English literature was further enclosed into fields of academic research. As a gesture of resistance, I wrote a history of English literature from 'The Dream of the Rood' to *The Remains of the Day*. The writing of this history uncovered a story, known to some scholars but not to most educated readers, of the recovery of the past and the re-introduction in the 1760s of new – medieval – models into modern literature, and gradually into other fields: politics, religion, architecture and art. The following essay in cultural history is an attempt to trace the very far-reaching results of this re-introduction.

Acknowledgements

The Middle Ages, blacklisted at the Reformation and looked down on in the Enlightenment, were long regarded as of little or no interest. Willed amnesia gave way, from about 1760 onwards, to curiosity and to gradual rediscovery, a rediscovery which had a variety of lasting effects.

'Medievalism' is an awkward term, referring not to the study of the Middle Ages but to the adoption of medieval models. Much of what is written on medievalism is grandly general ('Victorian medievalism was a reaction to the Industrial Revolution') or specialised, focusing on one field – Gothic Revival architecture, or Pre-Raphaelite painting – or one corner of a field, such as (an imaginary example) the use of heraldry in stained glass in Edwardian country houses. A more comprehensive account, longer in time and wider in scope, ought rightly to begin generations before the reign of Victoria and to continue for generations after it; and to look beyond architecture and the arts to the generation of new social and religious ideals. The following attempt, an essay in general cultural history, has its starting points in literature, since that has been my profession. I have made verse translations of Old English poems, and edited medieval texts, but my university teaching has, by choice, chiefly been of classical English literature since Chaucer.

During the writing of *A History of English Literature*, I became curious about the opening up, in the eighteenth century, of the Middle English literature which lay behind Geoffrey Chaucer. Thomas Percy's publication of medieval vernacular verse, in his *Reliques of Ancient English Poetry* of 1765, proved popular and was imitated. Missing links of medieval literature were imaginatively supplied by Macpherson and Chatterton. This romantic rediscovery of medieval romance was once quite well known, for it was promoted by the most influential writer of the nineteenth century, Walter Scott, whose own 'medieval' verse romances had a wild success. Coleridge had imitated medieval ballads and romances, Keats was to follow, and Tennyson's many readers mourned for the death of King Arthur. It was in Queen Victoria's palmiest days that medievalism was at its height. Yet medieval examples also acted with revived power upon Ezra Pound, T.S. Eliot and W.H. Auden. These modernist poets were loudly anti-Victorian, and Victorians were often medievalists. But this does not mean that modernist poetry is never medievalist. On the contrary, as is clearly laid out in the final chapters of this book, the leading modernists were very often medievalist. The more original parts of this book are the opening and closing chapters.

I began to explore the literature of the Medieval Revival with undergraduates at St Andrews, a university whose graduates include William Dunbar and Gavin Douglas. I thank the students who took this way through the backwoods of literary history, and my fellow explorer, Dr Chris Jones. He kindly read my drafts, as did Professor Michael Wheeler, who knows the literature and religion of the nineteenth century far better than I do. I thank him, and also Helen Cooper, then Professor of Medieval and Renaissance Literature at Cambridge, who kindly looked through the pages on Malory.

The text is the product of reading primary sources, medieval and modern; I have read little secondary literature, except in history and art history. I am grateful to the historian Dominic Aidan Bellenger, who improved my history, and to Chloe Johnson, who improved my art history. I owe much to books by Kenneth Clark, Arthur Johnston, Mark Girouard and Christopher Ricks, and to scholars whose names recur in the bibliography. I thank my agent Andrew Hewson, my publisher Robert Baldock and the skilled staff at Yale University Press, especially Rachael Lonsdale. Other debts go back to schooldays, to masters such as Peter Whigham, John Coulson and Hilary Steuert.

Parliamentary reports used to refer to 'sympathetic cheers'. Apologetic thanks are what I have to offer to those who have shared five houses with me and with *Medievalism*. One of them still does, in a sixth, and I have a special thanks for her.

* * *

For permission to reprint extracts from copyright material the author and publishers gratefully acknowledge the following: Faber and Faber and Harcourt Brace Jovanovich for lines from *The Waste Land* by T.S. Eliot; Faber and Faber and New Directions for lines from *The Cantos* and *Hugh Selwyn Mauberley* by Ezra Pound; Faber and Faber for lines from David Jones's *In Parenthesis*; Faber and Faber and Random House Inc. for lines from 'In Memory of W.B. Yeats', 'Memorial for the City' and *The Age of Anxiety* by W.H. Auden; and Faber and Faber, and Farrar, Straus and Giroux, LLC for lines from Philip Larkin's 'Going Going' from his *Collected Poems*, copyright © 1988 by the Estate of Philip Larkin.

Chronology

Introduction

This book traces the evolution of a neglected movement in English cultural history, chiefly by means of its literary manifestations. It begins, however, with two fires and a contrast.

Among the many buildings burnt down in the Great Fire of London of 1666 was the city's Gothic cathedral, St Paul's. The cathedral was eventually rebuilt by Christopher Wren in a modern style deriving from classical antiquity. In 1835, however, the year after fire had gutted most of the Houses of Parliament, a Select Committee of the House of Commons decided that the Palace of Westminster should be rebuilt in 'the national style', which it defined as 'Gothic or Elizabethan' (see Plates 1 and 2).[1]

It had seemed natural to leading Londoners in an age of new science that Old St Paul's, first built in 604, should rise again in a neater form and a very different style, of mathematic proportion. In 1835, on the other hand, Parliament, which had recently reformed itself to become a little more representative, decided that its Houses should be rebuilt in a medieval style. It is not surprising that the contemporaries of Christopher Wren, Isaac Newton and John Locke thought it inappropriate for the capital's cathedral to look Gothic, nor that the City of London rebuilt both it and its parish churches in a non-Gothic style. Yet a modern historian, introducing *The Houses of Parliament: History, Art, Architecture*, a collection of essays published in 2000, did find it surprising and even implausible that in 1835 Parliament should have specified 'Gothic or Elizabethan' as 'the national style' for so important a secular building.[2] The result, the Palace of Westminster, is less medieval on the inside than it looks from a distance, just as the new St Paul's is less classical than Wren had wished, since he was obliged to retain the long nave of its Gothic predecessor.[3] Yet it is fair to regard these contrasting decisions, separated by six or seven generations, as signalling an overturning of England's attitudes to her Middle Ages.

Why and how this revolution in attitudes came about is the subject of this book. Its focus, however, is not on architecture. Indeed, the prominence in many English towns of buildings of the Gothic Revival may obscure the fact that there was a larger Medieval Revival, of which the Gothic Revival in architecture is only one expression, if the most visible one.

The choice of a classical model for St Paul's Cathedral, the embodiment of the English Church, and then of a Gothic model for a reformed Parliament, the symbol of the British state, marks major changes in the direction of English cultural, political and religious life, changes which did not first appear in building. Indeed, the art historian Kenneth Clark, in his classic of revaluation, *The Gothic Revival: an essay in the history of taste* (1928), thought it obvious that the origins of the English Gothic Revival in architecture – 'perhaps the one purely English movement in the plastic arts' – were literary: 'We accept as axiomatic that in England a love and understanding of literature greatly exceeds, and indeed swamps, appreciation of the visual arts and a new current of taste is likely to be first felt in a literary channel.' True in 1928, this is far less true today.[4]

Clark's *Gothic Revival* was the first study of the movement since Eastlake's *History of the Gothic Revival* fifty-six years earlier. In 1872, the English Gothic Revival had been in full swing for a generation. But a generation after Eastlake, the taste for neo-Gothic architecture was overthrown by modernism, and by a decline in public professions of religious faith (Gothic Revival architecture implies, however faintly at times, a Christian orientation). Its English rehabilitation seems to have begun in the 1920s, when neglected Gothic Revival architecture became the subject of curiosity, and a minor cult, for which John Betjeman became the spokesman and later the mascot. Yet the larger Medieval Revival, that broad movement in general culture which was the parent of the architectural revival, has languished in an obscurity which the present study hopes to reduce. The Medieval Revival – the rediscovery, courtship and embrace of the medieval – amounted to a major change in how those living in England, and those who then looked to England, came to imagine their common history and to conceive their very identity. The magnitude of this change has never been sufficiently recognised.

What follows is the first attempt to write a coherent brief history of the Medieval Revival as a whole. As far as I am aware, it is the first book-length study of this phenomenon to attempt an account of its social, political, religious, architectural and artistic aspects, as these are recorded in literature. It focuses on England, for which I make no apology, for in no other country does the Medieval Revival seem as central, perhaps because the origins of the English Church, monarchy and Parliament (in that order) are medieval.[5] The Saxon kingdoms were converted in the seventh century by a mission sent from Rome, and English unity was ecclesiastical before it was political. Unified earlier than most European countries, England eventually turned out to be, for a time, the most influential of the nation-states which broke with Rome. The ten thousand medieval parish churches surviving in England were restored in Victoria's reign, and thousands of new Gothic churches were built – a striking contrast to the (equally vigorous) destruction of English abbeys at the Reformation.

Architecture plays a small part in this study. Yet the famous examples with which this Introduction began can be followed one step further. In Victoria's reign, schools were commonly built in the Gothic style, especially the new public schools for the sons of the middle classes. In London itself, to the west of the City, the Kensington campus of 'Albertopolis', comprising the Victoria and Albert Museum, the Natural History Museum and the Albert Hall, is largely, if variously, medieval in its stylistic inspiration, and the Albert Memorial is Gothic in form, though not in detail. Victorian Gothic town halls, corn-exchanges, polychrome Venetian banks and Early English railway stations survive by the score, and there are thousands of apparently Gothic hotels and public houses, and houses large and small, and non-Gothic houses with Gothic conservatories. The titles of Sir Walter Scott's historical romances provided names to houses, roads and townships throughout Britain's former empire. There is a Kenilworth Road in every Victorian city, and in Ivanhoe, a suburb of the Australian city of Melbourne, Victoria, eleven streets are called after characters in Scott's romance, from Athelstane Grove to Wamba Road.[6] The war memorials erected in most villages throughout that empire are Gothic in style, and these memorials are both civic and Christian.

If the Gothic Revival in architecture is put to one side, the Medieval Revival itself does not receive the recognition and approval enjoyed by other achievements of its period, such as Victorian engineering, or the nineteenth-century novel. If a list is made of leading examples of the Medieval Revival, not everything in it will command unqualified acceptance. Such a list might include Walter Scott's romances in verse and prose; John Keats's 'The Eve of St Agnes'; Alfred Tennyson's 'The Lady of Shalott' and 'Morte d'Arthur'; the first paintings of the Pre-Raphaelite Brotherhood; the Oxford or Tractarian Movement; the social thinkers who invoked medieval models, from the Whig Edmund Burke and the anarchist William Godwin (in his *Life of Chaucer*), to William Cobbett, A.W. Pugin, Thomas Carlyle, Benjamin Disraeli (in *Sybil*), John Ruskin, Karl Marx, William Morris, G.K. Chesterton and R.H. Tawney. From further afield, Leo Tolstoy, Mahatma Gandhi and Ezra Pound might be added to any list of those decisively affected by the thinking of John Ruskin.

Architecture, then, is merely the most public face of the Medieval Revival, a cultural iceberg with unacknowledged dimensions in literature and in social, political and religious thinking. The present essay in cultural history and revaluation is a study of the Medieval Revival in general. The impact of Pugin, Ruskin and William Morris on the decorative arts has been acknowledged in handsomely illustrated books of art history, and Victorian painting has undergone a full revival. These visible manifestations are not the focus of the present study, which looks rather at a set of ideals which underlay that art and architecture, pervading society, politics and religion, offering models of individual conduct, and finding expression in literature of various kinds. Medievalism, born in the mid-eighteenth century, boomed in the nineteenth and resonated well into the twentieth, though in constantly changing forms.

Medievalism is the offspring of two impulses: the recovery by antiquarians and historians of materials for the study of the Middle Ages; and the imaginative adoption of medieval ideals and forms. The second impulse gradually separated from the first during the lifetime of Walter Scott, who was born in 1771 and died in 1832. Antiquarian recovery does not simply precede imaginative revival, for the curiosity of the antiquarian can itself be a romantic impulse. The present study chiefly addresses the imaginative medievalism of the first half of the nineteenth century, though it begins with a look at the examples and materials provided by the antiquarian researches of the late eighteenth. It then takes the story down almost to the present day. Enlightenment antiquarianism was itself partly the product of scholarly *pietas*, nostalgia, or curiosity towards what had been relegated from national history and memory in the course of the Whig version of English history – a return of the repressed. The critical step in the Whig projection of history was the Protestant Reformation of the 1530s, by which the state assumed legal control of the Church, dissolved religious houses, took their property, and cut England's European links. Chief among the subsequent changes are the overthrow of the monarchy in the 1650s, the constitutional Revolution of 1688, and the succession to the British throne of the Hanoverian dynasty in 1714 on the death of the last Stuart monarch, Queen Anne. Catholics had already been excluded from the succession by the Act of Settlement of 1700.

The first research into English medieval origins did not come from disinterested scholarship or pious patriotism. Those who precipitated these radical remodellings of England – 'throwing the kingdom old / Into another mould', as Andrew Marvell put it – sought native historical precedent for their religious and political redefinitions of national identity. Those who seek for precedents in early history can generally find them. In the sixteenth century, the crown made itself head of the Church in England. In the seventeenth, Parliament decapitated a king and, a generation later, limited the powers of the crown. Research into the Middle Ages began under Elizabeth I's inquisitive Archbishop Parker. The aim of this research was to find evidence that Anglo-Saxon Christianity could be represented as independent of Rome. As the Anglo-Saxon Church, and the conversion of England, had been direct results of a papal initiative, Elizabethan efforts succeeded only in showing the absence from Aelfric's sermons on the Eucharist of the doctrine of transubstantiation, one which was developed long after 1066. In the seventeenth century, opponents of the Stuart monarchy were more convincing in finding medieval precedents for the royal duty to consult. The century following the Restoration of 1660 saw the development of a more disinterested antiquarianism and archaeology. By 1760 it was clear that in England neither Church nor crown would ever reclaim from their competitors the supreme authority which during the Middle Ages they had claimed and often enjoyed. Nor was a restoration of the Catholic Stuarts any longer a realistic prospect. Charles Edward's son and heir, Henry, Duke of York, Cardinal of Frascati, was eventually to be maintained, after Napoleon's invasion of Rome, by a secret subvention from George III.[7] It was in the 1760s that literary antiquarianism was quickened by the scholarly enthusiasm of dilettanti such as the Warton brothers, Thomas Percy, Thomas Gray and Horace Walpole. Medieval texts were recreated by 'Ossian' Macpherson and Thomas Chatterton, recovered, republished in 'improved' forms, imitated, and finally adapted in living forms. By 1815, this fanciful 'Gothick' mummery had deepened into a cultural reorientation which affected nineteenth-century England not only in its literature and art but also in wide stretches of its social, political and religious thinking and self-understanding.

A different account, less political and religious, more centred on cultural and intellectual elites, can be offered for this Medieval Revival. Renaissance humanists looked back on what they called *medium ævum*, a 'middle age', and some natural scientists eventually came to look down on it. Intellectual superiorismo reached its peak in Edward Gibbon's conclusion that the fall of the Roman empire had coincided with 'the triumph of barbarism and religion'. (Gibbon himself had in his youth briefly converted to Catholicism.) A generation before this notable sneer, enlightened disdain towards 'Gothic' had begun to transmute into aesthetic fascination, flirtation and playful pastiche. A year after Gibbon published the final volume of his *Decline and Fall of the Roman Empire*, the spectacle of the Revolution in France drew from the Irishman Edmund Burke, who had championed American independence, an idealised account of the bonds which held British society together. Burke foresaw that evil consequences would flow from the summary application of theoretical principles derived from abstract Reason, and he warned

Britain against following the French example. The Revolutionary Terror of 1792 to 1794 and the abolition of the French monarchy and Church made Burke's *Reflections on the Revolution in France*, published in 1790, seem prophetic. Indeed, his 'organic' social thinking now seemed salutary to many Britons who had at first supported the Revolution, among them the poets Wordsworth, Coleridge and Southey. Thirty years of war with France produced, or confirmed, a revision of English political attitudes towards the Revolution, except among intellectual radicals.

History-writing had been one of the eighteenth century's achievements. It was generally held, if not by Voltaire or Gibbon, that history showed improvement, but bloody events in France reminded her offshore neighbours of a skeleton in the English cupboard. Burke's *Reflections* repeatedly refuse to accept that the 'Bloodless' English Revolution of 1688 (which was not bloodless in Ireland) offered any parallel or precedent for the French Revolution, as its English admirers were claiming. But there is no mention in Burke's *Reflections* of an earlier English Revolution, still less of the execution of King Charles I. This parallel could scarcely have been denied. The French Revolution, and Napoleon's imperial ventures, prompted British readers to look to their national history. This interest contributed to the popularity of Scott's series of prose romances set in the Middle Ages, which began in the Regency with *Ivanhoe* (1819) and continued during the reign of George IV. Victorian readers were to take these Georgian romances more seriously.

The effects of the Industrial Revolution deepened an English revaluation of the Enlightenment, which the French Revolution had already brought to the boil. Thinkers such as Cobbett, Carlyle and Ruskin were among the first to see and to seek to understand the uglier effects of industrialism and capitalism on the economic, social and personal life of the country. Their searching analyses are no longer much read, partly because of their agonised and prophetic tone, and the frankness of their moralism. Their vision was largely shared by Charles Dickens, who shot it through with humour and relieved it with more beguiling visions, and also by Matthew Arnold, who substituted irony for high-minded denunciation. But Carlyle and Ruskin had a persistent influence on British attitudes, an influence long absorbed and largely forgotten, but feeding powerful movements of dissent within the national culture, movements which met with varying success: among them the Gothic Revival in secular architecture, 'Young England' Toryism, Anglo-Catholicism, Christian Socialism, British Marxism, the Socialist League, the Trade Union movement, the old Labour Party, the Arts and Crafts movement, the Society for the Protection of Ancient Monuments, the National Trust, the Garden Suburb and the New Town, and more generally in the cults of literature, of the arts and now of the environment. The society and conditions shaped by the Industrial Revolution met their first response in such thinkers, all of whom recoiled from the evident human cost of the strengthening influence of economic, commercial and utilitarian considerations on the life of the nation.

* * *

What does 'medieval' mean? The first recorded use in English of the word 'medieval' comes surprisingly late, in 1817, in a work on British monasticism. Both 'medieval and 'mediæval' are recognised UK spellings; 'medieval' is the spelling preferred here, on the ground that an 'æ' spelling classicises a vowel which in the Middle Ages was written as 'e'. American English also prefers 'medieval', following the lead of Noah Webster's *Dictionary of American English* of 1828.

In the 1830s, historians began to use 'medieval' in the place of 'Gothic', a word which had previously done very much the same job, but had negative associations of barbarism and irrationality – *except* in politics, where there was a long-standing belief that England had always had 'a Gothic constitution'. As a period term, 'Gothic' soon became confined to architecture, and, as we have seen, 'Gothic Revival' came to mean the revival of an architectural style. Some of the sense of repudiation formerly attaching to 'Gothic' transferred to 'medieval', a word still quite often used by journalists to mark something as barbarous, as if mass cruelty was unknown in modern Western civilisation. Yet it seems reasonable to say that, since Victoria's accession in 1837, educated people have rarely felt a simple and undifferentiated animosity to the Middle Ages, a period which saw the arrival of, among other things, England itself, its Church, monarchy, laws and Parliament, its hospitals, universities and cathe-drals. Anyone familiar with the history of Europe in the twentieth century cannot share the belief, common at its outset, in the inevita-bility of some automatic improvement in the conduct of human beings as a whole. In Britain at least, any simple anti-medievalism usually owes more to historical ignorance or to prejudice than to zeal for the Reformation, faith in the Enlightenment, or devotion to Petrarch, Copernicus, Bacon or Descartes, or even to Charles Darwin.

'Gothic', the predecessor term to 'medieval', is also the label for a kind of horror fiction or fantasy, which, after Horace Walpole's *The Castle of Otranto*, published at Christmas in 1764, squeaked into the cellars of literature. Walpole's experiment started a cult which was exploited by Mrs Radcliffe, 'Monk' Lewis and William Beckford, and mocked by Jane Austen in *Northanger Abbey*, where the heroine, a devotee of the Gothic novel and a guest at Northanger Abbey, is persuaded by what she has read of abbeys that her host, since he is a widower, must have had his wife horribly murdered. This sensational form of Gothic is too thriving to need reviving. Freak, horror and transgression sell tabloid newspapers, film and television, much as in Shakespeare's day they sold broadsheet ballads, and in imperial Rome had drawn crowds to the Coliseum. This genre of Gothic entertainment relishes more explicit versions of the same pleasures which Horace Walpole and his successors derived from imagining unspeakable threats to beautiful young women imprisoned by feudal tyrants in the bowels of their castles. Horror fantasy of the kind Bram Stoker cooked up in *Dracula* (1897) draws specifically on folklore, not historical writing. This kind of Gothic can be set in the future. It is fantasy, not history. As such, it forms no part of this study of the Medieval Revival.

The word 'medieval' derives from post-classical Latin *medium ævum*, itself first found in a British publication of 1604. The idea of a stage intervening between classical antiquity and the present day is found earlier in continental Latin writers. The noun *ævum* is 'age', the adjective *medius*, 'middle'.[8] In English, the *Oxford English Dictionary's* first recorded use of 'the middle age' is found in William Camden's *Remains* (1605). The second *OED* illustration is from Sir Henry Wotton's *Elements of Architecture*, written in Venice in 1624: 'After the reviving and repolishing of good Literature, (which the combustions and tumults of the middle Age had uncivillised . . .).' Wotton's 'the middle Age' intervenes between the ancient and the modern world: on the one hand classical antiquity, Greece and Rome; on the other, Reformation, and (later terms) Renaissance and nation-state. The thousand years which lay between had 'uncivillised' Europe. Latin informs French *le moyen âge* and Italian *medio evo*. In languages without a Roman past, 'the middle age' has given way to 'the Middle Ages' and to the German *mittelalter*. The plural forms suggest a less absolute mental category.

'Mediævalism' is first found in 1844, again with reference to monasticism. In 1854 John Ruskin wrote, in his Lectures on Architecture: 'You have, then, the three periods: Classicalism, extending to the fall of the Roman empire; Mediævalism, extending from that fall to the close of the fifteenth century; and Modernism.' Ruskin uses Mediævalism to designate a historical period.

Periodisation is an ancient human habit. To divide history into 'ages' is as old as history and literature, as in the dynasties of ancient Egypt and of China, or in Hesiod's ages of gold, silver and bronze. The Bible divides time into the periods before and after the Flood, the time of the patriarchs, the captivity in Egypt, and so forth. The tripartite division of recorded history into ancient, medieval and modern, to which Ruskin appeals, is enshrined in common use and often taken as axiomatic.[9] What is thought to be the first reference to the interval now called a middle age comes in a Latin poem, *Africa*, by Francesco Petrarca. Writing in 1341, the Italian humanist placed the end of antiquity and the beginning of a modern age at the point when Christianity was accepted in the Roman empire in the fourth century. Petrarch ended his poem: 'This sleep of forgetfulness will not last forever. When the darkness has been dispersed, our descendants can come again in the former pure radiance.'[10] This is often taken as prophetic of 'the Renaissance', which, at the time that Ruskin was lecturing on medievalism in 1853, was a newish concept. The term had not yet been popularised by the French historian Jules Michelet.

Underlying this three-period division is not a series of events falling naturally into three distinct phases, but a construing of these events, an interpretation of history, a narrative which enshrines value-judgements and forms habits of thought. This construal began in perception and became a conviction. It was adopted by Western historians and taught in schools, crystallising finally into a classroom convenience: 'the medieval period lasted from the 5th to the 15th century'. Yet 'medieval' also designates what is not modern: not a *datum* with dates, but a contradistinction and a negative category of otherness – a shifting category, since 'modern' denotes what is to be found in the present and is supposed, often incorrectly, not to have existed in the past. The fall of Rome to the Goths in 410 was a fact, and 'the reviving ... of good Literature' was, for Sir Henry Wotton in 1621, a given thing. But the tripartite periodisation of ancient, medieval and modern is not a fact, but an accepted perspective upon past lives: a historiographer's projection, much as Mercator's Projection is a cartographer's projection. Today, historians might wish to say more about the pre-classical era, and to subdivide the ancient, the medieval and the modern periods – 'late antiquity', 'early modern' and so forth. Yet, however misleading, the three-period paradigm will take time to die.

The habit of periodisation flatters the periodiser, as in Gibbon's comment on the triumph of barbarism and religion. It gives primacy to temporal sequence, and emphasises differences in human experience at the expense of continuity and survival, of eddies and of counter-currents. It concentrates on the avant-garde and upon elites. It also minimises or excludes other ways of conceiving history, whether providential, cyclical or dialectical. Periodisation is a convenient simplification which leaves out the atypical, the unrecorded, the moments which seem to stand outside time, and the less historical elements of human experience. Convenient to history teachers, this ancient/medieval/modern division lends itself to narratives which imply notions of progress or of decline (usually of progress), notions which have cultural authority. 'AMERICA was thus clearly top nation, and History came to a.' This is the close of *1066 and All That*, a parody of schoolroom history published by two history teachers, W.C. Sellar and R.J. Yeatman, in 1930. British historiography has since then become less progressive in its assumptions. Yet the very words 'medieval' and 'modern' lend an air of reason to a way of thinking which is circular.

The Medieval Revival may sometimes appear in the following pages as 'medievalism'. This word is used in the last of the three senses defined in the *Oxford English Dictionary*: 'Beliefs and practices (regarded as) characteristic of the Middle Ages; medieval thought, religion, art etc.; the adoption of, adherence to, or interest in mediaeval ideals, styles or usages.' The medievalism addressed in this essay is not the historical study of the medieval, but the conscious adoption of, or devotion to, medieval ideals or usages, whether of thought, art or life. Such a devotion grew partly out of the researches of eighteenth-century historians; not the philosophical historians such as David Hume, but the literary antiquarians: Bishop Hurd, the Warton brothers, Thomas Gray, Horace Walpole, Bishop Percy, George Ellis and Sir Walter Scott. Some of this antiquarian scholarship drew on manuscripts preserved by supporters of the Non-Jurors, the seven bishops who, bound by their oaths to James II, felt unable to swear the same oaths to William III.

As medievalism is a movement in general culture, it is approached in this book in historical sequence, rather than topic by topic. Literature plays a leading part, and although social and political thought, architectural theory, art and religion come to the fore at different points, and can dominate a chapter, it is literature which provides most of the evidence. The writer is a professor of English literature whose expertise is in medieval and modern poetry, not in history or art history. The chapters approach their topics in several different ways, including survey and close analysis, with occasional pauses for summary, explanation, reflection and what may look like repetition. In tracing the course of a movement which has lasted for more than two centuries, some topics and landmarks come into view more than once, and are seen from different angles. The story begins with the English literature of the 1760s.

CHAPTER 1

The Advent of the Goths

THE MEDIEVAL IN THE 1760S

He was a wise man, that friend of Fletcher of Saltoun, who said
that if a man were allowed to make the ballads of a people, he
cared not who made its laws.

Thomas Percy, *Reliques of Ancient English Poetry*[1]

'Ruin seize thee, ruthless king!' These are the opening words of
Thomas Gray's poem 'The Bard'. Gray's speaker is a Welsh bard,
and his words are addressed to King Edward I, the conqueror
of Wales. Gray believed the legend that this English king had in
1283 ordered the death of the Welsh bards, an honoured caste of
oral poets. 'The Bard', subtitled 'A Pindaric Ode', was printed by
Gray's friend Horace Walpole at Strawberry Hill, Walpole's house
at Twickenham. Gray's 'Elegy Written in a Country Churchyard' is
far better known than 'The Bard', and for good reason. Yet the
Medieval Revival, of which 'The Bard' (1757) is a very early instance,
is now a province of literary history less familiar than it deserves
to be.

Gray's Bard curses the Anglo-Norman invader and prophesies in
cloudy and cryptic detail the return of a British dynasty to the throne
of Britain – the Tudors, who were originally Welsh. The Bard also
foretells a revival of British poetry in Spenser, Shakespeare and
Milton, and their successors, of whom the last and least is Gray. Gray
thus opens up a way back to the remote and legendary British past.
His Bard makes a striking figure:

> On a rock, whose haughty brow
> Frowns o'er old Conway's foaming flood,
> Robed in the sable garb of woe,
> With haggard eyes the poet stood

(Loose his beard and hoary hair
Streamed, like a meteor, to the troubled air) . . .

The last Bard's last words are addressed to King Edward:

'Be thine Despair, and scept'red Care,
To triumph, and to die, are mine.'

He spoke, and headlong from the mountain's height
Deep in the roaring tide he plunged to endless night.[2]

Gray's poem had a lasting vogue, as is shown in John Martin's spectacular version, *The Bard*, painted sixty years later in 1817 (see Plate 3).

In 1760, three years after the defiant suicide of native British poetry was imagined in English, there appeared *Fragments of Ancient Poetry Collected in the Highlands of Scotland, and Translated from the Gaelic or Erse Language.* Both the collection and the translation were by a twenty-six-year-old Scottish Highlander, James Macpherson. He claimed that this 'ancient poetry' was the work of Ossian, a fourth-century poet, in Gaelic or 'Erse', the tongue brought by the Gaels from their native Ireland to north-western Britain. 'Erse' is an old spelling of 'Irish'. Macpherson turned oral Erse verses into printed English proses.

The eighth of Macpherson's *Fragments* begins:

By the side of a rock on the hill beneath the aged trees, old Oscian sat on the moss; the last of the race of Fingal. Sightless are his aged eyes; his beard is waving in the wind. Dull through the leafless trees he heard the voice of the north. Sorrow revived in his soul: he began and lamented the dead.

Fragment 8, 1–4[3]

A historical Ossian would have lived a thousand years before Gray's Bard, and Macpherson's Ossian is both a warrior and a poet. In other essentials, however, Macpherson's protagonist is suspiciously reminiscent of Gray's. Each is the last of a line of Celtic poets, aged and afflicted in eyesight; each feels constrained to speak by the plight of his conquered people; each is placed in a rocky situation, and in the mountain wind his beard is either waving or streaming.

Urban readers were taken with Gray's strange Ode and with Macpherson's hypnotic *Fragments*. It was intriguing to imagine a Britain that had preceded both England and modern Britain. Whereas Wales had been conquered in the thirteenth century, the Highlands had been finally subdued only thirteen years before Macpherson composed his translations. The end of the Stuart cause, and its residual Highland support, had come in 1746 at Culloden, near Inverness. Drawing rooms in Edinburgh in which Gaelic would have been unintelligible and unwelcome could now be moved by the word from the mountains – when put into English. It was time for empathy with the dispossessed. Macpherson followed up the success of the *Fragments* with a series of similar translations, for which he claimed written sources. The scholar and poet Samuel Johnson called Macpherson's bluff, asking for manuscript evidence for his 'impudent forgeries'. This was not produced. Thomas Gray, a poet and scholar as retiring as Johnson was robust, reacted very differently. Gray passed over the evident possibility that manuscript sources for the *Fragments* might be largely or entirely imaginary, and declared himself '*exstasié* with their infinite beauty'. Readers more remote were even more thrilled. Goethe thought Ossian superior to Homer. In his own Notes, Macpherson points out the remarkable resemblances between passages in his translations and passages in Homer and Milton. Macpherson had carefully fabricated these parallels, causing Madame de Staël to observe with some triumph that many of the beauties of English poetry were filched from Ossian. 'Ossian' was translated into Latin, and Napoleon had scenes from Macpherson painted on his bedroom ceiling. Gray's friend Horace Walpole 'appreciated' the Ossian poems, 'but he was convinced they were fake'.[4]

Horace Walpole was the youngest son of Britain's first Prime Minister, Sir Robert Walpole, and was to become London's first celebrity medievaliser. The unsigned Preface to *The Castle of Otranto, A Story*, published anonymously by Walpole at Strawberry Hill on Christmas Eve, 1764, says that its printed text had been 'found in the library of an ancient catholic family in the north of

England', and 'William Marshal, Gent.' appears on the title page as its translator 'From the original ITALIAN / of ONUPHRIO MURALTO, / CANON of the Church of St NICHOLAS at OTRANTO'. A discovered or translated manuscript was a common device in eighteenth-century fiction. Yet it seems that few readers saw through the name Onuphrio Muralto ('Humphrey Highwall' in Italian) to the name Horace Wal + pole, an aesthete who had for more than a decade been crenellating the walls of his suburban villa at Strawberry Hill, at Twickenham on the Thames, turning it into a 'little Gothic castle', with fan-vaulted ceilings in papier mâché.[5]

The purpose of the Preface to *The Castle of Otranto* by William Marshal, Gent., is to throw readers off the scent. His learned discussion of style, date, composition and provenance, and of the historical accuracy of the setting in twelfth-century Apulia, is very much that of a savant. There was nothing so obvious in the Preface as to arouse suspicion, although Marshal's Enlightenment prejudices today sound extreme. The Italian original, he writes, *'was printed at Naples, in the black letter* [i.e., in gothic type], *in the year 1529 ... The principal incidents are such as were believed in the darkest ages of christianity; but the language and conduct have nothing that savours of barbarism. The style is the purest Italian.'* Marshal judges that composition was *'little earlier'* than 1529: *'Letters were then in their most flourishing state in Italy, and contributed to dispel the empire of superstition, at that time so forcibly attacked by the reformers.'* The author was perhaps *'an artful priest'*, who was trying *'to confirm the populace in their ancient errors and superstitions ... The solution of the author's motives is however offered as a mere conjecture'*, so that *'his work can only be laid before the public at present as a* matter of entertainment' (final emphasis added). In the second edition of 1765, Walpole admitted that there was no original to be translated, that he had made it all up, that he was the author. He changed the subtitle from *A Story* to *A Gothic Story* – an adjective which became the name for a genre.

In style and incident, *The Castle of Otranto* is an eclectic medley of elements supposedly found in medieval romances. It is made up of five chapters, mirroring the five acts of a play. It is a hybrid of various genres, both a precious pastiche and a fantastic spoof. The plot of the story is ridiculous, and its characters are cardboard. In its opening scene, Conrad, the about-to-be-married heir to Otranto, crossing an interior courtyard of the castle, is 'dashed to pieces, and almost buried under an enormous helmet, an hundred times more large than any casque ever made for human being'. Conrad's father, Manfred, tyrant of Otranto, imprisons the suspected murderer inside the helmet, which is able to wave its black plume. Otranto is a long way from Twickenham.

In 1769 Walpole, who was a noted connoisseur of painting, received a letter from the young Thomas Chatterton, enclosing excerpts from 'The Ryse of Peyncteynge yn Englāde, wroten bie T. Rowleie, 1469'.* Chatterton revealed that Rowley was a prolific poet also. Walpole's Onuphrio Muralto was a Canon of St Nicholas, Otranto, and Rowley was also a Canon, of St Mary Redcliffe, Bristol. Walpole wrote warmly to Chatterton, asking where Rowley's poems were to be found. Chatterton replied that he had a transcript of a transcript. Walpole saw that 'the success of Ossian's poems had suggested the idea', and Mason and Gray wrote to Walpole that the poems were 'modern forgeries'. Since Rowley had supposedly flourished in the dark century following Chaucer's death, he seemed to constitute a missing, and welcome, link in the evolution of late medieval English poetry. Chatterton soon published a number of Rowley poems, all his own work. Then, in 1770, at the age of seventeen, he killed himself. William Wordsworth, who was born in that year, was to be much taken with the sad story of 'the marvellous boy', as were Samuel Taylor Coleridge, John Keats and Alfred Tennyson, all of whom wrote poems indebted to Chatterton's Rowley.

Chatterton's 'Mynstrelles Songe' begins: 'O! synge untoe mie roundelaie, / O! droppe the brynie teare wythe mee.'[6] The minstrel's invitation to weep along with him is made more authentically fifteenth-century by ending every word except 'O!' with a final -e. No careful reader would now be taken in by Chatterton's final -e, but in the 1760s the study of the English language between 1100 and 1470, of Middle English as it is now called, had not begun. Old English, the language of the Anglo-Saxons, had, however, been studied for two

---

* The bar, or *macron*, over the 'a' marks the omission of an 'n' or 'm' following the vowel; a habit of medieval scribes imitated by Chatterton.

centuries, and although more remote, was in some respects better understood. Although the poems of Chaucer had been read ever since his death in 1400, the English language itself had changed so greatly by 1500 that readers could not know whether a final -e should be pronounced. The cadence of Chaucer's verse was therefore uncertain.[7] Before 1775, when Chaucer's editor, Thomas Tyrwhitt, began to work out when a scribe's final -e retained a live grammatical function and actually meant something, and when it was simply a scribal habit, no one could be certain how to read Chaucer's verse.

The pages of Macpherson and Chatterton were not very often turned in the twentieth century, and more seldom still those of Richard Hurd's *Letters on Chivalry and Romance* and Thomas Warton's *Observations on the Faerie Queene*. These works of the 1760s have for more than a century been available in learned libraries only. They are known to most students of the eighteenth century by their titles, as having paved the way to Walpole's *Castle of Otranto*. Short examples of Gothic verse may now be included in multi-volume anthologies, but they do not fit what we have been taught to expect of the eighteenth century. The canon, established before the end of that century, has consecrated the Augustan poetry which ends with Johnson, and the critical prose which began with Addison and led to Johnson, Burke and Gibbon. By common consent, the role of innovator in the literature of that century has been taken by the Novel: Defoe, Fielding, Richardson, Sterne, Smollett, Frances Burney. Researchers in the wake of Roger Lonsdale have widened our idea of eighteenth-century verse, and feminist literary historians have added names to the roll. But since William Blake was rediscovered by D.G. Rossetti in 1847, no new major poet has been turned up. On all recent roadmaps of the eighteenth century, Gothic poetry still shows as a minor byway. Yet it proved to be the way to enchanted ground.

This has been a summary sketch of the advent of the Goths in the 1760s. A chronology of the decade offers a profile. At its beginning, the author of 'The Bard' was ecstatic about the translator-author of Ossian. By its end, the translator-author-publisher of *The Castle of Otranto* was sceptical about the fictitious Father Rowley. During the 1760s, the decade in which the Medieval Revival arrived, the movement gradually became less recherché, precious and theatrical, more self-critical and better informed. To advance with more security, we now take a step backwards to consider the Augustan matrix out of which the Gothic, its opposite, emerged.

* * *

'True wit is Nature to advantage dressed, / What oft was thought but ne'er so well expressed.'[8] Pope's couplet exemplifies what it defines: the value the Augustans put on truths of general validity. The lines Dr Johnson liked best in Gray's 'Elegy' were those such as 'The paths of glory lead but to the grave'; lines to which, he pronounced, 'every bosom returns an echo'. When judged by Pope's criterion, the last lines of Gray's Bard, 'Be thine Despair, and scept'red Care, / To triumph, and to die, are mine', express what had very rarely been thought, and had never been so expressed. Perhaps the imitation in English of the internal rhyming of medieval Welsh verse would have interested those in a position to appreciate it. The running headlines of cultural history advertise the period between the Restoration of the Stuarts in 1660 and the French Revolution as an Age of Reason (the title of a famous book by Tom Paine), and its literature is expected to shun Gothic singularity and extremity. It is true that the verse of Dryden, Swift, Pope and Johnson in the 'long' eighteenth century is characterised by cool social intelligence. But Sense is here a more helpful heading than Reason, for moral feeling was among the meanings of Sense in the earlier part of this period. It was only after the craze for sentimental fiction and drama of the 1770s that Sensibility became opposed to Sense, as in the title of Jane Austen's novel. It is to this craze that Wordsworth alludes in the Preface to *Lyrical Ballads*: 'The invaluable works of our elder Writers, I had almost said the works of Shakespeare and Milton, are driven into neglect by frantic novels, sickly and stupid German tragedies, and deluges of idle and extravagant stories in verse.'[9]

The suicide of Gray's Bard can be seen as fulfilling, though negatively and with Gray's own gloom, hopes which poets had been voicing for over a generation. In 1726 James Thomson, a Lowland Scot come to London, had called for a revival of the poetic sublime, which had inspired mankind 'from Moses down to Milton'. John Milton himself had conspicuously invoked the examples of Moses and the prophets of Israel, and the blind poet-prophets of classical antiquity: 'Blind Thamyris and blind Maeonides, / And Tiresias and Phineus prophets old' (*Paradise Lost*, III, 35–6). William Collins's 'Ode Occasioned by the Death of Mr Thomson' of 1749 opens 'In yonder grave a Druid lies'. (Druids, who are prominent in Tacitus' account of the crushing of the last British resistance in Anglesey, were in the eighteenth century credited with much, including the building of Stonehenge.) Gray's Bard descends from the Druids of Tacitus.

In the 1740s Dr Robert Lowth had lectured in Latin on the Sacred Poetry of the Hebrews, dwelling upon the sublime rhythms of the prophets. Among his Cambridge audience was Christopher Smart, who wrote 'mad' prophetic verse in the biblical rhythms later imitated by William Blake in his Prophetic Books. The Bible itself had always stood as a reminder that the sublime could be simple, and that it did not, as rationalist versions of neo-classical literary theory prescribed, require elevation of style. In 1754 Thomas Warton, the first academic historian of English literature, lamented that the Muses had been 'debauched at Court' after the Restoration, and regretted that polite life and familiar manners had become the only subjects of poetry. In 1756 Edmund Burke argued in *The Sublime and the Beautiful* that the aesthetic pleasure of the sublime arose from pain at the sight of the immense, the obscure and the traumatic. Poetry, then, could be found not only in a work of classic art but also in the 'infinite beauty' of fragments by an inspired bard, druid, or prophet. It was seen that antiquity offered a range of precedents, Hebrew as well as Greek, and a pre-classical sublimity as well as a neo-classical elegance. A sublime style could therefore be either lofty or simple. Eighteenth-century writers were smooth-shaven and wore wigs, but some of them liked to dream of ancestors who were rapt, bearded and vatic, and who addressed themes beyond polite life and familiar manners. Gray and Walpole were by upbringing and education smooth and refined, and exquisite by inclination.

The last major practitioner of Augustan verse, Samuel Johnson, looking back on the achievement of the first Augustan poet, wrote, in his *Life of Dryden*: 'What was said of Rome, adorned by Augustus, may be applied by an easy metaphor to English poetry embellished by Dryden: "he found it brick, and he left it marble".' It is not so well known that John Dryden himself, looking back over his career in his 'Epistle to . . . Mr Congreve' (1694), reflected that elegance had been achieved at a cost:

> Well then; the promis'd hour is come at last;
> The present Age of Wit obscures the past:
> Strong were our Syres, and as they Fought they Writ,
> Conqu'ring with Force of Arms, and dint of Wit:
> Theirs was the Gyant Race before the Flood . . .

That is, the 'Flood' of the Civil War and Interregnum had drowned the Giants: there would be no more Shakespeares and Jonsons. 'Our Age was cultivated thus at length; / But what we gain'd in skill we lost in strength.'[10]

Alexander Pope's *Essay on Criticism* and *Essay on Man* both assume that what Sir Henry Wotton had called 'the reviving . . . of good literature' had led to a general improvement in civilisation. Pope's only excursion into the Middle Ages is in 'Eloisa to Abelard' (1716). His prefatory Argument pleads a special case: 'Abelard *and* Eloisa *flourish'd in the twelfth Century; they were two of the most distinguish'd persons of their age in learning and beauty, but for nothing more famous than for their unfortunate passion.'* The poem opens in Eloisa's convent:

> In these deep solitudes and awful cells,
> Where heav'nly-pensive, contemplation dwells,
> And ever-musing melancholy reigns . . .[11]

Pope here bows three times in as many lines to Milton's 'Il Penseroso', and paints the convent in gloomy baroque colours. Milton's 'pensive man' had loved the 'storied windows richly dight, / Casting a dim religious light'. This becomes in Pope: 'Where awful arches make a noonday night, / And the dim windows shed a solemn light'. Solemnity and religion retire in the next line: 'What means this tumult in a Vestal's veins?' Eloisa, the '*person*' of '*the twelfth Century . . . distinguish'd . . . in learning and beauty*', pants for Abelard, from whose love she has been permanently cut off. This becomingly love-tormented nun was the kind of nun appreciated by the Enlightenment (see Jean-Jacques Rousseau's *Julie, ou la nouvelle Héloïse* (1761)). Walter Scott's verse romances, for example, have several such persons '*distinguish'd in ...* *beauty*' unwillingly cloistered.

Alexander Pope chose to keep the Catholic faith of his upbringing, but his celibacy was not chosen. Crippled by spinal tuberculosis in childhood, humpbacked and deformed, he loved women, but had no hope of marrying. So Pope sympathised with his Eloisa, and he shared the scepticism of his enlightened age towards the religious life, writing of 'happy Convents, bosom'd deep in vines, / Where slumber Abbots, purple as their wines' (*Dunciad*, IV, 301–2). The monasteries Pope satirises here are in France, where they were to flourish for another seventy years. English religious houses had been suppressed in the 1530s, and their property confiscated. In England, therefore, 'Convents' were indeed medieval, for none had survived the Reformation. Mary Tudor had brought the black monks back to Westminster Abbey, but her half-sister Elizabeth sent them back across the Channel again. Whereas Windsor Castle was inhabited by the King of England, Wales, Scotland and Ireland, and Alnwick Castle was lived in by the Duke of Northumberland, English abbeys, when inhabited in Pope's day, were lived in not by purple abbots but by sanguine English gentry whose ancestors had paid Henry VIII for them in services or in cash.[12]

Pope shows knowledge of no early writer in English. In his time, the recovery of writings in Middle English still lay in the future. In *The Dunciad* Pope mocks Thomas Hearne, a scholar of Old English manuscripts:

'But who is he, in closet close y-pent,
Of sober face, with learned dust besprent?'
'Right well mine eyes arede the myster wight,
On parchment scraps y-fed, and Wurmius hight.
To future ages may thy dulness last,
As thou preserv'st the dulness of the past!'   III, 185–9

The literary past that excited Pope was not early English but classical. He assumed the antediluvian view of the Middle Ages taken by

Enlightenment Protestants: 'A *second* Deluge Learning thus o'er-run, / And the *Monks* finish'd what the *Goths* begun'.[13] He also had the scorn of the humane generalist for the dilettante and the specialist, a scorn he showed not only to Saxonist bookworms, and to collectors of archaeological curiosities or butterflies, but also to minute textual critics of the Greek and Latin poets – to Richard Bentley, for example, whom he ridiculed in *The Dunciad*.

It is philosophical to prefer the broadly human to the minute and the material, yet Pope's censure now seems misplaced. We know that the eighteenth century saw European learning and knowledge expand far beyond Europe and its past, making possible the real achievements of historians, natural philosophers and encyclopaedists, and of comparative scholars such as 'Oriental' Jones and Linnaeus. The English products of this learning include Johnson's *Dictionary*, his edition of Shakespeare, his *Lives of the English Poets* (published in sixty-eight volumes), and Gibbon's *Decline and Fall of the Roman Empire* as well as the prose of some of the founding fathers of the United States, such as Jefferson and John Adams. High scholarship was to become specialist and exclusive, but the masterpieces of Johnson and Gibbon are humanely written for general readers. A permanent contribution of the eighteenth century to human self-understanding was the development of a comparative historical sense. In January 1793, in a letter to Lady Ossory, Horace Walpole wrote of 'the enlightened eighteenth century'.[14] He wrote with irony, for he was referring to the execution of Louis XVI and the beginnings of the Terror in France, but this is one of the first English references to 'the eighteenth century', and an early example of the modern habit of chronological self-classification.

We turn now to the rehabilitation of the romance, and the creation of Romance. One aspect of the growth of knowledge in that 'enlightened eighteenth century' is the recovery of the materials of later medieval literature and especially of Middle English verse romances, begun by Thomas Warton, Richard Hurd and Thomas Percy. In his *Enchanted Ground*, published in 1964 but still the defining study of this topic, Arthur Johnston observed that 'scholars from Percy to Scott thought more of the romances than of other medieval texts, or of any texts except those of Chaucer, Spenser,

Shakespeare and Milton'.[15] The antiquarian researches of these scholars went hand in hand with the imaginative medievalism of Gray and Walpole. These early lovers of medieval literature were characteristically men of letters and poets, amateurs not experts. Thomas Warton, the only university man of the three, was at different times Professor of Poetry and of History at Oxford, and Poet Laureate. Thomas Gray, who declined the Laureateship, later became Professor of Modern History at Cambridge, though he did not lecture. The medievalism of Walter Scott and George Ellis was, like that of Warton, Hurd and Percy before them, amateur scholarship offered to an audience which was cultivated and literary rather than learned. These men began a rehabilitation of romance in Britain which led both to the scholarly recovery of medieval romances, and also (as was their intention) to the revival of the romance genre in new writing. This revival of romances was later called the Romantic Revival and paved the way for the Romantic movement. Indeed, without the work of Warton, Hurd and Percy, that movement would have taken a different form and might not have been called Romantic. Romanticism and medievalism share a wish to re-enchant a world which Natural Philosophy had rendered too clear, and trade and industry had made too commonsensical. But this book is only accidentally an account of the rise of Romanticism.

Thomas Warton's *Observations on the Faerie Queene* (1754) was the first published study of medieval English literature. Chaucer's eminence and talent were generally acknowledged, and Dryden had written well about him, but Chaucer's verse was not easy to read. His elder contemporary, William Langland, had hardly been read for two centuries, and Malory's *Le Morte Darthur* (*c.* 1470) had last been printed in 1648. In 1754 the only English author who offered a window on the writing we now call medieval was Edmund Spenser (*c.* 1552–99). Spenser was a keen Renaissance humanist, and his *Faerie Queene* is a polemical Protestant allegory dedicated to the Head of the Church of England, then militant in Ireland, the Fairy Queen herself, Elizabeth I. His narrative of Arthurian knight-errantry is a verse romance, the traditional form for such stories, which were very popular with all classes during his lifetime, though they were increasingly being written in prose. Spenser applied a principle of decorum when he chose to use spellings, words and word-forms that were already antiquated and obsolete. Canto I opens:

A Gentle Knight was *pricking* on the plaine   *cantering*
Y *cladd* in mightie armes and siluer shielde   *clothed*[16]

This archaism was a historical application of the rhetorical theory that each genre had a style proper to it. Spenser decided that romance, as a Gothic 'kind', should be written in a Gothic style. He knew well that Protestant humanists such as Ascham had repeatedly condemned romances as immoral, 'low', unreal and childish. Moreover, popular romances came from manuscripts, and manuscripts came from monasteries, and in 1590 nothing good could be expected from that quarter. Thomas Nashe mocked romances as the 'fantasticall dreames of those exiled Abbie-lubbers'. Spenser chose to clothe his pure moral allegory in the form of a romance, then the most entertaining and widely accepted of literary genres. In this choice he was later followed by a writer purer still, John Bunyan in *The Pilgrim's Progress* (1678), though in prose. Bunyan might have put the romance on the stalls of his Vanity Fair, but he chose instead to use it to reach the widest possible readership.

A modern reader of *The Faerie Queene*, accustomed to notions of historical propriety, sees that Spenser inlays its polished surface with phrases designed to bring to mind older romances. We read these as signals that we are to enter the enchanted world of 'fairyland', a word coined by Spenser. In the next generation, however, Ben Jonson condemned Spenser for imitating the style of older romance: 'In affecting the ancients, he writ no language.' Yet eighteenth-century readers approached *The Faerie Queene* as a Gothic work in both style and content, not as a work of Renaissance humanism. Spenser borrowed elements of heroic gallantry and improbable fantasy from the recent sophisticated romances of Ariosto (*Orlando furioso*, 1516) and Tasso (*Gerusalemme liberata*, 1575), and purified them. Spenser's later readers, such as Walter Scott, accepted such Renaissance elements as medieval, but John Milton pointedly called him 'sage and serious Spenser', making clear that *The Faerie Queene*, though a romance, was not like the 'fantasticall dreames' mocked by the ungodly Nashe, but rather a moral allegory. When young, John Milton wrote glowingly of romance. He had at first planned to make his epic poem both Arthurian and national, following Spenser's example, but to write it in blank verse. Direct imitation of Spenser's style and stanza (and, less successfully, of his moral allegory) began with James Thomson's *The Castle of Indolence* (1748). Thomas Warton brought out a second, enlarged edition of his *Observations on the Faerie Queene* in 1762. By this time Warton had read many of the romances that Spenser had read, and so laid the foundations for his own *History of English Poetry*, published in three volumes between 1774 and 1781.

Spenser was read by poets, but medieval romances in prose or verse were still generally available, simply retold and retailed in cheap editions, and reprinted in chapbooks. They remained popular reading for children and less sophisticated readers. The adult Samuel Johnson sometimes read romances for relaxation: 'when a boy he was immoderately fond of reading romances of chivalry, and he retained his fondness for them through life'.[17] The Rev. George Crabbe regretted the days when, 'to care unknown', he 'Winged round the globe with Rowland or Sir Guy'.[18] Romances continued to enjoy popularity well into the reign of Queen Victoria, despite the rise of the novel. Mayhew reports a Victorian bookseller as saying, in 1851, 'there's plenty of "Henry & Emmas", & ... "Good Books for Good Boys and Girls"; but when people buys really for their children, they buys the old stories – at least they does of me'.[19] The apparent triumph of realism was neither complete nor permanent. Romance was not lost but only relegated.

Rather suddenly, in the middle of the eighteenth century, the verse romances which were earlier versions of 'the old stories' sold by Mayhew's bookseller were taken out of the nursery into the library, and studied by adult scholars interested in medieval life and literature. Arthur Johnston estimates that Thomas Warton read seven hundred medieval manuscripts. Warton later wrote, in his *History of English Poetry* (1774–81), that 'Only genuine survivals from the distant past can move'. Warton discovered the celebrated Harley Lyrics, and *The Kingis Quair*, attributed to King James I of Scotland, which he was the first to print. Warton also found the source of Chaucer's *The Knight's*

Tale in Boccaccio's *Teseide*. He gave the first critical account of several medieval authors, including Gower, Lydgate, Hoccleve and Hawes. Walter Scott wrote that Thomas Warton used the 'torch of genius to illustrate the ruins'. (Warton did not like prose romances, even Malory's, which he read in Caxton's print.)

The focus of the present study is on imaginative medievalism rather than on its scholarly and antiquarian sources, so we must leave Warton. In his influential *Letters on Chivalry and Romance* (1765), Bishop Hurd observed that the Augustans had brought 'a great deal of good sense', but in the process we had lost 'a world of fine fabling'. Hurd's urbane reporting of French romance scholarship prepared the way for a new attitude to medieval romance. This new view was historical, in two ways: on the one hand, romances should not be judged by the standards of modern taste, but understood as the products of their age; on the other, romances could be taken as reliable witnesses to medieval behaviour, and especially to the practices of chivalry. In the words of the French scholar Caylus, romances were *fabuleux pour les événements, historique pour le reste*. English commentators say that the stories of the romances were 'marvellous', but that the descriptions nevertheless provide evidence as to the 'facts and manners' of their (chivalric) ancestors. Few today would read romances for facts, but there was, in the 1760s, a desire to know how knights and ladies had actually behaved, what they ate and wore, how tournaments were conducted, and so on. At that point, there was no such thing as medieval social history, the sources of which were only just beginning to reach print.

It was Thomas Percy who reaped the harvest sown by Warton and Hurd. Percy's *Reliques of Ancient English Poetry*, published in three volumes in 1765, put into circulation the texts of medieval metrical romances and ballads, with brief introductions and notes, and gave them a widespread and lasting popularity. The *Reliques* went into three further series, each larger than its predecessor. Percy included three Essays – on the Ancient Minstrels in England, the Origin of the English Stage, and the Ancient Metrical Romances. The *Reliques* made the 1760s the decade in which medieval antiquarianism became widely fashionable and then popular. In the long run, Percy's anthology, with its accompanying explanatory prose, also had a defining effect on English Romanticism, as Wordsworth was to acknowledge in a Preface of 1815.

'Let Observation, with extensive view, / Survey mankind from China to Peru.' So Johnson begins *The Vanity of Human Wishes*, expressing for once the optimism, as well as the curiosity, of the Enlightenment. Percy had his share of both these qualities. He was an energetic amateur and virtuoso of what is now called Comparative Literature. In 1762 Percy wrote to the discoverer of *The Gododdin* (a Welsh heroic poem on the seventh-century Battle of Catraeth), of his own plans to translate poems from the Erse, Runic, Chinese, Arab, Hebrew, Indian, Lapland, Greenland and Saxon tongues. Percy, an eighteenth-century Ezra Pound, had already published the first Chinese novel to appear in English (in translation from Portuguese), and later brought out English translations of Icelandic, Hebrew and Spanish texts. Then, while staying at the house of Humphrey Pitt, Percy saw a folio 'being used by the Maids to light the fire'.

Old manuscripts had been put to baser uses than lighting the fire. Alexander Pope, in *The Dunciad* (published between 1728 and 1742), refers to 'the martyrdom of jakes [lavatory] and fire'. He goes on to describe the dullest library he can imagine: 'A Gothic Library! of Greece and Rome / Well purg'd' (I, 144–5). The shelves groan with medieval books:

> The Classicks of an Age that heard of none;
> There Caxton slept, with Wynkin at his side,
> One clasp'd in wood, and one in strong cow-hide.[20]

On an altar, the hero of the poem sacrifices to the Goddess of Dulness a hecatomb of the dullest books of all. The biggest and most boring volume makes the base of the pyre: 'A folio Common-place / Founds the whole pyle' (139–40). The words 'folio Common-place' exactly describe the kind of large manuscript miscellany which Percy later retrieved from Humphrey Pitt's fireplace, making it the foundation for his own 'Gothic Library', the *Reliques*. (Large vernacular manuscripts were usually miscellanies; not single works but a collection of various texts.) Another kind of Gothic Library is what Horace Walpole wanted, and, in the 1750s, built. Its arched bookcases are copied from a doorway in an engraving by Wenceslaus Hollar of Old St Paul's. (Strawberry Hill is full of copies of medieval things, carefully made in the wrong materials, and playfully misapplied.) In one generation, attitudes towards the word 'Gothic', and towards medieval manuscripts, had been reversed. Pope's poison had become Percy's meat. What is now called the Percy Folio was a hundred-year-old manuscript collection of poems, historical ballads, songs and metrical romances, composed between the fourteenth and the seventeenth centuries. Samuel Johnson encouraged Percy to print them. But in what form should antiquated popular literature be presented to those accustomed to 'polite' literature? To this problem there is still no simple solution. Modernisation of spelling, punctuation, typography and presentational layout is the general rule in popular or general trade editions of English classics composed after the time of Malory and Caxton. 'Normalisation', a partial modernisation of spelling and punctuation, is sometimes applied to Chaucer and to Middle English lyrics. Earlier texts cannot be modernised, and 'diplomatic' or old-spelling editions are rare for texts later than Shakespeare's.

The manuscript texts that confronted Percy, having been copied and recopied, were full of scribal errors. And before these could be tackled, there was the thorny question of spelling. Middle English was not written in a standardised form, and manuscripts exhibit a bewildering variety of dialects. A good example of how baffling spelling could be is offered by the word which in the UK is now spelled 'through'. *The Middle English Dictionary* gives no fewer than 118 different spellings of this word. No scholar before the late twentieth century could offer, for any one of the dialects of Middle English, a norm on the basis of which manuscript spellings could be standardised. In documents of the sixteenth century, more than eighty spellings of the name Shakespeare are recorded. The dramatist himself used various spellings when signing his name. The spellings of Johnson's *Dictionary* of 1755 eventually came to be taken as authoritative by printers and in official English, just as the spellings of Noah Webster's *An American Dictionary of the English Language* of 1828 became standard in the United States. Educated people did not standardise spelling in their letters, and Jane Austen saw no need to correct the spelling of the title of her early story, *Love and Freindship*.

* * *

> Late, very late, correctness grew our care
> Pope, *Imitation of the First Epistle of the Second Book of Horace*

Correctitude came to be prized in the eighteenth century, and it was usual to correct older texts when reprinting them. Editions of Shakespeare offer a case in point. By the end of the seventeenth century there were not enough copies of the four successive Folio editions of the plays to meet demand from actors and readers. The Folios are monuments made for ownership, admiration and consultation rather than for use, and their old spellings looked strange by 1700. In 1709 the playwright Thomas Rowe made a new edition of Shakespeare's plays in eight octavo volumes. He modernised spelling and punctuation, and improved the presentation of the text by adding a list of dramatis personae and dividing each play into acts and scenes. Editing Shakespeare in 1725, the poet Pope regularised the distinction between prose and verse. Later editors restored readings and added line numbers. Most readers today, if aware of such changes, would think them real improvements. A scholarly old-spelling text of a Shakespeare play would be of little use to most readers and of none to actors.

It is therefore not surprising that William Shenstone, poet, garden-designer and arbiter of taste, advised Thomas Percy to improve the texts of the ballads and romances he was putting into his *Reliques*. He should edit them for euphony and elegance, and not feel constrained by the criteria of authenticity and accuracy applied in biblical or classical editing; it would suffice if Percy italicised lines he had rewritten. Shenstone, a 'landskip' gardener, had built a pictur-esque ruined priory in his much-admired grounds at The Leasowes, near Halesowen, Worcestershire. Old texts had to be modernised and polished so that they could be read with ease. Readers who had nodded over Percy's *Runes* were currently enthusing over an 'Ossian' which had, to say the least, been much improved. The end of the practice of improving texts came through Joseph Ritson, whom modern students of Middle English romances regard as the first professional editor. Ritson established the rule of authenticity, and refused to modernise the spelling of a text, still less to 'improve' for euphony or sense. The Preface to his edition of *Metrical Romanceës* (1802) accepts only what is verifiable. Ritson, a lawyer, a Jacobin anti-clerical, and a vegetarian, savaged the editions of medieval romances made by Percy, a bishop, and Warton, a fellow of Trinity College, Oxford. Ritson calls to mind Johnson's 'A mere antiquarian is a rugged being.' He died by his own hand in 1803.

What Percy and his successors did to the medieval texts they published, however, went beyond modernising the spelling. Popular literature from such a period had to overcome strong prejudices against things Gothic. The classic early expression of the divided attitudes that educated humanists had towards early native literature was that of Spenser's patron, Sir Philip Sidney, in his *Defence of Poesy* (1580). Sidney says of the 'Ballad of Chevy Chase': 'Certainly, I must confess my own barbarousness, I never heard the old song of Percy and Douglas that I found not my heart moved more than with a trumpet; and yet is it sung but by some blind crowder [fiddler], with no rougher voice than rude style; which, being so evil apparelled in the dust and cobwebs of that uncivil age, what would it work trimmed in the gorgeous eloquence of Pindar.'[21] Here Sidney's 'barbarous' natural response is not quite suppressed by what he had been taught in Rhetoric. In humanist rhetorical theory, language is the dress of thought: 'heroic' poetry requires high heroic diction. Therefore the crude old ballad would, in principle, be nobler in effect if dressed in the 'gorgeous eloquence' and complex metres of the Greek poet Pindar, whose Odes had celebrated victors at the Olympic Games in the sixth century BC. The grip of humanist theory upon the educated was so tenacious that Thomas Gray chose to cast his avant-garde experiment 'The Bard' in the form of a Pindaric ode, observing the conventions of this most elevated, artificial and ancient of Greek lyric forms, while combining the Greek with *cynghanedd*, a technique of medieval Welsh verse, as in '*Ru*in seize thee, *r*uthless King'. At the same time, Gray interested himself greatly, just as Sidney had done, in a living representative of the oral tradition, a Welsh harper who visited Cambridge; the harper was blind, like Sidney's 'crowder', like Milton, and like Gray's own Bard.[22]

The outbreak of medievalism in the 1760s was in part simply the result of the melting away of the prestige attached by neo-classical literary theory to notions of correctitude. This collapse of standards allowed readers encountering newly discovered writings from earlier English literary history to follow their native instincts. In 1765, Shakespeare's discordant mixture of comedy and tragedy, which had seriously offended generations of neo-classical critics, was successfully defended by Dr Johnson. Other neo-classical precepts were gradually abandoned, and readers came to favour the rude style of a blind fiddler to a reputedly gorgeous eloquence which only the most learned could hope to appreciate.

The first eight titles in the table of contents of Percy's *Reliques* (see Plate 4), Series the First, Book One, are as follows:

1. The Ancient Ballad of Chevy-Chase[23]
2. The Battle of Otterbourne
3. The Jew's Daughter. A Scottish Ballad
4. Sir Cauline
5. Edward, Edward. A Scottish Ballad
6. King Estmere
7. Sir Patrick Spence. A Scottish Ballad
8. Robin Hood and Guy of Gisborne

The only items at all well known today are 'Edward, Edward' and 'Sir Patrick Spens', stark Scottish ballads from the sixteenth and seventeenth centuries, first printed in England by Percy. The ballad would later prove to be more popular than the romance. As Percy says in his headnotes, these two ballads do not come from his Folio manuscript. Indeed, only one-sixth of the poems in the Percy Folio are included in the *Reliques*, which remains a miscellany. Percy collected his texts from a wide variety of sources. He collated, edited, annotated, introduced, improved, arranged and ordered them himself. To supplement his texts, and to fill gaps in them, he collaborated with a range of other amateurs – for example, Lord Hailes in Scotland, Thomas Warton and David Garrick – and compared other manuscript versions in the Library of the newly founded British Museum. Among the popular romances Percy printed were *Bevis, Sir Guy, The*

Seven Champions and *Valentine and Orson*. He also published ballad versions of others. Percy's introductory 'Essay on the Ancient Metrical Romances', revised in subsequent editions, argued that these romances were better than the polished poems of Gower or Lydgate. He had prepared a further twenty-six metrical romances, which remained in manuscript. The 'Essay on Minstrels' treated these medieval entertainers kindly and with some reverence. Ritson, an acid specialist, observed that minstrels, as vagrants, could never have been admitted to a French-speaking court.

Percy's minstrels are relatives of Gray's Bard, and models for James Beattie's poem in Spenserian stanzas, *The Minstrel* (1771, 1774). The *Reliques* also provided a partial model for *The Scots Musical Museum* (1787–1803), to which Robert Burns contributed; and a complete one for Walter Scott's collection, *The Minstrelsy of the Scottish Border* (1802–3). Percy's anthology, and the essays which accompanied it, provided the materials, the theory, the models and the audience for Scott's first great success, *The Lay of the Last Minstrel* (1805), to be looked at in the next chapter.

Lyrical Ballads, published in 1798 by William Wordsworth and S.T. Coleridge, is today far better known than Scott's *Lay*. For a century, *Lyrical Ballads* was taken as inaugurating the great sequence of English Romantic poetry which closed with the death of Byron in 1824. (William Blake had printed his *Songs of Innocence* in 1789, but they were for seventy years largely ignored.) In the second edition of *Lyrical Ballads* in 1800, Wordsworth added his famous Preface, which defiantly presents the volume as a revolutionary departure from neo-classical poetic norms. The 1800 Preface is a grand manifesto, and some of the ballads are almost as remarkable as Wordsworth's deepest work. But the quality of the poems has meant that the Preface has often been mistaken for a reliable account of the condition of poetry at the moment when Wordsworth came upon the scene. This it is not. The Preface attacks the artifice of eighteenth-century verse, passing over its last forty years in strategic silence. Wordsworth denounces the abuses of a poetic diction which at the time he was writing was no longer used, except by George Crabbe, born in 1754.[24]

The present chapter began with a review of the Gothic Decade of the 1760s, which ended with the death of Chatterton. The advance of the hirsute Goths upon the Augustan Versailles implied by Wordsworth in his Preface of 1800 had actually occurred in the 1760s, when each departure from neo-classical norms had met with an eager welcome. The bearded barbarians were fêted in the six British universities. Indeed, half the Goths were professors: Gray at Cambridge, Warton at Oxford, Beattie at Aberdeen and Hugh Blair (Macpherson's champion) first at Aberdeen and then at Edinburgh. Neo-classic, which had never been the only kind of eighteenth-century poetry, had lost its battle, in England if not in Edinburgh, before Wordsworth was born. He might not have known this at Hawkshead, but must have discovered it at Cambridge. Wordsworth's silence on this point is partly due to his sublime egotism. Yet Wordsworth's silences can be conscious: the 1800 Preface makes no mention of Coleridge. In 1674, the critic Nicolas Boileau had written, of the arrival of regularity in French versification, *Enfin Malherbe vint* – 'at last Malherbe arrived'. The 1800 Preface announces that relief from the tyranny of the neo-classical is at hand, leaving the reader to guess the name of the leader of the relieving force.

Revisiting the topic in 1815, in a less well-known Preface, Wordsworth acknowledged that the Romantic poets had owed a large debt to Percy's *Reliques*. After justly remarking that Percy's texts had been 'collected, new-modelled, and . . . composed by the Editor', Wordsworth corrected one oversight in his 1800 Preface by declaring that Percy had 'absolutely redeemed' English poetry. He added that 'I do not think that there is an able Writer in verse of the present day who would not be proud to acknowledge his obligations to the *Reliques*.' In victory, magnanimity. The implausible Bards, Druids and Goths of the 1760s had won after all.[25]

CHAPTER 2

Chivalry, Romances and Revival

CHAUCER INTO SCOTT: *THE LAY OF THE LAST
MINSTREL* AND *IVANHOE*

The spirit of humanity, which distinguishes modern times . . . the
gallantry which prevails in our conversations . . . the point
of honour . . . which by teaching us to consider the importance
of others, makes us value our own; these circumstances arise
out of chivalry, and discriminate the modern from the ancient
world.

Gilbert Stuart, *A View of Society in Europe*, Edinburgh, 1778[1]

. . . excepting only the change which followed from the introduction of the Christian religion, we know no cause which has
produced such general and permanent difference between the
ancients and moderns, as that which has arisen out of the institution of chivalry.

Walter Scott, 'Essay on Chivalry', *Encyclopaedia Britannica*, 1824

To write a modern romance of chivalry seems to be much such a
phantasy as to build a modern abbey, or an English pagoda.

Francis Jeffrey, reviewing Scott's *Marmion*, 1808[2]

'The age of chivalry is gone – that of sophisters, economists, and
calculators, has succeeded; and the glory of Europe is extinguished
for ever.' The exclamation that launches this rhetorical climax is the
best remembered of Edmund Burke's *Reflections on the Revolution in
France*. Burke, a leader in the Whig opposition to the Tory government of William Pitt the Younger, had made his name as an eloquent
critic of British policy in India. A political thinker, his principle was
constitutional restraint upon absolutism, both in Britain and in
George III's empire, whether in India, in America or in his native
Ireland. Burke's immediate condemnation of the French Revolution

(he published his *Reflections* in 1790) shocked Thomas Jefferson and
some *philosophes*, and also the radicals in his own party. He flatly
denied the parallel between the revolution in France and the 'Glorious'
English Revolution of 1688, a parallel often claimed by British radicals and Dissenters in 1789. The constitutional settlement of 1688
had established the power of Parliament to limit the royal preroga-
tive, and contrived to tie up the outcomes of the Civil War in a formula
which was not much modified until the Great Reform Act of 1832. At
the outbreak of the French Revolution, England had been at peace
ever since the Young Pretender, Charles Stuart, retreated from Derby
in 1745.

Much of the excitement and most of any initial British welcome
for the French Revolution had evaporated by the end of 1792. In the
Terror of that year, hundreds of sympathisers with the French *Ancien
régime* of crown and Church had been guillotined. Thomas Paine, a
champion of and participant in the American Revolution, answered
Burke's *Reflections on the Revolution in France* with *The Rights of
Man*, an argument in favour of the radical egalitarianism of this
second Revolution. In Paris, Paine took part in the councils of the
revolutionaries. He argued against executing the King, which put him
in danger of the guillotine. In prison for nearly a year, he wrote *The
Age of Reason*, a title which contrasts with Burke's 'age of chivalry'. In
1793 the revolutionaries executed the King and then the Queen, and,
later that year, 17,000 opponents. The events of the Terror made
Burke's foresight seem truly prophetic. The Queen's execution recalled
his cry that the age of chivalry was gone from Europe. The following
passage might certainly have appealed to the young Walter Scott: 'All
the decent drapery of life is to be rudely torn off. All of the super-
added ideas, furnished from the wardrobe of a moral imagination,
which the heart owns and the understanding ratifies, as necessary to
cover the defects of our own naked shivering nature, and to raise it to
dignity in our estimation, are to be exploded as ridiculous, absurd,
and antiquated fashion.'[3]

Burke was determined that the chivalry and mutual forbearance
which had slowly built a more civilised British society should not be
surrendered. Chivalry was originally the ideal code of a chevalier, or
knight, in the era of the First Crusade – an aspiration, rather than a

description of usual behaviour. It received various formulations: ardently Christian orders of knighthood were founded; some epics and romances celebrated martial action, others celebrated love as well as war, some romances were spiritual. As education spread beyond the clergy, more peaceful roles for the leaders of lay society, and for those who served and advised them, were gradually articulated. A late example is Castiglione's *Il Cortegiano* ('The Courtier') of 1528. Codes of honour for the gentry and the nobility continued to evolve during the Tudor and Stuart centuries, and a neo-classical gloss was sometimes put upon the medieval mix of Christian and feudal ideals. The age of chivalry survived the age of cavalry. Long after battles were decided by artillery rather than by a few heavily armed horsemen, cavaliers and gentlemen aspired to ride well, and, in principle, dismounted with alacrity to help a lady in distress. In 1580, the chivalrous Sir Philip Sidney wrote the first formal English 'defence' of literature, beginning it with a discussion of the art of horsemanship. Sonnet 41 of Sidney's *Astrophil and Stella* is set at the tournament held by Queen Elizabeth I annually on her Accession Day: 'Having this day my horse, my hand, my lance, / Guided so well, that I received the prize.'[4] A lance won this cavalier the prize in the lists, but his death-wound at the Battle of Zutphen came from a bullet.

In Georgian Britain a nobleman usually rode not on a horse but in a carriage, with his coat of arms on the door, arms signifying rank and, ideally, possessions. Heraldry and genealogy were not hobbies, but had material consequences – for eldest sons, lawyers, tenants and neighbours and also for those whom eldest sons might marry. Conduct books were widely read; Lord Chesterfield's *Letters to his Son*, for example, was published in 1774. Among the worldly maxims Chesterfield offers his natural son is, 'Women, then, are only children of a larger growth.'

In 1765 Bishop Hurd's *Letters on Chivalry and Romance* gave chivalry a new historical and literary dimension. Richard Hurd and Thomas Percy were, like most antiquarians, members of the hierarchy of the Church of England. Percy's translating and editing were done in what time could be spared from more serious duties; a *Key to the New Testament* and a translation of the Song of Solomon are among his early works. An Anglican clergyman was by virtue of his office an honorary member of the gentry. Some Georgian gentry were descended from those whose services had been to Parliament or to the City of London, and whose business was diplomatic or even financial rather than military. Some had rendered personal services, especially under Charles II. It was always the crown, as fount of honour, which awarded titles. England, unified under the crown of Wessex since the tenth century, had evolved its Parliament, legal system, institutions and many social forms during the medieval centuries. It is not surprising that some scholarly clerics among the Georgian gentry were interested by accounts of early chivalry. Jane Austen, the daughter of a clergyman, gave the heroine of her most carefully planned novel a Norman name, and married her to a Mr Knightley. Yet her final novel, *Persuasion*, sharply caricatures a Somerset baronet who has more respect for titles than for rising naval officers whose service against the French has brought them fortune and national respect. Obligation is part of privilege, and only obligation and service can justify inherited privilege. Yet the moral justification of heritable rank in society was precisely what the French Revolution denied. As reliable information about what chivalry had been like, and how knights and ladies had behaved, was unobtainable in the reign of George III, the claim to be printing, or translating, from a manuscript lent a work authenticity. We saw in Chapter 1 that Macpherson, Walpole and Chatterton exploited this impression in different ways. Percy, though he 'improved' his texts, did print from real manuscripts. A manuscript's authenticity appeared to guarantee the genuineness of what it said.

As the writing of history was still based as much on literary as on documentary or archaeological evidence, medieval romances could be taken as authentic reflections of medieval 'facts and manners', and the romance code of honour accepted as a guide for how life was lived. Thus, in Chaucer's *Knight's Tale*, Duke Theseus, coming home to Athens to celebrate his wedding to Hippolyta, finds distressed widows kneeling in the roadway imploring his assistance; Creon has refused them permission to bury the bodies of their husbands, killed in the siege of Thebes. Chaucer's Theseus turns back from the gates of Athens, displays his banner, and rides immediately to Thebes to right the wrongs of these noble widows. Bishop Hurd assumed that medieval knights would have acted in this way in defence of ladies.

Hurd's readers were fascinated by chivalry, but had been taught to think of feudalism as tyrannical. This may perhaps explain Hurd's ingenuous proposal that the giants found in romances should be understood as representations of feudal lords. The bishop's desperate resort to allegory suggests the limits of literal exegesis. But when, as happens in medieval romances, something puzzling – 'the marvellous' – occurs, allegory is an obvious way out, the way of Hurd when faced with giants. Another way out is to assume authorial irony, the path taken by the comedian Terry Jones when faced with Chaucer's line, in the Prologue to the *Canterbury Tales*, 'He was a verray parfit gentil Knyght'. Hurd cannot take giants seriously, Jones cannot take chivalry seriously. Jones's reading of Crusade history confirms his mistrust of such an ideal. His book *Chaucer's Knight: Portrait of a Mercenary* (1980) shows that knighthood had fallen away from its Christian ideals by the time of Chaucer, and concludes that in Richard II's day there could not have been any such genuine, perfect and noble knight. But it does not follow from this that Chaucer is satirising knighthood, still less that he intended his audience to reject 'Trouthe and honour, fredom and curtesie', the ideals his Knight embodies. Chaucer's Knight was an ideal to be admired, not a satire upon actuality. Irony can lie in the ear of the hearer. Jones's Knight would have puzzled Chaucer.

In France, chivalric romances did not go out of fashion at the Renaissance, and had continued to interest scholars. In Germany, an edition of the medieval epic, the *Nibelungenlied*, appeared in 1757, and, as Thomas Carlyle later observed, 'books that had circulated only in mean guise for the amusement of the people, [became] important, not to one or two virtuosos, but to the general body of the learned'.[5] In England, popular romances were recommended in Hurd's *Letters on Chivalry and Romance*, and could be read in Percy's *Reliques*. This Europe-wide interest in the historic origins of the romance suggests a preoccupation with noble behaviour in love and war, the theme of French heroic plays and romances, English Restoration tragedies and Handel's opera. This preoccupation was not confined to rulers or to the gentry, for most of the romances now published were 'mean', not aristocratic. In earlier times, questions of honour had been the theme of the Renaissance romance of chivalry or romantic epic, from Ariosto to Sidney's prose *Arcadia*. It was from the *Arcadia* that King Charles I is said to have taken the noble Pamela's prayer to read on the eve of his execution, and the heroine of Samuel Richardson's first novel, a servant-girl who keeps her honour, is also named after Sidney's Pamela.

The medieval romances of chivalry, such as those of Chrétien de Troyes, and the English metrical romances, survived in forms of the medieval vernaculars distant from modern French and more distant from modern English. They were further still from the classical Latin of the academic curriculum, and from critical tradition. Historical curiosity about how knights and ladies had behaved was a reason, or a pretext, for reading Percy's medieval romances. Burke chose to regard the fact that so few Frenchmen had drawn swords to defend their Queen as a sign that the age of chivalry, the honour of Europe, had gone. For a century England had fought France abroad, but this war, culminating in Napoleon's blockade, came very close to home, and perhaps made England more aware of how long she had enjoyed domestic peace and order. Some sought reasons for England's relative stability in the historical record. Curiosity about chivalry, and the popularity of Percy's *Reliques*, gradually grew into something more than a fashion. It is hard not to think that some part of this must have been due to the guillotine and to Napoleon.

It was in any case through the verse romances of Walter Scott, a Unionist and a 'North Briton', that readers in Europe, the British empire and the United States were first able to imagine life in more chivalrous ages. History-reading had become popular in the eighteenth century, and the voluminous histories of England by David Hume and Tobias Smollett, both Scots, sold well. Scott devised a form of fiction which seemed historical. Comparative 'philosophical' history was popular also, and progressive models, such as Hume's four-age evolution of human history leading to the constitutional-commercial society of Georgian Britain, were widely accepted before the French Revolution. What then happened in Europe inclined British readers of Scott to dwell less on the rights of man, and woman, and more on what held society together. They enjoyed Scott's verse romances, the plots of which resemble those of Shakespeare's comedies, themselves taken from old romances. Considered politically, Scott's verse romances are benign fables of changes accommodated and differences contained and reconciled within the mutual obligations of idealised traditional societies. Indeed, Scott's romances offer a fictional demonstration of Burke's principle of mutual restraint, and of the theory advanced in his *Reflections on the Revolution in France* that courtesy was not only the oil which lent grace to social life and eased the social mechanism, but also a vital civic principle which allowed social and political change and development.

By the 1820s the reputation of Walter Scott was almost as high as it was broad. Hugely popular, he was for generations regarded as the greatest of British novelists, as he was by Charles Dickens and George Eliot. At 200 feet (61 metres), the Scott Monument in Edinburgh is the grandest monument to a British writer, and perhaps the grandest in the world. 'The block-heads talk of my being like Shakespeare – not fit to tie his brogues,' he wrote in his *Journal* for 11 December 1826.[6] But the career of the 'Wizard of the North' ended sadly. To pay the debts of his publishers, who had been bankrupted in the collapse of credit after Waterloo, Scott wrote book after book after book, diluting his reputation. His fame declined towards the end of Victoria's reign, and had far to fall. Although Scott currently enjoys an academic rally, the present writer, in thirty-three years in Scottish universities, met a number of university teachers of English literature who, if they had tried a novel by Scott, had failed to finish it. Scott's fame is a large black hole, though it is a hole with a certain shape, for the scale of his impact permanently altered the cultural landscape. He remains familiar by repute, unlike Robert Southey, and his works have stayed in print, unlike those of Chatterton and Macpherson. The Edinburgh Edition of the Waverley Novels has over twenty years brought out critical editions of the texts of all twenty-eight of Scott's novels. The first of ten volumes of Scott's verse is to appear in 2017 from Edinburgh University Press. No scholarly edition of his verse is currently in print, and professional students of Scott are not always very familiar with his verse romances. This academic revival of Scott seems unlikely to win back a popular readership, even for the historical fiction set in Scotland. Yet the frequency with which the name of this Scottish writer has to appear in a book about modern England testifies to his extraordinary and lasting impact.

Scott began as a poet, and with *The Lay of the Last Minstrel, The Lady of the Lake* and *Marmion* enjoyed a success more immediate than was enjoyed by the poetry of Wordsworth, Coleridge, Southey, Shelley or Keats, and achieved a far wider popularity. Many Victorians continued to think Scott equal or superior to his fellow Romantic poets. Indeed, Thomas Hardy, born eight years after Scott's death, 'never ceased to regret that the author of "the most Homeric poem in the English language" (*Marmion*) should later have *declined* on prose fiction.'[7] Another measure of Scott's worth as a poet is the fact that from the sales of *The Lady of the Lake* he earned £10,000.[8]

Scott's major writing came in three stages. His first original work, *The Lay of the Last Minstrel*, a verse romance of 3,077 lines, appeared in 1805, after which he was welcomed as a popular verse romancer. After *Waverley*, anonymously published in 1814, he became a popular novelist. In 1819, after nine historical novels, 'The Author of *Waverley*' published *Ivanhoe: A Romance*, set for the first time not in post-Reformation Scotland but in pre-Reformation England. He then became a popular prose romancer. So Scott's popularity was first and last as a writer of romance.

Fiction in verse or prose is only part of Scott's immense output. He published editions of Dryden, Defoe and Swift, a nine-volume *Life of Napoleon Bonaparte*, and much much more. What he wrote before *The Lay of the Last Minstrel*, though it is little read today, bears directly on the present story. Scott's first publication, in 1797, was 'William and Helen', a re-translation from German of Bürger's ballad *Lenore*, itself a translation from a Scottish ballad found in both Ramsay's *Tea-Table Miscellany* and Percy's *Reliques*. At the age of twelve, Scott had devoured Percy's miscellany of ballads, songs, historical poems and metrical romances, *The Reliques of Ancient English Poetry*, which begins with a border ballad. Scott's next publication was *The Minstrelsy of the Scottish Border*, which was a collection, in three volumes, of ballads from local singers and sources, made by Scott and some friends but edited and published by Scott. He then edited *Sir Tristrem*, a verse romance from the Auchinleck Manuscript, a large miscellany of medieval verse, one which is now well known to scholars, and may have been known to Geoffrey Chaucer. This manuscript had been presented to the Advocates' Library in Edinburgh in 1744 by Alexander Boswell of Auchinleck. Alexander, the father of James Boswell, had bought it from a professor at Aberdeen who was using leaves from the manuscript to make covers for notebooks. Scott was able to take the Auchinleck Manuscript home from the Advocates' Library between 1789 and 1800, and had it at Abbotsford again in 1801.[9]

Scott's first three publications follow the tradition and example of Percy. His *Sir Tristrem* was the most handsome edition of a medieval verse romance yet to appear, with large margins, a learned introduction and scholarly notes. The original text is incomplete, but Scott gave the story an ending in the same metre, composed by himself. He had been urged to do so by George Ellis, another amateur editor of medieval verse. Percy had sometimes filled in a gap, but to complete a text in this way would occur to few later editors of medieval texts. J.R.R. Tolkien was a partial exception to this, but his verse sequel to the Old English poem *The Battle of Maldon* is in modern English. Scott's edition of *Sir Tristrem* is now chiefly known to professional editors for negative reasons: he mistakenly thought that the language of the romance was Scots, and that its author was Thomas the Rhymer of Erceldoune. A more productive point is that the completion of *Sir Tristrem* set Scott on his career of composing verse and prose on historical subjects, supplying his own explanatory notes. He was thus fulfilling the hope of the generation of Warton, Percy and Gray that verse romance would enjoy a modern revival.

* * *

A digression is now necessary to arrive at some idea of what verse romances were like. Romance is less a literary form than a mode. The word comes from French *romauns*, and originally meant a story in one of the popular offshoots of the Roman tongue which are now called romance languages. Romance involves adventure and what the eighteenth century called 'the marvellous'. A common form of romance is the quest, in which the hero proves himself; the more courtly romances feature an exalted kind of love between the sexes, while the popular ones are filled with martial deeds of prowess. Romance is a narrative form less realistic than the novel, and often concludes in a union or reunion. In romances, as in the folk and fairy tales from which they derive, wishes come true: 'all losses are restored, and sorrows end', as in Shakespeare's *The Tempest*.

Examples may help to pinpoint the form more clearly than description can. A historical course in English literature, then, might include among verse romances *Sir Gawain and the Green Knight*, Chaucer's *Knight's Tale*, the tales of his Franklin or Clerk, perhaps his *Troilus and Criseyde*, and perhaps part of Spenser's *The Faerie Queene*. In the fifteenth century there were many prose romances too, notably Malory's *Le Morte Darthur*, printed by William Caxton in 1485. Malory has come to embody medieval romance to modern readers, thanks to the overwhelming popularity of his work, as mediated by Tennyson, with the Pre-Raphaelites and their followers, William Morris and Edward Burne-Jones, to whom *Le Morte Darthur* provided many subjects. Malory was the source of the Arthurianism which was so pervasive in Victorian literature and visual art. It comes therefore as something of a shock to realise that there is scarcely a trace of Malory in an English Romantic poet before Tennyson. The reason for this is that Malory was not reprinted in the eighteenth century. In 1815 the most recently printed version of *Le Morte Darthur* was Stansby's edition of 1634, which was to be reprinted with modernised spelling in 1816. For the English Romantic poets, Percy held the position later held by Malory, and – more crucially – 'romances' meant verse romances not prose romances.

The verse romances which held Percy's public, moreover, were not the art romances of Chaucer but popular romances, the metrical tales of knightly adventure which had been enjoyed ever since the days of the minstrels. (A sample from the romance of *Sir Isumbras* is given in note 14 to Chapter 8, on page 256.) When they are read rather than heard, the style of these popular romances is formulaic and uneconomical. In his tale of *Sir Thopas*, Chaucer wrote a parody of their artless language and inconsequential narration. He arranges for this hopelessly inept tale to be told by his fictive self, the pilgrim Chaucer:

> Listeth, lordes, in good entent,
> And I wol telle verrayment
>   Of myrthe and of solas,
> Al of a knyght was fair and gent
> In bataille and in tourneyment;
>   His name was Sire Thopas.

Sir Thopas, or Topaz, a Flemish knight, has 'lippes red as rose', rhyming
with his 'semely nose'. He rides out hunting but has no success:

> Sire Thopas eek so wery was
> For priking on the softe gras,
>   So fiers was his corage,
> That doun he leyde him in that plas . . .

Recalling a dream of a lovely 'elf-queene', he rides on to seek her out.
Reaching 'The countree of Fairye / So wilde', he is challenged by a 'greet
geaunt', but, not having his armour, Sir T. retires, the giant casting
stones at him. In the Second Fitt, Thopas returns to his house in the
town of Poperinge, and arms himself at length. The Third Fitt begins:

> Now holde youre mouth, *par charitee*,
> Bothe knyght and lady free,
> And herkneth to my spell . . .[10]

Sir Thopas, a Belgian J. Alfred Prufrock, rides out once more, with
a lily in his helmet. Chaucer tells us that he sleeps out of doors, using
his helmet for a pillow. But after several more stanzas, nothing has
happened, and the Host of the Tabard Inn cuts Chaucer short,
damning his 'rym dogerel', and throwing in the final comment that
Chaucer's rhyming is 'not worth a turd'. Rhyming was a point upon
which the Host's creator prided himself.

Chaucer's many writings show that after a few pages in the
romance mode, he felt a need of relief. The shaggy dog story of Sir
Thopas mocks minstrel romance for its cliché, bathos and inconse-
quence. But Chaucer also arranges that his own 'high' romance
should sometimes be lit unromantically from below. At the climax of
Chaucer's finest work, Troilus, kneeling by the bed of Criseyde,
swoons; Pandarus throws him into the bed and rips off his shirt.[11] In
the *Canterbury Tales*, the Wife of Bath opens her tale with 'In the olde
dayes of the king Arthour', a formula introducing a romance. The
Wife, who has proclaimed to the pilgrims that she would welcome a
sixth husband, relates how a young knight of Arthur's court, encountering a pretty girl walking by the river, ravishes her. The usual

penalty for this crime was death, but Arthur hands the rapist over to the Queen for punishment. Guenevere and her ladies decree that the young knight must die – unless, within a year and a day, he can tell the court of ladies 'what it is that women most desire'. One of the few things the Wife of Bath makes clear in the long preamble to her tale, is what it is that she most desires. Plot, situation and dialogue offer none of the refined sentiment prized in the more courtly romances of 'the olde dayes of the king Arthour'. Yet a surprising doctrine emerges clearly from the Wife's unlikely romance: that true 'gentillesse' is not 'descended out of old richesse' for 'Christ wol [wills that] we clayme of him our gentillesse'. Nobility is not an inherited rank, but a grace that comes with conduct modelled on that of Christ.

In the eighteenth century, romance was regarded as the literary genre which defined the Middle Ages. The remoteness and marvellousness of romance made a change from modern common sense and from the 'low' realism of Defoe, Richardson, Fielding and Smollett. In truth, romance is not especially medieval. At the dawn of Greek literature the *Odyssey* is full of romance, and prose romances survive from late Greek literature. Stories of this kind must precede literacy, and would survive it, since the genre in which the deepest human wishes come true is perennial. Realism was part of the novel's modernity, but realism in fiction is no longer modern and may have passed its peak. Romances are currently more popular than novels, if not more critically esteemed. British readers voted recently for their favourite book. Top of the poll was a romance written by a medievalist for his children, *The Lord of the Rings*, which has been made into a series of popular films. Second in this British poll came Jane Austen's *Pride and Prejudice*, which has also been filmed, and which video shops shelved under 'romance'.

The popularity of romance can make intellectuals suspicious, and in the hierarchy of disciplines in the medieval university, Logic occupied a place above Rhetoric. Rhetoric included secular literature, which had no prestige with theologians, especially if composed in the vernacular tongues. Clerical intellectuals often dismissed romance with contempt. When in the twelfth century Geoffrey of Monmouth brought out his Latin *History of the Kings of Britain*, releasing the legend of King Arthur into the bloodstream of Europe, the historian William of Newburgh sniffed at Geoffrey's tales of the 'once and future king' as a pack of lies invented to please the Britons. It did please the Britons, and the Bretons and their neighbours the Normans, then the Anglo-Normans and their Angevin successors, and eventually the English. William's view of Geoffrey is rather like Dr Johnson's reaction to the 'impudent forgeries' of Macpherson, or the reactions of Richard Bentley to Pope's version of the *Iliad*, of the Oxford historian E.A. Freeman to Scott's *Ivanhoe*, and of Thomas Babington Macaulay to Dickens and Thackeray. Scholars and imaginative writers do not always understand each other.

The original of King Arthur flourished, if at all, in the sixth century, winning victories against the Saxon invader. In 1190 a tomb was constructed at Glastonbury Abbey, bearing an inscription in an antique style, which declared that below lay the remains of King Arthur and Queen Guenevere. Modern scholars prefer to regard the tomb as a pious fraud to attract visitors to a holy place, later to be frequented by pilgrims to the Holy Thorn planted by Joseph of Arimathea. In 1278 Edward I, the addressee of the last speech of Gray's Bard (see page 1), reinterred the bones of the legendary Arthur at Glastonbury, making a point confirmed by his own conquest of Wales in 1282: Arthur may once have been a king, but he was dead and buried in England, and would not come again in Wales. The only *Arthurus redivivus* was Edward, King of Britain.[12] Arthur was evidently very popular in the twelfth century, and his cult was spreading and being spread in the thirteenth century. The fourteenth century saw another government-inspired revival, one which is still extant. Edward III used Edward I's reconstruction of King Arthur's Round Table for the Knights of the Garter, an Order of Chivalry which he, Edward III, created on St George's Day in 1348. The Knights of the Garter still meet in St George's Chapel at Windsor. Arthur's Round Table, the original of which may never have existed, can yet be seen in the Great Hall of Winchester Castle. Winchester was the capital of England under King Alfred, but William the Conqueror moved the capital to London. The table was used again by Henry VII, who was of Welsh descent, to invest the new Tudor dynasty with an Arthurian legitimacy.[13]

Literature does not always allow the mirror of truth to be obscured by the mist of fact. In medieval England, the story of Orpheus and

Eurydice was known chiefly from the versions in Ovid and Virgil, though King Alfred had translated Boethius, who has a moralised summary of the story. The classical Orpheus lived in Thrace, but the English one lived in Winchester. In the Auchinleck Manuscript of *c.* 1330, the manuscript which Scott had borrowed from the Advocates' Library (see pages 30–1), the romance of *Sir Orfeo* begins: 'Orfeo was a king, / In Inglond a heighe lording'. A little later the audience is told that:

This king sojourned in Traciens	*Thracians, i.e. Thrace*
That was a cite of noble defence,	
For Winchester was cleped tho	*called then*
Traciens withouten no.	*it cannot be denied*[14]

This is enough to show that, both in the *History of the Kings of Britain* of Geoffrey of Monmouth and in popular romance, Arthurian legend was given a local habitation and a name, and put to various uses: to satisfy historical curiosity about origins; to attract visitors and their revenue; to remind the Celts that the kings of Britain were Plantagenet; to bolster patriotic and chivalric morale; to reward service; and to bring home a good story. Geoffrey tells that Britain was founded by Brut, or Brutus, the grandson of Aeneas. On a map produced in Chaucer's lifetime, London appears as '*Troy Novaunt*', New Troy.

Some historians have tried to represent the Medieval Revival and the re-creation of tradition as inventions of the nineteenth century. But Virgil wrote Augustus into the legends of the founding of Rome, and Spenser did a similar thing for Elizabeth I. If medievalism is the creative reviving of the legendary ancestral past, we may seriously speak of it as having flourished in Geoffrey's work and at Glastonbury three centuries *before* the end of the Middle Ages. And three centuries earlier still, a poem introduced an unhistorical Beowulf into the historical ancestry of its intended audience. Such 'medieval' revivals long preceded the classical revival known as the Renaissance, and make a mockery of rigid periodisation. Time is not as compartmentalised as school history books suggest. There were survivals and revivals from the beginnings of history, and from before the invention of writing.

* * *

On completing the old romance of *Sir Tristrem*, Scott proceeded to compose one of his own, *The Lay of the Last Minstrel* (1805). It was the first decisive move of his career. Like James Boswell, he had strengthened a remarkable verbal memory by the practice of the law. In his youth he had ridden round the Borders collecting ballads and verse tales, 'makin' himsell a' the time', as his friend Robert Shortreed said, and committed much to memory.[15] In 1802 he heard Sir John Stoddart recite Coleridge's unpublished poem *Christabel*, a romance in a metre which, as Coleridge claimed when he finally published the fragment in 1816, was 'founded on a new principle ... counting in each line the accents, not the syllables'.[16] Scott borrowed *Christabel*'s verse-form, and some verbal details, for *The Lay of the Last Minstrel*, drawing also on Percy's ballads and romances. Thus, from the eighteenth-century cult of medieval Romance came the nineteenth-century Romantic poem. In a Preface to the *Lay*, Scott says that he adopted 'the measured short line ... that ... may be termed the Romantic stanza'. Scott tells us that he began to compose a medieval lay, and having read it aloud to some friends, decided to add 'an ancient Minstrel, the last of his race', a linking and framing figure who begins and ends each of the poem's six cantos.[17]

The Lay is improvised by the Minstrel for the Lady of Branksome Hall, in the Scottish Borders. The period is the 1690s. The Minstrel's *Lay* weaves legend, folktale and fantasy into the family history of the Montagu Douglas Scotts, Dukes of Buccleuch, a family to which Walter Scott could claim kindred. Branksome Hall belongs to these Scotts. The Lay has a series of dissolving time-frames, each less historically definite than the last. The Minstrel tells of events in the time of Mary Queen of Scots, the 1550s. Its characters are medieval knights and ladies, yeomen and armourers. More comprehensively medieval is the Monk of Melrose Abbey. He is said to be a hundred years old, but this is a gross underestimate. A Crusader in his youth ('in Paynim contries I have trod, / And fought beneath the Cross of God'), he was also a companion of the Wizard, Michael Scott, a thirteenth-century philosopher and alchemist, whose tomb in Melrose Abbey he now guards. With the introduction of Michael Scott *The Lay* dissolves from medieval into Gothic. The Wizard's old comrade, the Monk, seems the sole inhabitant of an Abbey which is already in ruins. The tomb of Michael Scott contains the Wizard's book of magic spells, which will be required by the plot; it is later disinterred by moonlight.

The main story of *The Lay*, like that of Coleridge's *Christabel*, concerns rivals and lovers from feuding families. These loving enemies live in the Border country between England and Scotland, much fought over, and the scene of many ballads. Thanks to chivalry and chastity – and to Michael Scott's magic spell – love is able to bring an end to this feud. The warring clans are reconciled in marriage, but the poem ends with Scott's translation of the *Dies irae* at a Gothic funeral at Melrose Abbey.

Whereas the heroine of Coleridge's Gothic *Christabel* is possessed by a witch, Scott's *Lay* lightens the demonic side, and provides the happy wedding with which Coleridge had intended to end his tale. In its turn, Keats's 'The Eve of St Agnes' revises the benign and genial medievalism of Scott's verse romance. In the next chapter, these three Romantic romances are compared more fully. The present chapter concludes with an extended look at the simplest form of literary medievalism, borrowing directly from a medieval text. Scott used the same passages from Chaucer in *The Lay of the Last Minstrel*, his first verse romance, and in his first prose romance, *Ivanhoe*.

One of Scott's sources for the *Lay* is the first of the *Canterbury Tales*, that of Chaucer's Knight. It tells of how love caused rival cousins to fight in the woods 'up to the ankles in their blood'; how the resulting tournament decreed by Theseus, Duke of Athens, ended in the death of one cousin, Arcite; and how, years later, Theseus wedded his niece Emelye to the other, Palamon. Shakespeare had borrowed Theseus and the young Athenian lovers for his *A Midsummer Night's Dream*, making the story into a comedy by adding a second lady and by allowing both cousins to live and to marry. Scott took from the *Knight's Tale* the single combat in the woods and the elaborate funeral of the defeated rival. He also added a second tournament.

Canto I of the Minstrel's *Lay* gives us, in its fourth stanza, the knights feasting in Branksome Hall:

> Ten of them were sheathed in steel,
> With belted sword, and spur on heel;
> They quitted not their harness bright,

Neither by day, nor yet by night;
They lay down to rest
   With corselet laced,
Pillow'd on buckler cold and hard;
   They carved at the meal
   With gloves of steel,
And they drank the red wine through the helmet barred.[18]

These are real knights: they drink through the bars of their helmets, perhaps with a straw picked up from the rushes on the hall floor. It might be difficult to pick up a straw when wearing gloves of steel, but Scott is not entirely serious. The description is heightened into genial comic hyperbole. This owes something to the comic excess of oral romance, to the fantasy of Ariosto, and to Horace Walpole's kitsch *Castle of Otranto*. It will be remembered that Walpole's cult romance had begun with a bridegroom being crushed to death by a falling helmet, and that Scott had described *Otranto* as 'the first modern attempt to found a tale of *amusing fiction* upon the basis of the ancient romances of chivalry' (emphasis added). Scott's *Lay* lacks Walpole's camp frisson, but its hyperbole is deliberate, a protective self-burlesque which pre-empts all the mockery which *Monty Python and the Holy Grail* was later to direct at Hollywood's Middle Ages. Scott's *Lay of the Last Minstrel* and *Ivanhoe* are both 'modern … tale[s] of amusing fiction' based upon the ancient romances of chivalry, and they are also romance comedies based upon the example of Shakespeare. It was a new genre which Scott was to perfect, and in *Ivanhoe* he gave the world a new form, the historical prose romance. Let us compare the Yeomen in the General Prologue to *The Canterbury Tales* and in *The Lay of the Last Minstrel*:

A *YEMAN* hadde he and servantz namo
At that time, for he liste ride so,
And he was clad in cote and hode of grene.
A *sheef of pekok arwes* bright and *kene*,
Under *his belt he baar* ful thriftily
(Well koude he dresse his takel yemanly;
His *arwes* drouped noght with fethres lowe),

And in his hand he baar a mighty *bowe*.
A not heed hadde he, with a broun visage.
Of wodecrafte koude he al the usage.
Upon his arm he baar a gay daggere
Harneised wel and sharp as point of spere;
A Cristopher on his brest of silver sheene.
An *horn* he bar, the *bawdryk* was of grene;
A forster was he, soothly, as I gesse.

General Prologue, 101–17

He was an English *yeoman* good,
    And born in Lancashire.
Well could he hit a fallow-deer
    Five hundred feet him fro;
With hand more true, and eye more clear,
    No archer bended *bow*.
His coal-black hair, shorn round and close,
    Set off his sun-burn'd face:
Old England's sign, St George's cross,
    His barret-cap did grace;
His bugle-*horn* hung by his side,
    All in a wolf-skin *baldric* tied . . .
His kirtle, made of forest *green*,
    Reached skantly to his knee;
And, at *his belt, of arrows keen*
    A furbished *sheaf bore he*;
His buckler, scarce in breadth a span,
    No larger fence had he;
He never counted him a man,
    Would strike below the knee . . .

The Lay, Cantos III, XVI and XVII[19]

Words borrowed by Scott are italicised. His yeoman remains yeoman-like, a type; but whereas Chaucer's Yeoman is bullet-headed – 'A nut head had he, with a brown visage' – Scott's figure is picturesque: 'His coal-black hair, shorn round and close, / *Set off* his sun-burn'd face'. The writer becomes a costume designer, adding antiquarian detail and touches of Gothic-grotesque: the *baldric* is now of *wolf-skin*. Scott also adds nationality – St Christopher becomes St George of England – and an instinctive chivalry: 'He never counted him a man / Would strike below the knee'. This is not the reported attitude of the archers at Crécy or at Agincourt.

Scott rhymes 'Knee' with 'had he' and 'bore he', and then with itself. He dilutes Chaucer's economy by restoring all the redundant verbal gesture of the popular romances, parodied by Chaucer in *Sir Thopas*. This minstrel redundancy and 'rym dogerel' did not prevent the *Lay* from becoming a smash hit in 1805. It was written to be read aloud. In his *Short History of English Literature* of 1898, George Saintsbury called the *Lay*, 'in some ways the most important original work in poetry, taking bulk, form and merit together, that had appeared for generations, though poetically it could not vie with the *Lyrical Ballads*.'[20] Scott's metrical romances are little read today, and the stanzas 'Breathes there the man, with soul so dead' and 'O Caledonia! stern and wild' are better known to Scots abroad than Scots at home.

Fourteen years later, Scott gave Chaucer's Yeoman a starring role in *Ivanhoe*, his first venture into the deep Middle Ages. The Yeoman appears in Chapter 7, at the Tournament at Ashby-de-la-Zouche. The chapter has an epigraph from *Palamon and Arcite*, Dryden's polished-up version of the *Knight's Tale*:

Knights, with a long retinue of their squires,
In gaudy liveries march and quaint attires;
One laced the helm, another held the lance,
A third the shining buckler did advance . . .

At the tournament, a Jewish money-lender pushes through the bystanders. 'One of these, a stout well-set *yeoman*, arrayed in Lincoln-green, having twelve *arrows* stuck in his belt, with a *baldric* and badge of *silver*, and a *bow* of six feet length *in his hand*, turned short round, and while his countenance, which his constant exposure to weather had rendered *brown* as a hazel *nut*, grew darker with anger . . .' (emphasis added).[21] This yeoman still has a mighty bow, arrows, baldrick and brown face. He wins the Ashby archery competition, splitting the willow wand (as in the Percy ballads), and

beating Prince John's champion. Who is this yeoman arrayed in
Lincoln Green and speaking 'Norman English', whatever that may
be? He turns out to be none other than Robin Hood, king of the
greenwood. Another hero, Richard Coeur-de-Lion, also emerges
from disguise, and finally reconciles Norman and Saxon in a united
England.

A British Prime Minister, Tony Blair, educated at Fettes, an
Edinburgh public school of Gothic design, named *Ivanhoe* as his
favourite novel. It is a suitable choice for a modern Prime Minister
– a popular fable of mutual understanding, acceptance and enlightened inclusiveness. Richard I's coronation, however, had been marred
by a riot against Jews.[22] Scott deals with this issue with the help of
Shakespeare: the money-lender Isaac (a Shylock very much light-
ened) has a darkly attractive daughter, Rebecca; who in an act of
obliging nobility surrenders Ivanhoe to the blonde Saxon princess
Rowena. In *Robin Hood, Prince of Thieves* (1991), a Hollywood film
made before the acts of terror carried out in the United States on 11
September 2001, Robin's merry men include a dark-complexioned
Saracen.

If a Yeoman is medieval, a Monk is more so. Following the
example of Spenser, Scott made a habit of providing each of his
chapters with a motto or epigraph, usually in verse – an allusion to a
literary text. When literary tradition offered nothing suitable, Scott
made something up and gave 'Old Play' as the source. As his chapters
have roman numerals, not titles, the epigraphs act as clues to what
follows. Thus the epigraph to Chapter II of *Ivanhoe* is taken from
Chaucer's portrait of the Monk:

> A Monk there was, a fayre for the maistrie,
> An outrider that loved venerie;
> A manly man, to be an Abbot able,
> Ful many a daintie horse had he in stable:
> And whan he rode, men might his bridle hear
> Gingeling in a whistling wind as clear,
> And eke as loud, as doth the chapell bell,
> There as this lord was keeper of the cell.
>
> CHAUCER

The chapter opens with a description of Prior Aymer, based on Chaucer's Monk but much changed: medieval Catholic irony becomes enlightened Protestant caricature. Scott takes 'venerie' as the pursuit not of hunting but of Venus, a sense attested only after Chaucer, whose Monk is luxurious, not lecherous.

Scott's use of sources in *Ivanhoe* can be indicated by listing the sources of the epigraphs to Book I:

i   Pope's *Odyssey*: Eumaeus the swineherd

ii   Chaucer's Monk (see above)

iii James Thomson's *Liberty*: 'And yellow-haired, the blue-eyed Saxon came'

iv Pope's *Odyssey*: Eumaeus the swineherd

v   Shakespeare's *The Merchant of Venice* (Shylock/Isaac; Jessica/Rebecca)

vi The same

vii Dryden's *Palamon and Arcite; Or, the Knight's Tale*: the tournament

viii The same

ix Dryden's *The Flower and the Leaf* (attributed to Chaucer): the Queen of Beauty

x   Marlowe's *The Jew of Malta*

xi Shakespeare's *Two Gentlemen of Verona*: an ambush

xii Chaucer's *Knight's Tale*: the tournament

xiii Pope's *Iliad*: archery games

xiv Thomas Warton: a chivalric feast

Only five of these epigraphs are medieval: two come from *The Knight's Tale*; two from Dryden's *Palamon and Arcite*, and one from Dryden's version of *The Flower and the Leaf*. (Dryden's Chaucer is still Chaucer to Scott.) The 1831 portrait by Sir Francis Grant (see Plate 5) shows Scott at work, a country gentleman, with dogs, transcribing from an old printed Folio into his own manuscript. This arranged pose is true to how 'the Wizard of the North' used a source: he concealed neither his methods nor his ingredients. Chaucer is only one source among many. Scott used old books not only for material, but also to signal genre.

Chapter I of *Ivanhoe* is known for its light-opera culture-wars between Saxon and Norman. It opens: 'In that pleasant district of merry England ... there extended in ancient times a large forest.' Scott's 'merry England' is a forest of 'oaks, which had witnessed perhaps the stately march of the Roman soldiery'. But now 'the laws of the chase, ... unknown to the ... free spirit of the Saxon constitution, had been fixed upon the necks of the subjugated inhabitants ...'. It was customary in a Roman triumph to parade captives under the *jugum*, or yoke. Chapter I of *Ivanhoe* popularised the 'Norman Yoke' theory of English social history. Scott makes the Yoke linguistic. Towards the end of the first chapter, the Fool Wamba, son of Witless, spells out the lesson to Gurth, son of Beowolf. Beowolf is a name taken from the Old English epic poem about Beowulf, the full text of which was published for the first time in Copenhagen in 1815. Scott owned a copy, but could not read the original and shows no sign of having read the accompanying Latin translation. The poem closes with the dying Beowulf lamenting that he does not have a son to succeed him and protect his people. Gurth was for a century to be more famous than Beowulf.

Scott has already told the reader that 'French was the language of honour, of chivalry, and even of justice', while Anglo-Saxon was 'far more manly and expressive'. Wamba, who is seated on a 'Druidical' stone, now informs Gurth that 'Alderman Ox continues to hold his Saxon epithet, while he is under the charge of serfs and bondsmen such as thou, but becomes Beef, a fiery French gallant, when he arrives before the worshipful jaws that are destined to consume him. Mynheer Calve, too, becomes Monsieur de Veau in the like manner ...'[23]

Merry England is a land full of names from old books, a pastoral greenwood whose oaks have seen the Romans come, conquer and go. Its comical but goodhearted Saxon folk are hard-ridden by their Norman seigneurs. Scott's historical ethnography is binary, but eclectic enough to use funny names. Wamba is Visigothic, Mynheer a Dutch title, and the name Beowolf is Geatish (sometimes equated with Gothic). Witless comes from a farcical Forest of Arden. Wamba now instructs Gurth in the names of animals: those who tend animals use their Saxon names, those who eat them use their French ones. Scott echoes an Englishman, Bottom the Weaver, discoursing on beef,

eating and gentility in an Athenian wood: 'Master Mustardseed ...
that same cowardly giantlike ox-beef hath devoured many a gentleman
of your house' (*A Midsummer Night's Dream* III.ii.183). The epigraph
to Chapter II, the portrait of Chaucer's Monk, would have been less
familiar in 1820 than the epigraph to Chapter I:

> Thus commun'd these; while to their lowly dome,
> The full-fed swine returned with evening home;
> Compelled, reluctant, to the several sties,
> With din obstreperous, and ungrateful cries.
>
> POPE'S *Odyssey*

'The full-fed swine returned with evening home ...' For Scott, the
Odyssey is not Pope's neo-classical epic, but an ancient metrical
romance with pastoral scenes. The *Odyssey*, which Scott read in
translation, also provides the epigraph to Chapter IV: 'With sheep and
shaggy goats the porkers bled ...'

Full-fed swine and bleeding porkers! Why did Scott pack his
epigraphs with pigs? Scholars of vernacular literatures can miss classical pearls. The epigraphs signal genre and also hint at the outcome
of the plot. Just as Odysseus' faithful swineherd Eumaeus saw through
his master's rags and helped him reclaim Ithaca at the end of the
Odyssey, so at the end of *Ivanhoe* the faithful swineherd Gurth helps
his disguised Saxon lord, Ivanhoe, to regain his inheritance and to
gain Princess Rowena. The disguised king restored is an established
theme of English romance, as in *Sir Orfeo*. In Homer, only the man
disguised as an old beggar can bend the bow of Odysseus, win the
archery competition, and Penelope, and bring the story to its right
end. The repeated Homeric pigs tell us that one tournament will be
won by the disguised, disinherited Ivanhoe, and another tournament
by the disguised, almost usurped King Richard; and that the archery
competition will be won by Yeoman Robin, disinherited king of
green England. In *Ivanhoe*, as in the *Odyssey*, the penalty for men
who bully or seek to force women is death. In Shakespeare's *King
Lear*, Edgar, the disinherited elder brother, beats the usurper Edmund
in single combat, and will rule Britain. Here, Richard, the elder
brother, defeats the usurper John. The obstreperous pigs grunt to us

that this is a broad romance comedy, and even suggest how it will all
end. Epigraphs serve not simply to remind readers of generic arche-
types – the Yeoman, the Monk – but also to signal the romance genre,
to create themes and to offer clues as to their chivalrous resolution.

So Scott cooks literary traditions – not just medieval ones, for he
is thoroughly eclectic – to make a new dish. He renders stock types of
romance narrative, of European literature, and of British political
discourse, into a new historical romance. The epigraphs use stock
types like stock cubes. This is neither high art nor popular culture but
popular art. Although Scott is today regarded as a second-division
British Romantic, he recreated the Shakespearean historical romance,
which, thanks to his example, still flourishes in the cinema and in
romantic fiction. A good lawyer, he wrote his literary authorities into
the record. The epigraphs invoke standard references identifying
the genre as romance comedy, one familiar to English readers. A new
romance of British national identities is offered in play: a 'matter of
entertainment', an 'amusing fiction' which celebrates past and present
and puts them into a new relation. This look at Scott's use of medieval
sources shows chiefly how saucy he was with them: his spirit is the
spirit of charades and house-party amateur dramatics; his approach
invokes the fun of dressing up and make-believe. If the message is
that the spirit of chivalry need not die, the medium is a hearty Scottish
variety of British stage humour, and the mode is the romance comedy
of *A Midsummer Night's Dream*, the third act of which ends:

> Jack shall have Jill,
> Naught shall go ill,
> The man shall have his mare again,
> And all shall be well.

CHAPTER 3

Dim Religious Lights

THE LAY, CHRISTABEL AND 'THE EVE OF ST AGNES'

The critical reputation of Scott, the acknowledged inventor of the historical novel, rests today on *Waverley* and the Scottish novels. He was first known, however, for the verse romances, beginning with *The Lay of the Last Minstrel*, which formed the groundwork for the Scottish novels. The verse romances also provided the foundation for the prose romances, beginning with *Ivanhoe*, which proved to be his popular legacy. Before considering the relation of Scott's *Lay* to verse romances by Coleridge and Keats, his other verse romances deserve brief mention. After the *Lay*, Scott wrote the 'epic' *Marmion* (1808) and the picturesque *Lady of the Lake* (1810), with some others of which *The Lord of the Isles* (1815) is of most interest. Typically central to these romances is an armed rivalry, complicated by wider feuds, for the hand of the heroine. The tale usually ends (though not in *Marmion*) with a wedding presided over by a gracious Scottish king, and the reconciling of enemies in the interests of civil society. The plots employ disguise and mistaken identity; the heroine, for example, often appears as a soldier or a page, as a nun, or even as a mute. The narrative patterns and the disguises are familiar from Percy's romances and from stage comedy. Scott's selection of motifs is benign, with a spice of Gothic.

Marmion, Scott's major effort in the new genre he developed, takes up 172 of the pages of *Poems by Sir Walter Scott* in the Oxford World's Classics edition of 1913. Besides the text, Scott wrote a dedication, a Preface, verse epistles and historical notes. Poets were more highly regarded – and rewarded – than novelists, and Scott protected his poetic reputation by publishing *Waverley* anonymously and his later fiction as by 'The Author of *Waverley*'. *Marmion* is a verse romance in six cantos, each introduced by an epistle to a friend. As with the *Lay*, the main text is framed by other kinds of text, and each canto has an inset poem, song or tale. The cantos are entitled The Castle; The Convent;

The Hostel, or Inn; The Camp; The Court and The Battle. These generic titles form a suite of picturesque medieval subjects – gifts to the illustrators and scene-painters who were soon to realise Scott's scenarios. Each is a standard 'topos' or commonplace. Together they show Scott creating a repertory of romance, and making it his own. Castles, convents, inns, camps, courts and battles were to be the settings, scenic and generic, of Scott's tales. His Enlightenment education made him think categorically and typically, and a neo-classical sense of genre informs the prefaces to the new hybrid form he developed.

An example of one way in which Scott built up his repertoire is his development of 'Merry England', a formula common in popular literature. A ballad in Percy's *Reliques*, for example, ends:

> King Estmere tooke that fayre ladyè,
> And marryed her to his wiffe,
> And brought her home to merry Englànd
> With her to lead his life.[1]

Merry England was green: another ballad, 'Adam Bell, Clym of the Clough, and William of Cloudesly', begins:

> Mery it was in the grene forest
> Among the levès grene,
> Whereas men hunt east and west
> With bowes and arrowes kene ...[2]

Scott's Merry England first appears as a subject, along with the older subject of Merry Christmas, in lines 80–1 of the Introduction to Canto VI of *Marmion*, an epistle to a fellow antiquarian and amateur of medieval romance, Richard Heber: 'England was merry England, when / Old Christmas brought his sports again.'

Scott goes on to trace the traditions of Christmas, beginning with the Danish *Iol*, Yule:

> When in his low and pine-built hall
> Where shields and axes decked the wall
> They gorged upon the half-dressed steer,
> Caroused in seas of sable beer ...[3]

Scott's ideas of the 'sports' of Christmas drew on the antiquarianism of Joseph Strutt, acknowledged in Scott's Preface to *Ivanhoe*, especially Strutt's *Glig-Gamena Angel-Ðeod* (1801), the first modern book with an Old English title. The subtitle translates as 'Of the Sports and Pastimes of the People of England'.[4] Scott's Merry England is the festive land of 'cakes and ale' invoked by Shakespeare's Sir Toby Belch in his retort to the puritan Malvolio on Twelfth Night, the end of the Christmas holiday. In pre-Reformation England, the twelve holy days of Christmas were the minstrels' high season, and it was at Christmas that interludes and modern plays were first played in larger households. In many romances, Arthur holds a twelve-day feast at Christmas, during which a challenger is permitted to ride into the hall of Camelot to crave a boon. The Church of Scotland had cut the Mass out of Christmas, calling it the Nativity. Scott later developed the Merry England celebrated in Percy's romances into the myth of the good old days of Robin Hood and King Richard. This is a major theme in the overture to *Ivanhoe*.

Scott developed Merry England by using recent scholarship to reanimate popular memory and legend. Like minstrels and their literary successors, Scott enjoyed embroidering the familiar. He composed narratives out of typical scenes set in picturesque parts of the 'land of the mountain and the flood' – the Borders, the Trossachs and the West Coast – and heightened sentiment with rhetoric. His scenarios transferred naturally to the stage and the lyric stage. Even in his decline, when leisureliness had relaxed into diffuseness and visualisation into description, Scott's narrative expertise can produce dramatic power.

Merry Christmas and Merry England revive popular nostalgia for lost medieval patterns of life. By contrast, a medieval feature very often mentioned in Medieval Revival literature but not found in medieval literature is stained glass, the technology of which had been invented in the Middle Ages but later lost. Stained glass became prominent in the first poem which might be called medievalist, and it plays a mood-changing role in the Romantic romances now to be compared.

Towards the end of John Milton's poem 'Il Penseroso', composed *c.* 1631, the thoughtful speaker offers a prayer:

> But let my due feet never fail
> To walk the studious cloister's pale,
> And love the high embowéd roof,

> With antique pillars' massy proof,
> And storied windows richly dight,
> Casting a dim religious light.[5]

This 'antique' church is clearly Gothic, and is described with a pictur-esqueness new in English verse though usual in Italian followers of Petrarch, who in his sonnets is 'solo e pensoso'. Milton's English disci-ples obediently roamed in churchyards, in ruins and near abbeys, in vacant or in pensive mood. Milton's meditative persona vows to 'love' the 'high embowéd' – that is, vaulted – roof, and the massy medieval pillars. He lingers on the richly decorated windows and on their effect. They are 'storied': historiated, telling sacred stories; not part of the 'clerestory', or clear storey above, which lets light into Gothic churches. The stained-glass stories which had been the scripture of the illiterate now cast the 'dim religious light' which appealed to private poets. Il Penseroso is alone as he seeks the cloister's studious confine. Cloisters were monastic, and still exist in cathedrals and colleges, and a few abbeys, for example at Lacock, Wiltshire. Il Penseroso, however, is not a member of a community but a solitary, and his Gothic fantasy is a solo dream. There had been cloisters at the London school Milton attended, St Paul's, by the old Cathedral. Other monastic foundations eventually became country houses, like Woburn Abbey, Newstead Abbey, or Jane Austen's Northanger Abbey, or survived as bare ruined choirs, like Tintern Abbey.

Milton's 'storied windows richly dight' are made of stained glass. Medieval stained glass seemed more medieval after the Enlightenment put clear glass into church windows. Stained glass became symbolic of Gothic endarkenment. This began to have its charm, and Horace Walpole called it 'gloomth'. Windows and stained glass, in abbeys, castles and towers, feature in the three Romantic poems now to be compared: Coleridge's *Christabel* (mostly composed in 1798), Scott's *The Lay of the Last Minstrel* (1805) and Keats's 'The Eve of St Agnes' (1819).

Christabel and 'The Eve of St Agnes' both take place in and around medieval castles, while the action of Scott's *Lay*, which is sung in a castle, takes place between this same castle and Melrose Abbey. All three castles are in the Border region of England and Scotland. After *The Castle of Otranto*, fictional castles became both seats of feudal power, arbitrary and dangerous – especially to innocent females – and also places of 'liminal' enchantment. These three romances have many further elements in common. The heroines bear the names of heroines of medieval romance: Christabel, Margaret and Madeline. Each is lovely, innocent, pure and good. Each loves and is loved by the son of her father's mortal enemy, as in *Romeo and Juliet*; the feudal is made to entail the feud. Each maiden has a bower in a tower.[6] Each of the ladies' chambers is the scene of critical action or critical restraint. Christabel's chamber is virginally enclosed, and lit by a curious lamp:

> The moon shines dim in the open air
> And not a moonbeam enters here.
> But they without its light can see
> The chamber carved so curiously,
> Carved with figures strange and sweet,
> All made out of the carver's brain,
> For a lady's chamber meet:
> The lamp with twofold silver chain
> Is fastened to an angel's feet.
>
> The silver lamp burns dead and dim;
> But Christabel the lamp will trim.
> She trimmed the lamp, and made it bright,
> And left it swinging to and fro . . .[7]

The swinging silver lamp helps cast a spell. In this Gothic chamber, the pious Christabel is bewitched by the beautiful Geraldine, a demon who mysteriously possesses her. In the projected sequel of which Coleridge sometimes spoke, there was to have been a happy ending: Geraldine has taken on the likeness of Christabel's betrothed and, in spite of the bride's obscure sense of revulsion, a wedding is about to be solemnised, when the true bridegroom appears – with the engagement ring! Geraldine vanishes – or would have vanished.

In *The Lay of the Last Minstrel*, Margaret spends much time in her chamber in the tower, 'all in her lonely bower apart', until her beloved, Lord Henry Cranstoun, passes unseen, due to a magic trick played by a mischievous goblin dwarf, into the castle yard:

A stately warrior passed below
But when he raised his pluméd head –
   Blessed Mary! can it be?
. . .
She started from her seat;
While with surprise and fear she strove,
And both could scarcely master love,
   Lord Henry's at her feet.[8]

A generation later, the Lady of Shalott looked out to see 'a bow-shot from her bower-eaves . . . the helmet and the plume' of 'bold Sir Lancelot'; who was never to kneel at her feet.

Margaret's exclamation, 'Blessed Mary! can it be?' is imitated from Coleridge's *Christabel*. Coleridge's pious heroine exclaims 'Jesu, Maria, shield her well!', and, less often, 'Mary mother, save me now!' and 'Praise we the Virgin all divine'. (Coleridge knew that the Virgin was not all divine, even in the Middle Ages, but popular romance needs popular religion.) After these maidenly prayers, Margaret and Henry do not fall into 'sin, and shame', as the dwarf had hoped. They feel not desire, but love:

True love's the gift which God has given
To man alone beneath the heaven:
   It is not fantasy's hot fire,
      Whose wishes, soon as granted, fly;
   It liveth not in fierce desire,
      With dead desire it doth not die;
   It is the secret sympathy,
The silver link, the silken tie . . .[9]

Love finds a way to end the feud. Lord Henry Cranstoun, disguised, kills the English champion in single combat. At the end of *The Lay*, a mass is said for the repose of the soul of Michael Scott in Melrose Abbey, to the accompaniment of a Miltonic 'pealing organ' and Scott's paraphrase of the opening of the *Dies irae*.

The stained glass of Melrose Abbey features earlier in *The Lay*. Canto II begins with advice to tourists: 'If thou would'st view fair

Melrose aright, / Go visit it by the pale moonlight'. Stained glass is translucent, and the Melrose moonlight casts a light more pictur-esque than religious:

> The moon on the east oriel shone
> Through slender shafts of shapely stone,
>> By foliaged tracery combined;
> Thou would'st have thought some fairy's hand
> Twixt poplars straight the ozier wand
>> In many a freakish knot, had twined.
> . . .
>> The silver light so pale and faint,
> Showed many a prophet and many a saint,
>> Whose image on the glass was dyed;
> Full in the midst, his Cross of Red
> Triumphant Michael brandishéd,
>> And trampled the Apostate's pride.
> The moonbeam kissed the holy pane,
> And threw on the pavement a bloody stain . . .

Why does silver moonlight throw a bloody stain? Because it shines through the stained-glass red cross of St Michael onto the grave of Sir Michael Scott. Michael Scott had dabbled in devilish arts, but his grave is protected by his patron, Michael the Archangel, who is shown trampling on Satan. Long ago, the Monk of Melrose had buried Michael Scott on the Wizard's feast-day, Michaelmas:

> When the floor of the chancel was stainéd red,
> That his patron's cross might over him wave,
> And scare the fiends from the Wizard's grave.[10]

Michael Scott's book of magic spells is later taken from the grave, illuminated by the red cross of St Michael: 'Slow moved the Monk to the broad flag-stone, / Which the bloody cross was traced upon' (II, xvii). The medieval Church appears here as a red-stained picturesque Gothic backdrop to wholesome human love: this love is the 'silver link, the siken tie' of secret human sympathy, the social bond of fellowship, valued by the eighteenth-century Edinburgh Enlightenment, here lightly sentimentalised.

All Scott's romances show the romantic love which leads to marriage as wholesome, and celibacy for a woman as a sad fate or a mistaken choice. His treatment of this point is consistent. In Canto III of *The Lady of the Lake*, after ' 'Tis Ellen or an angel sings', we hear Ellen singing: 'Ave Maria! maiden mild! / Listen to a maiden's prayer!' The first verse of her Hymn to the Virgin ends

> 'Maiden! hear a maiden's prayer –
> Mother, hear a suppliant child!
> Ave Maria!'

In *The Lord of the Isles*, the second (Spenserian) stanza of Canto V runs:

> But other duties call'd each convent maid
> Roused by the summons of the moss-grown bell;
> Sung were the matins and the mass was said,
> And every sister sought her separate cell,
> Such was the rule, her rosary to tell.
> And Isabel has knelt in lonely prayer;
> The sunbeam, through the narrow lattice, fell
> Upon the snowy neck and long dark hair,
> As stoop'd her gentle head in meek devotion there.

Ellen and Isabel eventually graduate from celibacy to married bliss. But in Canto II of *Marmion*, Constance de Beverley, who has broken her vows for love of Marmion, is solemnly sentenced to death: she is walled up to die. Her three judges are an Abbess, a Prioress and 'a blind old Abbot', who, 'Raising his sightless balls to heaven', gives his 'doom'. The judges are:

> All servants of Saint Benedict,
> The statutes of whose order strict
> On iron table lay.[11]

Scott seems to be making a point. But immurement and living death, though a Gothic punishment of the kind relished by the fans of 'Monk' Lewis, is as much a historical mistake as the iron table. There are no recorded instances of the Catholic Church having walled up erring nuns to die.[12] Scott is honoured for having enabled the Scots better to comprehend their country's divided past, for helping the English to begin to understand Scotland, and for helping his contemporaries to begin to imagine the Middle Ages. But Scott's later prose romances *The Monastery* and *The Abbot* show that the prejudices of his place and time limited the historical sympathy he could extend to pre-Reformation Christianity.[13]

The Lay of the Last Minstrel was, in its day, by far the most popular of these three poems. Today, only short poems can hope for popularity, and the best-known of these three verse romances is the shortest, Keats's 'The Eve of St Agnes'. In popular tradition, on the eve of the feast of the virgin martyr St Agnes, 21 January, a maiden could dream of the man she would marry. Madeline is a flesh-and-blood version of Margaret, Scott's chaste heroine, who is herself a revision of the unsuspecting Christabel. Christabel is the name of a noble and beautiful Christian maiden in an old romance. Margaret is the name of a canonised saint, the Queen who made Scotland more thoroughly Christian. But Madeline is named after St Mary Magdalene, the 'woman who is a sinner' of iconographic tradition, out of whom Jesus cast seven devils, who went to anoint his body, and who on Easter morning was told by the risen Christ not to touch him.[14] Keats summons up Scott's famous poem in order to rewrite it. Madeline has a bower with a window very 'richly dight':

> A casement high and triple-arched there was,
> All garlanded with carven imag'ries,
> Of fruits and flowers, and bunches of knot-grass,
> And diamonded with panes of quaint device,
> Innumerable of stains and splendid dyes,
> As are the tiger-moth's deep-damasked wings;
> And in the midst, 'mong thousand heraldries,
> And twilight saints, and dim emblazonings,
> A shielded scutcheon blushed with blood of queens and kings.

In the last Spenserian hexameter, emblazoned blood makes the shield blush, and the moon throws a blood-red light, not religious and not on a wizard's tomb: 'Full on the casement shone this wintry moon, / And threw warm gules on Madeline's fair breast . . .' 'Gules' is the French heraldic term for red; it derives from the word for fur ornaments, dyed red, and worn at the 'geule', the throat. Arthur Hughes's Ashmolean *In Madeline's Chamber* (see Plate 6), makes Keats more innocent: the colours of the stained-glass window in Madeline's chamber stream into her room but not onto her. In the poem, however, Madeline undresses and

> Unclasps her warmèd jewels one by one;
> Loosens her fragrant bodice; by degrees
> Her rich attire creeps rustling to her knees . . .[15]

We see all this exactly as Madeline's lover Porphyro sees it. The hot-blooded Porphyro has, with the help of a foolish servant, 'Angela the old', secretly hidden himself in a closet in Madeline's chamber, carrying with him a basket of candied and scented fruit. The answer to a maiden's prayer is what Porphyro plans to be. When Porphyro comes from the closet, the praying Madeline thinks that he is a vision, and in her dream they melt into each other's arms in 'Solution sweet'. The solution is not a dream, however, but actual. Feminists were not the first to censure the voyeurism and vicariousness here. Victorian readers regarded Porphyro's concealment and his secret observation of, and imposition upon, Madeline as unmanly. It is not the part of a gentleman to take advantage of a maiden half asleep. Porphyro's plan of action is not presented critically within the poem, however. Alec D'Urberville's still less chivalrous possession of the sleeping Tess, in Thomas Hardy's novel of 1891, makes an interesting comparison.

In 1842 Tennyson described King Arthur as 'most like a modern gentleman of stateliest port'. Arnold of Rugby wished to put 'a Christian gentleman in every parish'. J.H. Newman devotes a memorable page of his *Apologia* to the ideal of the gentleman. He also made nice use of a gentlemanly expression, writing that 'If I am obliged to bring religion into after-dinner toasts (which indeed does not seem to be quite the thing), I shall drink – to the Pope, if you please – still, to Conscience first, and to the Pope afterwards'.[16] Gentlemanliness is a theme also in Thackeray and Trollope. The Victorian gentleman knew that privilege obliged the rich to care for the poor, and the strong to protect the weak, as they do in Dickens's sunnier books. Such chivalric ideals are medieval in origin. Gerard Hopkins, S.J., wrote to Robert Bridges: 'if the English race had done nothing else, yet if they left the world the notion of a gentleman, they would have done a great service to mankind'.[17] This Victorian ideal was not the idea of a gentleman held either by Lord Chesterfield or by Lord Byron. (Byron, like Keats, also hid his hero in a closet in 1819, in Canto I of *Don Juan*.) The Victorian gentleman was improved by rediscovered Christian ideals, medieval in origin, and expressed in their highest form in the tale told by Chaucer's Wife of Bath. In the tale, the ugly hag who helps the knight knows very well that knights are not always 'parfit[ly] gentil' to women, whether young and beautiful or old and ugly. Her doctrine is that 'gentillesse' is the product not of 'old richesse' but of following Christ's example. Medieval social ideals of this kind, rekindled during the Medieval Revival, were to affect Tory paternalism, Christian Socialism, and the conception of society suggested by the words 'Welfare State', a medievalist formulation. An Archbishop of Canterbury, William Temple, was one of the first to use the phrase, in 1941.

Keats, however, was not a Victorian, and he idealised female beauty, not aristocracy or religion or chastity. Scholars have detailed the debts owed by 'The Eve of St Agnes' to the poems of Coleridge and Scott. But Keats's poem pointedly rewrites those poems by his predecessors, and offers a hostile critique of the religious and political aspects of their medievalism. Feudalism, in the person of Madeline's father, the Baron, is drunken and barbarous. The representatives of the Church, the Beadsman telling his beads and the wizened Angela, are chill, decrepit and witless. There is no angelic lamp, no Apostate-trampling archangel. Coleridge and Scott had chosen a Romeo-and-Juliet-like situation in order to take the feud out of the feudal; yet they show medieval popular religion as benign and its superstitions as harmless. For Keats, however, educated at a Dissenting academy, medieval popular Catholicism is repressive superstition.

Each of these embowered heroines behaves differently. Coleridge's motherless Christabel had found Geraldine in distress under an oak tree, believed her story of abuse, and taken her in to her father's castle – it was night – and offered her her bed. Geraldine turns out to be a sorceress and, when Christabel is asleep, suckles her at her witch's breast. Scott's Lord Henry and Margaret remain awake and remain chaste; while Madeline is united in her dream with a flesh-and-blood Porphyro. Porphyro's love for Madeline, and her response, are presented as natural, although Keats does not show love simply as leading to happiness: 'And they are gone: ay, ages long ago / These lovers fled away into the storm.' For Keats, the Middle Ages are gone. Yet he would not like young lovers in 1819 to be ruled by the feudal passions of parents, nor by the asceticism of clerics, nor even – as Scott's Margaret and Henry had been – by the mutual respect of chivalrous courtly love.

In historical conclusion, these three romances fulfil the hopes of Warton and Percy for a modern revival of romance; each is less Gothic and more realistically medieval than the last, as well as less fantastic and more modern. All the British Romantic poets revived the once popular genres of ballad and lyric as well as romance. Outstanding among these revivals are the songs of Robert Burns, Scott's 'Proud Maisie', Byron's 'So we'll go no more a-roving', and such ballads as Coleridge's 'The Rime of the Ancyent Marinere' and Keats's 'La Belle Dame Sans Merci'.[18] These poems could not have been written without the example of poems published or republished in eighteenth-century anthologies, chief of which was Percy's *Reliques*.

Scott was a good minstrel, not a great poet. He can be appreciated and should again be enjoyed as a deft, energetic and happy teller of stories in verse; he also made effective use of song in his novels. His poetry does not meet modern generic expectations, for, like much verse written before the twentieth century, it is narrative. Romanticism began to make the lyric the supreme kind of poem, and the poem was stripped down to its essentials, early in the twentieth century, by Ezra Pound and T.S. Eliot, by precept and example. That drastic concentration has since been relaxed, but in the hectic media competition for attention today, brevity commends itself to a poet who wishes to be heard. A poem should not now occupy more than one page. Length apart, contemporary readers are quite unprepared for the blithe metricality, the discursiveness, the open verbal weave and the shockingly slow build-up of Scott's verse narratives, which, like Fielding's novels or Byron's long poems, are written to be read at a good speed. Contemporary British poetry is sometimes written in regular verse, but it rarely tells a story longer than an anecdote. Baffled generic and stylistic expectations prevent Scott's romances from making the fresh impression they made on his own generation. They are theatrical and sentimental, like the novels of Dickens, but readers who try them will feel their charm. Whatever their final merits, Scott's verse fictions succeeded in introducing the public to life in Scotland as the Middle Ages ended (rather later than in England). Scott also recreated for poetry one of its oldest roles, that of remembrancer. Scott's Minstrel is a preserver of personal names 'whose memory feels a second death' (*Lay*, V, 20) if no poet is there to keep them alive. Of Scott's followers, Thomas Hardy especially honoured him for reclaiming this role for poetry.

In his verse, Scott reinvigorated the role of the minstrel, the medieval entertainer who compiled, retold and handed on the old stories. Scott added to this tribal role the more enlightened roles of author, editor and historian, and set out to understand old differences and to assuage ancient wrongs. Scott was a genuine Lowland version of what Macpherson had pretended to be, and his 'Last Minstrel' is both more pathetic than Gray's Bard, and also more prophetic of what romance might do in literature. Tennyson's 'The Lady of Shalott' and 'Morte d'Arthur' and Christina Rossetti's less medieval 'Goblin Market' were to show what verse romance could do.

Edmund Burke had proclaimed in 1790 that the age of chivalry was gone in Europe, and had done so in order that chivalry should not disappear from Britain. After decades of conflict with Revolutionary and Napoleonic France, the success of Walter Scott helped to foster ideals of chivalry and to create for his enormous public a first approximation of what chivalry might have been like. This discussion has maintained the distinction between Gothic fantasy and historical medievalism. Yet, however historical its attention to 'facts and manners', the Medieval Revival was always interested in how people should live now in the present as well as in how people had lived then in the past.

CHAPTER 4

'Residences for the Poor'

THE PUGIN OF *CONTRASTS*

To be born, or at any rate, bred in a handbag, whether it had handles or not, seems to me to display a contempt for the ordinary decencies of family life that reminds one of the worst excesses of the French Revolution. And I presume you know what that unfortunate movement led to?

Lady Bracknell, in Wilde's *The Importance of Being Earnest*

Every schoolboy knows who killed Montezuma, and who strangled Atahualpa.

Thomas Babington Macaulay, *Essay on Lord Clive*

Historians today would not presume that British pupils knew much about the French Revolution or about the Spanish conquest of Mexico. The favourite British bogey from European history is still Adolf Hitler. Historians of the Revolution often lament the durability in British minds of the guillotine, tumbrils and 'tricoteuses', and blame this on two books which fixed popular impressions, Thomas Carlyle's *French Revolution* (1837) and Charles Dickens's *A Tale of Two Cities* (1858–60).[1] It is said to be hard to get ideas into the heads of the English, supposedly a 'nation of shopkeepers'. Yet they eventually absorbed some of the Revolution's more liberal ideas. The Revolution famously abolished the nobility, the first of the three Estates in the French equivalent of Parliament, and, less famously, the Second Estate, the Church.

The Liberalism of the Revolution had a militant anti-clerical side, and French clergy went into exile en masse. About seven thousand of them went to England, and at one time a thousand French secular priests lived at the King's House, Winchester, which the government requisitioned for them in 1792. The possessions of religious orders were confiscated, and as the Napoleonic armies of the 'nouveau régime' advanced across Europe, they suppressed monasteries and convents. So it was that, not long after the Revolution, members of English religious communities in France and Flanders also crossed into England. One effect of the Revolution was thus that members of religious orders who had been chased out of England in the sixteenth century, and had then set up English houses abroad, were again chased out and re-crossed the Channel in the 1790s. Two examples of this are communities of English Benedictine nuns, in Paris and Cambrai, who were first imprisoned then allowed to go back to their native land. These religious refugees, Benedictines principally, began to set up communities in England, as, for example, the nuns who set up at Stanbrook and at Colwich. As they had on the Continent, the communities of men continued to offer a Catholic education, which had been forbidden in England from 1559 to 1778 by laws carrying the severest penalties.[2] After some years, they established their colleges once again, as for instance at Downside and Ampleforth. Walter Scott brings one of these unfamiliar beings, rare birds then in Scotland, into the Introductory Epistle to *The Monastery*: '"Am I to understand, then,...that I am speaking with a Catholic clergyman?" "An unworthy monk of the order of St Benedict" said the stranger "belonging to a community of your own countrymen, long established in France, and scattered unhappily by the events of the Revolution."'[3]

Only a small proportion of the *émigrés* of the 1790s were clerics, however, and some came for reasons neither religious nor political. One was a Charlotte Charpentier, who in 1797 married an Edinburgh lawyer, Walter Scott. Another *émigré* was Auguste Charles Pugin, who worked as a draughtsman in the London office of the architect John Nash in 1792. An associate of Daguerre, Charles Pugin built the Diorama in the new Regent's Park in 1823. He published *Specimens of Gothic Architecture* in 1821 and, in 1827, *Pugin's Gothic Furniture*. His son Augustus Welby Pugin grew up in the workshop, and at the age of fifteen designed Gothic furniture at Windsor Castle. In the previous year, 1826, the castle had received a visit from Mlle Charpentier's now celebrated husband. Walter Scott had been made a baronet at George IV's accession in 1820. In 1822 he stage-managed the first visit of a Hanoverian monarch to Edinburgh. George donned a kilt in the Stuart tartan, and drank a whisky; Scott went home with the King's glass in the tail-pocket of his coat, but forgot about it when he got there, sat on it and broke it. The Scott Monument stands, appropriately, in Prince's Street, Edinburgh.

On 21 October 1826, Sir Walter wrote up his Journal: 'After break-fast went to Windsor Castle, . . . examined the improvements going on there under Mr. Wyattville who appears to possess a great deal of taste and feeling for the Gothick architecture. The old apartments, splendid enough in extent and proportion, are paltry in finishing – instead of being lined with heart of oak the palace of the British Kings is hung with paper painted wainscot colour'.[4] Scott uses 'heart of oak' patriotically: the ships of the Royal Navy were built of oak, and 'Heart of Oak', a song of the Royal Navy, claims that its men also had hearts of oak. Oaks were English, and could, after the Battle of Worcester, be royal: the inn-signs of public houses called The Royal Oak show the head of Charles II against the foliage of an oak tree, because Charles had hidden in an oak after the defeat at Worcester. Windsor Castle was the ancestral residence of English, and then of 'the British', kings. It was at Windsor that Edward III had founded the Order of the Garter in 1348, and in 1788 that King George III had had Benjamin West paint Gothic scenes.[5]

These scenes, and the paltry paper 'wainscot' which disgusted Scott, belong to the playful, picturesque and theatrical phase of 'the Gothick architecture', a phase beginning early in the century with garden follies, to the self-amusing papier-mâché tracery of Horace Walpole, to the rise of William Beckford's terror-Gothic 'Abbey' at Fonthill (Plate 7), designed by James Wyatt in 1796 for the million-aire author of the Gothic tale, *Vathek*. In 1825, Wyatt's 278-foot tower collapsed upon its paltry foundations. By then Gothic architecture was moving from the fancy private estates of eighteenth-century gentlemen to the centre of power of what was becoming the world's most influential country. Scott's home at Abbotsford lies somewhere near the middle of this evolution. Its architecture is Scottish Baronial rather than Gothic. It is homely as well as picturesque, and had oil-gas and pneumatic bells. Another modern touch (or is it eighteenth-century?) is Scott's request for a parcel of old 'caricatures, which can be bought cheap, for papering two *cabinets à l'eau*'. This comes in a letter to the actor Daniel Terry, who dramatised some of the Waverley Novels and also supplied some of Abbotsford's decor. The decor is eclectic, most notably in the extraordinary collection of historical memorabilia made by Scott.[6]

The first half of the evolution of neo-Gothic architecture ended in the 1830s, at the point at which Augustus Welby Pugin made his first impact. By the time William IV died in 1837, the marginal was becoming the mainstream, and the eccentric had become the official. In 1829, Pugin had painted scenes and made costumes for an opera-ballet version of Scott's *Kenilworth* at the King's Theatre, London. In 1831, he designed Shakespeare's *Henry VIII* for Covent Garden. In 1833, his *Examples of Gothic Architecture* appeared. But in 1834, as he watched the Palace of Westminster burn down, he rejoiced at the sight of James Wyatt's 'composition mullions and cement pinnacles and battlements flying and cracking'.[7] The stagey and the inauthentic would no longer do.

Charles Pugin had died in 1832. In 1835, the twenty-two-year-old A.W. Pugin rejected the Presbyterianism of his English mother and publicly became a Catholic, 'a career-damaging move in protestant England'.[8] Pugin's contribution to the Palace of Westminster was for some years not publicised. The young designer's lively pencil had helped Charles Barry to win the commission to rebuild the Palace, and almost every detail that met the eye in the fabric of Barry's building, put up between 1836 and 1868, was by Pugin, as were its decoration and furnishing, from the finials to the inkwells. It is thanks to Parliament's decision and to Pugin's success that British architects began seriously to use medieval rather than classical models for the construction of public buildings other than churches and schools.

The Church of England had in the 1820s begun to build city churches in what came to be called Commissioners' Gothic. By this date the Church Commissioners were alive to the fact that Gothic rib vaulting allowed a large space to be roofed, and lit by large windows in the thin walls between the columns; slender pillars of iron could also be used. Thus, a large Gothic church could be built using less stone than a smaller classical one. The Commissioners' appreciation of the economic advantage of building in Gothic was a side-effect of

the serious scholarly attention given to Gothic buildings over three
decades. The architect John Carter had drawn and measured the
cathedrals and abbeys of England, the Society of Antiquaries
publishing his albums of engravings from 1795 onwards. John
Milner, a Catholic priest at Winchester, was the first to realise that
the key to Gothic was not the decorativeness which had attracted
eighteenth-century amateurs, but the engineering of the pointed
arch. Milner used Carter as his architect for a chapel at Winchester.
Milner also saw that the styles of Gothic churches had changed
over time. Archaeology had shown the columns of classical temples
evolving from simple Doric to fine Ionic to flowery Corinthian
(the classical 'orders'), while late Roman building in cement had been
quite different. The stage-by-stage evolution of classical orders
offered Milner a model, which itself seemed to imply an analogy to
the growth and decay of living things. This organic analogy suggested
a further correlation with the rise and fall of civilisations: Gibbon's
Decline and Fall of the Roman Empire had been followed by the fall of
the thousand-year French monarchy. In 1811 Milner identified three
stages in the historical evolution of Gothic, calling them First, Second
and Third Pointed, of which the Second or Middle Pointed order,
illustrated by the forms of York Minster of about 1300, was the apex
of the pointed style.[9]

In 1819 the architect Thomas Rickman published his *Attempt
to Discriminate the Styles of English Architecture*, with the practical
aim of making churchmen 'more capable of deciding the various
designs for churches in imitation of the English styles'.[10] Rickman,
an enterprising Quaker, was to win a large number of these church
commissions for himself. He took over Milner's three 'pointed
orders', but called them 'English styles': Early English, Decorated
English, Perpendicular English. He added an introductory fourth
period, before Early English, for the Romanesque of Durham
Cathedral. This style he called Norman. Milner had seen the
evolution of the pointed orders as exhibiting growth and decline.
Mr Rickman's 'English' titles proved more popular than Father
Milner's ordinal numbers. Northern European Romanticism was
nationalist, and English patriotism had been stimulated by Napoleon.
Rickman's *Attempt* appeared in 1819, the same year as *Ivanhoe*, in

which 'Norman' (Prince John) also gives way to 'English' (King Richard I, supported by Robin Hood). It was not until rather longer after the final defeat of Napoleonic France at Waterloo in 1815 that it was generally admitted that the first language of the kings of England from 1066 until 1413 had been French; that the patriotism of the rulers of Anglo-Norman and Plantagenet England had not been insular; or that Gothic architecture, though it had developed differently in the part of the kingdom known as Outre-Manche, had originated about 1140 in the Île de France. By 1841, however, scholarship had advanced enough for the readers of Pugin's *True Principles of Pointed or Christian Architecture* to be reasonably informed about church architecture in the Middle Ages.

The aim of this study is to link, correct and supplement received accounts of various aspects of the Medieval Revival rather than to rehearse those accounts. Pugin's achievements as an architect are not reviewed here; rather, one or two points are offered on his orientation and his reputation. Pugin did not begin as an architect and was both more and less than an architect. His gift was for design, which came to him as readily as fiction came to Dickens. He designed furniture, buildings and objects of many kinds in various media, including glass, clay, metal, cloth, paper, wood and stone.[11] He also designed books, and wrote incisively. Except for architectural historians, Pugin's contribution is not best conveyed by listing the quantities of furniture, churches and other buildings that he designed and made. This profusion came from his grasp of the fundamentals of design and his quickness of hand and eye, but also from the total conviction of his faith. The craftsman became an apostle of *The True Principles of Pointed or Christian Architecture*.[12] Pugin declared that good architecture is not an elegant arrangement of neo-classical appearances clothing a well-proportioned body but springs naturally from fitness to purpose and truth to materials. The functionalism which distinguishes modernist from Victorian architecture originated with A.W. Pugin. One of his 'true principles' was that an honest chair or table, door or house expresses the society which makes it. Pugin was the first to define principles which John Ruskin later elaborated with equal zeal and at far greater length. Pugin was also the first in his generation (as William Cobbett had been in his, and

William Blake in his) to see the warping effects of much of England's industrial prosperity upon the lives of her people, to attack it with passion and wit, and to offer a moral critique of architecture as expressing social ideals. This was the principle enunciated at Ruskin's inaugural lecture in 1870 as Slade Professor of [Fine] Art: 'the art of any country is the exponent of its social and political virtues'.[13] Pugin's critique was shared, and expressed with differing emphases, by Thomas Carlyle and then by others, including Benjamin Disraeli, John Ruskin, Charles Dickens, Friedrich Engels, Karl Marx and William Morris. Pugin also pioneered, without theorising it, the kind of working relationship between individual craft and design and high-volume workshop production for which Morris is admired. According to Clive Wainwright, 'Pugin was setting new standards for craftsmen and reviving lost craft techniques twenty years before Morris and Co. was founded.'[14]

The leaders of the Medieval Revival came from very different backgrounds. Pugin was a designer who grew up in the workshop. Carlyle, the son of a stonemason, worked hard to establish himself as a writer. As a lay preacher, he commanded a national audience in the 1840s. By contrast, Ruskin had available to him the fortune his father had made as a sherry importer, and William Morris, his disciple, inherited capital his father had accumulated on the stock exchange. As wealthy Oxford undergraduates, Ruskin and Morris dreamed of becoming working men. As adults, they lectured and wrote advocating the ideal of the craftsman. Ruskin founded the medieval Guild of St George, and Morris tried to recreate a medieval workshop. A talented draughtsman and painter, Ruskin was primarily a writer, and Morris much more a writer than is now remembered. Yet in their copious publications, and in those of Carlyle, there is nowhere an acknowledgement of the fact that a master of design, who was also a master of craftsmen, had already achieved in many fields what they were to advocate, before they had begun to advocate it. 'Morris, like his mentor Ruskin, never paid public tribute to his debt to Pugin.'[15]

This silence about Pugin on the part of the leading advocates of a return to medieval ideals was not professional jealousy but anti-Catholic prejudice. Pugin's ardently avowed Catholicism meant that he received no public commissions; for his work at Westminster he was discreetly paid by Barry. Any explicit Catholicism was unacceptable to many in England in 1835, and not only to those of strongly Protestant upbringing such as Carlyle and Ruskin. It was against his own inclinations and in the teeth of opposition that the Duke of Wellington, an Anglo-Irish Prime Minister concerned for the future governability of Ireland – a part of the United Kingdom since 1800 – had in 1829 forced Catholic Emancipation through Parliament. His Catholic Relief Act, lifting most of the remaining civil disabilities imposed on British Catholics, was unpopular in the 1830s and became more unpopular in the 'Hungry Forties', during which 220,000 of the Queen's Irish subjects crossed from the smaller to the larger of the British Isles.[16] It was only after Pugin's campaigning Catholicism faded from public memory that English architects who admired his 'true principles' began to imitate his churches. The Pugin exhibitions and publications of the 1990s said little about his Catholicism.

Pugin first announced his new convictions in 1836 in the first edition of *Contrasts: or, a parallel between the noble edifices of the fourteenth and fifteenth centuries, and similar buildings of the present day; shewing the present decay of taste*. *Contrasts* is the most entertaining and influential manifesto in the history of English art and architecture. The text is short, but each page-opening carries copper engravings satirically juxtaposing the worst in modern urban building – and social provision – with the best of their idealised medieval counterparts.

In the upper half of the engraving 'Contrasted Residences for the Poor' (see Plate 8), Pugin's 'MODERN POOR HOUSE' is based upon Jeremy Bentham's design for a 'Panopticon', his Greek name for a device in which all can be seen. This was Bentham's ingenious idea for a rational and economical modern prison in which the pens for prisoners could be overseen by a single warder in a central turret. The lantern in the turret is so designed that the overseer can see without being seen, and absent himself for periods during which the prisoners will still feel that they are being watched. (Bentham's design unconsciously parodies the rational idea of God as an all-seeing but invisible landlord favoured by Deists and Freemasons of the eighteenth century, when the divine was sometimes represented by a large Eye set high in the triangle of a classical pediment.) The entrance to the Poor House has a pediment, and the windowless octagon occupies a blank space cleared within a pleasantly bosky landscape; the parish church is remote and diminished. The surrounding panels show One of the Poor Men; the Master, with leg-irons, manacles and scourge; the Diet of gruel; the Convoy of the coffin, marked 'For Dissection', and a dissecting table superscribed with 'A Variety of Subjects Always Available for Medical Students'; and 'Discipline', a mother about to be locked away from her children. These gaolers and dissectionists are precisely the unfeeling agents of social control caricatured in the early novels of Charles Dickens, who was, like Pugin, born in 1812.

The 'Contrast' below is an 'ANTIENT POOR HOYSE', an idealised monastic set-up which sits happily in a leafy and cultivated land-scape. The Gothic buildings look natural in a wooded landscape, an organic analogy which appealed to Romantics north of the Alps, notably Ruskin.[17] In this engraving, Pugin's buildings are weirdly prophetic of some of the public schools erected later in the century. The left range of buildings is probably almshouses, for this imagined community is dedicated to that charitable care for the poor which is enjoined upon Christians: the hospitality of the hospital and the hospice, institutions which medieval Christianity developed to serve the community. The panels again show the Poor Man and the Master; the Ale, Cider, Bread, Meat and Cheese which formed the Diet of hospitable medieval England; the clergy burying their Brother; and a gentle fraternal kind of Discipline: Merry England as Merciful England.

To his revised edition in 1841, Pugin added further Contrasts, in which the letterpress is more explicit. Thus the 'Catholic Town in 1440' has a key identifying sixteen buildings, only one of which, 'Guild hall', is not ecclesiastical. Set in a rural landscape, a river flows outside a city wall bordered by trees, and church spires point heaven-wards. In 'THE SAME TOWN IN 1840', the spires have largely been replaced by factory chimneys, and the riverside is dominated by a wall of rectangular factories and warehouses. The trees have gone. The key identifies a Lunatic Asylum, Iron Works and the chapels of several sects. Christian unity has been replaced by sectarianism and the madhouse. The Panopticon appears again, as The New Jail, situated on open ground previously available for public recreation, lying between the new Gas Works and the New Parsonage House and Pleasure Grounds. The parson's gentlemanly family home, a neo-classical building, stands pleasantly, with its private garden, on top of the medieval graveyard and in front of the medieval church.

Contrasts is an original combination of several traditions: witty polemical cartoon, architectural satire and a polarised moral vision of a prophetic, revolutionary and Romantic kind. Early examples of the latter were Blake's *Songs of Innocence* (1789) and *Songs of Experience* (1794), also illustrated with the author's engravings. Pugin's vision of English life during the Wars of the Roses is amusingly serene, and should be taken not literally but symbolically. His extreme caricature serves a satirical purpose. For Pugin, the increase of industrial production has come at a dire human and spiritual cost, visible in the greed, cruelty, social division and harshness of urban life. In setting the present against the best of the past, *Contrasts* uses the technique of the English neo-classical satirists Dryden, Pope and Johnson. But Pugin's standard of a good society is taken from Catholic Christendom in late medieval England, not from the Rome of Augustus and Maecenas. To object that his Christendom is idealised is to mistake the genre; the English Augustans did not dwell on the fate of Cicero at the hands of Mark Antony or of Ovid under Augustus, nor upon the lot of women, slaves or gladiators.

In the same year as the second edition of *Contrasts*, Pugin published *The True Principles of Pointed or Christian Architecture*. These he states with his usual directness: 'First, that there should be no features about a building which are not necessary for convenience, construction or propriety; second, that all ornament should consist of enrichment of the essential construction of the building.' In 1843 he produced *An Apology for the Revival of Christian Architecture in England*. The words 'Pointed or Christian' in the first title depart from family tradition. Between them, Pugin *père et fils* had published three titles on 'Gothic' architecture and furniture, illustrated with specimens or examples, which were also samples of what might be supplied by the Pugins. The son now called the architecture he professed not Gothic but Christian, and offered not examples but principles.

Pointed architecture is Christian and classical architecture is pagan, a polemical simplification not derived from history. Nero had indeed martyred Christians, and classical temples were dedicated to the worship of pagan gods. Yet in the fourth century, when Christianity was first tolerated and then supported by the Emperor Constantine, the first public Christian assemblies were held in halls of a kind known as basilicas. A basilica, or 'royal' hall, had a double colonnade. Today the four Major Basilicas in Rome are rectangular: they are not pointed but they are Christian. Only from the mid-twelfth to the late fifteenth century was Gothic the style for building churches in parts of Western Europe. Church architecture in Italy had returned to classical models before the Reformation: Bramante levelled old St Peter's to build the basilica which Michelangelo was to complete. The architecture of the Catholic Reformation is not Gothic, and in 1843 the Gothic churches of England, Wales, Scotland and Ireland, though originally Catholic, were in Protestant hands. Most Catholic churches in post-Reformation Britain were neo-classical.

Historically, therefore, as Catholic critics pointed out, the equation asserted by Pugin in 'Pointed or Christian' holds true only in Northern Europe and in the parts of the Mediterranean conquered by Normans or Franks, and only for four of the ten centuries of Catholic Christendom. Pugin's fundamental interest, however, was not in the historically accurate but in the authentically sacred. His imperative was not that the old northern architecture should be archaeologically recreated, but that churches should again be built which not only glorified God but also enabled the fullest worship of God in the liturgy. His view of classical architecture as indelibly pagan owes less to European history than to family history. To the son of a French architect who had left Paris at the time of the Revolution, classical architecture radiated the chill of those eighteenth-century academicians and *philosophes* who regarded the Gothic as irrational superstition and the classical as human reason rightly expressed. The Temples of Reason erected by French Revolutionaries were classical in form, and they installed neo-classical statues of the goddess of Reason in the Gothic churches they desecrated. For Pugin, the Gothic was holy, the classical unholy. His passionate conviction that a real church required a rood-screen seemed fanatical to some English Catholics, including J.H. Newman. Nevertheless, for many English people to whom Pugin's imperatives are quite foreign, the idea of a church is not easily dissociated from the forms of the Gothic.[18]

By a curious irony, the fire at Westminster in 1834 was the accidental result of a decision to modernise the government's accounting system. The fire was lit by officers of Parliament in the stack of wooden tally sticks which had been used by the Exchequer ever since medieval times to record the transactions of expenditure, and which had accumulated in the cellars. The flues caught fire, and, although there was no human casualty, the effect on the fabric exceeded the worst that might have been hoped for by Guy Fawkes. The bonfire got rid of the tally sticks but also of pretty well everything else above ground, except for Westminster Hall and St Stephen's Chapel. The Commons Select Committee, appointed in March 1835 to report on plans 'for the permanent Accommodation of the Houses of Parliament', decided in December that the new building must be in the 'national' style, specifying 'Gothic or Elizabethan'. (These were stylistic alternatives, not two names for the same style.)

The Houses of Parliament, an illustrated volume by various hands, appeared in the year 2000, introduced by the then Director of the Institute of Historical Research at London University, David Cannadine. Professor Cannadine remarks that the 'national' style 'was deemed, rather implausibly, to be Gothic (or Elizabethan)' by the Commons Select Committee. It is true that Gothic had not been much used for buildings other than churches or colleges for a long time.[19] But that Parliament should choose Gothic as the English style should not seem implausible to a historian. Parliament is a medieval institution, as Parliamentarians knew. Since the eighteenth century, children's history books had told how England had been ruled by kings and queens for nine centuries, but also that in English law the monarch was obliged to consult Parliament and required Parliament's consent. The same books pointed out that some kings had neglected this duty, and that sharp reminders of it had successfully been presented to a few of them, including King John, Edward II, Richard II, Charles I and James II.

Parliament chose also to rehouse itself on its old site, a place surrounded by Gothic buildings, standing reminders of the medieval origins of the English nation, Church and state. Amid the smoking ruins of 1834 stood Westminster Hall and St Stephen's Chapel, and, close by, Westminster Abbey. Edward the Confessor had founded his minster to the west of the city, but governmental buildings had crept out towards it. Edward's successors were crowned in the Abbey and many of them were, like him, buried there, including Henry VII, who, at the east end of the Abbey, had built a Lady Chapel in the richest Perpendicular style. This splendid model is across the road from the west end of the parliamentary precinct. The Abbey had been 'finished' by Christopher Wren, and Nicholas Hawksmoor had given its West Front Gothic towers; for to the neo-classic mind, a Gothic abbey should be regularly and completely Gothic. Westminster Hall, the scene of the deposition of Richard II and such trials as those of Thomas More and Charles I, had been built by William Rufus, son of the Conqueror, and rebuilt with great magnificence by Henry Yevele for King Richard II, who in Plate 9 is shown admiring the great roof. Perhaps the largest civic building in the Europe of its day, Westminster Hall still stands with Hugh Herland's original hammerbeam roof. For part of the period of construction, the Clerk of the King's Works was Geoffrey Chaucer, who in 1400 was buried in Westminster Abbey in what became Poets' Corner.

Professor Cannadine describes the Royal Commission appointed to judge the competition as 'essentially conservative' and its members as 'all of them patrician amateurs with interests in the Gothic and the picturesque'. Since the Select Committee had already determined upon 'Gothic or Elizabethan', an interest in Gothic architecture was a qualification in a Commissioner. The amateurs did well in awarding the prize to Barry, though his Palace is indeed both Gothic and picturesque. Internally, Barry's building answered the requirements of his brief and of a site which contained two older structures.[20] Externally, Barry's river frontage has an 800-foot facade of notable symmetry. Perpendicular has few pointed arches. Pugin, sailing along the Thames, remarked to a friend: 'All Grecian, Sir: Tudor details on a classic body.'[21]

But the Select Committee's choice of 'Gothic or Elizabethan' had more to do with political theory than with architecture. This point has been overlooked because word-usage has changed. In 1835, 'Gothic' and 'Elizabethan' were not simply architectural terms. Today, 'Gothic' is an adjective which (except in popular culture) expects an architectural noun, as 'Elizabethan' does not. In 1835, the narrowing of 'Gothic' to its specialist meanings had hardly begun; the first recorded use of the word 'medieval' is dated 1817. In 1834, the wider sense of 'Gothic' was current, and, for Parliamentarians, the bearing of the word was not architectural but ideological. 'Gothic' had long been a standard term in accounts of English constitutional law, and current in political discourse.

The *Oxford English Dictionary* defines the second of the senses of 'Gothic' as follows: 'Formerly used in extended sense, now expressed by *TEUTONIC* or *GERMANIC*.' The *Dictionary*'s first illustration of this sense is dated 1647 and taken from 'N. BACON, *Disc. Govt. Eng.* I. xl. 96.' Nathaniel Bacon was a Puritan MP who held office under Oliver and Richard Cromwell. The title of Bacon's treatise is *The Historical Discovery of the Uniformity of the Government of England from Edward III to Elizabeth*. The Dictionary quotation is: 'Nor can any Nation upon earth shew so much of the ancient Gothique Law as this island hath.'[22] Bacon, a Parliament man, saw national history as rooted in 'ancient Gothique Law'. Such Puritan and Parliamentary ideas were music to Whigs, but in the eighteenth century were also accepted by the Tory opposition, as is shown by two of the *Dictionary*'s further illustrative quotations: '1721 SWIFT *Letter to Pope* 10 Jan Wks. 1841 II.551/2 As to Parliaments, I adored the wisdom of that Gothic institution which made them annual. 1735–8 BOLINGBROKE *On Parties* 102 Maintaining the Freedom of our Gothick Institution of Government.'

Jonathan Swift had begun his career as secretary to Sir William Temple, but joined the Tory opposition when the Whigs failed to support the Church of England. Bolingbroke was the exponent of democratic Toryism. These quotations from the *Dictionary* show both sides of English Parliamentary politics appealing to 'ancient Gothic law'. Swift adores annual Parliaments, and Bolingbroke sees the 'Institution of Government' as Gothic. The manner in which these political writers use the word implies that 'Gothic' had a self-evident value, rather in the way in which Western politicians now use the word 'democratic'. Enough has been said to show that Parliament had long felt entitled to think of itself as historically a Gothic institution, in a sense of the word which has since become obsolete. For its architectural choice, then, Parliament had historical and constitutional reasons which had nothing to do with aesthetics, the picturesque or amateurism.

To step back a stage, the success of the Whigs in securing the succession of the German-speaking George I of Hanover in 1714, and in having ensured that the British monarch would be Protestant, was accompanied by a revival of the idea that the English constitution had originally been Germanic, northern and free, not Roman and absolutist, like that of Louis XIV. It was believed that in Anglo-Saxon times, under what Swift refers to as 'that Gothic institution', kings had ruled by the consent of regular meetings of the Witenagemot, or assembly of the wise. Later in the nineteenth century, William Stubbs published much historical evidence tending to substantiate this view of early English constitutional history. There is also literary evidence that early English kings used to consult. In his account of the conversion of Northumbria in 632, Bede has King Edwin say to the Roman missionary Paulinus that he would accept the new religion if this had the consent of his wise men, whom he then proceeds to consult.[23] Likewise, the formula used by King Alfred in writing to the Bishop of Worcester shows a king deferring in exactly this way: 'me thyncth betre, gif eow swa thyncth' – 'it seems to me better – if it also seems so to you'.[24] The 'Norman Yoke' view of British history, at one time treated by academic historians as an English joke, is like all historical generalisations an interpretation of selected evidence: a legal construction. Its real origins, however, lie less in Germanic customary law than in the legal fiction, in Thomas Cromwell's preamble to Henry VIII's Act of Supremacy, that England had never accepted Roman jurisdiction.[25]

There is no evidence that the Saxon conquerors of Britain, for all their respect for law, were instinctive practitioners of village-green yeoman democracy of the kind we read of in medieval Iceland. Saxon war-leaders, before they settled down and became kings, made slaves of some of those they had conquered in battle. Also, the first written Old English laws, those of Ethelbert of Kent of 604, are already Christian. According to the popular version of (de-Romanised) Gothic-Germanic constitutionalism, the Francophone companions of William the Bastard were high-handed aristocrats and their kings autocrats, until they were checked by 'English' barons at Runnymede, as recorded in Magna Carta, 1215. Such national and racial designations can mislead, since if the Angles, Saxons and Jutes were originally of Germanic stock, so were the Danes, the Normans and indeed the Franks. The idea that the 'Norman Yoke' was thrown off by liberty-loving Englishmen, first elaborated in the period leading up to the Civil War, informed the Whig historiography of Macaulay's *History of England* of 1849–55. As the Gothic theory was invoked by eighteenth-century Tories such as Swift and Bolingbroke, the theory became Parliamentary, not Whig.

In 1741, Richard, Viscount Cobham, a prominent Whig, had erected in the gardens of his house at Stowe a 'Temple of Liberty'. Cobham had this remarkable building designed for him by James Gibbs, a Scottish Catholic and a classical architect best known for his St Martin-in-the-Fields, on what is now Trafalgar Square. Cobham's Temple was dedicated to Liberty, and had accordingly to be in the Gothic style. 'Temple of Liberty' plays on Cobham's family name, Temple. It has statues of the Seven Saxon Worthies, and bears the motto 'I am not a Roman'. 'Roman' alludes to the Church of Rome, the Roman empire, and to the continental empires of France and of Spain, whose Catholic monarchs ruled absolutely: without the due consultation of their free people such as had in the past been observed by Germanic kings such as Alfred of Wessex – and should in future be observed by the dynasty who had come to England from Hanover.[26]

Ivanhoe had opened with 'the . . . free spirit of the Saxon constitution', and propounded the 'Norman Yoke' view of social history, in words addressed by a fool, Wamba, son of Witless, to a thrall, Gurth, son of Beowolf. In 1843, Thomas Macaulay pronounced that the history of England was emphatically a history of progress.[27] In the same year, Thomas Carlyle compared Gurth's position favourably with that of a modern industrial worker in free and democratic England. The work in which he did so, *Past and Present*, uses the technique Pugin pioneered in *Contrasts* (1836, 1841). Two years later, similar contrasts between ideal medieval and modern industrial conditions were invoked by Benjamin Disraeli in *Sybil*, as we shall see in the next chapter.

CHAPTER 5

Back to the Future in the 1840s

CARLYLE, RUSKIN, *SYBIL*, NEWMAN

> He [Pugin] was a Catholic convert ... who thought the
> medieval world better than his own time ... This profoundly
> conservative, anti-democratic, anti-utilitarian and anti-industrial
> vision was partly derived from such recent writers as Sir Walter
> Scott ... and had much in common with the 'Young England'
> movement that was fashionable among some Tories during
> the 1840s.
>
> David Cannadine, Introduction to *The Houses of Parliament*[1]

The aim of this essay in cultural history is to draw together elements
of the Medieval Revival, so that it may be seen as a whole. This
chapter looks at four representative figures who brought ideals
borrowed from the Middle Ages to bear upon the 1840s, a decade of
serious economic unrest. Some aspects of this story, and some of its
principal actors, are better known than others. In the case of a well-
known figure, it may be enough to refocus an accepted view. John
Ruskin, for example, is known to anyone interested in the history of
art and architecture, or in Victorian society, and such readers must
be among the audience of this book. If the first thing suggested by
the words Medieval Revival might be neo-Gothic architecture, the
first name to come up in a discussion might be that of John Ruskin.
He accordingly receives in this essay a more summary treatment
than would be found in a more systematic survey of the period.

Thomas Carlyle's *Past and Present* hinges on a simple contrast
between an ideal past and the concerns that were most urgent in
1843, when it was written. Carlyle's contrasts are less absolute than
Pugin's: the monastery of the twelfth century evoked in his pages is
less idealised than Pugin's fifteenth-century monastery. Unlike
Pugin's, it is not devoted to 'the corporal works of mercy'. The impact

which *Past and Present* had upon public opinion suggests that popular antiquarianism, and the romances of Walter Scott, had enabled readers for the first time to imagine a distant historical period neither classical nor biblical but part of national history, and to engage with an open mind in an imaginative comparison of such a past with the present state of society. The facing panels of Carlyle's diptych of 'Past' and 'Present' are entitled 'The Ancient Monk' and 'The Modern Worker'. The monk is drawn from Jocelyn of Brakelonde's *Chronicle* of the monastery of Bury St Edmunds, which was published by the Camden Society in 1840. The Ancient Monk is Carlyle's idea of Jocelyn's hard-working abbot, Abbot Samson, one of the 'great men' by whom, according to Carlyle in his lectures, *Heroes and Hero-Worship*, history is made. Had there been a seventh lecture in the series, Samson could have exemplified Hero as Administrator.

Abbots had not featured in post-Reformation English history as good, and had regularly appeared in fiction as bad: at best, they were depicted as lazy, and at worst as depraved, as in Matthew Lewis's *The Monk* of 1796 (see Plate 11), in which the monk of the title rapes a young girl in a charnel house. For educated eighteenth-century Protestant readers, English monasticism lay below the horizon of worthwhile historical enquiry. Rightly had its institutions been dissolved and rightly did its lands belong to those who held that the Church was safely governed by the state. The road back to the Middle Ages had been dug up, and the making good of this road was not an early priority of the heirs of the Enlightenment. John Lingard's *History of England* in three volumes (1817–30) removed the grounds for this prejudice, if not the prejudice itself. Carlyle describes the life of a monastery of the twelfth century as 'covered deeper than Pompeii with the lava-ashes and inarticulate wreck of seven hundred years'. 'Monks', he assures his readers, are 'an extinct species of the human family'. When Carlyle wrote this, there were monks in England, English monks, between one hundred and two hundred of them – Cistercians at Mount St Bernard, and Benedictines at Downside and Ampleforth. Confident in a revealed sense of the direction of history, Carlyle dismisses these 'live specimens which still go about under that character' as 'too evidently to be classed as spurious in Natural History'. Monks, then, are like those monsters who had survived the

Deluge, but ought not to have done so. Carlyle treats English history as a theme park, and for him any monks found in this green and pleasant land must have strayed from the Jurassic section. Thus did Carlyle quieten any fears aroused by praise of a twelfth-century abbot.

Carlyle's dismissal of live specimens of the religious life as spurious does not treat history in the spirit of the motto from Schiller that he quotes at the head of his treatise: 'Ernst ist das Leben' – 'Life is earnest'. The medieval is a stalking horse for Carlyle's primary target, the condition of workers in the present. His remedy for this condition is leadership, but his wish for a working aristocracy is the weaker part of his thesis. His contention is that the modern factory worker is worse off than the medieval worker. To this end, he makes repeated use of Gurth, a character from the opening chapter of Scott's most popular title, a romance of the late twelfth century. *Ivanhoe* is set in the very period chronicled by Jocelyn of Brakelonde. Gurth is first introduced in Chapter III of Book I, 'Manchester Insurrection': 'Gurth, a mere swineherd, born thrall of Cedric the Saxon, tended pigs in the wood, and did get some parings of the pork'.[2]

In Chapter V of 'The Ancient Monk', entitled 'The Twelfth Century', Carlyle tells us that in that Past: 'A Feudal Aristocracy is still alive ...; everywhere governing the people, – so that even a Gurth, born thrall of Cedric, lacks not his due parings of the pigs he tends ... Governing; – and, alas, also game-preserving; so that a Robert Hood, a William Scarlet and others have in these days, put on Lincoln coats, and taken to living in some universal-suffrage manner, under the greenwood-tree!'[3] The last phrase comes from a song in *As You Like It*, a pastoral comedy which prefers the glad poverty of the Forest of Arden to the envious corruption of court and town. Carlyle's greenwood tree shelters Robin Hood's 'democracy' of innocent outlaws in *Ivanhoe*, itself derived from the Robin Hood ballads published by Percy.

'Democracy', a chapter of 'The Modern Worker', produces the fullest statement of Carlyle's message in *Past and Present*:

> Gurth, born thrall of Cedric the Saxon, has been greatly pitied ...
> Gurth, with the brass collar round his neck, tending Cedric's pigs
> in the glades of the wood, is not what I call an exemplar of human

felicity: but Gurth, with the sky above him, with the free air and tinted boscage and umbrage round him, and in him at least the certainty of supper and social lodging when he came home; Gurth to me seems happy, in comparison with many a Lancashire and Buckinghamshire man of these days, not born thrall of anybody! ... Gurth had superiors, inferiors, equals. – Gurth is now 'emancipated' long since; has what we call 'Liberty'. Liberty, I am told, is a divine thing. Liberty when it becomes the 'Liberty to die by starvation' is not so divine![4]

The insecure livelihood of the millions of factory workers is again alluded to in the 'Permanence' chapter of Book 4. In the twelfth century, Carlyle writes, 'Gurth was hired for life to Cedric, and Cedric to Gurth.'[5] Although the hospitable Cedric is not as good an exemplar of energetic leadership as Abbot Samson, Carlyle's paradox that Cedric was 'hired for life' to Gurth has some historical validity. Yet 'hired', though taken from a New Testament parable, is the wrong word, for Carlyle wants to say that the obligations binding lord and man were not financial and temporary, but should be understood, despite inequality of rank, as lifelong mutual service and protection. Carlyle's application of feudal social theory was read with interest in societies less equal than England's, as in the Southern United States.

Carlyle's pronouncement that 'With our present system of individual Mammonism, and Government by *Laissez-faire*, this Nation cannot live' was soon to be amplified and broadcast by John Ruskin.[6] The standards of social and economic justice to which Carlyle appeals are as old as the first books of the Old Testament and inform Christian social teaching. It first received full and notable expression in English in William Langland's radical *Piers Plowman*. The dignity of labour and the principles of economic justice are at the core of medieval social thought, and at the heart of the General Prologue of Chaucer's *Canterbury Tales*, in the paired portraits of the ideal Ploughman and his brother, the ideal Parson. Carlyle's moral denunciation of industrialism and laissez-faire economics set the tone for one side of national discussions of these subjects for a hundred years or more. He saw human relations as sadly shrunken in comparison with older notions of mutual service, and he memorably crystallised the new relationship as 'the cash nexus between man and man'. The acceptance of workhouses as part of the virtuous circle of an industrial economy meant that material interests, whether of individuals or of the economy as a whole, had finally triumphed over residual ideals of mutual obligation between different ranks of society, the ideals which Burke had intended to embrace and consecrate in his inegalitarian 'chivalry'. Carlyle's analysis was admired by Karl Marx, but instead of Carlyle's remedy, of vertical cohesion under a working aristocracy, Marx prescribed class war and prophesied a dictatorship of the proletariat.

John Ruskin (1819–1900) is Britain's great art critic, and was also a lifelong critic of the moral insensitivity with which Victorian Britain exploited its raw materials, natural or human. He was an insistent advocate both of Gothic art and of medieval ideals, not only in his eloquent chapter of *The Stones of Venice* on 'The Nature of Gothic' and his loving analyses and detailed descriptions of medieval buildings and carvings, but also at every turn of his later discussions of economics and in his prophetic vision of the polluting of the natural world in 'The Storm-Cloud of the Nineteenth Century'. Ruskin's historic role and wide influence are acknowledged, and the aim of the present work is not to blow the dust off accepted reputations. Yet the impression left by the name Ruskin upon the general reading public is now very general indeed. Few have read far into his copious and discursive writings. As he grew older, he engaged with more immediate political issues, and with increasing anger. Although a page of Ruskin can enlighten and possess, he can be distracted by a favourite topic, and his work is not easy to represent either as a whole or in selection. Voluminous idiosyncrasy does not lend itself to summary, but there is no alternative.

The only child of a Scottish evangelical family living in London, Ruskin grew up on the Bible and on British literature, especially the Scottish Romantics, Scott and Byron. His formal education did not conventionalise his tastes, and he had no academic training in the history of art or in philosophical aesthetics, but had instead been taught drawing, water-colour, geology and natural history. A love for Gothic art, carving and architecture developed on family holidays in Normandy. The neglect, destruction or over-restoration of the medieval buildings he saw in Italy caused him to suspend work on *Modern Painters*, a defence of J.M.W. Turner and other British artists, after its second volume, so that the fifth and final volume appeared only in 1860. Ruskin threw himself instead into writing *The Seven Lamps of Architecture* (1849) and, from 1851 to 1853, *The Stones of Venice*. He championed the Gothic spirit in art both for its own sake but also, and increasingly, because for him it made a painful contrast with the unbeautiful buildings and manufactures of the new England which came into being in his lifetime. Among his prophetic denunciations of prospering England, a favourite maxim was that 'there is no wealth but life.'

The point to be dwelt on here, in considering Ruskin and the Medieval Revival, is that for him medieval workmanship lacked the machined finish of the factory product, which he held in abhorrence, for reasons not aesthetic but ethical: because it was turned out by machine operators who could, like their machines, be discarded when worn out. Ruskin's biblical outrage at the reduction of the modern worker into a disposable tool was such that he extended his distrust of perfectly finished art to include classical as well as neo-classical art and architecture. Perfect finish indicated that the workman was a slave, whereas free-hand meant that he was free. Thus, though by a different route, Ruskin, like his predecessor Pugin, arrived at a generally negative attitude to the art of the classical world. Both Ruskin and Pugin, had they known of it, would have agreed with William Blake's declaration that 'Grecian Art is Mathematic Form; Gothic is Living Form.'[7]

It is well enough known that Thomas Carlyle and, more insistently, John Ruskin criticised contemporary industrial practice and utilitarian theory, contrasting them with ideals drawn from the Middle Ages. That Benjamin Disraeli (1804–81) also did so is less generally known. He began a trilogy of novels between 1844 and 1847, setting out his political beliefs with *Coningsby* and *Sybil; or, The Two Nations*. The third novel, *Tancred*, has not lasted so well. (Dickens's anti-industrial *Hard Times* appeared later, in 1854.) Disraeli's essays in fiction are more romances than novels; as *Sybil*'s subtitle suggests, they are also treatises of ideas, sometimes in dialogue form. In this they resemble the satires of Thomas Love Peacock, and the Platonic discourses of Kenelm Digby's *The Broad Stone of Honour* of 1822.

Sybil is not familiar today and lends itself to quotation. It addresses 'the condition of the people' in the decade of Chartism, but it opens by contrast in a London club in St James's, where gilded youths are gambling fortunes on the results of the 1837 Derby. It focuses then on the owners of Marney Abbey:

> The founder of the family had been a confidential domestic of one of the favourites of Henry VIII, and had contrived to be appointed one of the commissioners for 'visiting and taking the surrenders of divers religious houses'. It came to pass that divers of these religious houses surrendered themselves eventually to the use and benefit of honest Baldwin Greymount.[8]

Early in the seventeenth century, a Greymount was elevated to the peerage as Baron Marney:

> The heralds furnished his pedigree, and assured the world that, although the exalted rank and extensive possessions enjoyed at present by the Greymounts had their origin immediately in great territorial revolutions of a recent reign, it was not for a moment to be supposed that the remote ancestors of the Ecclesiastical Commissioner of 1530 were by any means obscure. On the contrary, it appeared that they were both Norman and baronial, their real name Egremont, which, in their patent of peerage, the family now resumed. In the civil wars the Egremonts, pricked by their Norman blood, were cavaliers, and fought pretty well. But in 1688, alarmed at the prevalent impression that King James intended to insist on the restitution of the church estates to their original purposes, to wit, the education of the people and the maintenance of the poor, the Lord of Marney Abbey became a warm adherent of 'civil and religious liberty', the cause for which Hampden had died in the field, and Russell on the scaffold, and joined the other whig lords, and great lay impropriators, in calling over the Prince of Orange and a Dutch army, to vindicate those popular principles which, somehow or other, the people would never support.[9]

Later the 'lay abbots of Marney' become members of the Whig oligarchy which figures as 'a Venetian constitution' in Disraeli's projection of English history. 'During the seventy years of almost unbroken whig rule, from the accession of the House of Hanover to the fall of Mr. Fox, Marney Abbey had furnished a neverfailing crop of lord privy seals, lord presidents and lord lieutenants.' This oligarchy is what Disraeli wants to end. If 'a Greymount' can turn into 'Egremont', Marney can turn into Money, the love of which motivates Egremont's elder brother, Lord Marney.

One of Disraeli's successors as Prime Minister, Harold Macmillan, once said that television was not for looking at but for being on. This recalls Disraeli's 'When I want to read a novel, I write one', supposedly said in answer to the suggestion that he might read George Eliot's Zionist novel, *Daniel Deronda*. Disraeli wrote sixteen novels or romances, to advance his fortunes, his fame and his ideas. (In his youth he wrote a verse epic on the French Revolution, which was not a success.) Though written at hectic speed, and unpredictable in quality, Disraeli's witty analyses of the life of high society were imitated by Oscar Wilde and Evelyn Waugh.

Egremont, the novel's leading man, is a younger son of the 'lay abbots of Marney'. Egremont is modelled on Walter Scott's impressionable observer protagonist, Edward Waverley. In Scotland, Waverley had encountered two nations unknown to him, Lowlanders and Highlanders, and was charmed by each in turn. Egremont is, like Waverley, a young gentleman who falls for a young beauty from another social world, encountering her first in a Romantic landscape. Waverley had come upon Flora MacIvor gazing at a Highland waterfall, her 'small Scottish harp' held by an attendant, while 'the sun now stooping in the west, gave a rich and varied tinge'. Disraeli's Egremont first sees Sybil at sunset, after having overheard a lengthy discussion between two speakers previously unknown to him upon:

'two nations; between whom there is no intercourse and no sympathy; who are as ignorant of each other's habits, thoughts, and feelings, as if they were dwellers in different zones, or inhabitants of different planets; who are formed by a different breeding, are fed by a different food, are ordered by different manners, and are not governed by the same laws.'

'You speak of –' said Egremont, hesitatingly.

'THE RICH AND THE POOR.'

At this moment a sudden flush of rosy light, suffusing the grey ruins [of Marney Abbey], indicated that the sun had just fallen; and, through a vacant arch that overlooked them, alone in the resplendent sky, glittered the twilight star .... when from the Lady's chapel there rose the evening hymn to the Virgin. A single voice; but tones of almost supernatural sweetness; tender and solemn yet flexible and thrilling .... in the vacant and star-lit arch on which his glance was fixed, he beheld a female form. She was apparently in the habit of a Religious, yet ... her veil ... had fallen on her shoulders, and revealed her thick tresses of long fair hair.[10]

This is not 'the fair phantom of some saint haunting the sacred ruins of her desecrated fane', as Egremont at first imagines, but Sybil, the daughter of Walter Gerard, who is to lead the Chartists. Sybil is a religious sister, and, like the Sybil of antiquity, a source of spiritual wisdom. The speaker who has just instructed Egremont on the economic actualities of contemporary English society is Morley, a political journalist, a friend of Walter Gerard, and in love with his daughter. Walter Gerard ideally represents the People. Sybil, though she seems rather a free-range nun, represents the Church.

Readers familiar with the fortunes of nuns with lovely hair in the verse romances of Walter Scott will not have been surprised at the conclusion of Sybil's penultimate chapter: ' "We will never part again," said Egremont. "Never," said Sybil.'

Like Sybil, Waverley is a political fable, but as it is a novel as well as a romance, it has to have a more balanced ending. After the defeat of the Jacobite rising in 1746, Edward Waverley weds Rose, a Lowlander. Flora, on the other hand, the proud Highland lady by whom Waverley had previously been fascinated, goes into exile in Paris, to become a Benedictine nun. Sybil's trajectory is in the opposite direction.

Disraeli wished to promote his vision of a triple alliance of People, Church and Crown against the Whig plutocracy, a vision he eventually furthered when he presided over the extension of the popular franchise with his Reform Act of 1867. Disraeli's presentation of his case in *Sybil* draws directly upon an updated version of the 'Norman Yoke' theory expounded by Wamba to Gurth in Scott's *Ivanhoe*. Disraeli speaks of Merry England and Old England, and applies the epithet 'Saxon' variously to the 'race', the 'people' and the 'multitude', the 'yeoman', the 'thrall' and the 'serf'. He refers to 'the drink of Saxon kings'.[11] Thus a Saxon (or Gothic) people is opposed to a (pseudo-) Norman aristocracy, as in *Ivanhoe*. It was handy for Disraeli's purpose that the name of the new Queen's family was Saxe-Coburg-Gotha.

The Greymount-Egremonts, ignoble impropriators of an abbey founded by Norman knights, are further rewarded for the surefootedness of their placehunting. The de Mowbray family is similarly descended: from Warren, a waiter in a St James's club, who became first the valet, and then the agent, of a Governor of Madras (a glance at Warren Hastings). Warren used a fortune made by buying rice cheap and selling it dear in India to burrow into British public life. Having bought a seat in the Mother of Parliaments, he sells his vote dearly, to emerge as Baron Fitz-Warene, 'his Norman origin and descent from the old barons of this name having been discovered at Heralds' College.'[12] The rightful heirs of Mowbray Castle, burned down by a Chartist mob in the Gothic ending of the novel, turn out to have been Walter Gerard, who dies in the assault, and his daughter Sybil, who survives to marry Egremont. In these ways, *Sybil; or the Two Nations* rewrites the plots of both *Waverley* and *Ivanhoe*.

Disraeli's *mythos* of English history gives prominence to the former role of the Church in securing what is the only 'duty of power: the social welfare of the PEOPLE'.[13] The social provision made by the medieval Church is not a theme of Carlyle, nor of Ruskin. Cobbett and Pugin had preceded Disraeli in attacking the Dissolution of the Monasteries, but neither Cardinal Gasquet nor Hilaire Belloc could have improved on the rhetoric of the case against the Dissolution put to Egremont by Walter Gerard in Chapter V of Book II in *Sybil*. This takes place in the ruins of Marney Abbey (which is based upon Fountains Abbey in Yorkshire).

Egremont remarks that the monks 'would hardly have forfeited their restingplace had they deserved to retain it', to which Gerard replies that 'their history has been written by their enemies; they were condemned without a hearing; the people rose oftentimes in their behalf; and their property was divided among those on whose reports it was forfeited'. Among the points Gerard makes are that 'the Monastics were easy landlords'; that 'there were yeomen then, sir: the country was not divided into two classes'; that 'the great majority of the heads of houses were of the people' (like Abbot Samson); that the bare ruined choirs are 'the children of violence, not of time'. He describes the Dissolution as 'worse than the Norman conquest; nor has England ever lost this character of ravage'.[14] Gerard concludes: 'I don't know whether the union workhouses will remove it. They are building something for the people at last. After an experiment of three centuries, your gaols being full, and your treadmills losing something of their virtue, you have given us a substitute for the monasteries.' New workhouses for old monasteries: the Oxford editor of *Sybil* notes that 'the graphic equivalent of this argument can be found in A.W.N. Pugin's *Contrasts*,' citing 'Contrasted Residences for the Poor' from the 1841 edition.

A final quotation from *Sybil*: ' "Ah!" said Gerard, "if we could only have the Church on our side, as in the good old days, we would soon put an end to the demon tyranny of Capital." '[15] Such claims as these, made by Disraeli's spokesmen for 'the PEOPLE', may surprise readers who know of him only that he was the first Jew either to lead the Conservative Party or to become Prime Minister. But Benjamin Disraeli had been baptised, and remained a worshipping member of the Church of England. The Anglican Church adheres in its Creed to 'one Catholick and Apostolick Church'. Since 1833 some leading Anglicans at Oxford had, in a series of Tracts, tried to awaken the Church of England to this clause in its creed. How far Disraeli in 1845 entertained a true attachment to the historic faith of England is hard to tell, but he was historian enough to know that had there been no Catholic Christians there would have been no Christianity to reform. Pro-Catholic sentiment had for Disraeli the advantage of undermining the legitimacy of Whig claims. Wondering what Disraeli really thought was to become a national preoccupation. As for the (Anglo-) Catholic sympathies of *Sybil*, Sir George Smythe, one of Disraeli's associates in 'Young England', a Gang of Four in the politics of the

1840s, remarked with political cynicism that 'Dizzy's attachment to moderate Oxfordism is something like Bonaparte's to moderate Mohammedanism'.[16] Despite his reverence for the medieval Church, Disraeli had within a few years become hostile to the impact upon British politics both of Irish nationalism and of the Vatican. Walter Gerard's hatred of 'the demon tyranny of Capital' did not prevent his creator, when, much later, he was Prime Minister, from borrowing £4 million from Baron Rothschild, on the security of the British government, to buy Egyptian shares in the Suez Canal Company.[17]

The historian Robert Blake in his classic biography of Disraeli remarks severely that he 'had no real historical sense; he wrote propaganda, not history; and projected the circumstances of his own times into the past'.[18] It is nevertheless striking that a novel of the 1840s could make such a thesis so central. It was Disraeli's Conservative government which in 1867 extended the popular franchise, against Liberal opposition.

Of the Medieval Revival, Robert Blake wrote:

Just as the Oxford movement set up for its ideal the revival of a pure, uncorrupted, pre-Reformation church which had never existed, in order to counter the Erastian and latitudinarian tendencies of the day, so Young England resuscitated a no less mythical benevolent feudal system to set against the radical centralizing Benthamism which seemed to be carrying all before it in the 1830s and 1840s. Yet if this may be its social explanation, and if one may easily laugh at some of its more absurd follies, the movement should not be dismissed as wholly ineffective ... In *Sybil* even the Reformation is looked at with a jaundiced eye and there is much nostalgia for monasteries and the Old Faith.[19]

This kindly putting aside of Medieval Revival policies in Church and state, by a distinguished Conservative political historian, has something in common with David Cannadine's list, at the head of this chapter, of Pugin's disqualifications: 'Catholic convert ... thought the medieval world better than his own time ... profoundly conservative, anti-democratic, anti-utilitarian and anti-industrial vision ... Sir Walter Scott ... "Young England" ... fashionable among some

Tories.'[20] These two modern historians, of different generations and political persuasions, appeal to the journalistic assumption that only the contemporary is real and that past ideals are delusive. Cannadine reports that Pugin 'thought the medieval world better than his own time', as if no more needed be said. Yet the medieval Church passed on the command that the neighbour should be cherished in the same way as the self, and practised this command – to an extent – by relieving the poor and needy, and by running hospitals and other charities. This social duty is one which the state did not – to any extent – assume until the twentieth century. Pugin's juxtaposition of a medieval Christian ideal with the harsh treatment of the unemployed recommended by Benthamite liberal economists is not to be dismissed in the way Professor Cannadine implies. It was not dismissed by Carlyle, Ruskin or Disraeli, nor by their readers. The 1840s were, like the 1930s, a decade in which economic crisis and social unrest showed that the usual parliamentary politics were not working. What can be rejected is the suggestion that medieval revivalists were all 'profoundly conservative', if conservative meant conserving the status quo. In this respect, Ruskin is representative in calling himself both a Tory of the school of Homer and Sir Walter Scott, and also 'a communist, reddest of the red'. In that sense, Karl Marx and William Morris were medievalists, a tradition carried on into the third quarter of the twentieth century.[21] In such a medievalism there is more of machine-breaking than of nostalgia.

All revivalists hold up for admiration a selective version of the past, whether their chosen ideal is medieval or classical, secular or Christian, Tory or republican. The architecture chosen by Thomas Jefferson for his house at Monticello and for the University of Virginia, which he founded, was to remind the world of the ideals of Cincinnatus and of Marcus Junius Brutus, or at least of John Locke. He also proposed that US coins should bear on the obverse the figures of the Saxon leaders Hengest and Horsa, to represent Saxon democracy. As Republican Rome was to imperial Rome, and Saxon England was to Norman England, so would the United States be to the England of George III. The world in which revivalists live seems to them to lack something which they believe to have been present in the culture of another time. Such a belief can hardly be proved or disproved. Yet medievalism is too often dismissed simply as nostalgic or escapist; the social medievalism of the 1840s was neither.

The first in Professor Cannadine's list of Pugin's disqualifications is that he was a Catholic convert. Catholics know that the Church is an earthen vessel and holds itself to be *semper reformanda*, always in need of reform. During the age of the Catholic Church's fullest influence in Europe, when she was developing universities, cathedrals and hospitals, and patronising learning and the arts – the period of Aquinas and of Chartres – that most Catholic poet Dante Alighieri put two Popes in his Inferno. The Church then was, its members well knew, in drastic need of reform. Reformers have no language to express their hopes for the future which is not taken from the past; whether they prophesy a Christian future or a secular one, or, like most Victorian visionaries, a bit of both. The least supernatural book of the Bible records the maxim that 'where there is no vision, the people perish' (Proverbs, 29:18).

* * *

This chapter has so far considered the use made of medieval comparisons by writers addressing what in the 1840s was called 'the condition of England'. Carlyle contended that the permanent bond between a feudal lord and a 'thrall' was more real than the freedom of a factory hand in a market economy. To Ruskin, the free-hand carving of the medieval stoneworker was living and visible proof of an organic and healthy society, very different to the one he saw around him, in which wage-slaves operated machinery supplying finished goods to the rich. Disraeli has a Chartist leader stand by a wrecked abbey, contrasting the charity to the poor of the former monastic landlords with the sordid conditions imposed on workers in Manchester and the Black Country, described luridly and at length in *Sybil*. Elsewhere in the novel, the Catholic Traffords are kindly paternalists, in contrast to the ruthless 'lay abbot', Lord Marney. The focus of all three authors is on the desperate conditions of those whose labour was making Britain the richest country in the world. All present the contemporary treatment of the poor, and an influential contemporary theory about how the poor should be treated, as falling below the theory and practice of the medieval Christian past. It is a very tenable view.

Carlyle and Ruskin have little to say about the Christianity of Britain in the past, although when abroad Ruskin admired the old communal spirit of Venice, and attended cathedral services in France. Both had had a markedly Protestant upbringing. It is striking that of the three social commentators of the 1840s that we have considered, it was not the lay pulpiteers who praised the social provision of the medieval Church but the political dandy. This aspect of Disraeli's creed in 1845 is as polemically black and white as Pugin's cartoons of 'Residences for the Poor' are in *Contrasts*. Unlike Disraeli, the Scots Carlyle and Ruskin avoid England's eight Catholic centuries, the elephant in the living-room of her history – and of Scotland's history. Like Pugin, Carlyle ventured boldly into medieval social history, but his humbly born abbot is a hard worker, an exemplar not of the monastic life of prayer and worship, but of 'worth' and 'social vitality'. Ruskin turned a blind eye to the fact that the art which he loved was produced by Christians who venerated images, and that the images he admired were created as aids to prayer. When in Italy, Ruskin worshipped with the Waldensians, the sect about whom John Milton wrote his sonnet 'Avenge, O Lord, thy slaughtered saints'. At thirty-nine, however, Ruskin rejected the Waldensian creed as stunted.[22]

Unitarianism has been defined as the belief that there is, at most, one God; Unitarians can be more Deist than Christian. Benjamin Disraeli, an Anglican of Jewish birth, had attended a Unitarian school, and had in his twenties visited the Levant and Jerusalem. Throughout his life he maintained a synthesis of three traditions: the Israel of the Old Testament, the Messiah of the New, and the history of English Christianity. He held that 'Christianity is completed Judaism'. This repeats Christ's claim to fulfil the Law, and is unacceptable to Jews, for whom Jesus is not the promised Messiah. 'Completed Judaism' was in 1845 a formulation strange to English ears, though since 1945 it has become more familiar to European Christians, who have had to reconsider what they owe to Judaism, and how they have treated Jews. Disraeli is said to have remarked to Queen Victoria that he was the blank page between the Old and the New Testaments.[23]

Disraeli approached pre-Reformation English Christianity with a mixture of romanticism and pragmatism: it was part both of providential history and of family history. Dizzy's DIY ecclesiology side-stepped the concerns of Anglicans who held that their bishops inherited from the medieval Catholic hierarchy the powers conferred on the apostles, and equally of evangelicals within the Church of England, and Dissenters outside it, who looked upon the Pope as the Antichrist, and the Middle Ages as a Babylonian captivity. Disraeli's Egremont, in conversation with St Lys, a High Church parson devoted to the poor, is doubtful about ceremonious forms of worship, observing that 'the people of this country associate them with an enthralling superstition and a foreign domination'. St Lys replies to Egremont that 'forms and ceremonies existed before Rome' and, more surprisingly, that 'the Church of Rome is to be respected as the only Hebraeo-christian church extant'.[24] Disraeli's religious history was, like his political history, very special. He had the courage of his convictions, and if his convictions changed, he remained an Anglican.

The medieval revivalists reviewed in this and earlier chapters all appropriated, or misappropriated, those aspects of the Middle Ages which appealed to their taste or suited their purposes. The manner of these appropriations became increasingly serious after the Reform Act of 1832 and in the 1840s. In *Ivanhoe* (1819), for example, the swineherd Gurth is instructed by the Fool, Wamba. In 1843 Carlyle used this puppet from light romantic fiction earnestly to instruct the public. In Victorian times medieval ideals could still be used for decorative or light purposes, but they were also given serious social applications. Ruskin taught drawing at the Working Men's College, which the Rev. F.D. Maurice had founded in 1854. He himself founded the Guild of St George, and an Oxford college for working men was named after him. His disciple, Morris, later started up a workshop named Morris, Marshall, Faulkner and Co., also known as Morris & Co., and as 'the Firm': a firm which, although it used some modern industrial processes, tried to preserve a guild spirit and produced 'medieval' and modern work to the highest craft standards. Morris also founded the Socialist League. Alfred Tennyson and Anthony Trollope wrote seriously, if differently, about chivalrous gentlemen, while Ruskin and Coventry Patmore idealised chivalrous ladies, and Charles Kingsley chivalrous lads. Painters and poets, following Rossetti and the Pre-Raphaelites, used medieval romance to explore the themes and emotional states of extramarital love. The Gothic Revival radically transformed Victorian architecture, which in the period of George Street, William Butterfield, George Gilbert Scott and William Burges had great achievements. Yet the most serious form of Medieval Revival, and the one which caused most controversy, was the attempt to revive the sacramental religion of the Middle Ages within the Church of England. The Oxford Movement within the English Church strove, between 1833 and 1845, to revive the Catholicism to which Anglicanism lays claim. In the Book of Common Prayer of 1662, still used in some Anglican churches, the Apostles' Creed ends: 'I believe in the Holy Ghost; The holy Catholick Church; The Communion of Saints; The Forgiveness of sins; The Resurrection of the body; And the life everlasting. Amen.' These claims remain in all Anglican creeds.

The Oxford or Tractarian Movement had begun in 1833 with a sermon by John Keble on 'National Apostasy'. It aimed at resisting Broad Church Liberal theology, restoring the High Church ideals of the Caroline period in the seventeenth century, and reviving the sacramental dimension of pre-Reformation Christianity. John Keble, John Newman and Edward Pusey – senior members of Oxford University – and their many supporters, emphasised the Church of England's share in the Apostolic Succession of the Catholic (or universal) Church. The strictly Tractarian phase of the Oxford Movement came to a halt with John Henry Newman's *Tract XC*. In this last of the series of Tracts for the Times, Newman had argued that all the Thirty-Nine Articles of the Church of England could be interpreted in a Catholic sense.

The Elizabethan ecclesiastical settlement had been presented by Richard Hooker as a *via media* between Catholicism and the Protestant sects, and a 'high' version of this Middle Way or troika theory of the Church of England was sustained under Charles I, in opposition to the Calvinism which had gained much ground. But this high Caroline Anglicanism fell with Archbishop Laud and Charles I, and was effectively repudiated at the Succession crisis of 1688. Although the Church of England's episcopate has in each generation repeated its claims to apostolical continuity, many Anglicans feel a greater loyalty to her Protestant origin. It is therefore not surprising that Newman's *Tract XC* was censured by his bishop. He resigned his position as Vicar of the University Church of St Mary the Virgin, and after a period of reflection left the Anglican to be received into the Catholic Church in 1845, the year of the publication of *Sybil*. Newman's move was an event of national importance. As late as 1870, Disraeli could still write, in the Preface to *Lothair*, that 'the secession of DR NEWMAN ... dealt a blow to the Church of England under which it still reels'.[25] (The protagonist of *Lothair* is a Scottish nobleman, based on John Patrick Crichton Stuart, 3rd Marquess of Bute (1847–1900), who as an undergraduate at Christ Church, Oxford, converted to Catholicism and became a pioneer scholar of early liturgy and of Byzantium. He devoted his great wealth to reversing the iconoclasm of the Reformation. Heir to much of the Welsh coalfield, Bute gave Cardiff £3 million to construct new docks, and built Cardiff Castle and another spectacular Gothic Revival castle, Mountstuart, on the Isle of Bute. Crichton Stuart also endowed churches and several buildings at Scottish universities. When Rector at St Andrews, Scotland's first university, Bute began to rebuild the cathedral there, Scotland's equivalent of Canterbury Cathedral, destroyed at the Reformation by the supporters of John Knox. For a photograph of Bute, see Plate 12.)

One of the starting-points of the present study of the Medieval Revival is a passage concerning the origins of the Oxford Movement to be found in Newman's *Apologia pro Vita Sua* of 1864. This account confirms and repeats the terms of an assessment Newman had given in 1839. Newman's defence of the conduct of his life was prompted by the Rev. Charles Kingsley's having remarked in print that Dr Newman, as a Catholic clergyman, would not feel under any obligation to tell the truth. In his defence, Newman undertook to explain the history of his religious opinions, and traces the reasons which had brought him to leave the Anglican Church nineteen years earlier. He described the Oxford Movement as:

a reaction from the dry and superficial character of the religious teaching and the literature of the last generation, or century; and as a result of the need which was felt both by the hearts and the intellects of the nation for a deeper philosophy; and as the evidence and as the partial fulfilment of that need, to which even the chief authors of the then generation had borne witness. First, I mentioned the literary influence of Walter Scott, who turned men's minds in the direction of the middle ages . . .[26]

Newman mentions Coleridge, who 'made trial of his age, and succeeded in interesting its genius in the cause of Catholic truth', as well as Robert Southey's fiction and Wordsworth's philosophical meditation.

Newman refers here to what he had written in the *British Critic* in 1839, that Walter Scott had:

> prepare[d] men for some closer and more practical approxima-
> tion to Catholic truth . . . stimulating their mental thirst, feeding
> their hopes, setting before them visions, which when once seen,
> are not easily forgotten, and silently indoctrinating them with
> nobler ideas . . . while history in prose and verse was thus made
> the instrument of Church feelings and opinions, a philosophical
> basis for the same was under formation in England by a very orig-
> inal thinker . . . who instilled a higher philosophy into inquiring
> minds, than they had hitherto been accustomed to accept . . . it is
> only since the death of Coleridge that these results of his writings
> have fully shown themselves . . . Two living poets [Southey and
> Wordsworth] have addressed themselves to the same high princi-
> ples and feelings, and carried forward their readers in the same
> direction.[27]

Newman's account is surprising. It is easy to understand that he should have seen Coleridge as instilling a philosophy higher than that of empiricism. It is also clear that the Oxford Movement owes much to what is now called Romanticism. But how could a deeper and more Catholic religion be seen as having developed from reading the 'history in prose and verse' of Walter Scott? Scott's representations of Catholicism are barely tolerant. On reading *Waverley* at the age of eighteen, Newman wrote: 'O what a poet! his words are not like a novelist . . . Author of Waverley, thou art a second Shakespeare.' Newman's reaction is typical of his period and is not due simply to

the age at which he read the book. Educated people today no longer read *Waverley* as history, and know that *Ivanhoe* is fiction. But Newman's rapture was shared by two generations of European adults, for whom Scott filled a historical void exposed by fading Reformation certainties, and spoke to the emotional and imaginative deficit left by Enlightenment intellectualism. It is probable that an evangelical home such as that into which Newman was born in 1801 had no historical knowledge of the Middle Ages. It seems that Scott's 'history' (we would call it historical fiction) not only turned men's minds in medieval directions but for the first time enabled readers to imagine in detail a pre-modern way of life – the life of their ancestors. The recovery of the Middle Ages had been begun before Scott by antiquarians and was completed after Scott by historians. The transition from antiquarianism to history took place during his life, and his work was the bridge between the two.

One of the attractions of the Church of Rome for Newman was, as he wrote as an Anglican in *Tract XC*, that 'She alone, amid all the errors and evils of her practical system, has given free scope to the feelings of awe, mystery, tenderness, reverence, devotedness, and other feelings which may be especially called Catholic.' Newman's warm approval of the devout piety he observed among Catholics is the counterpart of his view that the '[Anglican] religious teaching and the literature of the last . . . century' had been 'dry and superficial'. Coleridge wrote in his notebooks of his despair at the refrigeration of high and dry Anglicanism and the fierce emotionality of the chapels of Dissent: 'Socinianism moonlight – Methodism a Stove! O for some Sun to ignite heat & Light!'[28] The Oxford Movement was an answer to this prayer. Newman's approval of piety agrees with the value Pugin gave to worshipful devotion. Yet the Gothic Revival of Pugin and Ambrose Phillips de Lisle did not have Newman's support. Phillips's 'strong conviction that Gothick is Christian architecture, and Italian or Grecian Pagan', classifies the basilica built over the tomb of St Peter as a pagan building, as Newman pointed out. His own view was that the Church's liturgy, which changed 'according to the times', required a 'living architecture'. Gothic was 'now like an old dress, which fitted a man well twenty years back but must be altered to fit him now'. In Milan, Newman preferred the brightness, grace and simplicity of the classical style to Gothic: 'as the young prefer autumn and the old spring, the young tragedy and the old comedy, so in the ceremonial of religion, younger men have my leave to prefer gothic, if they will but tolerate me in my weakness which requires the Italian … my heart has ever gone with Grecian. I loved Trinity Chapel at Oxford more than any other building.'[29] Trinity was Newman's undergraduate college at Oxford; its chapel is in the restrained English baroque of which Christopher Wren was the chief exponent.

The religious society which Newman chose to join after his conversion to Catholicism – the Oratory –was not medieval but had been founded by Philip Neri in the sixteenth century. The Oratory is neither contemplative nor enclosed. Oratorians are secular priests living in community under a simple vow of charity, open to the world and obliged to care for the poor. The Oratory Newman himself founded was in Birmingham, and its work was among the poor. 'Birmingham people have souls', as he pointed out to an English Monsignor in Rome.

Newman had a scholarly mind with an exceptional range. Rather than the churches of the fourteenth century, the chief object of Newman's historical enquiry was the Church of the fourth century, when Christian communities in the Roman empire emerged from persecution to toleration and from acceptance to establishment. Amid the hubbub of competing theological voices, the General Councils of the Church were driven to defend and therefore to define core Christian beliefs about the two natures of Christ, both human and divine, in a single person. Arians, who denied that Christ was truly divine, were adjudged, at the Council of Constantinople of 381, to have strayed from the common faith which Christ's followers had received from the apostles. What Arius taught was ruled out as incorrect. Newman's studies led him to conclude that the position of Anglicans in the nineteenth century was comparable to that of Arians in the fourth century. For all the sensitive compassion towards human frailty which Newman shows in *Gerontius* and elsewhere in his verse, he was, as a controversialist, acute, disciplined, strategic and tough-minded. His feelings were under control. He was thus very far from the kind of aesthete or 'cultural Catholic' who in the

1890s and afterwards was captivated by what is often referred to as 'smells and bells'. This smiling dismissal of ritualism is itself a ritual reaction to the worship of churches whose services use much ceremony. In England today, such a church may well be Anglo-Catholic rather than Roman Catholic.

Newman, then, wanted a revival not of medieval churches or liturgy, nor of the medieval Church, but of a fuller living of Christianity in the present. He did not think of Catholic Christians in the way that Carlyle classified monks, as a species whose natural habitat was medieval or continental.

CHAPTER 6

'The Death of Arthur was the Favourite Volume'

MALORY INTO TENNYSON

...the windows of the castle commanded an extensive view of the country: and Lancelot, having observed at some distance on the plain a procession accompanying a lady in a veil, in whom he recognised a likeness to the fair Guenevere, suddenly fell down in a swoon, an accident very usual with amorous knights, but always productive of wonder and curiosity in the bystanders.

George Ellis's summary of Chrétien's *Le Chevalier de la Charette*[1]

The first three chapters looked in turn at literary antiquarianism, at the uses Scott made of medieval literary remains, and at various revivals of verse romance. The fourth and fifth chapters, on Pugin's 'Christian Architecture', and on the applications of medieval ideals to the social problems of the 1840s, show that the mock Gothick of the eighteenth century had given way, with Scott, to a less fantastic and more historical Medieval Revival, dwelling less on what the Enlightenment called 'the marvellous' and more on 'facts and manners', and finally on values.

The values attributed to reason and imagination changed in the course of the eighteenth century: to see reason as needing supplementation is an infallible sign of Romanticism. A clear if trivial example of this is the change in the way writers portray the habit of seeing 'pictures in the fire' on the domestic hearth. This is treated by Pope as innocent in childhood but silly in an adult, whereas Coleridge in his 'Frost at Midnight' and Dickens in many places present it as a privileged access to supra-rational vision.

Reason and imagination have a classic debate towards the end of Shakespeare's *A Midsummer Night's Dream* (V.i.1–8, 14–17):

HIPPOLYTA: 'Tis strange, my Theseus, that these lovers speak of.
THESEUS: More strange than true. I never may believe

These antique fables, nor these fairy toys.
Lovers and madmen have such seething brains,
Such shaping fantasies, that apprehend
More than cool reason ever comprehends.
The lunatic, the lover, and the poet
Are of imagination all compact.
... And as imagination bodies forth
The forms of things unknown, the poet's pen
Turns them to shapes, and gives to airy nothing
A local habitation and a name.

To the cool Athenian reason of the strategist, the young lovers' reports of their night's transfigurations are not credible; his betrothed replies that they may nevertheless be true. Immediately after this exchange, the grown-up couple react very differently to the play of Pyramus and Thisbe, offered by Bottom and the 'rude mechanicals' of Athens, Warwickshire. Hippolyta, who had found truth in the lovers' dreams, dismisses the craftsmen's comically inept love-tragedy as 'the silliest stuff that ever I heard'. But her man thinks it reasonable to lend his imagination to amend the imperfections of a well-meaning effort: 'THESEUS: The best in this kind are but shadows [actors], and the worst are no worse if imagination amend them' (V.i.211–13). A hint from a playwright to his patrons.

'Things unknown' is a category which in the Enlightenment included the 'facts and manners' of medieval life. The enlightened were confident that these were among the things not worth knowing, a point of view still occasionally encountered. Educated but unimaginative folk were to remain serenely incurious about the Middle Ages for some decades after antiquarians began to publish medieval things in the 1760s. But early in the next century, Walter Scott's 'histories' in verse and prose gave 'A local habitation and a name' to inhabitants of the medieval vacuum. Unknown things bodied forth by Scott were reimagined by others, and the values attributed to them went well beyond aesthetic values. The exotic medievalism which had formed 'matter of entertainment' for the leisure of some of King George III's subjects, and the metrical romances which it had amused George Ellis to excerpt and summarise in 1805, were taken by a more serious generation and converted into various forms of 'applied medievalism'. In the reign of Victoria, medievalism was pressed into social service. The games and dreams of one generation took more concrete forms in the next. Some modern art had begun to imitate medieval life, and modern life began to imitate aspects of this medievalising art.

Within a year of its publication in 1819, five versions of *Ivanhoe* were put on the London stage and Ballantynes were printing a third edition.[2] Guests at an *Ivanhoe* Ball in Brussels in 1823 had to dress either as persons from Scott's romance or in twelfth-century costume. The climax of the Coronation dinner in London in 1820 was a ceremony in use from the fourteenth century: a King's Challenger rode into the hall, threw down his gauntlet thrice, and asked aloud who dared dispute the right to the throne of 'King George, the Fourth of that name'.[3] On his visit to Edinburgh in 1822, George IV wore a version of what became known as Highland Dress, which had been forbidden to Highlanders after 1745. Beau Brummel's 'fat friend' liked dressing up, and, as his Brighton Pavilion suggests, his tastes were various and garish. In 1839 Archibald Montgomery, thirteenth Earl of Eglinton, staged a large-scale tournament, where the flower of society competed, armed and on horseback, before the eyes of Britain, for the hand of a 'Queen of Beauty'. To the delight of the London press, and of those who had not been invited, the Eglinton Tournament was ruined by rain (though it was successfully held two days later). A spectator noted that the Marquess of Londonderry 'clad in complete steel, with casque and nodding plume on his head ... hoisted an umbrella'. Despite this celebrated fiasco, the dressing-up aspect of chivalry could be put to serious purposes by those who wished to defend gentle status or to claim it. A notable example of this is Landseer's painting, reproduced on the front cover of this book, of Victoria and Albert appearing at a fancy dress ball dressed as Queen Philippa and King Edward III.[4] As Britain prospered, crenellations were constructed, disused armour was polished and displayed, and family coats of arms were carved on walls and installed in stained-glass windows. The walls and windows of many large houses and some churches testify that this armorial movement ran until the First World War ended the Austrian and Russian empires, and heraldry became more of a hobby. The bow and arrow which had conquered at Agincourt, and won prizes for Robin Hood, became a pastime for ladies as well as gentlemen at country-house parties. In the 1960s, a bow-shot from Marble Arch and the Tyburn Convent, in London W1, the untended lawns of the Royal Toxophilite Society were still to be found.

We have seen how, in the 1830s and 1840s, Pugin, Newman, Carlyle, Ruskin, Disraeli and others drew religious, ethical, social and political lessons from Scott's 'histories' of the Middle Ages and applied them to a number of national issues: the harshness of the factory system, and of a liberal economics which seemed to justify this inhumanity; the end of the Anglican monopoly on the entrée to a public career; the Catholic origins of English Christianity, and what to make of them; the future roles of Crown, Lords and Commons, housed anew in buildings which proclaimed that the reformed government of England had a 'Gothic constitution'. Such a historical view of the English polity did not come readily to a philosophical rationalist like Jeremy Bentham, or to a political realist such as Lord Palmerston, who violently opposed a Gothic design for a new Foreign Office. In such quarters an Enlightenment tone persisted, as in Ellis's amused summaries of medieval romances, or in Thomas Love Peacock's satirical romance set in sixth-century Wales, *The Misfortunes of Elphin* (1829), now best remembered for 'The War-Song of Dinas Vawr', a parody of the Dark-Age battle-poem delighted in by antiquarians:

> The mountain sheep are sweeter,
> But the valley sheep are fatter;
> We therefore deemed it meeter
> To carry off the latter ...
>
> We brought away from battle,
> And much their land bemoan'd them,
> Two thousand head of cattle,
> And the head of him that owned them:
> Ednyfed, king of Dyfed,
> His head was borne before us:
> His wine and beasts supplied our feasts,
> And his overthrow our chorus.[5]

* * *

What are the chief material evidences for Victorian medievalism? A quantity surveyor instructed to report on its visible remains would first note the profusion of neo-Gothic buildings of various sizes, shapes and colours; then, perhaps, the high incidence of medieval subjects in painting and in the decoration of public and private places, from over-ambitious murals in the Houses of Parliament, and the amateur frescoing by the Pre-Raphaelites of the ceiling at the Oxford Union, to the wardrobe chest painted by Edward Burne-Jones as a wedding present to William Morris, and the more satisfying furniture and decoration of Morris's Red House, to stained-glass windows showing sportsmen in knightly attitudes, and to many illustrated books. In the world of books, our surveyor would find that *The Lay of the Last Minstrel* and *Ivanhoe* and their progeny had helped change the cultural climate in the decade of the Regency, preparing the ground for Pugin's impact on practice and theory in architecture and design in the reign of William IV. The advent of a major medievalist revival in poetry dates from the early 1830s, and its subjects came overwhelmingly from Arthurian romance. The adventures of knights and ladies, whether picturesque, gallant, moral, tragic or spiritual, provided Victorian romancers in verse with a range of medieval subjects. Favourite among these were the relationships of single knights with ladies, nearly always single ladies. The major exception to this rule proves crucial, however: the love of Guenevere and Lancelot du Lac. In Malory's version of the Arthurian story, it is the public 'outing' to Arthur of the mutual love of his queen and his best knight that leads to the break-up of the fellowship of the Round Table. Most of these Arthurian subjects were drawn from a book which, when *Ivanhoe* appeared in 1819, had been out of print for 185 years.

Sir Thomas Malory completed his *Morte Darthur* in 1469 or 1470. It was first printed by William Caxton in 1485. The English throne was seized in that year by Henry of Richmond, of a family Welsh in origin, the Tudors. Henry VII called his eldest son Arthur, and had the Winchester Round Table painted in Tudor colours. No fewer than five printed editions of Malory appeared during the reigns of Henry Tudor's second son, Henry VIII, and his children, the fifth and last appearing in 1577. The popularity of the *Morte* throughout the century following its composition is shown by allusions in Sidney, Spenser and Shakespeare, and by the denunciations of educationalists. Roger Ascham, whose book *Toxophilus* had won him a pension from Henry VIII, was tutor in Greek to Queens Mary and Elizabeth. He wrote in *The Scholemaster*, published posthumously in 1570:

> In our forefathers tyme, whan Papistrie, as in a standyng poole, covered and overflowed all England, fewe bookes were read in our tong, savyng certaine bookes of Chevalrie, as they sayd, for pastime and pleasure, which, as some say, were made in Monasteries, by idle Monkes, or wanton Chanons: as one for example, *Morte Arthure*: the whole pleasure of which booke standeth in two speciall poyntes, in open mans slaughter, and bold bawdrye: In which book those be counted the noblest Knightes, that do kill most men without any quarell, and commit fowlest adulteries by sutlest shiftes . . .[6]

This prosecuting counsel's reduction of chivalry to manslaughter and adultery is shrewd enough to suggest that Ascham knew this *Morte Arthure* well. Malory's book says more than once that it was composed in prison. But Ascham is less interested in the composers of immoral romances than in those 'idle Monkes' who, 'as some say', copied them: Nashe's 'abbey-lubbers'. Hundreds of religious houses had indeed stood in the England of Ascham's birth in 1515, but printers were then taking over from the professional lay scribes who copied romances.

The sole surviving manuscript of Malory's work is dated *c.* 1471–83. It was discovered in 1934 in the Fellows' Library at Winchester College, founded in 1378 by the Bishop of Winchester (motto: 'Manners Makyth Man'). The Fellows' Library at Winchester College is the right place for the manuscript to have been found, since Camelot, seat of the legendary Arthur, King of Britain before the Saxon conquest, was often identified with the historical Winchester, seat of the historical Alfred of Wessex and capital of England before the Norman conquest. Malory refers to 'Camelot, otherwyse callyd Wynchester'. The Round Table, the top of which hangs in the hall of

Winchester Castle, is thought to have been made in the reign of King
Edward I, the conqueror of Wales, the 'ruthless king' of 'The Bard', or
possibly that of Edward II, hammered by the Scots at Bannockburn,
or that of Edward III, the victor of Crécy and Poitiers, and the
founder of the Order of the Garter.

In 1577 Nathaniel Baxter, formerly tutor in Greek to Sir Philip Sidney,
wrote a Dedicatory Epistle to his own translation of Calvin's sermons on
the book of the prophet Jonah. Baxter is less donnish than Ascham. He
attacks: 'vile and blasphemous, or at least … prophane and frivolous
bookes, such as are that infamous legend of King Arthur … with the
horrible actes of those whoremasters, Launcelot du Lake, Tristram de
Liones, Gareth of Orkney, Merlin, the Lady of the Lake, with the vile and
stinking story of the Sangreall, of King Peleus, etc.'[7] Sidney, Baxter's pupil,
learned to read Greek. Like Ascham, he too seems also to have read the
vile, blasphemous, profane, frivolous, infamous, horrible, whoremasterly,
vile and stinking book of Sir Thomas Malory, which had the advantage
of being written in a clear and vigorous English. The chivalrous Sidney
will have warmed to Malory's accounts of knightly deeds and his appeals
to English honour: he tells us, in his Defence of vernacular literature, that
his heart had been stirred by the old ballad of Percy and Douglas, 'more
than with a trumpet'. His addition, that it would have sounded better
'clothed in the gorgeous eloquence of Pindar', may have been prompted
by a memory of Baxter's tutorials.

The chronology of editions of Malory's *Le Morte Darthur* offers a
profile of its popularity, and editors' prefaces suggest how knights of
romance were seen. In 1634, during the Caroline calm before the Civil
War, William Stansby published his edition of the *Morte*, the sixth. A
Preface recommends Malory to readers capable of appreciating the
style and manner of antiquity: 'the reader may see the best forme and
manner of writing and speech that was in use at those times'; further,
the Morte 'may passe for a famous piece of antiquity, revived almost
from the gulf of oblivion'. In 1748 William Oldys wrote apologetically
in *Biographia Britannica* that Malory's work 'seems to have been kept in
print for the entertainment of the lighter and more unsolid readers'.
In 1765 a reader neither light nor unsolid wrote in the Preface to
his edition of Shakespeare that 'Nations, like individuals, have their
infancy … The study of those who then aspired to plebeian learning

was laid out upon adventures, giants, dragons, and enchantments. The Death of Arthur was the favourite volume.' By 'plebeian learning' Dr Johnson meant popular literature in the vernacular (from *verna*, 'a slave born in the house'). The boy Samuel had devoured the books in his father's shop and grew to make many major contributions to plebeian literature and learning, though he was also a distinguished poet in Latin. Early in the next century it was rumoured that Walter Scott was about to edit the *Morte Darthur*. But Malory was not restored to print until 1816.[8] In that year Stansby's edition of 1634 received two separate reprints, inexpensive and in modernised spelling. Wordsworth, Keats and Tennyson owned copies of the 1816 editions of the *Morte*.

Declining the Poet Laureateship in 1813, Walter Scott had mentioned the name of Robert Southey. In 1817 Southey's elaborate and scholarly edition of the *Morte* appeared. The Laureate flatters the discerning reader, observing that 'the fashion for such works has passed away; and now for the full enjoyment of them a certain aptitude is required, as it is for poetry and music: where that aptitude exists, perhaps no works of imagination produce so much delight.' In 1824 Walter Scott wrote in his 'Essay on Romance' in the *Encyclopaedia Britannica* that 'Sir Thomas Malory, indeed, compiled from various French authorities, his celebrated *Morte d'Arthur*, indisputably the best Prose Romance the language can boast.' Malory's prose romance (compiled from English verse romances as well as from French prose authorities) soon eclipsed metrical romance in general, and Percy's *Reliques of Ancient English Poetry* in particular, as the chief source of a renewed literary medievalism. Of higher literary and narrative quality than most of the English verse romances which had preceded it, and very much easier to read, *The Death of Arthur* again became 'the favourite volume' among aspirants to 'plebeian learning'. The high status accorded to it by Walter Scott was, interestingly, not challenged on moral grounds by Victorian schoolmasters. *Idylls* from the betrayed king's story were dedicated by the Poet Laureate to the Queen.

In 1822 the young Sir Kenelm Digby illustrated his *The Broad Stone of Honour*, variously subtitled 'Rules for the Gentlemen of England' and 'The True Sense and Practice of Chivalrie', with many exemplary quotations from Malory, all tending to the doctrine of 'noblesse oblige'. Digby's magnificently idiosyncratic, innocent and influential work raised Malory's tone for generations. His 'philo-sophic history of chivalry' opens:

> 'Where do you wish that we should sit down and read this tale of ancient chivalry?' said one of our company, as we walked on a Spring morning through the delicious groves that clothe those mountains of Dauphiny which surround the old castle of the family of Bayard. We proposed to turn aside along the banks of the stream, and there sit down in peace. We were all familiar with Plato, and this spot reminded me forcibly of that charming episode where Phaedrus and Socrates . . .[9]

Digby's work is 'a moral history of the heroic age of Christendom'. The atmosphere of *The Broad Stone of Honour* is suggested by its locale: 'a fortress like that rock upon the Rhine which appears to represent, as it were, Knightly perfection, being lofty and free from the infection of a base world'. The 'rock upon the Rhine' is called Ehrenbreitstein.[10] The elevation of style and sentiment suggest that Digby had read not only Plato's dialogues but also Sidney's *Arcadia*. The Plato with whom Sir Kenelm and his friends were all familiar was not the Plato of Ascham and Baxter, though each might have accepted the ideal of the 'Philosopher Kings' put forward in Plato's *Republic*. For all his studied grace, Digby was perfectly in earnest in his Christian idealism, and his work was warmly received by its intended audience, the gentlemen of England. Perhaps for this reason, it is now rarely read. This is not the case with the works which stand at the head of the Arthurian tradition of the nineteenth century, Malory's *Morte Darthur* itself, and two poems by Tennyson, 'The Lady of Shalott' and 'Morte d'Arthur'.

Alfred Tennyson was not a Victorian poet, not at first. Yet as it turned out, he was Victoria's Laureate for half his life, and dedicated the first volume of *The Idylls of the King* to her late husband. In 1869 he published the twelfth and last book of *The Idylls*, entitled 'The Passing of Arthur'. In an epilogue 'To the Queen', Tennyson reminds her, with some awkwardness, of the *Idylls*' original dedication:

> But thou, my Queen,
> Not for itself, but through thy living love

For one to whom I made it o'er his grave
Sacred, accept this old imperfect tale,
New-old, and shadowing Sense at war with Soul,
Ideal manhood closed in real man,
Rather than that gray king, whose name, a ghost,
Streams like a cloud, man-shaped, from mountain peak,
And cleaves to cairn and cromlech still . . .'[11]

Thus did Alfred Tennyson close the ideal manhood of King Arthur in a real man, Prince Albert, now dead. Algernon Swinburne called the poem the 'Morte d'Albert, or Idylls of the Prince Consort'. Father Hopkins wrote to Canon Dixon in 1879 that Tennyson 'shd. have called them *Charades from the Middle Ages* (dedicated by permission to H.R.H. etc.)'.[12] But the *Idylls* also close a real man whom Tennyson remembered, one who had died very young, not in 1864 but in 1833: his friend Hallam.

Readers who, like the present writer, first encountered Tennyson's 'Morte d'Arthur' in a school anthology of the 1950s may like him have received Arthur's dying speech as representing the Victorian age at its most funereal. It begins, if that is not too lively a word:

And slowly answered Arthur from the barge:
'The old order changeth, yielding place to new
And God fulfils himself in many ways . . .'[13]

It comes as a surprise to find that these heavy lines had been composed by a man of twenty-three, shortly after the unexpected death of an Arthur who was his dearest friend. Arthur Hallam had died of a brain haemorrhage while visiting Vienna in September 1833, aged twenty-one. In the next two months Tennyson wrote remarkable poems on early death, old age and survival: 'Morte d'Arthur', 'Ulysses', 'Tiresias' and 'Tithonus'. This was also the year in which he began his major work, *In Memoriam A.H.H.*, published in 1850. After her husband's death, the Queen changed 'Tears of the widower' to 'Tears of the widow' in her copy of *In Memoriam*, and 'his' to 'her'.[14]

In the year of Byron's death in Greece, 1824, Wordsworth, Coleridge and Scott were writing, as was William Blake. But Keats

had died in Rome in 1821, and Shelley had drowned in the
Mediterranean in 1822. In a received view of English literary history,
these early deaths in exile broke the rainbow of Romantic poetry. Yet
seven years later Alfred Tennyson composed 'The Lady of Shalott', a
poem whose familiarity from school anthologies may have prevented
its worth from being recognised. It is in the nature of things that
Poets Laureate should write better before their appointment than
after it, though John Dryden may be an exception to this rule.
In Tennyson's case, many of his best poems were composed not
only before Wordsworth's death in 1850 but even before Victoria
acceded to the throne in 1837. He is not simply a Victorian poet. The
Arthurian poems in Tennyson's *Poems* of 1832 and of 1842 provided
Dante Gabriel Rossetti and other artists with some of their first
subjects, and Victorians often approached Malory through
Tennysonian arches.

'The Lady of Shalott' was begun in 1831 and finished in May
1832, before the death of Hallam. Tennyson, who was a voracious
reader, seems to have been interested in Arthurian legend before he
read Malory, for he later testified that the story of his verse romance
was 'taken from an Italian novelette, [La] *Donna di Scalotta*. The
Lady of Shalott is evidently the Elaine of the *Morte d'Arthur*, but I do
not think that I had ever heard of the latter when I wrote the former.'[15]
Much of the real success as well as the initial charm of this piece
comes from its opening: 'On either side the river lie / Long fields of
barley and of rye'. A picturesque medieval landscape is simply
presented, but the reader comes to see that its decorated and pageant-
like quality stands in special relation with the tapestry the Lady
weaves in her bower, showing what her glass shows her of life outside:
a reflection of a reflection, as in Plato's fable of the Cave. 'The Lady of
Shalott' is usually first met with in school, but it is not an immature
work.

> And moving through a mirror clear
> That hangs before her all the year,
> Shadows of the world appear.
> There she sees the highway near
>   Winding down to Camelot: ...

Sometimes a troop of damsels glad,
An abbot on an ambling pad,
Sometimes a curly shepherd-lad,
Or long-haired page in crimson clad,
　　　Goes by to towered Camelot . . .

Or when the moon was overhead,
Came two young lovers lately wed;
'I am half sick of shadows,' said
　　　The Lady of Shalott.

Part III brings into the picture not a shadow but a man:

A bow-shot from her bower-eaves,
He rode between the barley-sheaves;
The sun came dazzling through the leaves,
And flamed upon the brazen greaves
　　　Of bold Sir Lancelot.

The shock which this sight delivers, comparable to the effect on Lancelot of the distant sight of Guenevere in Ellis's amused summary at the head of this chapter, is well conveyed:

The helmet and the helmet-feather
Burned like one burning flame together . . .

She left the web, she left the loom,
She took three paces through the room,
She saw the water-lily bloom,
She saw the helmet and the plume,
　　　She looked down to Camelot.
Out flew the web and floated wide;
The mirror cracked from side to side;
'The curse is come upon me,' cried
　　　The Lady of Shalott.

In a short song or ballad, Romantic poets could, when on top form, sustain an effect hardly distinguishable from that of their late medieval models. Examples of this are Scott's 'Proud Maisie', Byron's 'So we'll go no more a-roving', and Keats's 'La Belle Dame Sans Merci'. This timeless illusion could not be sustained in the longer verse romances essayed by all the Romantic poets, such as Coleridge's *Christabel* and 'Rime of the Ancyent Marinere' and Keats's 'Eve of St Agnes'. Even the best of these poems has difficulty in blending modern viewpoints and 'Gothic' elements into supposedly medieval stories.

It was therefore a remarkable achievement for a twenty-two-year-old to write a poem which for 171 lines adjusts means to ends as perfectly as Keats had managed in the forty-eight lines of 'La Belle Dame Sans Merci'. Compared with Keats, Tennyson is more pictorial, less sensuous, and has a less explicit preoccupation with the relation of art, and the artist's life, to the life around them. It may be thanks to Keats that in 'The Lady of Shalott' Tennyson uses genre to much better effect than he had in previous poems of any length.

Following on from the revived romances of Coleridge, Scott and Keats, Tennyson distils a purely artistic idea of the world of Arthurian romance, deploying without strain an echoing stanza form, the rhyme-scheme of which runs aaaa4b3ccc4b3. He then succeeds in making this elaborated landscape organic to the working out of the poem's meaning. This youthful performance entirely lacks the 'authentic' costume detail which encrusts medievalist description in *The Lay of the Last Minstrel*, *Ivanhoe* and the medieval historical novel down to Stevenson's *The Black Arrow*. To lay on detail with a trowel was the vice of historical novelists, from Scott to Bulwer Lytton and Harrison Ainsworth, from Flaubert's *Salammbô* to Marguerite Yourcenar.

In Tennyson's poem such detail is decorative, not obtrusively 'authentic': this is a world of legend and romance, not of history – a difference with consequences for the future. 'The Lady of Shalott' is as vividly coloured as a landscape in a Book of Hours – part of its attraction for anthologists – but bewitchingness of representation becomes part of the poem's theme. A deeper virtue lies in the poem's use of psychological symbolism. Here Tennyson shows artistic tact of a high order, for 'The Lady of Shalott' is a finer poem than 'The Eve of St Agnes', if less ambitious. In considering such a judgement, members of the jury should ask themselves whether they are more affected by understatement ('She saw the helmet and the plume') or by overstatement ('His heart made purple riot'). Edinburgh critics accused Tennyson of 'Cockney' vices of style, less violently than they had accused Keats of such vices. Tennyson had read Homer in the original.

Tennyson's other notable Arthurian poem from this early period, his 'Morte d'Arthur', was finished in 1834, though not published until 1842. In the 1842 *Poems* it is grouped among 'English Idylls' and appears framed by 'The Epic', a poem set in the present, which opens 'At Francis Allen's on the Christmas-eve'. In it Tennyson, thinly disguised as the poet Everard Hall, says that he had burnt 'His epic, his King Arthur, some twelve books', written at college. Encouraged by his friends, Hall now reads aloud to them the eleventh book of this epic, the 'Morte d'Arthur', the manuscript of which, we are told, Francis Allen had retrieved from the fireplace when they were at college together. The parson sleeps through the recital, but the narrator later has a significant 'Christmas' dream. The note of apology in the introduction to 'The Epic' struck Leigh Hunt as insincere. Tennyson, he wrote, 'gives us to understand that he should have burnt his poem but for the "request of friends"'. 'Request of friends', a formula to excuse the vanity of publishing, was an ancient pretext for backing into the limelight. Alexander Pope has a desperate poetaster who 'Rymes e're he wakes, and prints before *Term* ends, / Oblig'd by hunger and Request of friends.'[16]

Much in 'The Epic' is conventional authorial modesty, a convention to which Tennyson kept throughout his life, calling *The Idylls of the King* an 'old imperfect tale'. What is conventional can be sincere, however, and in this case 'request of friends' was no fiction. Friends, from Hallam onwards, repeatedly requested Tennyson to publish what he had written, often in vain, and Tennyson's publishers had to twist his arm to get him to do so. Other details in 'The Epic' correspond to actuality, notably the twelve-book Arthurian epic, although at college Tennyson had only dreamed of what he represents Everard Hall as having written and burnt. Tennyson later incorporated the full text of 'Morte d'Arthur' into the twelfth and last of *The Idylls of the King*, 'The Passing of Arthur'. The poet's concern about how his 'Morte' might be received was justified, for 'his matter was new'.[17] John Sterling, a member of the Cambridge 'Apostles' (a Socratic circle to which both Hallam and Tennyson also belonged), criticised the 'Morte' in print as 'inferior'. Sterling thought any modern treatment of the legend of Excalibur 'a mere ingenious exercise in fancy'. Tennyson was highly sensitive to criticism, especially from a fellow Apostle. Sterling's review discouraged him from continuing his epic for many years. The 'Morte d'Arthur' purports to be a fragment plucked from the burning of a completed epic, but in the event was a trial instalment of an epic that Tennyson contemplated but deferred.

John Milton's notebook, held like Tennyson's at Trinity College, Cambridge, shows that he too had thought of taking the Arthurian story as the subject of his epic. He later decided against the subject as fantastic and historically unreliable. In Tennyson's 'The Epic', his spokesman, Hall, is conscious that the story of Arthur is largely legend and from a remote period. 'Why take the style of those heroic times?' Hall asks himself: 'For nature brings not back the Mastodon, / Nor we those times; and why should any man / Remodel models?' This, Hall says, is why he had burnt his epic: 'Those twelve books of mine / Were faint Homeric echoes, nothing worth.' Yet the heavy frame of 'The Epic' serves its purpose well; the country-house Christmas Eve fireside setting disliked by Leigh Hunt now seems right. Prologue and Epilogue are there for the same reasons as Scott's in *The Lay of the Last Minstrel*: to introduce unfamiliar material, to provide a sense of temporal recession, to tune the expectations and mood of the audience, and to point a moral. Scott habitually furnished editorial paratexts for his imaginative narratives, a Scottish Enlightenment dissociation of head and heart, found also in James Hogg and Thomas Carlyle. The visitor, fictional narrator, or editor who tells a strange tale set in the past is a device as old as fiction itself. In the *Odyssey* XI, the disguised Odysseus tells the court of King Alcinous of his visit to Hades. The answer to Hall's rhetorical question about remodelling models is provided in the Epilogue, when the narrator, asleep on Christmas Eve, dreams of 'a bark that, blowing forward, bore / King Arthur, like a modern gentleman / Of stateliest port'. A remodelled Arthur is offered as a model to modern gentlemen, just as, towards the end of the Wars of the Roses, Sir Thomas Malory's Arthur had been the model of chivalry for his intended audience. Malory makes despairing asides on the inconstancy and factiousness of English knights in his day. Caxton, a businessman of letters, recommended Malory's work as a guide to gentle conduct. The preface to Stansby's 1643 edition likewise commends Malory's work as a book of knightly conduct lent charm by antiquity.

What constitutes superior conduct in a man has interested audiences from before the 'gentillesse' of Chaucer through to Tennyson's 'modern gentleman', and since. As early as 1833, Tennyson made a note: 'The Round Table: liberal institutions'.[18] The passage from the 1816 edition of Malory on which he based his 'Morte' is reproduced in Ricks's edition of *The Poems of Tennyson*. This allows a comparison of a medievalising poem with its source-text, a comparison like that offered earlier between Scott's characters and their Chaucerian originals. A brief extract is chosen to illustrate the differences between (i) a scholarly edition of the manuscript text in modernised spelling, (ii) the 1816 modernisation of Caxton which was Tennyson's source, and (iii) Tennyson's adaptation.

The passage comes at the point when the dying Arthur has repeated his order to Sir Bedivere to throw Excalibur into the lake, which Bedivere had secretly decided to disobey on the first two occasions. This is how the passage stands in Helen Cooper's edition of *Le Morte Darthur: The Winchester Manuscript*:[19]

> 'What sawest thou there?' said the King.
>
> 'Sir,' he said, 'I saw nothing but waters wap and waves wan.'
>
> 'Ah, traitor unto me and untrue,' said King Arthur, 'now hast thou betrayed me twice! Who would ween that thou that hast been to me so lief and dear, and also named so noble a knight, that thou would betray me for the riches of the sword?'

The second text is from the 1816 edition, which modernises Caxton:

> 'What saw ye there,' said the King. 'Sir,' said he, 'I saw nothing but the water wap and waves wan.' 'Ah, traitor, untrue,' said King Arthur, 'now hast thou betrayed me two times, who would have wend [weened] that thou hast been unto me so self [*for* lief] and dear, and thou art named a noble Knight, and wouldest betray me for the rich sword.'

Finally, Tennyson's verse:

> Then spoke King Arthur, breathing heavily:
> 'What is it thou hast seen? or what hast heard?'
> And answer made the bold Sir Bedivere:
> 'I heard the water lapping on the crag,
> And the long ripple washing in the reeds.'
> To whom replied King Arthur, much in wrath:
> 'Ah, miserable and unkind, untrue,
> Unknightly, traitor-hearted! Woe is me!
> Authority forgets a dying king ...'

Comparison shows Malory's prose as rapid, and Tennyson's verse as slow. Malory wrote directly, for reading aloud; Tennyson for the recitation of a poet 'mouthing out his hollow oes and aes'. The speech of his King Arthur is consciously poetic and noble. Malory's eye is for action, Tennyson's for description and effect; his ear is an echo-chamber for Homer, Virgil, Shakespeare and Milton. Malory is laconic, Tennyson's poetic strain has a dying fall. The stylistic qualities of the two passages are of opposite kinds. Tennyson's variation upon a theme from Malory has an effect comparable to that of the 'art' settings of English folksongs by composers from Vaughan Williams to Benjamin Britten: long-drawn out and lacking the simplicity of the original; finely modulated, but nostalgic. Helen Cooper points out that the hand which in Malory clutched Excalibur 'shook it thrice and brandished', whereas in Tennyson the arm is 'clothed in white samite, mystic, wonderful': priestly, feminine, ethereal.[20]

I hope that readers of the nine lines from Tennyson given above will prefer the first five of them. Malory's king sounds angry whereas Tennyson's makes a speech 'much in wrath'. Better by far is Bedivere's ' "I heard the water lapping on the crag, / And the long ripple washing in the reeds." ' This both makes more sense and sounds better than 'I saw nothing but the water wap and the waves wan' (1816). Tennyson here can stand comparison with what Malory may actually have written: 'I saw nothing but waters wap and waves wan'. Bedivere's evasive answer is glossed by Helen Cooper to mean 'I saw nothing but the waters lap and the waves darken.' Tennyson elaborates a beautiful pattern, but does it very well, achieving something different from Bedivere's enigmatic words yet almost as desolate.[21]

The same reader can at different times yield to the spell of each of these works. Malory's seven-hundred-page romance is an extraordinary achievement, both historically and artistically: the best prose romance, as Scott told the readers of the *Encyclopaedia Britannica*, but also the first major work of prose in an English which is all but modern. (Previous English medieval romances had been in verse.) By taking 'Morte d'Arthur' as his title, Tennyson acknowledges that his poem derives from Malory. The king's death is indeed the climax of Malory's *Le Morte Darthur*, and Tennyson gives it epic treatment. It is a great subject, but Tennyson deserves credit for having selected it and selected well from it. Much of the power of Tennyson's 'Morte' comes from its parent legend, and the impersonal skill with which Malory shaped and retold the legend, or legends, in the 1460s. Yet there was nothing inevitable in Tennyson's choice of Malory, nor his choice of Arthur's end, nor about the success of his 'Morte'. Even as an amplification of an episode, it remains extraordinarily evocative.

Tennyson submerges himself in his source while remaking it entirely, as in 'The Lady of Shalott'. The difference is not only in the change of form from prose to verse and to a symbolic mode. Both poems also add much in the way of decorative and atmospheric detail. Further, 'The Lady of Shalott' adds many key narrative features to the bare bones of the source, most significantly the web and the mirror. Tennyson's 'Morte', on the other hand, leaves out stark physical moments such as that immediately preceding the action, when Sir Bedivere and his brother Sir Lucan de Butler attempt to move the wounded Arthur: 'and in the lifting Sir Lucan fell in a swoon, that part of his guts fell out of his body, and therewith the noble knight's heart brast. And when the King awoke, he beheld Sir Lucan, how he lay foaming at the mouth, and part of his guts lay at his feet.'

If Tennyson leaves things out of Malory's plain report of actions, he elaborates what remains. In Malory, Bedivere on his third and final visit to the mere 'threw the sword as far into the water as he might'. Tennyson builds a Miltonic simile:

> The great brand
> Made lightnings in the splendour of the moon,
> And flashing round and round, and whirled in an arch,
> Shot like a streamer of the northern morn,

Seen where the moving isles of winter shock
By night, with noises of the northern sea,
So flashed and fell the brand Excalibur ...[22]

The burden of Tennyson's 'Morte d'Arthur' remains the myth of the dying king's possible return: a myth of special moment to a poet suddenly bereft of so close and admired a friend. This is why Tennyson borrows details of Arthur's dying face from the prophecy of the Suffering Servant in Isaiah, 52–3. What sticks in the mind of the reader of the 'Morte', however, as much as the story itself and what it portends, is its desolate landscape of loss, which is Tennyson's. Here are some of the lines which create this quality:

So all day long the noise of battle rolled
Among the mountains by the winter sea ...

A broken chancel with a broken cross
That stood on a dark strait of barren land.

But the other swiftly strode from ridge to ridge,
Clothed with his breath, and looking, as he walked,
Larger than human on the frozen hills.

Then loudly cried the bold Sir Bedivere,
'Ah! my Lord Arthur, whither shall I go?'

Long stood Sir Bedivere
Revolving many memories, till the hull
Looked one black dot against the verge of dawn,
And on the mere the wailing died away.

Plotted on a chronological graph of the Medieval Revival, the two early poems of Tennyson are substantial steps into the world of legend. These romances, though they derive from medieval texts, lack the historical grounding and antiquarian colouring which had made Scott's medievalist fictions more credible than the sensational-istic fantasy of earlier Gothic fiction. In his 'Eve of St Agnes' and

'Belle Dame', Keats had produced a first synthesis of Coleridge's magical experiments and Scott's historical minstrelsy. Tennyson began where Keats left off, writing medium-length poems of such artistic tact that the authenticity of their medievalism, or the credibility of their Gothicism, are not questions which arise even for the most historically minded reader. Tennyson's poems are beautiful, are wholly grounded in Arthurian legend, and are set in landscapes almost entirely created by himself.

Poetry showed the way. 'The Lady of Shalott' and the 'Morte d'Arthur' were written in 1833, before the fire at Westminster, before Pugin had designed a church, and before the lay pulpiteers of the 1840s had begun to clear their throats and to call upon medieval precedents. The poetry of the Medieval Revival was henceforward very often to operate in Malory's world as reimagined by Tennyson, the world of Arthurian legend and symbol. After Scott, imaginative historical writing went in two directions, following the change in his own fiction after *Ivanhoe*. The historical novel which stemmed from *Waverley* and Scott's Scottish novels was typically set in a post-medieval time. The romances which followed in the mode of *Ivanhoe*, whether medieval or not, are not really historical, but adventure stories and romantic stories loosely situated in 'history'. Victorian historiography sought confirmation for its narratives in political and constitutional documents. It made strong assumptions, but was interested in facts, not ideas, and later became more analytic than narrative. The rise of professional history cramped the style of the writers of medievalist fiction in prose or verse. They increasingly moved away from texts into the world of legend or of adventure, though this glamour was implicit in their originals. It was Tennyson who led them onto this enchanted ground.

CHAPTER 7

History, the Revival and the PRB

WESTMINSTER, *IVANHOE*, VISIONS AND REVISIONS

In the 1840s and 1850s, the Palace of Westminster rose ever higher on the banks of the Thames, an 'argument in stone' at the centre of the British empire, a public reminder of the long-standing arrangement whereby the country was governed by 'The Crown in Parliament under God'; and a sign, also, that this arrangement should continue. The appearance chosen for the new Palace for those who governed Britain in the Queen's name testified to a sense that English (and by extension British) government had a long history, and also that it was 'Gothic' in the sense that the governed were a party to their governing; Gothic, or as people had begun to say, 'medieval'. Two of the three Estates of the realm, Lords and Commons, went back to the twelfth century, and a united England to the tenth. A historical case for this 'Gothic' understanding of the constitution can be made out. But at the time when Parliament was deciding on the proper style for a new Palace of Westminster, this understanding was an inherited assumption, persuasion or conviction, not a claim requiring justification. It is also worth mentioning that Barry's building gives more space and splendour to Crown and Lords than to Commons.

It is in the 1840s that the Medieval Revival can be said to have arrived, at much the same time as the steam railway. Research and development had been done, and it was now time for application, and production. In one of the bays of the Crystal Palace in Hyde Park, the huge glasshouse built for the Great Exhibition of British manufactures in 1851, there was a 'Mediæval Court' also known as 'Pugin's Court', devoted to the works of A.W. Pugin and of his manufacturers. It was visited and admired by the Queen and Prince Albert, and by many others, not all of them as well dressed as those who in top hats and bonnets inspect the exhibits in Joseph Nash's lithograph of the Medieval Court (Plate 13). Pugin, who had once designed chairs for

George III, had a conference lasting three-quarters of an hour in the Mediæval Court with the Prime Minister, who had personally led the political opposition to the restoration of the Catholic episcopal hierarchy. This was Lord John Russell, whose family, earls and dukes of Bedford, were beneficiaries of the Dissolution of the Monasteries, residing at Woburn Abbey and developing Russell Square, Bedford Square and Bloomsbury on their London estate. The *Illustrated London News* judged that the Mediæval Court was the best thing in the Exhibition: 'To Mr Pugin, then, who furnished the design for this gorgeous combination, is the highest honour due; and he has marvellously fulfilled his own intention of demonstrating the applicability of Mediæval art in all its richness and variety to the uses of the present day.'[1] Pugin died the following year.

England's Church and state, and areas of her social, economic and artistic life, were either taking new bearings from medieval ideals, or being urged to do so. The medieval was variously seen as offering examples more inspiring or edifying than the rational self-interest of Enlightenment civilisation and the greed and squalor of what Dickens was soon to portray in the Coketown of his *Hard Times*. A hundred years earlier, after the days of the Non-Jurors and their scholarship, the idea that the English present had much to learn from the remote English past was not voiced by those with access to the public ear; certainly not within the Establishment, although some outside the Church of England valued ideals which had prevailed at times in the past. In the 1740s some marginal poets had wished that the roles and subjects of contemporary poetry were not confined to the polite world. They had dreamed of Bards and Druids, role-models not historically English but primitively Celtic. A hundred years later the Medieval Revival, which had already made a strong and varied contribution to literature, was becoming the style for public architecture, and its example was increasingly urged from pulpits and lecterns.

Yet a revival cannot establish itself quite in the way that the steam railway established itself, or pointed-arch church architecture had established itself in the twelfth century, or new institutions such as universities and hospitals had established themselves in Europe. For the conscious revival of a style presupposes a number of models to choose from, a choice of examples from history. Before about 1750, the subject-matter of history was highly selective. If one project of the Enlightenment was to let Observation 'survey mankind from China to Peru', another was to survey how humans had lived between classical antiquity and the present day. Such a survey could not exclude the life of Europe in the centuries between Marcus Aurelius and Petrarch. This vast interval had been authoritatively surveyed by Edward Gibbon on the eve of the French Revolution, and pronounced to be 'the triumph of barbarism and religion'. But the history of twelve centuries can be told from more than one point of view. The decline and fall of the Roman empire can also be seen as the coming into being of a culture with a different hope. A notable recent account is entitled *The Rise of Western Christendom*.[2]

To the west of Westminster, early in the eighteenth century, a Chinese pagoda was added to the Gardens at Kew, not far from Lord Burlington's Palladian villa; not far, either, from Alexander Pope's villa, with its garden grotto. All over England, vistas punctuated by small pillared temples, and perhaps an obelisk, began to acquire other things to interest the eye: Gothic cottages, new-built ruined abbeys, a Turkish tent or minaret, the whole to be viewed from a belvedere or gazebo, or a hermitage on a bosky hill, by an owner taking a rational pleasure in his property and his picturesque improvements, rather than by a hermit renouncing the world and choosing poverty.[3] Some estate owners even advertised for a hermit to reside in their hermitages. As Observation's view extended, these eye-catching garden pavilions gradually evolved into a more fully imagined museum of history, and Walpole, Beckford and Scott chose to build the houses of their dreams and even to live in them. So, part of the time, did the Prince Regent at his Pavilion in Brighton. Queen Victoria spent much time at Windsor, but she preferred her more romantic modern castle at Balmoral.

The increase in historical awareness provided a range of possible models, and the embarrassment of choice.[4] The Renaissance and Enlightenment had favoured classical models, and public buildings of the Victorian period often continued in this style; a classical revival coincided in time with the Medieval Revival. 'Classical' architects from Wren to Gibbs had turned their hands to Gothic, and, before his Palace of Westminster, Sir Charles Barry had designed the Renaissance palazzo of the Reform Club in Pall Mall. Victorian Oxford acquired the Ashmolean Museum (eclectic Graeco-Roman) in 1841–5, and in 1854–60 the neo-Gothic University Museum devoted to Natural History, which was later to house a dinosaur skeleton. The Enlightenment wish to understand all human history eventually led to the recovery of the ages between the conversion of the Emperor Constantine and the Reformation. Yet an increase in historical information did not cause the Medieval Revival. So major a change is brought about not by an improvement in knowledge, but by changes in what people think they need. A sense that something is missing comes first to people of imagination and vision, and is then recovered by scholars and recreated by artists. The order of these stages can vary. Materials and models were required, but historical imaginings do not live by authenticity alone. A lot of learning can be a dangerous thing. George Eliot's *Romola* is a fine novel, but it is set in a Renaissance Florence which is too archaeologically recreated.

From the 1840s onwards, a historical sense came to be a normal part of the thinking of educated people, and academic history gradually became a profession. Anyone who reads English literature historically can see that Walter Scott jumbles Elizabethan material with medieval material, and that the style of his medieval romances mixes Chaucer, Spenser and Shakespeare with ballads and metrical romances. Scott's fictions gleefully draw on an eclectic range of sources, some of which are themselves mixed in genre, notably Shakespeare's history plays. As Shakespeare dramatised reign after reign for the stage, kneading and shaping each story from various chronicles, he evolved a new kind of English play, of which *Henry IV*, Parts I and II is the best example, mingling high and low, tragedy and comedy. This was the model of history which provided Scott with the essential form for his fiction: theatrically conceived, and mixed in genre ('tragical-historical-comical-pastoral', as Polonius puts it). Scott followed Shakespeare in adding realism to stories shaped by the currents of romance. He also took motifs and structures from Shakespeare, such as scenes in taverns and at court, the loyal daughter, the king in disguise, fools, witches and songs.

As audiences became better informed about historical fact, they began to read modern medieval English romances through spectacles which made Scott's historical bravura seem hasty. In *Ivanhoe*, Robin Hood is described as speaking Norman English. Brian de Bois-Guilbert, a Knight of the Temple of Jerusalem, has black slaves and is a secret atheist. The twelfth-century fool, Wamba, bears the name of a seventh-century Spanish Visigothic king. His master, Cedric, bears the name of a sixth-century king of Wessex, properly spelt Cerdic and pronounced 'Cherdtich' (pronounced like '*Ich*' in German). The swineherd, Gurth, has a Scandinavian name, and is clearly labelled as a 'thrall', a Norse term for a serf or slave: ' "Gurth, the son of Beowolf, is the born thrall of Cedric of Rotherwood"'. The witch Ulrica invokes various pagan Teutonic gods.

The names Wamba, Cedric, Gurth and Ulrica are early Germanic, or 'Gothic'. None would have been common in the England of the 1190s. Scott, however, was not historically so uninformed as to confuse the twelfth century with the sixth. The anachronism of the names he gave his English characters is so uniform as to make a point. It tells us that Scott believed that the Germanic – or Gothic – settler tribes who formed the English people preserved ancestral attitudes about the way political things should be arranged. These social and political attitudes made them constitutionally different from their French rulers. Scott presents this cultural difference as essential, making it almost as strong in 1190 as it had been in 1066. So Scott's most glaring historical 'mistake', his portrayal of Saxons and Normans as still at enmity after several generations of cohabitation, was deliberate. Scott was a lawyer and knew how to make a case seem natural and self-evident. Although *Ivanhoe* ends with the English accepting Richard as their rightful king, one of the book's morals is that the 'Gothic' tradition of participatory democracy is fundamental to the English character. In 1819 this tradition was held to be the key difference between Georgian Britain and an imperious France, whose twenty-year attempt to dominate Europe had ended in 1815, in the most recent of many battles on the border between Latin-speaking and German-speaking Europe. In the year of Waterloo, or very shortly after it, the Author of *Waverley* ordered a copy of a new book, *De Danorum rebus gestis secul. III & IV, poema danicum dialecto anglosaxonica* ('A Danish

Poem in Anglo-Saxon Dialect on Exploits of the Danes of the Third and Fourth Centuries'), edited by G.J. Thorkelin, and published in Copenhagen. At this time, Scott also began to think about a new kind of book, which came to fruition in *Ivanhoe*.

The many implausibilities of *Ivanhoe* would not have bothered those contemporary readers who noticed them. They would not have taken implausibilities for historical mistakes, since they would not have mistaken *Ivanhoe* for history. *Ivanhoe* is subtitled *A Romance*, a classification which signals fiction and legend. Yet in the 1870s Edward Augustus Freeman, Regius Professor of History at Oxford, felt obliged, in the fifth volume of his *History of the Norman Conquest in England*, to take Scott to task for such inaccuracies. The reason for this seems to be that *Ivanhoe* had been mistaken for English history by the French historian Augustin Thierry. *Ivanhoe* was so popular in France that Cedric is today a first name more common across the Channel than it is in England. Popular history is a genre in which wishes can come true. Some French writers found it congenial to think of the Anglo-Saxons as beef-witted skin-wearing hut-dwellers who recognised the arrival of Guillaume le Conquérant as a civilising mission. The truth is that the romance *Ivanhoe* is not much more historical than one of its remote descendants, the film *Braveheart*, which has sometimes been taken for history, not only in Australia and the United States but even in Scotland.

A last word on Beowolf (or Beowulph, the more Gothic spelling adopted by Scott in the Magnum Opus edition), the father of Gurth in *Ivanhoe*. A man of this name in the 1190s could not be the Beowulf of the Old English epic, who, according to the edition owned by Scott, lived in fourth-century Scandinavia. Beowulf's people, the Geats, were conquered after his death, and disappear from history. Some nineteenth-century scholars of Anglo-Saxon (not of Scott) identified the Geats as Goths. Others speculated that Geats may have fled to what is now Yorkshire.[5] Is Gurth's father the descendant of a Gothic immigrant who has taken the name Beowolf? As *Ivanhoe* is not history, the question should not arise. The name of the fictional Gurth's fictional father evokes the Beowulf of the old epic, a literary not a real person. Beowolf was a name unfamiliar in any spelling in England in 1819. Thorkelin's was the first edition of the full text of the poem about Beowulf.[6] Vernacular works in early manuscripts normally have neither title nor author. Editors invented titles and tried to find authors. Thorkelin, an Icelander who saw the manuscript when studying in the British Museum, became Denmark's National Archivist. The Danish court in 1815 would have been unsurprised to be told that a poem set at the court of King Hrothgar the Dane and concerning the deeds of Danes was a Danish poem, though written in Anglo-Saxon dialect. Had not England been part of the Danish empire, ruled by the Danish King Cnut? The manuscript is now dated c. 1000–10 – before the reign of the king whom English history books call Canute. The poem was first called *Beowulf* by John M. Kemble in 1833.[7]

Thorkelin made two transcripts of the unique manuscript in the British Museum: the first he commissioned from a scribe in 1787, the other he made himself in 1791. Back in Copenhagen, he worked on the text for years, his research being seriously interrupted in 1807 when his papers in the Royal Library were destroyed by the British bombardment of a French fleet in Copenhagen harbour. Thorkelin's Latin translation, which faces the text in his edition, is described by the authoritative Klaeber as 'practically useless'. In Britain in 1815 only a very few could have begun to understand the poem. Some of its diction is so archaic that it seems not to have been fully understood by the man who copied it into the manuscript at the beginning of the second millennium. Beowulf is the nephew of a historical king, Hygelac, who died in about 521, and the guest of another historical king, Hrothgar (Roger). Thorkelin put the action of the poem two centuries too early. Beowulf himself is thought to be an invented figure, though in 1815 no one was yet in a position to show why this might be so. Yet he lives in a stylised version of a real historical world, and his career embodies a secular ideal of heroic conduct modified by Christian attitudes. Scholarship interested the savant in Scott, but would not have worried the author of *Ivanhoe*, who was more taken up with ideal characters, the idea of 'Gothic' British democracy, and the colour, texture and feel of history – so long as it was picturesque history – than in the accuracy of individual components of his story.

Literary medievalism had begun to divide, before Scott's death in 1832, along lines already visible in his work. On the one hand,

Tennyson's imaginative poetic treatments of legends, as in the poems of 1833 we have looked at, were no longer cast in the 'medieval' verse-forms favoured by Coleridge and Scott, and had none of the notes they supply. On the other hand, scholarly editions of medieval texts had begun to appear. Soon after Scott's death appeared the first English editions both of *Beowulf* and of what is generally reckoned the finest Middle English verse romance, *Sir Gawain and the Green Knight*. The editor of *Beowulf*, J.M. Kemble, was friendly with Tennyson, who had himself tried his hand at translating a few lines of the poem in 1830. *Gawain* was edited by Sir Frederick Madden for the Bannatyne Club in 1839. Imagination and the scientific philology pioneered in Germany had begun to go their separate ways.

* * *

In 1848, the year of revolutions in Europe and of Marx's *Communist Manifesto*, three art students at the Royal Academy Schools, one of them a drop-out, disliking the Academy's canons of taste and its teaching programme, enrolled four friends into a Brotherhood of seven, to be known as the PRB. The three letters were to appear on all of their paintings, under oath that they were never to be explained. In 1849 a PRB journal appeared, entitled *The Germ*. The PRB was the first in England of those revolutionary in-groups of artists whose controversial magazines capture a trend.[8] The names given to these groups sometimes stick with journalists, chroniclers and historians. The PRB leader, the drop-out from the Academy Schools, was Dante Gabriel Rossetti, then twenty. His father, Gabriele, had long been a political exile from Italy, where he had been a member of a secret society. Dante's English-born mother was also half Italian. The first three Brothers were Rossetti, William Holman Hunt and John Everett Millais. The PR in their strange device stood for 'Pre-Raphaelite'. Once the initials were spelled out in words, they needed no further explanation at the Academy Schools. The accepted academic model of Renaissance painting had for generations been Raphael (1483–1520), the painter of *The School of Athens* and of much else in the Vatican, as well as of many Madonnas painted for churches. Raphael is the most regular of the painters of the High Renaissance canon-ised in Georgio Vasari's *Lives of the Italian Painters* and praised in the

Discourses of Sir Joshua Reynolds. In Raphael's balanced composi-
tions the forms of the actual are purified towards the ideal, colours
are harmonised, and parts subordinated to the whole. In the English
eighteenth century this neo-classical tradition was personified in
Reynolds, Founder and President of the Royal Academy: a figure
attacked then by the obscure engraver William Blake, and in 1848,
although Sir Joshua had died in 1792, by the PRB.

To the Brotherhood in 1848, the Royal Academy's programme
seemed stale. They proposed a different approach, painting from an
observed nature rather than from its ideally conventionalised forms.
Such a simple directness was 'medieval' only in that it did not imitate
neo-classical norms. As a device, 'Pre-Raphaelite' has less effrontery
than the 'or' in Pugin's *Pointed or Christian Architecture*. Yet this
hyphenated word neatly turns the academic canon on its head,
putting medieval example above that of the Renaissance. A similar
rearrangement of the ancestors was made early in the twentieth
century by two highly educated Americans in London: Ezra Pound
and T.S. Eliot. They elevated the example of Dante above that of
Milton. The avant-garde overturns the immediate past in the hope
that the future may resemble a remoter past.

A liking for the Italian painters before Raphael was not new; it was
found among Jacobites in Rome; and in Paris the prices fetched by
Italian primitives rose in the late eighteenth century. Imitation of
such paintings was pioneered by a group of German painters in Rome
in the 1820s, the Lukasbrüder. They called themselves Brothers of St
Luke since he is the patron saint of religious artists; tradition shows
him painting an icon of the Virgin Mary. They are known also,
because of their love of scenes from the life of Jesus of Nazareth, as
the Nazarenes. The idea of a Brotherhood, and some of the early
subjects of the PRB, may have come from these German artists.
Timothy Hilton notes that 'Prince Albert, Victoria's German consort,
made a collection of pictures which included works by Van Eyck,
Roger van der Weyden, Duccio, Fra Angelico and Gentile da
Fabriano.'[9] British painting had previously seen nothing like this.
Although Blake and Stodhard had engraved Chaucer's pilgrimage,
and Samuel Palmer's Shoreham paintings have a visionary quality,
there were no oil paintings corresponding to the medievalist verse

romances of Coleridge and Scott. In 1844, Ford Madox Brown, an older and independent painter who had visited the Nazarenes, came to live in England, at a time when painting was perhaps the only visible form of medieval art not being produced by A.W. Pugin. In 1845 Brown began to paint his *Chaucer at the Court of Edward III*, which he describes as 'a vision of Chaucer reading to knights and ladies fair, to king and court, amid air and sunshine'.[10] The picture derives from a full-page illustration in a fifteenth-century manuscript of Chaucer's *Troilus and Criseyde*, kept at Corpus Christi College, Cambridge. D.G. Rossetti admired Brown's work. In 1846, in Volume II of his *Modern Painters*, John Ruskin, in full cry against the classical pictures in Catholic churches, had referred to 'the clear and tasteless poison of the art of Raphael'. Ruskin wrote to his tutor: 'St Peter's I had expected to be *disappointed* in. I was *disgusted*. The Italians think Gothic architecture barbarous. I think Greek heathenish.'[11] Ruskin also thought St Peter's would make a nice ballroom.

The Pre-Raphaelites were a Brotherhood for a few years only. But when *The Times* attacked them, John Ruskin defended them. The first artists to rally to what the Pre-Raphaelites stood for were Ford Madox Brown, then Edward Burne-Jones and William Morris, not yet Oxford undergraduates. The earliest PRB paintings, such as Rossetti's *Girlhood of Mary Virgin* of 1848–9 and Millais's related *Christ in the House of his Parents* of 1849 (Plate 14), treated traditional Christian subjects with an apparently artless simplicity and an unpolished naturalism which, though reverently intended, shocked those who expected a painting of the Holy Family to glow and provide 'uplift'. Millais 'first exhibited this work without a title, but with the Biblical quotation "And who shall say unto him, What are these wounds in thine hands? Then he shall answer, Those with which I was wounded in the house of my friends" (Zechariah, 13:6)'. Millais was inspired by a sermon heard in Oxford. These 'Gothic revivalists' in paint were 'part of the Oxford Movement, and . . . enchanted by Oxford's Catholic past'.[12] The boy Jesus has hurt his hand; the wound, the tools behind his head and his mother's compassion foreshadow the Crucifixion. The figure of St John the Baptist, on the right, bringing a bowl of water to his wounded cousin, prefigures his baptism of Christ, also symbolised by the dove perched in the background. Baptism itself,

and the nature of its effects, were at the time of Millais's painting the
subject of violent public controversy, prompted by the Gorham
Judgement. Archdeacon Robert Wilberforce had preached that 'To
deny the doctrine of the baptismal regeneration of infants is a "virtual
denial that Jesus Christ is come in the flesh".'[13]

The analogy between the physical and the metaphysical, basic to
Catholic art, was a principle being revived in the Church of England
by the Oxford Movement. The Tractarians admired *The Analogy of
Religion, Natural and Revealed, to the Constitution and Course of
Nature*, written by Bishop Butler in 1736. Butler's *Analogy* countered
the Deist view of God as a distant artificer, who, having created
Nature, took no close interest in its workings. Analogy is here given
a fresh application by the twenty-year-old Millais, whose unusual
and rather successful painting was inspired by the sermon he had
heard, and by the example of Rossetti.

But if the symbolism is orthodox or (in England) neo-orthodox,
the painting is naked of style, without vanishing point or perspective,
techniques within the capacity of Millais if not of Rossetti. It shows
the house of Mary and Joseph as a humble carpenter's workshop,
inhabited by an overworked family who seem pious and homely
rather than holy. The painting was often referred to as 'The Carpenter's
Shop'.[14] A popular magazine described Millais's Jesus as 'a hideous,
wry-necked, blubbering, red-haired boy in a night-gown', and his
mother as a woman 'so horrible in her ugliness that ... she would
stand out from the rest of the company as a monster in the vilest
cabaret in France or in the lowest gin-shop in England'. This infuri-
ated attack on modern medieval art was written, not in an outraged
Letter to the Editor, but *by* the Editor of this magazine, Charles
Dickens, whose Christianity is usually described as Unitarian, undoc-
trinaire and liberal.[15]

The earliest PRB paintings are often of medieval subjects. When
religious, they attempt to combine detailed naturalism with the
symbolism of European Christian art. For example, Rossetti's painting
of the Annunciation (1849–50), now in the Tate Gallery, shows the
Angel Gabriel offering the lily of perpetual virginity to Mary, who
looks more 'troubled' (Luke, 1:29) than ready to accept with 'Behold
the handmaid of the Lord' (Luke, 1:38), as in the painting's title, *Ecce*

Ancilla Domini. The dove on the windowsill represents the overshadowing of the Holy Spirit by whom Mary is to conceive. Analogy between natural and supernatural, traditional in Christian thought and in its artistic manifestation, does not blend easily with naturalism, and is opposed to mere materialism, then being posited by some natural scientists. There was also a more basic problem for Protestant middle-class people who now, for the first time, aspired to buy works of art – people such as the parents of Ruskin, Browning or William Morris. They had no first-hand familiarity with religious painting, and its traditions were alien to them.

The Reformation had channelled English energies into the culture of the word, removing the stained glass from the parish church and whitewashing its wall paintings, replacing them with the Tables of the Law, and words from the pulpit. The Catholic Ten Commandments were renumbered by Anglicans, who promoted the second part of the First Commandment into a separate prohibition. This forbids the making and reverencing of graven images, and likenesses of anything that is in heaven above or in the earth beneath. If Scripture is sufficient to salvation, a religious painting could be an invitation to idolatry. Those who wanted sacred art, King Charles I for example, imported it from Catholic countries. In 1850, English culture was literary. Artists were often foreigners. To English ears, the word 'painting' suggested a portrait. There were landscapes, too, and history paintings had academic approval, but the sacred was not a subject for art. Nor were there all the colour reproductions supplied by today's visual supermarket. The art students of the PRB pored over black and white engravings of the frescoes in the Campo Santo in Pisa; their first paintings are flat and linear. Most English people would have had no idea of what Michelangelo's frescoes in the Sistine Chapel looked like, and no mental image of Leonardo's *Last Supper*. Even in the 1870s, it would not have occurred to an English admirer of Botticelli's *Birth of Venus* that the painting might express ideas taken from Christian Neo-Platonism. In this respect, the assumptions of Pater, writing about Renaissance art, are as reductive and naturalistic as those of Browning in 'Fra Lippo Lippi'.

These are among the reasons why John Ruskin, in his 1851 letter to *The Times* defending the PRB against the newspaper's attacks, expressed reservations about what he saw as the 'Romanist and Tractarian tendencies' of PRB paintings. 'My real introduction to the whole school', Ruskin recalled in 1882, 'was by Mr Dyce, R.A., who dragged me, literally up to the Millais picture of "The Carpenter's Shop" which I had passed disdainfully, and forced me to look for its merits.' Dyce, born in Aberdeen in 1806, was an accomplished painter, a High Churchman who had learned from the Nazarenes. The symbolic code employed in 'The Carpenter's Shop' (more properly, *Christ in the House of his Parents*, Plate 14) was alien to the literal understanding of the Bible in which Ruskin had been brought up, although he had no difficulty with it in Italian painting. 'In 1847 Holman Hunt had read to Millais Ruskin's analysis of the iconography of Tintoretto's *Annunciation* in *Modern Painters*, Volume II, where carpenters' tools also have symbolic significance.'[16] The biblical literalism of Ruskin's upbringing conflicted with the metaphysical dimension of the Gothic vision to which the adult Ruskin later committed himself, and this led to a crisis of faith. But for John Ruskin in 1851, the symbolism used in Italian Gothic art rang 'No Popery' alarms when used by England's modern painters. From this time onward the difficulty of marrying a literal modern naturalism to the symbolism traditional in visual art became a problem for Christian artists, notably William Holman Hunt. The strain shows in Holman Hunt's *The Scapegoat*, painted from a live goat on the shores of the Dead Sea in 1854. Christian symbolism (and Tractarian influence) faded from most Pre-Raphaelite art. Millais moved on from medieval and religious to literary subjects, and then to modern ones. Rossetti mingled medieval motifs with an esoteric symbolism of his own, as can be seen in his verse. A similar tension, though dealt with differently, can be felt in the poetry of the Catholic poets Coventry Patmore and Gerard Hopkins.

Rossetti's sensibility shows in 'The Blessed Damozel', written at seventeen, and the first poem he published, in *The Germ* in 1849:

> The blessed Damozel leaned out
>   From the gold bar of Heaven;
> Her eyes were deeper than the depth
>   Of waters stilled at even;

She had three lilies in her hand,
   And the stars in her hair were seven.

Her robe, ungirt from clasp to hem,
   No wrought flowers did adorn,
But a white rose of Mary's gift
   For service meetly worn;
Her hair that lay along her back
   Was yellow like ripe corn.

The lilies and stars seem to be meaningful, and the numbers seem symbolic; but of what? These emblems are opaque rather than clear, as they would be in Dante or the Quattrocento art which the poem invokes. Commentators mention Swedenborg and Blake, yet the three lilies and the seven stars remain mysterious. The Damozel wears on her neck a white rose, given by the Blessed Virgin Mary 'meetly', we are told. Yet Rossetti tells us that he wrote the poem to reverse the situation in which an earthly man longs for a beloved woman dead and gone to heaven. 'I determined to ... give utterance to the yearning of the loved one in heaven'.[17] The Damozel is unmeetly miserable in heaven and would rather be with her lover on earth. She leans and leans 'until her bosom must have made / The bar of heaven warm' – a lay Eloisa yearning for her Abelard.

Romantic poets often wrote of an unattainable lady in a tower. Rossetti's Damozel leans warmly on the 'bar of Heaven', longing for an unattainable man. Seventeen-year-old males have often dreamed of beautiful women who yearn for them, and men have often painted them, but rarely as obsessively as Rossetti, or in such numbers as Burne-Jones. The 'bar of Heaven' makes Rossetti's Damozel more unattainable than a lady in a tower. But if, as we are invited to do, we study the Damozel's deep eyes, hair 'like ripe corn' and 'robe, ungirt from clasp to hem', the details place her within imaginable distance of a woman of a different kind, often painted by French Impressionists: a lady in a towel. The PRB sought out attainable young women in bars and theatres. Such behaviour is not confined to artists, but the PRB sought such 'stunners' (Rossetti's term) as models, or as muses, and two of the most stunning of them agreed to become Mrs D.G. Rossetti and Mrs William Morris. 'All beautiful women were "Stunners" with us', wrote Val Prinsep, one of the band of Pre-Raphaelites who frescoed the Oxford Union in the summer of 1857. 'We copied his [Rossetti's] very way of speaking. Wombats were the most beautiful of God's creatures. Medievalism was our beau idéal.'[18]

Rossetti was fond of wombats and other Australian fauna, and later kept wombats, wallabies and kangaroos in the garden of his house in Cheyne Walk, Chelsea. Wombats, stunners and medievalism make an engaging combination, but in 'The Blessed Damozel' Rossetti does not combine the sensuous with the spiritual so much as confuse them. A lighter version of this youthful mixture appears in early Yeats. But Yeats eventually grew out of it, whereas Rossetti grew into it. Two years after their marriage, his wife, Elizabeth Siddal Rossetti, took a fatal drug overdose. He buried with her body the original manuscript of his poems, but later exhumed it from her coffin and published the poems. His life was in some respects a horrible version of the fantasy of 'The Blessed Damozel'. An admirer of Poe's 'The Raven', he painted a version of 'The Blessed Damozel' towards the end of his life, in 1875 to 1878. His sometimes unfinished paintings, like his uneven poems, have a striking but willed emotional intensity.

Rossetti's paintings became increasingly preoccupied with images of women who are very unlike the shrinking and immature figure of the Annunciata in *Ecce Ancilla Domini*. He filled these commanding figures with an obscure symbolism and a brooding sensuality not seen in Italian painting before Raphael. In medieval terms, the goddesses who dominate Rossetti's later paintings are icons who are well on the way to becoming idols. He typically links erotic love with death in a way which anticipates the art of the Æsthetes and the Decadents. Algernon Charles Swinburne and Simeon Solomon stayed at Rossetti's house in Cheyne Walk, along with the wombats, and so did James McNeill Whistler. Whistler's exhibition of *Nocturne in Black and Gold, The Falling Rocket* in the Grosvenor Gallery in 1877 led Ruskin, in his *Fors Clavigera*, a series of letters to the workmen of England, to accuse the American painter of imposture: 'I have seen, and heard, much of Cockney impudence before now; but never expected to hear a coxcomb ask two hundred guineas for

1. St Paul's, London's Cathedral, designed by Christopher Wren – an image of *c*. 1890. See page xvii.

2. The Palace of Westminster, designed by Barry and Pugin, in an image of 1878. See pages xviii and 71–3.

3. John Martin, *The Bard*. In 1817 Martin painted this to illustrate Gray's poem of 1757. The 'ruthless' Edward I and his army appear on the left, below Conway Castle (built later by Edward). The defiant bard, top right, with beard, is about to plunge into the Conway below. See pages 1–2.

4. The title page of Percy's *Reliques*, 1765. A harp stands before ruined Gothic arches and pillars. Below is the motto *Durat opus vatum*: 'The work of the poets endures'. Between the harp and the ruins, the trunk of a tree produces new leaves: the ancient oak of English poetry is about to revive. See pages 15–22.

5. *Sir Walter Scott* by Sir Francis Grant, painted in 1831, a year before Scott's death. See page 43.

6. A study by Arthur Hughes for his *In Madeline's Chamber*, 1856, illustrating John Keats's 'The Eve of St Agnes'. See pages 56 and 145.

7. Sublimity without religion. The Great Western Hall at Fonthill, leading to the central tower (see page 62). Built by James Wyatt for William Beckford between 1796 and 1812, Fonthill had the plunging perspectives of Gothic. The 278-foot tower fell down twice. 'Improving' Salisbury Cathedral, Wyatt removed roodscreen, chapels and tombs.

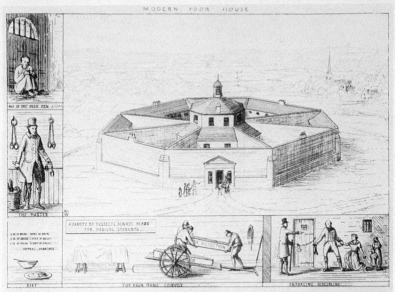

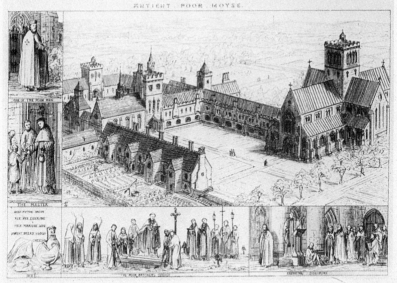

'Contrasted residences for the poor', from Contrasts *by Augustus Pugin (revised edition, 1841).*

8. 'Contrasted Residences for the Poor' from A.W. Pugin's *Contrasts*, 1836. See page 67.

9. Frank O. Salisbury, *The Great Roof* (detail), 1924. Hugh Herland shows King Richard II the new hammerbeam roof in Westminster Hall, rebuilt by Henry Yevele. See page 72.

10. Daniel Maclise, *Sir Francis Sykes and Family*, 1837. A well-armed baronet, with dogs, children and wife Henrietta. She descends their medieval stair in more than medieval glamour. Sir Francis ended the marriage after finding her in bed with the Irish painter of this canvas.

11. James Gillray, *Tales of Wonder*, 1802. Ladies listen in horror to Matthew Lewis's new book. A copy of Lewis's *The Monk*, 1796 (see page 77), lies on the table. The watch of the fashionable young reader shows it is past midnight.

12. John Patrick Crichton Stuart, 3rd Marquess of Bute, in a monk's cowl. Photograph by Thomas Rogers, *c.* 1896. See page 93.

13. Joseph Nash, *The Medieval Court at the Great Exhibition*, 1851. See page 118.

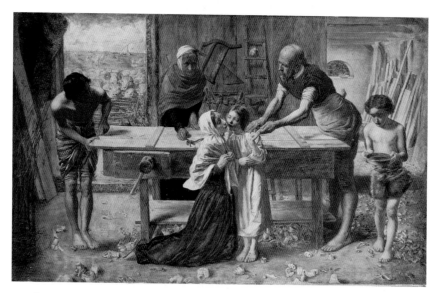

14. John Everett Millais, *Christ in the House of his Parents*, 1849. Discussed on pages 127–8.

15. 'Music' from *King René's Honeymoon*, stained glass, Morris and Co., 1862. This window shows King René of Provence, a character who in Walter Scott's *Anne of Geierstein* is a lover of the arts – and of beauty. Designed by Rossetti. Now in the Victoria and Albert Museum.

16. John Everett Millais, *Mariana*, 1851, after Tennyson's poem 'Mariana', an expansion of a detail in Shakespeare's *Measure for Measure*. Mariana waits five years for her fiancé, Angelo. Millais had studied the stained glass of Merton College Chapel, Oxford. 'On the whole the perfectest of his works, and the representative picture of that generation' (John Ruskin, 1878). See page 146.

17. Millais, *A Dream of the Past: Sir Isumbras at the Ford*, 1857. See pages 147–8.

18. Frederick Sandys, *A Nightmare*, 1857. See page 148 and note 15 to Chapter 8.

19. Ford Madox Brown, *Work*, 1852–65. Discussed on pages 153–4.

20. Dante Gabriel Rossetti, *Lancelot in the Queen's Chamber*, 1857. See pages 156–7 and 201, and note 7 to Chapter 9.

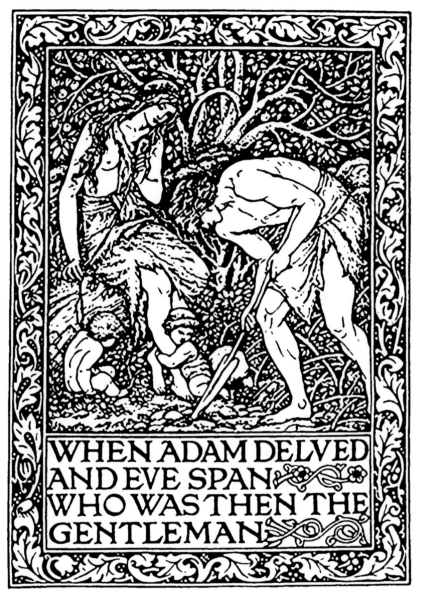

WHEN ADAM DELVED
AND EVE SPAN
WHO WAS THEN THE
GENTLEMAN

21. Edward Burne-Jones, *When Adam Delved and Eve Span*, illustration for Morris's *A Dream of John Ball*, 1886–7. See page 164. A modern man awakes to find himself in 1381: the Peasants' Revolt. The Peasants' question turns the punishment pronounced on Adam and Eve into a challenge to rank and privilege. Adam works for his bread, Eve has the toils of motherhood, a spindle and a Burne-Jones languor.

22. Edward Burne-Jones, *The Beguiling of Merlin*, 1874, exhibited in the Grosvenor Gallery in 1877. In *Le Morte Darthur IV*, Merlin is enchanted by Nenyve, a name changed by Tennyson in *Vivien*, 1859. Burne-Jones follows a French romance in which Merlin's pupil makes him fall asleep, and by a spell (taken from the book she holds) confines him in a hawthorn. Vivien is given a bewitching *contraposto*, a lovely face and a serpentine headdress. See pages 152 and 178.

23. George du Maurier, 'Ye Æsthetic Young Geniuses', *Punch*, 21 September 1878. See page 180.

24. Cover of Baden-Powell's *Young Knights of the Empire*, 1916. St George, as a boy scout, displays the Scouts' fleur-de-lys emblem. Courage cages the dragon.

25. *Gareth and Linet*: 'Faugh Sir! You smell of ye kitchen.' H.J. Ford's illustration of Andrew Lang's *Book of Romance*, 1902, a retelling for children of Tennyson's version in *The Idylls of the King*. Gareth rescues Lynet, but she scorns him as a scullion: he had worked in the kitchen.

ONGYREDE·
hINE·þaGEonð
·hÆLEð:þÆT·
WÆS·GOD·✠
ÆLMIhTIG·
SʒRANG·anD
·STIðMOD:
GESTAh·hEor
·GEALGAN·hE
annE:moDIG
ON·manIGRA·
GESIhðE:þa·he·uuolðE
·manncȳnn·lȳʃan:

26. David Jones, 'The Dream of the Rood' inscription. Jones used his watercolour of lines 39–41 of the Old English poem to illustrate his long poem *The Anathemata*, 1952. Christ as victor over death: 'The young hero ungirded himself, he that was God Almighty, strong and resolute. He mounted the high gallows, brave in the sight of many, for his will was to redeem mankind.'

27. J.R.R. Tolkien's illustration for *The Hobbit*, 1937. Bilbo Baggins ventures into the wood. A late example of the fairy-tale medievalism of the Edwardian nursery, seen also in Plate 25.

throwing a pot of paint in the public's face.' Whistler sued Ruskin, was awarded derisory damages of a farthing, and went bankrupt.

Colour reproduction has familiarised us with the stunning, and stunned, images of Elizabeth Siddal, who became Mrs Rossetti, and of Jane Burden, who became Mrs Morris but was worshipped by Rossetti in his decline. The attractions and significance of these women, and of Rossetti's 'Blessed Damozel', have little to do with medieval art, except in details of the way Rossetti sometimes envisaged them. Rather, they form part of the cult of the image of Woman, a cult which sometimes referred its origins and its authority back to an oft-invoked but ill-understood aspect of medieval culture, which was recovered in the nineteenth century and is usually known in English as Courtly Love. Medieval scholars today are not sure that there ever was a real-life Code of Courtly Love, and regard the work of Andreas Capellanus (who flourished in the 1180s), entitled *De Arte Honeste Amandi*, translated as *The Code of Courtly Love* and later taken as a serious treatise, as at least half a joke. The relationship between life and literature is rarely simple, and whether or how far life imitated art in various courts across Europe between 1100 and 1300 or 1400 will never be known. This love is first expressed in the lyric poetry of the troubadours at the courts of Provence in the twelfth century, creating a literary fashion which spread throughout European verse, and not only in the Romance languages. In German it is 'Frauendienst' – 'the service of women'. It is no coincidence that the cult of the Blessed Virgin Mary rose to a new height at the same period. There were, indeed, courts at which questions of love were discussed, but these came much later than the poetry of the troubadours and were more of a parlour game than an alternative religion. Rossetti was steeped in the poetry of Dante and his circle, publishing his verse translations from them under that title in 1861; all his life, he identified with the Florentine after whom he had been named. Christened Gabriel Charles Dante, he renamed himself Dante Gabriel. It is clear from his painting, however, that despite his intimate knowledge of the earlier poetry of Dante Alighieri, he subscribed to the romantic image which held such appeal for his literary contemporaries. Gabriele, D.G. Rossetti's father, identified with the obdurate advocate of civic virtue eating the bitter bread of exile. Gabriele's son focused instead on what he saw as the poet's tragic love-life. An exaltation of romantic love into an absolute ideal had been a feature of continental romantic fiction in the generations since Rousseau's Emile and Goethe's Werther. In some nineteenth-century novels and operas, if not in the midland counties of England, an adulterous passion was regarded with sympathy, approval and even admiration, especially if it ended in death.

Nineteenth-century readers of medieval romances were accordingly taken with Dante's story, in *La Vita Nuova*, of how as a child he was smitten with love for Beatrice, who was to marry another and to die young, and also with the inspiring role which Beatrice plays in the *Divine Comedy*. Reading Dante's verse literally and autobiographically, and turning his life-story into the legend recorded in several paintings by Rossetti and others, they seized upon the episode in *Inferno V* of the adulterous love of Paolo and Francesca, slain by the Lord of Rimini, Francesca's husband and Paolo's brother. The punishment of the lovers is to be blown around, locked in each other's arms, kissing, and burning with desire, for all eternity. Such a fate did not seem to the young Rossetti an undesirable one. In his *Paolo and Francesca da Rimini* (1855) he painted '*O lasso!*' between the figures of Dante and Virgil – Dante's exclamation on seeing the embracing lovers: 'Alas!' Romantic readers read this scene in the opposite sense to that which it must chiefly bear, placed as it is in Hell, in the Circle of the Lustful. Leigh Hunt's *The Story of Rimini* (1816) had proved lastingly popular, and in the next century the episode still held a romantic meaning for Gabriele D'Annunzio and Ezra Pound.

Women are first accorded an elevated place in Western European culture in the twelfth century: in the cult of the Blessed Virgin Mary in France and England, and in the poetry of the troubadours in Provence. But the role of *fin amors*, or Courtly Love, in medieval life, as distinct from medieval literature, was generally misunderstood by late nineteenth-century scholars such as Gaston Paris, and taken to imply an inherent approval of adultery. It is obvious that some medieval romances, notably that of Tristan and Iseut, lend colour to such a view, and the story of Lancelot and Guenevere, in some versions, can also be taken or mistaken as doing so. Under the Provençal title of *lo gai saber* – 'the happy science' – a special interpretation of this literary fashion became, in France and elsewhere, a late Romantic cult of love, involving troubadours, jongleurs, nightingales, lovely ladies, lords absent on crusade, and high-spirited adultery. Its more gnostic devotees idealised the Albigenses, adherents of a Cathar heresy popular in the Pays d'Oc, but crushed by the Church. The detail of Catharist belief is disputed, but they were dualists, believing in two creators: a good god, creator of the soul, and an evil god, creator of the body. They condemned procreation and marriage as bringing evil into the world. The forbidden nature of troubadour love, the death of Tristan, and the extirpation of this mysterious 'pure' Cathar cult (Greek '*katharos*': pure), proved irresistible to some late Romantics and Decadents. The cult of a love made more special by being forbidden and also, by illogical association with the Cathars, *persecuted*, is a powerful motif in the work of Wagner, Wilde, Proust, D'Annunzio and Pound. Here it is worth recalling the dry account given by George Ellis of the love of Lancelot for Guenevere: 'It is necessary to the dignity of his mistress, that she should still share the bed of Arthur, and that, protected in her reputation by the sword of her lover, she should lead a life of ceremonious and splendid adultery. This point is accomplished, and their intercourse continues as usual.'

The 'code' of Courtly Love, the cult of *fin amors*, the Provençal *gai saber*, seemed to some nineteenth-century adepts to sanctify extramarital love. The story of the fatal passion of Tristan and Iseut was still taken as typical of medieval attitudes to love by Denis de Rougemont in a work of *haute vulgarisation* translated in 1940 as *Passion and Society*. Scholars do not regard Tristanism as typical of attitudes to adultery in medieval literature, still less in medieval life. This was a nineteenth-century cult. Mr and Mrs D.G. Rossetti were perhaps its first British victims. The first two figures Rossetti asked Elizabeth Siddal to model for were Iseut and Queen Guenevere.

Christina Rossetti, the best of all English woman poets in the judgement of Virginia Woolf, understood her brother. Her poem 'In An Artist's Studio' gives us his doomed world:

One face looks out from all his canvases,
One selfsame figure sits or walks or leans . . . .
Not as she is, but was when hope shone bright;
Not as she is, but as she fills his dream.[19]

Christina kept a Pre-Raphaelite truth to nature in her verse, which, when pictorial, has bright colours and clear edges. She was twice engaged to be married – first to a member of the PRB, James Collinson – but renounced both engagements on religious grounds. Collinson had re-joined the Catholic Church. Christina, a devout Anglo-Catholic, cared for her family and wrote fine lyrics, often religious, in a purified ballad style, whose models derive ultimately from Percy's *Reliques*. For ten years she undertook voluntary work to help ex-prostitutes. Delicacy and fancy are features of her verse, and she wrote well for children, but she is much more than girlish. Her secular masterpiece, 'Goblin Market', is a charged fairy story of forbidden fruit, of two sisters, and of innocence lost and redeemed. It is an early poem, but its adult themes, close to her brother's, are managed with a tact and discipline beyond him, and a sensuous verbal and rhythmic energy. This remarkable poem, though itself of high artistic achievement and moral seriousness, indicates one of the trajectories which the Medieval Revival was to take: legend to fairy story to illustrated books for children.

This chapter began by remarking on the arrival of the Medieval Revival in the 1840s, and spoke of the stage of research and development as complete. The stage of application has already been sketched in Chapter 5, on Carlyle, Ruskin and Disraeli. That the stage of production had also been reached is shown by the verdict on the Great Exhibition: that Mr Pugin had demonstrated 'the applicability of Mediæval art in all its richness and variety to the uses of the present day'. But in *Pugin: A Gothic Passion*, the closing tribute to Pugin in Alexandra Wedgwood's chapter on 'The Mediæval Court' is ominous for the future: 'As the *Illustrated London News* had noted, he [Pugin] was the originator of all the ideas; without him there was no development.'[20]

CHAPTER 8

History and Legend

THE SUBJECTS OF POETRY AND PAINTING

The working definition of medievalism adopted at the outset of this essay in cultural history included a historical or textual component, so that a work might not be considered part of the Medieval Revival if it referred to a world of Gothic fantasy rather than to a historical or textual Middle Ages. The reverence for a historical Middle Ages felt by some artists and poets, if not the general public, reached a high-water mark in 1851, when the 'Mediæval Court' won plaudits at the Great Exhibition. This was also the year in which Ruskin, at the prompting of Coventry Patmore, wrote his letter to *The Times* defending the Pre-Raphaelites, an intervention which began the process of their acceptance.[1] Soon they were being asked to paint everywhere.

It might seem tempting to regard the restoration of the English Catholic hierarchy in 1850 as part of the Medieval Revival. In England, Catholicism can seem medieval. Yet the Catholic Church existed before and after the Middle Ages, and is not limited to the millennium in which it helped to form England. The installation of Wiseman as Archbishop of Westminster, and of other Catholic bishops in England and Wales, was met by violent public protest. 'Papal Aggression' was represented as political, even territorial.[2] Wiseman's response was that the only subjects of Queen Victoria he coveted were the poor who clustered in the 'rookeries' of Westminster. What Newman in a sermon of 1852 called 'The Second Spring' of English Catholicism (the first being Augustine's conversion of Saxon England) was mocked by *The Times* as 'the Italian mission to the Irish'. In the course of the controversy surrounding the restoration of Catholic bishops there was much appeal to history, especially to the rights and wrongs of the English Reformation.

Since Pugin had published *Contrasts* (1836), and its second edition in 1841, he had been a leading public advocate of medieval ideals. In

1851 he published *An Earnest Address, on the Establishment of the Hierarchy*, which includes a surprising retractation. By some, Pugin writes, 'All, anterior to the Reformation, is regarded and described as a sort of Utopia: – pleasant meadows, happy peasants, merry England ... bread cheap, and beef for nothing, all holy monks, all holy priests, – holy everybody. Such charity, and such hospitality, and such unity, when every man was a Catholic. I once believed in this Utopia myself, but when tested by stern facts and history it all melts away like a dream.'[3]

This dream of the charity and piety of pre-Reformation England had inspired Pugin's own 'Contrasted Residences for the Poor' of 1836 (see Plate 8). With one sweeping gesture, Pugin confesses that his youthful dream of the Middle Ages cannot stand up against history. What led him to apply the test of 'stern facts and history' may have been a new fact, the restoration of the hierarchy. After three penal centuries, English Catholics were permitted to practise their faith openly. A few penalties remained – they could not leave money to the Church, for example, or attend Oxford or Cambridge – but they had their bishops, the heirs of the apostles. For Pugin, this new fact melted an old dream: something of what England had lost was now to be restored to her, or to her Catholics. This retractation may also acknowledge that the Medieval Revival had won public acceptance. Pugin died in the next year, having done his work.

It was from about this time that a younger generation of Gothic Revival architects felt at liberty to move away from archaeological exactitude and to develop new forms.[4] In a kindred development, medievalist poems and paintings were henceforward less likely to start from a medieval text or event than from a legend. Medievalism did not now have to be based on copying medieval things accurately. The decision that the Palace of Westminster would be Gothic led to Pugin's success at the Crystal Palace. Since medieval ways were accepted as part of modern life, a new 'medieval' venture no longer had to take careful bearings from attested precedent, or to reproduce medieval forms in the manner of a brass rubbing. The academic history of the Middle Ages developed, with the researches into English charters of William Stubbs, later Bishop of Oxford. Scientific philology had already begun to recover more and more of the texts of Old and Middle English literature, as in the editions of *Beowulf* and *Sir Gawain*.

The publications of the gentlemen of the Bannatyne Club and the Roxburgh Society gave way, under the impetus of F.J. Furnivall and Walter Skeat, to the editions of the Early English Text Society. Germanic linguistic science would eventually be instituted in university courses in the new subject of English. Medieval Revival literature now derived less from medieval history than from medieval story.

Pugin's retractation applied the modern distinction between history and story, history and legend, fact and fiction, fact and interpretation. It is a distinction easy to grasp but hard to apply to large questions. A major instance of this problem arose for Victorian Christians in the new challenge offered by geological findings to literal readings of the two accounts of Creation given in Genesis, Chapters 1 and 2. Some Victorian Protestants read Scripture very literally. A founding Protestant principle is *sola scriptura*: all that is necessary to salvation is to be found in the Bible, its truth guaranteed by divine inspiration and available to the individual reader. A more extreme position is that every sentence in the Bible is literally true: every brick in the wall. Such an implicit faith in the inspiration of (translated) words now clashed, in Britain and in the United States, with the prevailing assumption of Anglo-Saxon culture that the truth of any proposition was to be ascertained empirically or historically, by the tests of natural science. Recent geological discoveries forced the conclusion that if the universe was created in the year 4004 BC, it had been created with rocks and fossils designed to make it look very much older. The 4004 BC calculation accepted in the Anglican Church was that of Archbishop Ussher, who in the 1650s refined an old calculation based on figures given in the Old Testament.[5] It was now clear, however, that sedimentary rocks held what were evidently fossils of life-forms many thousands, perhaps millions, of years old. The accounts of Creation given in the opening chapters of the Bible failed the empirical test of truth favoured in England. The faith of John Ruskin, a lover of rocks, was seriously troubled by geological proof that scripture could not be literally true. He wrote to his friend Henry Acland, M.D., on 24 May 1851: 'If only the Geologists would let me alone, I could do very well, but those dreadful Hammers! I hear the clink of them at the end of every cadence of the Bible verses – and on the other side, these unhappy, blinking Puseyisms; men trying to do right and losing their very Humanity.'[6] For Catholics, trusting not to a literal reading of scripture but to the consensus of the community from which these writings came, geology could not threaten foundations; nor did the later findings of Darwin. Newman wrote that he 'could go the whole hog with Darwin'.[7] The Catholic Church takes the New Testament as the witness of her early members, and its essential implications as having been defended in the Ecumenical Councils.

In the 1970s, the validity of the distinction between history and story was denied by French post-structuralists who insisted upon the primacy of language in representation, and on language's indeterminacy. In British universities this denial was taken less seriously in philosophy departments than in departments of language and literature. Using a linguistic theory to reclassify history as a form of story is a modern expression of ancient scepticism as to the possibilities of knowledge and the limitations of language. In practice, of course, the most unphilosophical and fact-grubbing historian is well aware that each attempt to write history is regarded, at least by other historians, as no more than a version of the truth. Conversely, the most historically ignorant of theoretical sceptics relies in practice on the reality of historical events, such as, for example, the German defeat of France in 1940.

The English language contains both 'history' and 'story', two words from one root. Like other technical words in English, 'historia' was a Greek term adopted by Romans. It came into English twice, first crossing the Channel as 'estoire', which in the thirteenth century produced 'story'. 'History' came from Latin in the fifteenth century and gradually attracted the meanings associated with the true relation of historical events, leaving 'story', which had previously included these senses, to indicate 'anecdote, entertainment, fiction'. Words such as 'myth' and 'legend' show a similar semantic split. A history is now expected to be a connected narrative of past events, derived from records, and scholarly history is based upon empirical evidence. A story, whether oral or written, is simply a narrative, either fictional or with some relation to real events. Thus English has different and distinct terms for factual and fictional narratives. In romance languages, however, the word derived from 'historia' includes both aspects: the Italian 'storia' and the French 'histoire' designate narratives which can be either factual or fictional.

Historical knowledge of a reliable kind was the justification given by eighteenth-century scholars for their interest in an earlier literature with no classical prestige and of questionable Christian value. It will be remembered that Bishop Hurd held that romances provided evidence of the 'facts and manners', following Caylus: 'fabuleux pour les événements, historique pour le reste'. Walter Scott might have thought of his own historical romances in this way. But after Scott history played a diminishing role in the Medieval Revival, as literature began to divide into imaginative and non-imaginative. The later fiction of the Author of *Waverley* became less historical the more of it he produced. The Scottish novels are historical, but the romances are set in periods much further back, in a pre-modern past known to Scott only through literary and historical texts. His early Scottish verse and prose had been set in a world whose traditions, local beliefs and social and religious attitudes he had himself experienced. But the formal structure of Scott's thinking and learning derived from his Enlightenment education. The intellectual part of Scottish society had modernised itself so fast that by 1800 curious minds in Edinburgh had around them in their native land a hugely varied social landscape to observe and to understand. Walter Scott had, at an impressionable age, been sent to older relatives in the Border country to recover his health, and he profited from his stay. When in the Borders, he read Percy's *Reliques*, but he also received an informal education from the stories and ballads he heard, and in the process recovered more than his health.

Subsequent historical novelists such as Bulwer Lytton and Harrison Ainsworth rarely set their stories in the Middle Ages, though Robert Louis Stevenson and Arthur Conan Doyle were to continue Scott's medieval adventures. 'Medieval' stories in prose became adventure stories set in an exotic land of knights, ladies and castles, with decorative historical detail, often concentrating upon arms. This prose tradition informs the imperial adventure fiction of Rider Haggard, John Buchan and (in mutant form) Ian Fleming. Many poets had followed Tennyson into the enchanted world of Arthurian legend. Malory's unhistorical prose replaced verse romance as the ultimate source of subjects for poet and painter. Medieval literature was no longer valued for the social history which could be extracted from it, but for the magic casements it opened onto the world of legend. Indeed, the literature upon which the mid-Victorian writers of the Medieval Revival depended for their immediate inspiration was no longer, generally speaking, the medieval ballad or romance, the writings of Chaucer or even Malory's *Le Morte Darthur*, the most influential among the medieval texts then coming into circulation. For the Medieval Revival is typically a mediated thing. Byron was right to call Scott the Ariosto of the North, for Scott's romances are more like Ariosto than like Percy. Malory was freshly available in modern spelling, yet Victorian versions of Arthurian subjects are often not taken direct from his pages. The immediate source was often not the *Morte* but what Tennyson had made of it.

Arthur aside, amateurs of the Middle Ages after 1850, in poetry as well as in painting, found their subjects either in the writings of the Romantic poets or in Shakespeare, who was treated as a Romantic poet. (To Elizabethans, Shakespeare was a 'poet'; the word 'playwright' is first recorded in English in 1605, 'dramatist' in 1678.) To the Romantic poets, Shakespeare was not the rapt Bard of the 1760s but the National Poet: the author of dramatic poems, romances better performed in the reader's imagination than on public stages. Charles Lamb and Coleridge liked the theatre but held that Shakespeare was far richer on the page. Poetry, Wordsworth thought, was 'the rock of defence of human nature'; Shelley held that poets were our 'unacknowledged legislators'. Since then, Shakespeare has more often been taught as literature than as theatre.

Tennyson shows the dependence of Medieval Revival poetry upon previous literature. Keats wrote poems 'on first looking into' Chapman's Homer, and 'on sitting down to read *King Lear* once again'. One of Tennyson's best early poems, 'Mariana', makes a minor character in *Measure for Measure* into the protagonist of a poem of eighty-four lines (see Plate 16). Browning holds the record for literary expansion with 'Childe Roland to the dark tower came'. This line in *King Lear*, quoted from a lost ballad, became a verse romance of thirty-four six-line stanzas, ending in a line which repeats the title. The magnification of poetic detail is the source of much Medieval Revival painting. 'King Cophetua and the Beggar Maid' is among eighteen 'Ballads that illustrate Shakespeare' in Percy's *Reliques*. Quoted or alluded to in four Shakespeare plays, and the subject of an early poem of Tennyson, it gave to Edward Burne-Jones both the title and the layout for one of his most famous paintings.[8]

From their preoccupation with Christian painting before Raphael, the Pre-Raphaelites moved on to scenes from poetic literature. Subjects were taken from the verse romances of Coleridge, Scott and Keats, but more often from the romances of Tennyson and of Shakespeare. Scott paved a path for Keats and Keats for Tennyson, and their medieval tales in prose and verse inspired Pre-Raphaelite paintings and stained glass (see Plates 6 and 15). Whereas medieval revivalists of the 1760s had claimed that early literature was a useful source of historical evidence, revivalists in the 1850s evacuated legendary subjects of historical content. The titles of poems by Tennyson and Browning show how miscellaneous were the subjects they picked from history, literature, legend and myth. Whereas Scott's historical romances in verse and prose are set in the past, and loosely based on real characters and events, this is less true of Victorian verse, though Browning is an exception. Tennyson's chief source is legend. Rossetti admired the pictorial qualities which made the Laureate's poetry 'the Bible of the Pre-Raphaelites'. Rossetti had already done a *Mariana in the South*, and in 1857 he was happy, along with Millais and Holman Hunt, to accept the invitation of Tennyson's publisher, Moxon, to illustrate a grand edition of the Laureate's *Poems*.[9] Much Pre-Raphaelite and Victorian art is illustration, either of literary classics or of topics from history and mythology.

Before he associated himself with the Pre-Raphaelites, Ford Madox Brown produced a number of history paintings, tableaux from the pageant of English history: *The Execution of Mary Queen of Scots*, *Wycliffe reading his Translation of the Bible to John of Gaunt* and *Chaucer at the Court of Edward III*, which was exhibited in 1851. In the original version of this last painting, entitled *The Seeds and Fruits of English Poetry*, now in Oxford's Ashmolean Museum, the Black Prince, England's military hero, places a friendly hand on the shoulder of the Father of English Poetry, who (like Madox Brown's Wycliffe) is reading to the court. The idea for the subject presumably came from the famous frontispiece of an early fifteenth-century manuscript of

Chaucer's *Troilus and Criseyde* (now at Corpus Christi, Cambridge). This full-page illumination shows the poet reading to courtiers in an emblematic landscape.

In 1845 Madox Brown had begun *Seeds and Fruits* by dividing the canvas into three arches, evoking the format of the medieval triptych, a tripartite icon painted on hinged wooden panels, with the outer leaves opening to reveal the centrepiece. Brown idealises the role of the poet, but not in the manner of the illustrator of the Corpus Christi manuscript, though neither seeks to depict an actual event. If the Black Prince knew Geoffrey Chaucer, it is unlikely that he would have shown such public favour to a junior member of the royal household simply because the fellow was a poet in his spare time. (Not one of the four hundred instances in which Chaucer's name is found in surviving contemporary records suggests that he was a poet.) It is even less likely that Wycliffe should have read aloud to a willing John of Gaunt from the extremely literal running gloss on the Bible which not he, but some of his followers, had produced. Such improbabilities are, however, evident only to a historical knowledge which developed after Madox Brown's paintings were made. Few early viewers would have raised a pedantic eyebrow.

Seeds and Fruits presents English poetry as an organic growth which springs naturally from the earth of England – much as French commentators saw the Gothic arch as springing from that of France. The scheme is genealogical: a family tree, like the Tree of Jesse (a sacred subject common in stained-glass windows), with Geoffrey as Jesse. Jesse is the father of David, from whom Joseph of Nazareth is descended. The offspring of Chaucer's metaphorical seed are (left arch) Milton, Spenser and Shakespeare and (right arch) Byron, Pope and Burns, with, in the roundels above, Goldsmith and Thomson. Below, 'the names of Campbell, Moore, Shelley, Keats, Chatterton, Kirke White, Coleridge and Wordsworth appear in the cartouches held by the standing children in the base'.[10] In the larger version, *Chaucer at the Court of Edward III*, now in the Tate Gallery, Chaucer's poetic offspring have disappeared and the Gothic frame has been replaced by a sunny English Pre-Raphaelite landscape. History and genealogy give way to Nature. Brown's patriotic history conceived as a pageant – as in Walter Scott's *Tales of a Grandfather* – is absent from the work of the PRB proper. They were more interested in religion, nature and literature, especially poetry.

Much of the painting of the Pre-Raphaelites during the three years in which they were a Brotherhood owed its inspiration to medieval or medievalist romance, as can be shown by listing some of their canvases from this period.

1. William Holman Hunt, *The Eve of St Agnes* (1848); based on Keats's verse romance, discussed in Chapter 3. (Porphyro and Madeline were illustrated with more success by Arthur Hughes in 1856, in a triptych with the same title: see Plate 6.)

2. John Everett Millais, *Isabella* (1849); based on Keats's *Isabella, or the Pot of Basil* (1820), itself taken from a story in Boccaccio's *Decameron* of c. 1350.

3. Millais, *Ferdinand Lured by Ariel* (1849); from Shakespeare's *The Tempest*.

4. Dante Gabriel Rossetti, *Dante drawing an Angel on the First Anniversary of the Death of Beatrice* (1849); a scene from Dante's *Vita Nuova* (1290–4), later translated by Rossetti.[11]

5. Holman Hunt, *Claudio and Isabella* (1850); from the scene in Shakespeare's *Measure for Measure* in which the novice nun is asked by her brother to save his life by agreeing to go to bed with the judge who has condemned him to death.

6. Walter Deverell, *Twelfth Night* (1850); from Shakespeare's play.

7. Holman Hunt, *Valentine Rescuing Sylvia from Proteus* (1851); an incident from Shakespeare's *Two Gentlemen of Verona*.

8. Millais, *Mariana* (1851); based on Tennyson's 'Mariana' ['in the Moated Grange'], an expansion of a detail of Shakespeare's *Measure for Measure*. See Plate 16.[12]

Shakespeare contributes directly or indirectly to five of these eight paintings. In every case the source is a romance comedy, a love-tangle ending in marriage. Each tableau illustrated shows love or attraction between the sexes (Ferdinand is lured by Ariel to meet Miranda). This is true also of the three other paintings, which illustrate incidents taken from Keats, Dante and Tennyson. I drew up this list to demonstrate the Pre-Raphaelite preoccupation with medievalist romance. A second look at the list shows much overlap in the subjects and genres of the PRB: poetry, romance and drama. A third look shows that the Brotherhood's interest in illustrating the literature of medieval, or medievalist, romance took a naturalistic form not very surprising in a group of twenty-year-old men. Some of these narrative paintings, notably numbers 1, 5 and 7 in the above list, fix the reader's interest pointedly upon What Happened Next, or what might have happened next. Porphyro elopes with Madeline; Claudio is tempted to wish that his sister would accept Angelo's corrupt and indecent proposal; and Proteus, had Valentine not intervened, was about to ravish Sylvia. All three works are by Holman Hunt, a man who hated sin as much as Rossetti gazed at femmes fatales.

Millais's *Mariana* (Plate 16) is the most assured and successful of these eight paintings, and the only one whose subject is a single figure. The young woman is bored: what happened next was nothing; Mariana waited for her fiancé for five years in the moated grange. *Mariana* shows also that an interest in the stained glass of the Middle Ages was not confined to the middle-aged, any more than it had been for the youthful author of 'The Eve of St Agnes'. The storied windows of Madeline's bedchamber pour colour into the central panel of Arthur Hughes's triptych of 1856, although their focus is less sensual than the coloured beams of Keats's poem. It was *The Lay of the Last Minstrel* and 'The Eve of St Agnes' which put romance of a more and a less innocent kind into the modern medievalist romance. Young love became an essential ingredient of medievalist poetry and of Pre-Raphaelite painting. In 'The Lady of Shalott', Tennyson used medieval imagery to treat the subject of the sudden sexual attraction felt by a woman for a man – the female gaze. The love of Elaine le Blank for Sir Lancelot is the basis of the original medieval romance. (Another casualty of love is shown in Millais's *Ophelia*, in the Tate Gallery.) Tennyson's version is so satisfactory because he did not give the romance motif the raw naturalistic treatment often found in the paintings of the Pre-Raphaelites, who have their share of Victorian bad taste. Rather, he thoroughly reimagined the original situation and story, and was not too explicit. For later Romantic poets, the

Middle Ages provided a dark glass in which dangerous matters could be dealt with by means of images, symbols and allegories.

A curious final instance of the end of the historicist phase of 'medieval' art is Millais's large painting *A Dream of the Past: Sir Isumbras at the Ford* (see Plate 17). It was first exhibited in 1857 at the Royal Academy, accompanied by lines from 'A Metrical Romance of Sir Ysumbras'. An elderly knight uses his horse to give two frightened children a lift across a river, against an evening sky, in a chivalric analogue of the legend of St Christopher and the Christ child. The painting, with its humanity and pathos, and its broadly painted picturesque background, had an obvious appeal for family-minded Victorians, who appreciated Millais. He was the youngest ever entrant to the British Academy Schools, at the age of eleven. At fifteen, he won the gold medal for painting *The Young Men of Benjamin seizing their Brides*, a prophetic choice of subject; as his *Mariana* was also to prove. By 1853 he had become Ruskin's candidate for the mantle of Modern British Painter relinquished by J.M.W. Turner, who had died in 1851. But in 1855 Millais had become the husband of Ruskin's former wife, Effie. Despite the scandal attaching to the court proceedings by which, at her suit, Effie's marriage to Ruskin had been annulled, Ruskin still pinned his hopes for British art on Millais. 'I am not sure,' he wrote in 1856, 'whether [Millais] may not be destined to surpass all that has yet been done in figure painting, as Turner did all past landscape.' But Ruskin disliked *Sir Isumbras*, and pronounced judgement: 'The change in [Millais's] manner from the years of *Ophelia* and *Mariana* to 1857 is not merely Fall – it is Catastrophe; not merely a loss of power, but a reversal of principle.'[13] The principle Millais had betrayed was that of fidelity to nature, nature observed in detail. This tenet was one which some Pre-Raphaelites had begun to leave behind, but their public champion had adopted it before 1848 and was not going to give it up. It is a constricting principle, but in seeing the change in Millais's work, and interpreting it, Ruskin showed his acuteness of vision and trenchancy of judgement.

Confirmation that the Medieval Revival's historicism had passed its peak came with the advertisement exhibited with the painting. This suggests that *Sir Isumbras at the Ford* is an illustration of the metrical romance exhibited below it; an authenticating reference in the manner of Walter Scott. But although the incident can be found in *Sir Isumbras*, the lines Millais exhibited cannot. He had commissioned them from Tom Taylor, a journalist.[14]

Earnestness and intensity are characteristic of much of the work not just of Holman Hunt or of the PRB but of the Victorians; who had too many styles to choose from. Architects were conscious of this problem, and Pugin tried to solve it. It seems, as Mordaunt Crook argues in *The Problem of Style*, that this problem, a consequence of the explosion of knowledge, is one which cannot be resolved. Now that history provided a museum of styles, none seemed authentic. This was among the preconditions for the Romantic Revival and for Victorian earnestness. Millais and Rossetti had been caricaturists since their days at the Academy Schools. Millais's mock-source for *Sir Isumbras* suggests that a venerable textual origin was not really needed to authenticate this kind of painting, and also that a painting did not need to be ethically sourced in history or in a real text. The booster rocket of literature falls away from artistic medievalism. Millais's facility took him to success, the Presidency of the Royal Academy, a baronetcy, and the production of the winsome *Bubbles*, advertising Pears Soap. He was thus the first British pop-artist, perhaps the first post-modernist. This Ruskin had sensed.

In 1857 the artist Frederick Sandys, a friend of Millais, produced a caricature of *A Dream of the Past: Sir Isumbras at the Ford*, entitled *A Nightmare* (see Plate 18). The knight is replaced by Millais, the children by Rossetti and Holman Hunt, and the noble steed by a braying ass branded with the initials 'J.R. / OXON.' This in-joke relieved a debt of ingratitude. But it also suggests both that the medieval had lost its kick, and also how useful Ruskin's vocal support had been for these young artists: it was Ruskin who had got them across. Ruskin's first major publication had been Volume I of *Modern Painters, by a Graduate of Oxford*. Underneath *A Nightmare* appeared the unkind verse:

> A Tournor's asse he annes had bene,
> Millare him cleped Russet – skene,
> But dames y wis and men konninge,
> Cleped him Graund Humbugge.[15]

CHAPTER 9

The Working Men and the Common Good

MADOX BROWN, MAURICE, MORRIS, HOPKINS

As we saw in the last chapter, the aspects of the Medieval Revival activated by Pugin and the PRB had by the middle of the nineteenth century gained in England the kind of approval which the Romantic Revival in literature already enjoyed. The resurrection of the Palace of Westminster had paved the way for the commercial cathedral of the Crystal Palace, erected in Hyde Park for the Great Exhibition, and for Albert's cultural campus at Kensington. Literature, architecture, religion and social thought had all drawn fruitfully on medieval models, as, more recently, had painting. The Medieval Revival was now acknowledged as contributing to English life, and all-out resistance ceased, though not without harrumphing in certain quarters. Accordingly, for the next generation, a medieval inspiration, in literature, art or design, felt less obligation to refer back to a medieval poem, document, building, or precedent. The varying impulses of the Medieval Revival could be expressed with a greater freedom of form and given various application. Application was something that Victorian England was good at. Research and development were over, manufacture had begun, product recognition was high, and commercial take-off led in some areas to high volumes of output. A tour of the horizon will indicate how medieval models were applied in several fields. The quantity of these applications means that generalisation becomes both inevitable and less safe, and that examples may be less representative. The chapter ends with a discussion of a special case.

Victorian Gothic architecture abandoned correctitude and native models. It borrowed and combined examples from North Italian and Northern European civic architecture, devising applications which range in success from splendid, bold, graceful and appropriate to odd, clumsy, garish and grotesque. Among the welter of new Gothic architecture, Street, Butterfield, Waterhouse, Webb and Burges, and the dynasties of Pugin and George Gilbert Scott, produced many successful public buildings. Indeed, if we compare the work of Pugin and of his Cambridge admirers at *The Ecclesiologist* with the fire-work display of Gothic building which followed Pugin's death, there are, to an unarchitectural eye, two obvious differences. First, Pugin's successors designed public, civic and corporate buildings: town halls, museums, hospitals and schools; insurance company buildings, banks, railway stations and hotels; monuments and war memorials; and private houses great and small. Before Pugin, neo-Gothic was first found decoratively in and around country houses, then seriously in churches, clergy houses, church schools and colleges. The Palace of Westminster is the first grand civic exception to these generalisations. Second, Gothic building after 1850, whether in stone or in brick, is richer than Pugin could normally afford to be; more flamboyant and more riskily polychromatic.

As the major Pre-Raphaelite painters left the Brotherhood behind, their painting was affected by medieval exemplars but they took fewer subjects from medieval history. The PRB and company had plenty of patrons wishing to beautify churches, public buildings and large houses. They also found plenty of buyers for their oil paintings, as art galleries in Birmingham and other cities still show. Canvases do not have to remain permanently on show, but buildings stand until destroyed. In the mid-twentieth century, curators of museums built by Victorians often withdrew Victorian canvases from public view. It was harder to hide the Midland Grand Hotel, designed by George Gilbert Scott for St Pancras Station in the 1860s. 'Saved' in the 1960s, after the employees of British Railways had walked out of the building ('leaving the lights on', according to a guide to the building), this tomato brick mega-Schloss is once again a luxury hotel. Behind it, St Pancras railway station houses the Eurostar terminal.

As Pre-Raphaelite painting went on, the early Christian component declined, except chez Holman Hunt. New sacred art gave way to new applications of Christian morality and pity to real and present misfortunes which might befall the middle-class family. In an age of comfort and gain, scenes of distress and loss struck home. Painters often depicted the dire consequences of sexual irresponsibility, in men and in women; the ruin to which gambling could lead; a child's grief at the sudden loss of a parent; emigration. The scrupulous reproduction of pristine natural detail, a foundational principle for Ruskin and for the PRB, passed into the naturalism and realism characteristic of the period. The nature represented began to include human nature: populated English fields and shores, or the suburban greenery of Clapham Common, rather than the primal rocks, waters, grasses and mountains prized by Ruskin. Solo uplift gave way to social downfall, or to the mediocrity of ordinary life. The gradual departure of Victorian painting from academic conventions of representation and composition, and from academic subjects, was in part due to the PRB's revolt against the Academy at which they had studied and in which Millais and Holman Hunt now exhibited. It was also due to the emergence of a new class of patrons, who wanted to see themselves represented, preferably in modern dress.

William Morris (1834–96) and Edward Burne-Jones (1833–98), the leading artists of the second growth of the Pre-Raphaelites, devoted themselves to differing goals: to social good and to dreamy beauty respectively. Morris was not an architect, nor quite the poet that many of his contemporaries thought him, nor did he persist with his painting. Rather, the energy he put into his various enter-prises, and the cumulative output of Morris and Co., had a wide-spread and permanent effect on British design, in the applied arts of house-building, furniture-making and printing, and on the decora-tive arts, especially wallpaper and fabrics. Among the enterprises of this human dynamo must be included the work done for him, espe-cially the construction of the Red House at Bexleyheath, London, his first marital home, completed in 1859: medievally built and furnished by Philip Webb for William and Jane Morris, and painted by their friends. Its vernacular boldness embodies the best ideals of the Pre-Raphaelites in their younger years.

The PRB went to art school, Morris and Edward Burne-Jones to Oxford. Burne-Jones went up from King Edward VI School in Birmingham, where the handsome Gothic hall had been decorated by Pugin. Although Burne-Jones developed his talent and became a highly skilled painter, he seems, in comparison with Rossetti, Holman

Hunt, Millais and Madox Brown, a painter and decorator. His most outstanding paintings made a great impact, but the cumulative effect of his unstinted production is decorative, his repeated motifs taking the form of lovely young women, rather than the plants and birds of William Morris's designs. Burne-Jones began by replicating Rossetti's dreamy interest in Woman, though his symbolic female forms do not have the afflicted gaze which Rossetti exchanged with his single images. As Burne-Jones passed into the gravitational field of Morris, he came under the spell of mythology. His serial female forms, and the graceful patterns in which he poses and drapes them, become more highly involuted, while the faces remain expressionless. The cult of beauty evoked from him some of Rossetti's stunned and stunning qualities, in a whiter shade of pale. Never a naturalistic painter, the trajectory of his career seems in retrospect to illustrate how the raw vigour of the PRB turned into the passive, aesthetic, symbolic and almost abstract kinds of mood-painting which emerged in the 1870s, though there are exceptions to this, for example the stained glass at Birmingham's Anglican cathedral (1885–7). Another grand exception, *The Beguiling of Merlin* (Plate 22), was exhibited at the Grosvenor Gallery in 1877, a gallery which launched Whistler and George Frederick Watts, and a style which became more stylised and, among the Decadents of the 1890s, eroticised or (as in this instance) post-eroticised. Sir Edward Burne-Jones (he was eventually made a baronet, like Millais) was admired by two of the most gifted artists of that decade, men who personified its opposed tendencies. Rudyard Kipling, Burne-Jones's nephew, 'adored' his uncle; Aubrey Beardsley 'idolised' him.[1]

For English people not specially interested in art the legacy of the PRB, in the dilutions of Morris and Burne-Jones, might today appear as accessories in the lifestyle of a stylish older lady: a Liberty scarf, Morris wallpapers, curtains and cushion-covers, children's fairy stories illustrated by Arthur Rackham. However faded these might now seem, they are items in that new world of consumer capitalism, the coming of which revolted Ruskin, a world to which the young PRB was fiercely opposed.

Even more opposed to it, and ever more opposed, was William Morris, although his Firm had to take on some mass-production processes to ensure its survival as a business. It could not afford to be a guild. Social concern was something that Morris could express in words but not in paint. Ford Madox Brown could, as is shown, for example, by two of his paintings of the 1850s, *Work* and *An English Autumn Afternoon*. The latter painting, now in Birmingham, has no 'message'. It shows an ordinary young couple looking down towards 'a literal transcript of the scenery around London, as looked at from Hampstead', as Madox Brown put it in the catalogue. 'What made you take such an ugly subject?' asked Ruskin. 'Because it lay out of the back window,' came the answer. Madox Brown painted exactly what he saw, which is what Ruskin had enjoined. He may be the first English artist to portray the poetry of the suburb.[2] This achievement is all Madox Brown's, but he would not have done it had he not been exposed to the Pre-Raphaelite programme. *An English Autumn Afternoon* is not a fruit sprung from the seeds of the Medieval Revival. But by their very rejection of Renaissance conventions as to elevation of subject and of style, and their reliance, instead, on unacademic principles of fidelity to perception, the PRB helped painters to look at an unstylish modern world, and allowed some of them to 'find the living world enough'. Though ugly to Ruskin and ordinary to Madox Brown, the setting now seems semi-rural and almost idyllic.

The urbanisation of Hampstead is recorded in *Work*, a small and crowded canvas reproduced as Plate 19; its details repay careful study. Title and painting handily illustrate the central subject in a society which was being transformed by the pressures of the industrial economy – in this instance, by London's growing need for drains. The human worth of physical labour, assumed and praised by Chaucer and Langland, and saluted in passing by Shakespeare, was not a preoccupation of the Augustan poets. It is not in Alexander Pope that the ploughman homeward plods his weary way. Rude forefathers and rural labour are idealised first by Gray, and then by Wordsworth, as in the elegiac figures of the shepherd and his wife in *Michael: A Pastoral*. In *Past and Present* and *Heroes and Hero-Worship*, Thomas Carlyle glorified hard work. His *Latter-Day Pamphlets* of 1850 were admired by Marx.

Now, for the first time since the illuminated manuscripts of the Middle Ages, manual work was depicted in English art. Ford Madox

Brown's picture has a programme. Hard labour – urban, not rural – is celebrated at the centre of the painting. Generations of American and Russian artists celebrate similar themes with less humour. Brown described his subjects: 'the British excavator … the young navvy in the pride of manly health and beauty; the strong, fully developed navvy who does his work and loves his beer; the selfish old bachelor navvy … the Paddy with his larry and his pipe in his mouth.'³ They cheerfully dig up the pavement in Heath Street, Hampstead, making the bare-footed and the nicely shod edge past on the left; the hole they are digging blocks entirely the passage of a mounted lady and a gent in a top hat at the back of the painting. That is their bad luck! The dogs in this painting have similarly symbolic functions. Leaning against a railing on the right are two believers in work and in workers, Thomas Carlyle, eyeing the onlooker from beneath the brim of his hat, and a smaller man in clerical dress, F.D. Maurice.

Madox Brown himself worked long and hard at his paintings. He began *Work* in 1852, adding in 1856 the figures of Carlyle, the prophet of the gospel of work, and Maurice, the Founder and Principal of the new Working Men's College in Great Ormond Street, London. *Work* was then exhibited. The Rev. Frederick Denison Maurice, who had attended Cambridge and Oxford and had been Professor of English Literature and of History at King's College, London, and then of Theology, had since 1848 been drawn into Christian Socialism: he wanted to apply the lessons of the gospel to the English poor. Associates of his in this work were the Rev. Charles Kingsley and Thomas Hughes, who in 1857 was to publish *Tom Brown's Schooldays*. Maurice had founded the college in 1854, and at a meeting held to raise funds, 'Ruskin's chapter "The Nature of Gothic" from *The Stones of Venice* had been given away as a pamphlet, with the words "and herein of the true function of the workman in art" significantly added to the title.'⁴

Ruskin taught drawing at the college, as did Rossetti, who was succeeded by Ford Madox Brown. If some fine artists taught in Great Ormond Street, so did some great owls. The Working Men studied grammar with F.J. Furnivall, a barrister who was behind the *New English Dictionary*, which became the *Oxford English Dictionary on Historical Principles*, edited by James Murray, now known as the

OED. Furnivall was also the founder of the Early English Text Society, the Chaucer Society, the Ballad Society and the Wyclif Society. The non-medieval societies he founded were fewer in number, but included the New Shakespeare Society, the Browning Society and the Shelley Society.[5] Some of the teachers at the college were not advocates or practitioners of medievalism. Thomas Hughes, for example, taught boxing. But the Working Men's College proves that medieval revivalists cannot be dismissed as escapists dwelling in ivory towers. The teachers at the college can certainly be charged with idealism and a willingness to serve. Social inequality was something Victorian society could both admit and address. Most of these teachers, like most of the revivalists, inclined to Christian Socialism; others were Christian Tories (Ruskin called himself a 'communist, reddest of the red'). Their paternalism and quixotism did some good, and exemplified the medieval ideals of chivalry, generosity and charity.

The men who taught the Working Men were, by later standards, factually ignorant about the Middle Ages whose virtues they commended; Pugin had confessed to this. An ignorance so widely shared is not culpable, but it made the Middle Ages a handy source to authorise one's wishes. A case in point is Madox Brown's picture of John of Gaunt listening to a running glossary of the scriptures in the vulgar tongue read aloud by a theologian to a court which preferred to speak French (see page 143). More transparently self-persuaded is the argument offered by Professor F.D. Maurice in 1866 to disprove the notion that Chaucer might have been a Wycliffite: 'He is not that. He is simply an Englishman. He hates Friars, because they are not English and not manly.'[6] Chaucer's Friar is wanton, but this acid portrait is not evidence either of a personal hatred of friars, or of a national conviction that all celibates are traitors, philanderers, wimps or worse. Thousands of friars have been as English as F.D. Maurice – Carmelites (such as St Simon Stock), Dominicans, Austin Friars, and Franciscans, such as Roger Bacon, John Peckham, Archbishop of Canterbury, and William of Ockham, whose Razor is still used by philosophers. Some of these friars had, like Maurice, held chairs at English universities. But Maurice, if thinking, was not thinking of history, one of the subjects he professed. Rather, as a married Anglican clergyman, he felt a present horror, as did Kingsley and other clergymen conscious of their manliness, at the return of celibate religious orders to the Anglican Church, at first for women, but now also for men. Maurice's reactions have less to do with the Middle Ages than with the foundation of the Cowley Fathers in 1865.

In one of the few surviving recordings of the voice of W.B. Yeats, the poet can be heard defending the way he is about to read poems including 'The Lake Isle of Innisfree'. He says, or rather declaims: 'I am going to read my poems with great emphasis upon their *rhythm*. I remember the *great English poet* William Morris coming in a rage out of some lecture hall where somebody had recited a passage out of his *Sigurd the Volsung*. "It gave me a *devil* of a lot of trouble", said Morris, "to get that thing into verse." It gave *me* a devil of a lot of trouble to get into verse the poems I am going to read, and that is why *I will not read* them as if they were *proose*.' Few today remember Morris as a great poet. He wrote a great deal of poetry, but his first volume, *The Defence of Guenevere* (1858), remains his best. Like Froissart and Malory, Morris writes of knights, but his tales have more gore than glamour. In the title poem, a remarkable dramatic monologue, Guenevere defends herself at length. This is shortly after the point at which King Arthur asks Sir Gawayne to 'bring my queen to the fire and there to have her judgement'. Malory resumes: 'And so the Queen was led forth without Carlisle, and anon she was despoiled into her smock. And then her ghostly father was brought to her, to be shriven of her misdeeds.'[7] In Morris's poem, Guenevere is beautifully dressed as she tells the listening knights how the friendship grew between her and Sir Lancelot. She beguiles her masculine audience with her beauty, to which her words often draw attention. She asks the listening knights how they could look at her white throat and believe that she could have been guilty of betraying her lord Arthur. Thus she turns the accusation back on her accusers, while also keeping the audience spellbound until Lancelot rides up to rescue her. As in Rossetti's and Burne-Jones's paintings, the theme is the almost irresistible power of female beauty, and an acknowledgement that the action of this power is indifferent to conventional morality.

Glamorous adultery was a theme enacted in the lives as well as the art of several of the Pre-Raphaelites and their circle. The taking of Lancelot and Guenevere as role-models (see Plate 20 and note 7) was an unhappy effect of the Medieval Revival, similar to the effect which the reading of D.H. Lawrence had on university English departments in the mid-twentieth century. We have seen that Rossetti did not heed the warning Dante gives in the story of Paolo and Francesca, who read together the story of Lancelot, and of how Love took charge of him, 'di Lancialotto, e come amor lo strinse'. This led them to a kiss with fatal (in Dante, eternal) consequences. Chaucer, in his *Nun's Priest's Tale* of Chauntecleer the Cock, Pertelote his favourite Hen and Reynard the Fox, also issues a sly warning against reading about Lancelot and Guenevere. The Nun's Priest says, of his story of talking animals:

This storie is also trewe, I undertake,
As is the book of Launcelot de Lake,
That wommen holde in ful greet reverence.

Another of the Nun's Priest's jokes at the expense of the Prioress who employs him is to have Chauntecleer translate, for the benefit of Pertelote, the Latin tag 'Mulier est hominis confusio' – 'Woman is Man's downfall' – as follows: 'Madame, the sentence of this Latyn is, / "Womman is mannes joye and al his blis." '[8]

The fatal power of love over men became a constant theme in the work of W.B. Yeats, who admired Rossetti as well as Morris. This Pre-Raphaelite theme of love's enchantment was first cast by Yeats into mythological forms taken from medieval Irish saga, and later into the more familiar types of Greek mythology. Yeats makes the beauty of Helen the sole cause of the Trojan War. Helen's beauty, destructive of men, of ships and of cities, persists as a theme of Ezra Pound's early *Cantos*. Yeats's early tales of Aengus bewitched or of Cuchulain led by the nose by beauty were in the tradition of the verse romances of William Morris in *The Earthly Paradise*. In this capacious common-place book, Morris retells many of the world's old stories, and with much skill. The form of the work is modelled upon Boccaccio's *Decameron* and Chaucer's *Canterbury Tales*.

Morris later visited Iceland, which had since its settlement been a democracy of farmers, with an annual parliament, and so for Morris an example of an ideal society. Partly for this reason, but more for love of the old stories and their world, he became devoted to retelling the heroic tales of the Germanic North, writing a verse epic, *Sigurd the Volsung*, and several long verse romances, *The House of the Wolfings*, *The Roots of the Mountains*, *The Story of the Glittering Plain*, *The Wood beyond the World* and *The Sundering Flood*. As their titles suggest, these tales are directly ancestral to J.R.R. Tolkien's prose romance *The Lord of the Rings*. The debt is overlooked, for Morris's long poems now lie unread. Poems of one hundred pages in length, such as Scott's *Marmion*, Tennyson's *The Idylls of the King*, Browning's *The Ring and the Book* and Longfellow's *Tales of a Wayside Inn*, were popular in their time. Thomas Hardy, who thought Homer's *Iliad* 'in the *Marmion* class', was a popular nineteenth-century novelist, but his epic verse drama *The Dynasts*, appearing in the twentieth century, was not popular. In the twenty-first century, English graduates who read poems read short poems, and long poems in selection. The gentle reader who is shocked at this is asked when he or she last read a poem of more than twenty pages in length.

At the end of his life, William Morris, who relaxed from a day's work at 'the Firm' by turning out a few score lines of verse, translated *Beowulf* into verse, with the help of a prose version made by the Anglo-Saxon philologist A.J. Wyatt, publishing it in 1895 as *The Tale of Beowulf Sometime King of the Folk of the Weder Geats*. It has been said that in order to read Morris's translation it is necessary to learn Anglo-Saxon. There is some truth in this unkindness. One line reads: 'Brake the bale-heedy, he with his wrath bollen'.[9] A more intelligible line describes the reception given by Grendel's mother to the hero of the poem when he dived into her underwater cave: 'She sat on her hall-guest and pulled out her sax'. This is clearly not the conduct prescribed to a noble Anglo-Saxon hostess, but to visualise the scene the reader must know that a 'seax' is a stabbing knife. Furnivall would have had no difficulty with this line, and many Victorian readers, keen on folk-etymology and folk-origins, will have recognised a 'sax' as a knife. Carlyle had reminded them that the Saxons of the Dark Ages were known for their use of the 'seax'. Hengist ordered his men to attack their British hosts with the words 'Saxons, draw your saxes', according to a story from Nennius's *History of the Britons* (c. 830), repeated by Geoffrey of Monmouth. The arms of the county of Essex are three saxes.

Before he reached for *Beowulf*, William Morris had already fallen into what J.R.R. Tolkien calls 'the etymological fallacy'. In his enthusiasm for democratic Saxon roots, he proposed that the Old English word 'leeds' should be resurrected to replace 'people', a word which in French use can sound *de haut en bas*. Morris also urged that instead of 'omnibus', a Latin word imported to England from France in 1809, to mean '[a carriage] for all', the English should substitute Morris's own compound word, 'folk-wain'. 'Folk-wains' would have anticipated the cars developed for the German 'Volk' in the 1930s, Volkswagen. I have read both Morris's *Beowulf* and his *Sigurd the Volsung*, the latter with pleasure. *Sigurd* swings, but *The Tale of Beowulf Sometime King of the Folk of the Weder Geats* does not. W.S. Mackail, Morris's biographer, reports, of the old man's habit of translating a few lines of *Beowulf* each day, that as the work progressed, 'his pleasure in the doing of it fell off'.[10]

Morris is known today as a designer and manufacturer. He also founded the Socialist League, and wrote the utopian fables *News from Nowhere* and *A Dream of John Ball* – Ball was the leader of the 1381 Peasants' Revolt (see Plate 21). Morris's fables are hardly read now. His most popular poetic work was *The Earthly Paradise* (1868–70), which begins:

Forget six counties overhung with smoke,
Forget the snorting steam and piston stroke,
Forget the spreading of the hideous town;
Think rather of the pack-horse on the down,
And dream of London, small, and white, and clean,
The clear Thames bordered by its gardens green.

These are the only lines usually quoted, by critics who then shake their heads at Morris's escapism. The contrasted cities are remarkably similar to those drawn by Pugin in his *Contrasts*, except that Christianity has been replaced by nature, a common Victorian substitution. The contrast between 'Forget . . . And dream' and Morris's later political activism is often remarked, and indeed John Betjeman would have been proud to have written the lines quoted above. On the eve of the Second World War, Auden wrote, in his elegy for W.B. Yeats, that 'Poetry makes nothing happen'. This lesson, drawn by

Auden from his own recent experience, has provoked protest, perhaps because, at the level of wars between nations, it is so evidently true. But 'In Memory of W.B. Yeats' ends with an act of faith – that poems can make things happen in the lives of individuals:

> In the deserts of the heart
> Let the healing fountain start,
> In the prison of his days,
> Teach the free man how to praise.[11]

To recall other views of the use-value of art, it is enough to mention two sayings of Yeats: 'In dreams begins responsibility', the epigraph of *Responsibilities* (1914), and a remark of his, recalled by Ezra Pound: 'Nothing affects these people / Except our conversation',[12] a seigneurial version of Shelley's claim that poets are the world's legislators.

As the opening lines of *The Earthly Paradise* suggest, the movement of its verse and the unfolding of the sense are pleasantly clear and fluent, and Morris's narrative runs well. There is the charm of a novel manner. Yet after some pages, pleasure in the reading falls off. There seems no reason why the story or the poet should stop or why the reader should go on. Morris can almost be heard to hum as he turns his verses. There is an analogy with the tapestries and wallpapers produced by Morris and Co.: wallpaper should please the eye but not detain it for long.[13] Burne-Jones's friezes and frescoes are properly decorative, but it is unsatisfactory to find the same quality in the saints of his stained-glass windows. *The Earthly Paradise* is less passive than Burne-Jones's work, but similarly mesmeric. It is well done, but why is it being done at all?

During his detention in a US Army centre outside Pisa in 1945, Ezra Pound found a Roman Catholic chaplain's handbook:

> 'I have not done unnecessary manual labour'
>   says the R.C. chaplain's field book
>   (preparation before confession)[14]

The question to which the first line is an answer is a medieval one, but William Morris might not have liked to answer it. *The Earthly*

Paradise has a parallel in the Kelmscott Chaucer, which Morris designed with the help of Burne-Jones, and produced himself. It imitates the black-letter typography of those early printed books which imitated the handwritten letter-forms used in manuscripts, and whose black-and-white woodcuts replaced hand-painted manuscript illuminations. The Kelmscott Chaucer is an original which looks like a facsimile: a fascinating object, it is a trophy of art rather than a book to read. The problem with *The Earthly Paradise* is not that it is escapist, but that its purpose escapes the reader, who likes it, lays it down and forgets to pick it up again. The stories of Tennyson's *Idylls of the King* can flag, but they are unified by common characters, and their themes glance at the present. Tennyson also knew why some poetry has to be written:

> But, for the unquiet heart and brain
> > A use in measured language lies;
> > The sad mechanic exercise,
> Like dull narcotics, numbing pain.
>
> > > > *In Memoriam*, v

Like King Arthur, Morris had plenty of pain in his later life, but in his narcotic later poetry he does not seem to have known very well what he was doing.

* * *

It is a contention of this book that the French Revolution occasioned reflections, in Edmund Burke and others, which gave a sudden and more serious turn to the revived British interest in the romances of chivalry; and also that the vogue for Scott's 'histories' in verse and prose intensified and popularised this development. After the defeat of Napoleon, however, it was the Industrial Revolution, and its social consequences, which began to fuel the Medieval Revival. What could or should be done about Disraeli's Two Nations, the Rich and the Poor? Cobbett, Pugin, Disraeli, Carlyle and Ruskin thought that there was something to be learned from the Middle Ages here. But on how to approach Disraeli's problem, medieval revivalists, like others, divided. Many of the heirs of Ruskin, 'a Tory of the school of

Homer and Sir Walter Scott', were Socialists, notably Morris. Many Victorians, for whom the Christian dignity of human labour was an article of faith, were troubled by the harsh conditions of English industrial workers. Some of them, like Mrs Gaskell's husband, worked as clergymen in industrial parishes. This chapter concludes by looking at the case of Gerard Manley Hopkins, who spent most of his adult life in prayer, in study or in parish work of this kind. In considering the pressures which, at this juncture, society and religion brought to bear upon a sensitive and conscientious man, Hopkins is clearly a special case, if a case of special interest. He was not an advocate or exponent of the Medieval Revival, for by his day the medieval had already been revived and was available to those who wanted it. Yet the medieval informed key aspects of his life and work.

Newman's *Apologia pro Vita Sua*, a response to Kingsley's smear that Newman, like the Catholic clergy generally, did not hold truth for its own sake to be a virtue, was published during Hopkins's second year as a classical scholar at Balliol College, Oxford. In his *Apologia* Newman explains that the Tractarians regarded Anglican bishops as successors to the apostles, and the Church of England as part of the divinely instituted universal Church, the mystical body of Christ. In the eighteenth century such a view, although a central part of the English Church's own formulas, would itself have been regarded as something of a Gothic survival. When Newman, in *Tract XC*, had interpreted the Anglican Thirty-Nine Articles in this sense, his bishop, the Bishop of Oxford, had disagreed; and Newman had resigned, in 1842. His *Apologia* satisfied many readers that Dr Newman was not a stranger to the truth. The undergraduate Hopkins went to Birmingham to ask Newman to receive him into the Catholic Church – to the acute distress of his family. He then joined the Society of Jesus, and after the long Jesuit training served as a priest, chiefly in industrial parishes. His last appointment was as Professor of Greek at the new Catholic university in Ireland. Newman had been the first rector there, delivering the lectures which became *The Idea of a University*. In Dublin, Father Hopkins S.J. felt 'at a third remove', and died there of typhoid in 1889. Like Newman, Hopkins conceived of the Catholic Church as an organic continuation of the church of the apostles, and his conception of society was likewise organic and visionary, but not egalitarian. Hopkins's letter to Robert Bridges of 2 August 1871 indicates some of his attitudes to this question:

> I am afraid some great revolution is not far off. Horrible to say, in a manner I am a Communist. [*Hopkins adds a footnote: 'I have little reason to be Red: it was the red Commune [in Paris in 1870] that murdered five of our fathers recently.'*] Their ideal bating some things is nobler than that professed by any secular statesman I know of ... Besides it is just. – I do not mean the means of getting to it are. But it is a dreadful thing for the greatest and most necessary part of a very rich nation to live a hard life without dignity, knowledge, comforts, delight, or hope in the midst of plenty – which plenty they make. They profess that they do not care what they wreck and burn, the old civilisation and order must be destroyed. This is a dreadful look out but what has the old civilisation done for them? As it at present stands in England it is itself in great measure founded on wrecking. But they got none of the spoils, they came in for nothing but harm from it then and thereafter. England has grown hugely wealthy but this wealth has not reached the working classes; I expect it has made their condition worse. Beside this iniquitous order the old civilisation embodies another order mostly old and what is new in direct entail from the old, the old religion, learning, law, art, etc and all the history that is preserved in standing monuments. But as the working classes have not been educated they know next to nothing of all this and cannot be expected to care if they destroy it ...[15]

Hopkins wrote several poems on people in humble roles, and on young people about to choose their way in life. Three of his poems are on working men: 'Felix Randal', and a later pair, 'Tom's Garland' and 'Harry Ploughman'. Other poems also involve the Christian dignity of labour, including 'The Windhover', which Hopkins thought the best thing he ever wrote. A line towards the end of this sonnet includes the sentence 'sheer plod makes plough down sillion shine'. 'Sillion' is 'furrow', archaic in English but familiar in French. It comes in the refrain of the first verse of *La Marseillaise*, the revolutionary anthem of the French Republic, which encourages *citoyens* so to defend themselves against their enemies '*[Qu'un sang impur]* / *Abreuve nos sillons*': '[That an impure blood] / should slake our furrows'. The Christian Hopkins associates the furrow made by the plough not with the impure blood of enemies but with daily sweat for daily bread: the lot of mankind since Adam (see Plate 21). For medieval Christian social thought, as seen in *Piers Plowman*, this gave physical work a special value: hence the maxim *laborare est orare* – 'to work is to pray'. It also made the ploughman the archetype of man: the labourer whose labour provides the archetypal food for all. That is why, for Hopkins, the ploughman's hard work makes the earth turned over by the plough to shine in the eye of heaven. His two poems on working men refer to this. The first, a sonnet written in Liverpool in 1880, begins: 'Felix Randal the farrier, O is he dead then? my duty all ended'. It ends: 'When thou at the random grim forge, powerful among peers, / Didst fettle for the great grey dray-horse his bright and battering sandal!'

Felix Randal was a parishioner to whom Hopkins had brought the sacraments. Tom and Harry, the protagonists of the other poems, have typical names. Perhaps Hopkins recalled the Song sung by Winter at the end of Shakespeare's *Love's Labour's Lost*:

When icicles hang by the wall,
And Dick the shepherd blows his nail,
And Tom bears logs into the hall,
And milk comes frozen home in pail.

The Tom of 'Tom's Garland' has a mate, Dick; Harry is the third. 'Harry Ploughman' begins: 'Hard as hurdle arms, with a broth of goldish flue / Breathed round; the rack of ribs; the scooped flank . . .' Admiration for a masculine physique was expressed easily by Victorian men, as with Ford Madox Brown and his British and Irish navvies. Madox Brown was the painter, Hopkins the poet, but the poet's analysis of the Ploughman's physique is almost as anatomical as a study by Leonardo. In the sonnet's octave, Hopkins makes a 'roll-call' of Harry's features, and orders his 'one crew' to 'fall to'. The sestet begins: 'He leans to it,

Harry bends, look. Back, elbow and liquid waist / In him, all quail to
the wallowing o' the plough: 's cheek crimsons ...' Hopkins portrays
this ploughman from head to foot, ending with his heavy boots and
the gleam of the turned furrow, the 'sillion' of 'The Windhover':

> ... broad in bluff hide his frowning feet lashed! raced
> With, along them, cragiron under and cold furls –
> With-a-fountain's shining-shot furls.

The previous poem ended with the drayhorse's 'bright and battering
sandal'. We do not see Harry's horse but Harry following the plough
as it wallows. He is the type of the unselfish hard worker, like Chaucer's
Ploughman, and is presented externally, like the horse he guides. In
Christian analogy, Harry is a type of humanity (he is much more a
type than a person). The horse has shared man's labour since the
Middle Ages. At the time of the Paris Commune, ploughs were drawn
by horses (the poem was finished in Ireland, but Hopkins thinks of
England). In one of the poems in A.E. Housman's *A Shropshire Lad*
(1896), the voice of a dead farm worker asks 'Is my team ploughing?'
Although ploughing with horses was not so common by 1945, George
Orwell chose a horse to stand for the uncomplaining worker, the
sacrificial Boxer of *Animal Farm*.

The first poem in the pair, 'Tom's Garland: upon the Unemployed',
was also finished in Dromore in September 1887. Tom is not a farm
worker, but 'Tom Navvy', a carefree labourer: 'Tom seldom sick, /
Seldomer heartsore'. Tom then bursts out with:

> Commonweal
> Little I reck ho! lacklevel in, if all had bread:
> What! country is honour enough in all us.

Social inequality wouldn't worry Tom, if all had bread; to be English
is enough of an honour. Hopkins explained the poem to Bridges in a
letter of 10 February 1888:

> ... As St. Paul and Plato and Hobbes and everybody says,
> the commonwealth or well ordered human society is like one

man; a body with many members and each its function; some
higher, some lower, but all honourable, from the honour which
belongs to the whole. The head is the sovereign, who has no
superior but God ... The foot is the daylabourer, and this is
armed with hobnail boots ... the garlands of nails they wear ...
But presently I remember that this is all very well for those who
are in, however low in, the common weal; but that the curse of
our times is that many do not share it, that they are outcasts from
it and have neither security or splendour; that they share care
with the high and obscurity with the low, but wealth or comfort
with neither. And this state of things, I say, is the origin of Loafers,
Tramps, Cornerboys, Roughs, Socialists and other pests of
society.[16]

Hopkins died in 1889, and most of his poems were published by
Bridges in 1918. The letter gives up its analogy in a baffled outburst
which helps with the sonnet's abrupt final couplet. The despair and
rage caused by unemployment make the day-labourer, who is the
admirable 'foot' of the body of the Commonweal, degenerate into
dog and wolf: 'This, by Despair, bred Hangdog dull; by Rage, /
Manwolf, worse; and their packs infest the age.'

Lilies that fester smell far worse than weeds. Tom is not a lily, but
Hopkins has an exalted idea of this 'foot', this member of the body of
society. The poet's exaltation comes from a high-strung Christian
idealism, an intense sense of human splendour and misery, and of
insoluble social inequities.

Hopkins found some of his ideas on poverty and the unemployed
confirmed in William Cobbett's *A History of the Protestant Reformation
in England and Ireland; showing how that Event has Impoverished the
main Body of the People in those Countries; and containing a List of the
Abbeys, Priories, Nunneries, Hospitals, and other Religious Foundations
in England, and Wales, and Ireland, Confiscated, Seized on, or Alienated,
by the Protestant 'Reformation' Sovereigns and Parliaments, in a series
of Letters addressed to all Sensible and Just Englishmen*, produced in
parts from 1824 to 1825, and published in two volumes in London in
1829. Hopkins wrote to Dixon: 'the most valuable and striking part of
[Cobbett's *Reformation*] to me is the doctrine about the origin of

pauperism'.[17] (Tudor law punished 'sturdy beggars'. Cobbett blames
the Reformation for making unemployment a social misdemeanour,
and for categorising paupers as a burden on the state which the state
should seek to avoid.) Hopkins accepted inequality as a fact, and took
seriously the obligations it entailed: the rich to care for the poor, the
strong to protect the weak – medieval chivalric ideals. The marriage
of 'One Nation' Tory paternalism with a maternal Christian Socialism
produced the Welfare State.

The idiosyncrasy and extreme abridgement of Hopkins's expression meant he often had to unpack the meaning of his poems, even
to Bridges and Dixon, both of them classicists and Christian poets
like himself. Hopkins began the above letter: 'I laughed outright and
often, but very sardonically, to think you and the Canon could not
construe my last sonnet; that he had to write to you for a crib. It is
plain I must go no further on this road: if you and he cannot understand me, who will?'

Canon Dixon (1833–1900) had been at school in Birmingham
with Burne-Jones. At Oxford, he became an associate of the PRB.[18]
Dixon became a clergyman, and briefly taught Hopkins at Highgate
School, London, where T.S. Eliot was later 'the American master'
when Betjeman was a pupil. Young Hopkins, like Dixon and Rossetti,
admired the poetry of Keats. Minuteness of detail is the most Pre-
Raphaelite feature of Hopkins's poetry, as is already apparent in his
schoolboy poem, 'The Escorial'.

In a letter of 1 December 1881, Hopkins gave his old teacher a
lesson in the history of the 'Prae-raphaelites': 'This modern medieval
school is descended from the Romantic school (Romantic is a bad
word) of Keats, Leigh Hunt, Hood, indeed of Scott early in the
century ... Keats's school chooses medieval keepings, not pure nor
drawn from the middle ages direct but as brought down through that
Elizabethan tradition of Shakspere [sic] and his contemporaries
which died out in such men as Herbert and Herrick.'[19] Hopkins goes
on to the Lake poets, Byron's school and other subjects, and ends:
'Now since this time, Tennyson and his school seem to me to have
struck a mean or compromise between Keats and the medievalists
on the one hand and Wordsworth and the Lake School on the other.'
Literary genealogy interested Hopkins and Dixon, for both were

members of that 'modern medieval school' of 'Keats and the medievalists'. Hopkins concludes that, 'The Lake School expires in Keble
and Faber and Cardinal Newman'.[20]

Hopkins's adult poems are medieval when the subject requires, as
in 'Duns Scotus's Oxford', where the 'dapple-eared lily' and the city
'branchy between towers' are Gothic. In this poem he calls that phil-
osophical friar, 'Of realty the rarest-veinèd unraveller'. Likewise, in
'The Windhover', the 'dauphin' of the kingdom of daylight brings in
French chivalry, 'chevalier' and the 'sillion' made by the plough.
Hopkins's language is medieval when appropriate. He has little of the
archaism common in Victorian poetry; exceptions are the 'housel' of
'The Bugler's First Communion'; or ' 's cheek crimsons', quoted above.
Hopkins once wrote to Bridges, who was trying to interest him in the
'Saxon' English of Doughty's *Arabia Deserta*:

> You say it is free from the taint of Victorian English. H'm. Is it
> free from the taint of Elizabethan English? Does it not stink of
> that? for the sweetest flesh turns to corruption. Is not Elizabethan
> English a corpse these centuries? No one admires, regrets,
> despairs over the death of the style, the living masculine native
> rhetoric of that age, more than I do; but ' 'tis gone, 'tis gone, 'tis
> gone' . . . to write in an obsolete style is affectation . . .

Hopkins's idioms – 'these centuries', ' 'tis gone' – mock 'Elizabethan'
English.[21] Hopkins's use of older English was more radical than archaic.
He often chooses Saxon words, to 'rinse and wring the ear'; physical
words like 'thicket' and 'thorp', 'banks' and 'brakes', 'delve', 'hew' and
'hack'. More idiosyncratically, he coins words, such as 'selve', meaning
to show a unique nature, and 'unselve' – to destroy it. His use of the
compound nouns held to be natural to Germanic languages is both
old and new. Anglo-Saxon had used compound nouns to extend its
wordhoard, as Morris wished modern English to extend its wordhoard with 'folkwain'. But the compound words in Anglo-Saxon poetry
are traditional – their 'whale-road' was to them as everyday as 'railroad'
is in American English. In marked contrast, Hopkins's new-coined
compounds are 'original, spare, strange', and singular. Sometimes, as he
knew, he went too far on this road.

Hopkins's 'sprung rhythm', a topic where many have ventured to tread, owes little to medieval English verse, and less than is often supposed. In the Preface to his unpublished poems, Hopkins says that 'the old English verse seen in *Pierce Ploughman*' is 'in sprung rhythm', a claim discussed below.[22] He claims also that sprung rhythm is 'the rhythm of common speech and of written prose'. English is indeed a stressed language, but in a discussion of English versification this is a first step only. Hopkins finds sprung rhythm in nursery rhymes and weather saws, illustrating this elsewhere with 'Ding dong bell, pussy's in the well'.[23] Finally, he believes that no post-Elizabethan English poem is in sprung rhythm. This may be so, although, as we have seen, Coleridge had explained in the Preface to his metrical romance, *Christabel*, that its metre is 'founded on a new principle: namely, that of counting in each line the accents, not the syllables'. To the modern reader, the effect of the metre of *Christabel* and *The Lay of the Last Minstrel* is reminiscent of Percy's ballads and romances, and consciously so. All too often, however, the verse of the metrical romances relaxes into what Chaucer calls 'doggerel', which is also the word used of Langland by Hopkins. This weakness also affects Coleridge's 'The Rime of the Ancyent Marinere'. Hopkins's style lacks any such redundancy.

Hopkins's reference to the 'old English verse seen in *Pierce Ploughman*' has been misunderstood. For though the English of Langland is old, it is not the Old English of historical linguistics: the Anglo-Saxon of *c*. 600–1100. Langland wrote in what scholars have since classed as Middle English, dating from *c*. 1100 to 1470. Hopkins's claim about *Piers Ploughman*, and the confusion of 'old' with 'Old', has created the widespread but erroneous belief that his sprung rhythm is modelled on Anglo-Saxon. Hopkins did not claim this, and knew that *Piers Ploughman* was not an Anglo-Saxon poem. His point is that its versification counts stresses rather than syllables. In fact, however, Langland's versification and language lack the economy of Old English verse, which differs from his in crucial respects. When Hopkins tried to read *Piers Ploughman*, he was disappointed in it, and judged that its version of 'Anglo saxon verse' was 'in a degraded and doggerel shape'. He twice mentions in 1882/3 that he is beginning to read Anglo-Saxon in order to ascertain whether or not it is a precedent for the sprung rhythm he had been practising since 1876. We don't know what he began to read. That is all the evidence we have that Hopkins had read Anglo-Saxon verse. We do not know that he could have understood its sense, still less its metre. The true basis of Anglo-Saxon versification began to be understood in Germany in 1873, too late for Hopkins to hear about it.[24]

Since it is hard to be certain of understanding Hopkins's ideas of sprung rhythm, one cannot say whether Old English or Middle English verse is 'sprung'. But it is certain that Anglo-Saxon verse was not the model for Hopkins's verse. All they have in common is the English language. Old English verse alliterates regularly and system-atically, whereas Hopkins does so gratuitously. Hopkins uses rhyme, which is the opposite of alliteration, and is rigorously stanzaic, whereas Old English verse adds line to line without limit. Indeed, all the poems so far discussed are sonnets with Italian rhyme-scheme, octave and sestet. Hopkins was not influenced by Old English verse, but by reading American books about the nature of English words: books of a nativist and primitivist tendency, which affected his ideas about word-choice and word-formation.[25]

Hopkins's poetry is medievalist when he writes on medieval occasions, as in: 'To What Serves Mortal Beauty'. His answer to this question is that the faces of some boys in the Roman slave market caught the eye of a future Pope, Gregory the Great: 'lovely lads once, wet-fresh windfalls of war's storm, / How then should Gregory, a father, have gleanèd else'. Gregory decided that these angelic-looking but pagan Angles should be evangelised. *Ergo*, mortal beauty serves immortal beauty. Hopkins reminds the English that it was a Roman, indeed a papal, mission which brought Christianity to Canterbury.

The question, 'To what serves' is medieval: Latin, Thomist, Aristotelian, teleological. Philosophy is the final aspect in which Hopkins might be considered medievalist. He delighted in the indi-viduating and intuitionist philosophy of Duns Scotus, a Franciscan from Duns in Berwickshire, who had taught in Oxford. Scotus persuaded Paris that the Virgin whom the angel hailed as 'full of grace' must have been so since her conception. Hence the sonnet's last line: 'Who fired France for Mary without spot'. (Immaculacy is an additional reason for the 'lily' in 'Duns Scotus's Oxford'.) Hopkins

liked Scotus and was grounded in the theology of Aquinas, the official theologian of the Jesuits. The Society of Jesus is not medieval, but
Aquinas was made the standard of orthodoxy at the Council of Trent.
Hopkins's translations of Aquinas's Eucharistic hymns are in common
use, and probably known to more people than his poems are.

Another poem medieval in subject is 'The Blessed Virgin Mary
Compared to the Air We Breathe'. This comparison is more metaphysical than medieval, but Hopkins was a nature poet who saw all of
nature, not simply human nature, as transformed by the Incarnation.
Whether medieval or metaphysical, what now seems most sadly pre-
modern about Hopkins is his habit of thinking and envisioning in
terms of analogy and symbol: everything in creation speaks of Christ.
Hopkins is the clearest sign that the 'medieval' strand in English literature would henceforward be linked with a vision of the world and of
human life rooted in Christian beliefs, and that this vision would
eventually identify itself as explicitly Catholic or Anglo-Catholic.

'The Windhover', admired for the intensity of its natural description and empathy, is dedicated to Christ our Lord. It is incarnational
from its first line, and based on analogy: 'I saw this morning morning's minion, king-'. The bird is the darling son of the morning,
coming as heir apparent to the kingdom of daylight. We do not readily
recognise this as a natural augury of the Second Coming, the dawning
of the Kingdom of Heaven. Modern natural philosophy, what Blake
called 'single Vision, and Newton's sleep', saw no evidence of a supernatural element in nature, and doubted the hypothesis of a supernatural element in human nature. Hopkins had made scientific
contributions to the journal *Nature* concerning the effect of the erup-
tion of Krakatoa on the earth's atmosphere. He asserts metaphysical
vision with urgency, because the natural science of his day had begun
to see no need for it. In his 'Hurrahing in Harvest' Hopkins wrote: 'I
walk, I lift up, I lift up heart, eyes, / Down all that glory in the heavens
to glean our Saviour'. A record of personal experience, this is also an
act of faith, drawing on the injunction in the Mass to 'Lift up your
hearts', and on the Psalms: 'The heavens shew forth the glory of God,
and the firmament declareth the work of his hands'; and 'I have lifted
up my eyes to the mountains, from whence cometh my help'. After the
harvest, he 'gleans' our Saviour, looking carefully at the earth, and at

the heavens, for the remaining grains are very fine, and as easily missed as a violet by a mossy stone.

A true medieval lyric such as 'I sing of a maiden / that is makeles' employs the biblical image of the 'dew in Aprille that falleth on the grass' as an analogy for Mary's conception of Jesus. In the Middle Ages, natural supernaturalism needed no assertion; the particular was the universal. To assert or reassert such a vision is, then, medievalist rather than medieval. Yet it is also Romantic. Hopkins asserts the significance of nature, what it signifies. In this he is the heir of the Coleridge who in 'Frost at Midnight' had prayed for his baby son:

> so shalt thou see and hear
> The lovely shapes and sounds intelligible
> Of that eternal language, which thy God
> Utters, who from eternity doth teach
> Himself in all, and all things in himself.
> Great universal Teacher! He shall mould
> Thy spirit, and by giving make it ask.[26]

Coleridge called his son Hartley, after the associationist philosopher who had developed Locke's empirical derivation of ideas from sensations, but his second son Berkeley, after the idealist philosopher Bishop Berkeley. Coleridge held that the mind is divinely inspired, that its creativity comes from God, and that the perception of phenomena by the mind is a repetition of, and participates in, the continuous agency of divine creation. Of this he almost convinced Wordsworth, at that time a pantheist. Hopkins, however, sees in Nature, not only God the Creator, but Christ our Saviour.

CHAPTER 10

Among the Lilies and the Weeds

HOPKINS, WHISTLER, BURNE-JONES, BEARDSLEY

Then was he ware where there came from a wood there fast by a
knight all armed upon a white horse, with a strange shield of
strange arms.

> Sir Thomas Malory, 'Sir Lancelot and Queen Guenevere',
> *Le Morte Darthur*, Book XVII[1]

I'll tell you everything I can;
There's little to relate.

> Lewis Carroll, 'The White Knight's Song',
> *Through the Looking Glass*

The reader has been presented in earlier chapters with the Medieval
Revival in its successive aspects. The focus has moved from literary
history to political thought, to poetry, to the ethical implications
of architecture, to social and religious thought, and to painting,
returning regularly to literature. All are outworkings of the Medieval
Revival, which took different forms as times changed, and was felt in
different areas. But after the early 1850s, when the revival had
succeeded, developments which are both new and truly medievalist
become rare. From this point onwards, the Medieval Revival passes
into general medievalism. Furthermore, after 1870 or so, medievalism has no single story. Gradually leaving behind its historical/
textual moorings, it diffused into general culture in various combi-
nations, sometimes as a minor component, whether vital or merely
decorative. What is looked at in the following pages may not be part
of a main stream, and does not follow a single course. Medievalism is
variously hybridised in the eclectic culture of late Victorian England.
What is selected may strike specialists as atypical, depending on the
illustrations chosen, and the field.

To some, the latter part of the last chapter will already have suggested this clearly enough. There, the case of Gerard Manley Hopkins was held up to the question, 'Is he significantly indebted to medieval example?' To which the answer was, 'Up to a point'. And however special and interesting the case of Hopkins may be, 'Up to a point' might be the verdict in any other case arising between 1860 and 1900. Some of the original revivalists persisted in the same causes, notably John Ruskin and William Morris. Academic medievalism developed, for instance, in the volumes of the Early English Text Society (founded 1864), and in Walter Skeat's edition of Chaucer, in the work of such notable historians as F.W. Maitland, and in the collection and conservation of medieval manuscripts in libraries and objects in museums. Some exponents of the Medieval Revival, however, went on to follow other courses and causes.

As far as poetic medievalism is concerned, three extracts from a letter which Hopkins wrote to Dixon show how things were going. It was in this letter from one poet to another, written at Stonyhurst on 4 June 1878, that Hopkins first made contact with his former teacher: 'Your poems had a medieval colouring like Wm. Morris's and the Rossetti's and others but none seemed to me to have it so unaffectedly.' Certain poems of Dixon's, Hopkins writes, were '... purer in style, as it seems to me, and quite as fine in colouring and drawing as Morris' stories in the *Paradise*, so far as I have read them, fine as those are.' The straightforwardness of these comparisons shows how far medievalism had been accepted. A further sentence of praise for the Canon's poetry sounds a new note: 'The extreme delight I felt when I read the line "Her eyes like lilies shaken by the bees" was more than any single line in poetry ever gave me and now that I am older I could not be so strongly moved by it if I were to read it for the first time.'[2] This has both Hopkins's naked susceptibility and his self-analytic turn. What is new, almost shocking, is the aesthetic feeling. Aestheticism had begun to affect the lives of artists who lacked Hopkins's discipline. Public misgiving about the direction in which some poetry and art were going had begun to appear. Dixon's line is striking, and it may seem excessive to pay much attention to the reaction to it of so unusual a person as Hopkins. But the rarest human beings take some colour from their times. Nevertheless it is odd to think that this reaction could almost have appeared in a letter by Walter Pater, one of Hopkins's tutors at Oxford, and a sponsor of English aestheticism.

The strength of Hopkins's reaction to the line in question is, in the frankness of its emotion, generally Victorian. Victorian art and society easily expressed the kind of intensely subjective reaction which we find in Keats's 'Oh for a life of sensations rather than thoughts', and Shelley's 'I fall upon the thorns of life, I bleed.' Confessions of emotion are found at climactic moments of works by Tennyson, Browning, Dickens and George Eliot, and not only at such moments or in the works of artists of this order. Victorian painters and writers were drawn to domestic distress and public disaster. The artless William McGonagall, self-styled 'Poet and Tragedian', knew that audiences would listen more readily to the ballads he composed and recited if they told of things such as the Tay Bridge disaster. His poem on this collapse of a railway bridge in a storm, when a train plunged into the Tay, and seventy-five passengers and crew lost their lives, begins 'Beautiful Railway Bridge of the Silv'ry Tay'. A shipwreck, with loss of life, is the subject of G.M. Hopkins's two longest poems, 'The Wreck of the Deutschland' and 'The Loss of the Eurydice'. Shipwrecks were a preoccupation of the Hopkins family, since the father, Manley, made his living by marine insurance. More to the point, Gerard, in the year in which he first wrote to Dixon, also began a verse play on the martyrdom of St Winefred. His three longest works are about the sudden death of Christians, in a universe created and ruled by divine providence. These poems resemble *Lycidas*, Milton's elegy upon the death of a fellow student intended for the priesthood, who drowned crossing the Irish Sea. Hopkins's three poems concentrate upon the shock of 'what the unsearchable dispose / Of highest wisdom brings about', the closing words of *Samson Agonistes*.

But Hopkins's reaction to 'Her eyes like lilies shaken by the bees' – shaken in the way the Lady of Shalott was by the sight of Sir Lancelot – is aesthetic as well as emotional. Much late Victorian poetry and art took an ocular and aesthetic turn, a turn most conveniently illustrated here by the changing career of D.G. Rossetti, already sketched in Chapter 7, but now to be looked at from another side. In 1849 Rossetti had exhibited *The Girlhood of Mary Virgin*, a painting now in the Birmingham Museum and Art Gallery, accompanying it

with two sonnets of explanation, one of which was inscribed on the
picture frame. The more awkward of the two, printed in the exhibition catalogue, begins, 'These are the symbols'. In the picture, in front
of Mary and her mother Anne, in a vase placed on top of a pile of
books, stands a lily, emblem of purity. 'Mary Virgin' translates the
Italian 'Maria Virgine', and the whole sonnet is in an early Tuscan
form of English:

> The books (whose head
> Is golden Charity, as Paul hath said)
> Those virtues are wherein the soul is rich:
>
> Therefore on them the lily standeth, which
> Is Innocence, being interpreted.[3]

Elizabeth Prettejohn's 1997 book about Rossetti and his circle in the
years after the break-up of the PRB is biographical and psychological. But it clearly shows, not least by means of its illustrations, just
how far the image of Woman became central to Rossetti's art after its
Pre-Raphaelite phase – erotic on the one hand, exotic and occult on
the other: mysterious, and also full of sexual yearning.

At Tudor House, Cheyne Walk, D.G. Rossetti was at the centre of
a bohemian circle of men, including the poet Swinburne and the
painter Solomon and also James McNeill Whistler, who had studied
art in Paris. Visitors included Morris and Burne-Jones, and also
George Meredith, the model for Wallis's *The Death of Chatterton*.[4]
The poet-painter himself attracted gossip as well as fame, and
managed his own PR better than his unhappy life. It could have been
of this set that Hopkins was thinking when he wrote to Robert
Bridges on 3 February 1883 that, 'As a fact poets and men of art are, I
am sorry to say, by no means necessarily or commonly gentlemen.'[5]
Rossetti did not exhibit publicly after the year 1850, when he was
twenty-two, but published his poetry. He arranged that his *Poems*
of 1870 should be reviewed by his friends, Swinburne and Morris.
But in the next year these poems drew a stinging attack, entitled
'The Fleshly School of Poetry', a general denunciation of the tendencies of Rossetti's artistic circle. The (pseudonymous) review was by

Robert Buchanan, a young Scot embittered by criticisms he had received from Swinburne and W.M. Rossetti. Buchanan began by saying that:

> the fleshly gentlemen have bound themselves by solemn league and covenant to extol fleshliness as the distinct and supreme end of poetic and pictorial art; to aver that poetic expression is greater than poetic thought, and by inference that the body is greater than the soul, and sound superior to sense; and that the poet, properly to develop his poetic faculty, must be an intellectual hermaphrodite, to whom the very facts of day and night are lost in a whirl of aesthetic terminology.[6]

'Hermaphrodite' alludes to Swinburne's poem in praise of the statue of the classical Hermaphrodite in the Louvre. This was one of his *Poems and Ballads* of 1866; others celebrate Sappho's love, and compare the Virgin Mary unfavourably with Venus.

Some of Buchanan's barbs drew blood, but his pseudonymous attack had less effect than the thunderbolt Ruskin launched at a painting by Whistler, exhibited on the opening day of the Grosvenor Gallery in 1877, a society event attended by seven thousand people. Rossetti had written a letter to *The Times* explaining why he was *not* exhibiting – he was not sufficiently satisfied with anything he had done. Instead, he recommended the work of his protégé, Edward Burne-Jones – 'a name', Rossetti wrote, 'representing the loveliest art we have'. The work of Burne-Jones featured largely in the exhibition, as did that of painters outside Rossetti's circle, such as G.F. Watts and Frederick Leighton, and some French artists. The Grosvenor Gallery, owned and built by Sir Coutts Lindsay in New Bond Street, Mayfair, was an opulent new venture, a new kind of gallery filling a gap in the market between private showings and Royal Academy grandeur. Lindsay's 'curious mixture of aesthetic elitism, high-society glamour, and commercial opportunism, was an instant success'.[7] Whistler's *Nocturne in Black and Gold, The Falling Rocket* provoked Ruskin's celebrated attack in his *Fors Clavigera; Letters to the Workmen and Labourers of Great Britain*, No. 79, which advised both the gallery's owner and the American painter that it would have been better not to have exhibited such an apology for a painting. Ruskin's words, already quoted, are given again here in fuller form:

> For Mr. Whistler's own sake, no less than for the protection of the purchaser, Sir Coutts Lindsay ought not to have admitted works into the gallery in which the ill-educated conceit of the artist so nearly approached the aspect of wilful imposture. I have seen, and heard, much of Cockney impudence before now; but never expected to hear a coxcomb ask two hundred guineas for throwing a pot of paint in the public's face.

Although one can see why Whistler sued Ruskin (see pages 132–3), the terms used here by England's great art critic are prophetic of public reaction to some modern art – that they can't see the art in it. Equally prophetic of modern misunderstandings was an exchange which took place at the trial (at which Burne-Jones was a reluctant witness on Ruskin's side). The judge asked whether another of Whistler's paintings, *Nocturne: Blue and Gold – Old Battersea Bridge*, was 'a correct representation of Battersea Bridge'. Whistler: 'As to what the picture represents, that depends upon who looks at it.'[8]

If all is subjective, the true subject is the mood of the onlooker. There is no call for the painter to explain 'the symbols', as Rossetti had tried to do in 1848. The only symbol is the butterfly with which Whistler signed his work, aping the manner of Japanese woodcuts. Before denouncing Whistler's apparently slapdash work, *Fors Clavigera* 79 had praised as 'immortal' the clear-edged paintings exhibited by Burne-Jones at the Grosvenor Gallery. One was *The Beguiling of Merlin* of 1874 (see Plate 22). The turn of medievalising art away from history towards legend has already been noted. In painting, legend now gives way to dream, non-realism, symbolism. It is clear enough that Merlin has been conquered by a sensuous beauty, and, to those who had read their Malory or their Tennyson, that the power used by the enchantress to extract all Merlin's secret knowledge is sexual.[9] Another subject taken from Malory, *The Madness of Sir Tristram* (1862), is a further instance of the fatal effect of love upon a man.[10] Some of the other works shown at the Grosvenor, opaque and mysterious, did not invite 'being interpreted' by reference to a literary source, still less by reference to what

'Paul hath said', owing more to Walter Pater. In 1873, Pater had concluded *The Renaissance* on the cadence: 'the desire of beauty, the love of art for art's sake'. With the opening of the Grosvenor Gallery in 1877, this Parisian doctrine now had a foot in Mayfair, a well-shod foot.

Burne-Jones once wrote, in words often quoted: 'I mean by a picture a beautiful romantic dream of something that never was, never will be – in a light better than any light that ever shone – in a land no one can define; or remember, only desire ...'[11] The painter Walter Crane, aged twenty, wrote of the effect of Burne-Jones on himself and his friends:

> The curtain had been lifted, and we had had a glimpse into a magic world of romance and picture poetry, peopled with ghosts of 'ladies dead and lovely knights,' – a twilight world of dark mysterious woodlands, haunted streams, meads of deep green starred with burning flowers, veiled in a dim and mystic light, and stained with low-toned crimson and gold, as if indeed one had gazed through the glass of
>
> > Magic casements opening on the foam
> > Of perilous seas in faerylands forlorn.[12]

There is in such a medievalism no consciousness of the Witenagemot, Magna Carta or John Ball. Crane misquotes Keats slightly, and his 'dim and mystic light' recalls the stained glass of Madeline's bedchamber in 'The Eve of St Agnes' rather than the magic casements of 'Ode to a Nightingale'.

In Crane's watercolour of 1870, *The White Knight*, the knight emerges from a mysterious woodland to cross a glade. This knight is alone, and if not 'palely loitering', he is as white and errant as Chaucer's Sir Thopas.[13] 'The White Knight's Song' in Lewis Carroll's *Through the Looking-Glass* seems oddly appropriate: 'I'll tell you everything I can; / There's little to relate.' The picture does not ask us to imagine what had happened in the wood, nor what might happen next. The knight has a strange helmet but no identifying shield, and the scene calls for no definite interpretation. It seems too passive for Sir Lancelot du Lac.

In 1877, the Grosvenor Gallery made aestheticism fashionable. 'Ye Æsthetic Young Geniuses' (Plate 23) is the caption to a caricature in *Punch* in 1878, the year in which Hopkins wrote to Dixon of the delight given him by 'Her eyes like lilies shaken by the bees'. The artist was George du Maurier, who in 1865 had written a parody of William Morris's verse sagas, entitled *The Legend of Camelot*, with his own Pre-Raphaelite illustrations. Du Maurier illustrated the novels of Mrs Gaskell, Meredith, Hardy and Henry James. In 1894 he published *Trilby*, a novel set among art students in Paris, which depicted a life currently being sampled by some British aesthetes. The 'Ye' in 'Ye Æsthetic Young Geniuses' preserves an archaic confusion. The Old English symbol for the initial sound of the word 'The' (known as the Thorn) was in late Middle English often written indistinguishably from the letter 'Y'. 'Ye' is a muddle perpetuated by early modern typesetters. Du Maurier's mock-archaic wink acknowledges the medievalist origins of aestheticism, but the geniuses depicted are weedy rather than merry. Men so grey, limp and lachrymose would not have lasted long in Sherwood Forest.

Confirmation of the widespread recognition that the apostles of Beauty had had medievalist godparents came with the comic opera *Patience, or Bunthorne's Bride* (1881), with words by W.S. Gilbert and music by Sir Arthur Sullivan, and particularly in the song, 'If You're Anxious for to Shine in the High Aesthetic Line'. The male leads of Gilbert's story, Bunthorne, A Fleshly Poet, and Grosvenor, An Idyllic Poet, borrow post-Pre-Raphaelite features from Algernon Swinburne, Oscar Wilde, James Whistler and others. Wilde and Whistler sat in the front row at the first performance, and Wilde was sent by D'Oyly Carte on a lecture tour of the United States to be, in the words of Max Beerbohm, 'a sandwich board for *Patience*'.[14] Gilbert and Sullivan had a confident rapport with a broad public such as had been enjoyed by Dickens and Trollope, and even by the seriously intellectual George Eliot. But the advent of a mass reading public in the last quarter of the nineteenth century meant that writers could no longer reach the whole of that public in the way that Dickens had. The aesthetes, already marginal, marginalised themselves further by treating the heartier social conventions with conspicuous scorn. Some ended up by becoming as precious as they had pretended to be; the mask grew onto their faces. Before beginning his Song, 'If You're Anxious for to Shine in the High Aesthetic Line', Bunthorne confesses:

> I am not fond of uttering platitudes
> In stained-glass attitudes
> In short, my medievalism's affectation,
> Born of a morbid love of admiration.

The Song itself ends:

> Then a sentimental passion of a vegetable fashion
>   must excite your languid spleen,
> An attachment à la Plato for a bashful young potato,
>   or a not-too-French French bean!
> Though the Philistines may jostle, you will rank as an apostle
>   in the high aesthetic band,
> If you walk down Piccadilly with a poppy or a lily
>   in your medi-*e*val hand.
>   And everyone will say,
>   As you walk your flowery way,
> 'If he's content with a vegetable love which would certainly not
>   suit *me*
> Why, what a most particularly pure young man
>   this pure young man must be!'[15]

Vegetarianism and homosexuality are not particularly medieval, and the potato came in with the Renaissance. But the word 'medi-*e*val' is printed in the libretto in this broken form, and the *e* is italicised to make sure that it gets a sustained *forte* at the stanza's climax. The soporific poppy and the pure lily are well aimed, and flowers also get the last, artistically mangled word in the final Chorus of *Patience*. All sing:

> In that case unprecedented,
>   Single he must live and die –
> I shall have to be contented,
>   With a tulip or li-*ly*.

The doubts of 'everyone' as to the purity of the particularly pure young man turned out to be well founded. As Wilde himself remarked, the truth is rarely pure and never simple. As for lilies, Ruskin had in 1865 published his *Sesame and Lilies*, two lectures on the separate and contrasting roles he thought fit for men and for women. The confidently eclectic Ruskin took the texts of his lay sermons from widely different sources. Sesame is from 'Open, Sesame', the key words in the Persian tale of *Ali Baba and the Forty Thieves*. Lilies come from the second chapter of the Song of Solomon, verse 16: 'My beloved is mine and I am his; he feedeth among the lilies'. Lilies are the standard biblical comparison for female beauty. Gilbert's male leads reverse the normal tastes, if not roles.

Ruskin believed in work, and that it was not just dutiful but holy. He believed also that what is holy is beautiful. At its simplest, the history of medievalism after 1850 is that it gradually separated out into those who thought work holy, those who found holiness in beauty, and those who sought the beauty of holiness. After Ruskin, Morris was the standard-bearer for the first view, the sanctity of labour. His conviction that work was a good greater even than beauty was expressed in his increasing political activity in the cause of Socialism, though he also worked incessantly at his art-work. After his death, his followers went into the Trade Union movement and the Labour Party and also into the Society for the Protection of Ancient Buildings (which he founded in 1877), and later the Arts and Crafts movement, and lived in Hampstead. Those who found their holiness in beauty are the artists and poets whose trajectory we have been following. Endorsing this tendency was the art criticism of Walter Pater, which is not about the art of the Middle Ages but gives his own gloss to Hellenic ideals. Those who sought true beauty in holiness included many of the followers of Keble and Newman, such as Christina Rossetti and G.M. Hopkins, J.M. Neale, the hymn writer and founder of the Camden Society, and a mass of those Anglo-Catholics sometimes called Ritualists: the patrons and vicars of many a Victorian country parish and slum church. (Ritualists, as Michael Wheeler points out, were *second*-generation Anglo-Catholics.) But believers in the beauty of holiness also included Christians evangelically opposed to the Oxford Movement, such as the Rev. Charles

Kingsley, the author of the gibe 'Truth for its own sake has never been a virtue of the Roman clergy.' In the 1850s, Kingsley, Cardinal Wiseman and Dr Newman all wrote novels about virgin martyrs: respectively, *Hypatia* (1853), *Fabiola, or the Church of the Catacombs* (1854), and *Callista, a Martyr of the Fourth Century* (1856).

In the 1890s there was a remarkable collapse into each other of the aesthetic and the religious, in the strange case of the group known as the Decadents. Before coming to them, the most singular talent of this odd group deserves separate treatment in any discussion of medievalism. The aesthetic Decadents were not medievalist, but the most talented artist among them, Aubrey Beardsley, continued the central Pre-Raphaelite tradition of illustrating literary texts. He began with the text most central to the Victorian Medieval Revival. Beardsley's opening into the profession into which Burne-Jones's example had drawn him came in a commission from John Dent to illustrate a new edition of Malory's *Morte Darthur*. Art history was repeating itself: forty years earlier, Moxon had invited Rossetti and his friends to illustrate Tennyson's poems. Beardsley rapidly produced over 351 designs for Dent's elaborate Art Nouveau edition of the *Morte*, which appeared in two volumes in 1893–4.[16] The preparation of Beardsley's Malory will therefore have overlapped with that of *The Works of Geoffrey Chaucer*, designed by Morris with illustrations after woodcuts by Burne-Jones, regarded as the supreme product of the Kelmscott Press, which appeared slightly later, in 1896.

Beardsley's angle of approach to the Arthurian legends was further from the approaches of Morris and Burne-Jones than their approaches were from that of Alfred Tennyson. Beardsley's next notable piece of illustration was in 1894, for an English translation of Oscar Wilde's play *Salome*, a work which could scarcely be less medieval. From the beginning, the style of Beardsley's illustration had owed as much to Japanese prints as it did to early printed books: he rapidly and deci- sively refined his own idiosyncratic manner. An enthusiast for Richard Wagner, Beardsley wrote a version of *Tannhäuser*, which Wagner had in 1845 based on a medieval legend. Beardsley's novel, *The Story of Venus and Tannhäuser*, shows the influence of Swinburne's poem *Laus Veneris* of 1866. The (unfinished) text is more porno- graphic than the illustrations; a shorter and less suggestive version appeared as *Under the Hill* in the *Savoy Magazine*. Beardsley died of consumption in 1898, aged twenty-seven.

J.M. Dent, Beardsley's first publisher, was in 1905 the publisher of the original Everyman's Library, in which a minimally illustrated *Morte Darthur* appeared in 1906. The Art Nouveau endpapers of this series of popular classics carry the Library's motto: 'Everyman, I will go with thee and be thy guide, / In thy most need to go by thy side.' Everyman's Library is a good example of the educational mission of the Medieval Revival, which was to offer the best of the past to every member of society. The words of the motto come from *Everyman*, a Morality Play of the very early sixteenth century. They are addressed to the protagonist, Everyman, by a character called Knowledge. Knowledge's offer expresses a sentiment common to those who founded the Working Men's College in 1854 and the Workers' Educational Association in 1903, and indeed the public libraries of Great Britain. 'I will go with thee and be thy guide' is part of what William Morris called the dream of John Ball, a democratic universalism full of healthy aspiration. The promise of Knowledge here is not that knowledge is a good in itself, the idea of liberal education. Yet it implies a nobler form of self-improvement than its distant relative, the column in *Readers' Digest* entitled 'It Pays To Increase Your Word-Power'. More than a century after the foundation of Everyman's Library, it is strange to think that a publisher could then suppose that the public either had heard of *Everyman* or would respect it as a name. Probably it was the word 'Everyman' that appealed. Those who read the play *Everyman* to its end will note that Knowledge breaks his promise to Everyman and deserts him at his 'most need', as death approaches.

With Aubrey Beardsley's wicked realisation of the erotic possibilities of one kind of medievalism, we seem to reach a terminus. Yet medievalism outlived the nineteenth century. In assimilated forms it remains part of the modern world. But Gilbert's mockery, and Beardsley's travesty of the styles and ideals which had formed his art, suggest that the major phase of medievalism had reached a crisis, and prompt a look back over the life-cycle of this style. When a style no longer fits society well enough to be taken seriously, it is used for comic or satirical purposes. In the noonday of Augustanism, Pope used Gothic for unworthy things: 'Chaucerian' language to tell a bawdy joke in verse, and 'Anglo-Saxon' archaism to deride Wurmius's taste for old manuscripts. As Augustan certainties waned, Thomson's *Castle of Indolence* experimented with Spenserian stanza and narrative, with skill but without conviction: the first canto is a *jeu d'esprit* and a spoof, the second a guilty effort to extol the Knight of Industry, the opposite of Indolence.

The Medieval Revival proper had begun in the 1760s with various attempts to make copies of medieval exemplars. All the exemplars and copies appeared to be genuine, though only Percy's *Reliques* were so. The copyists' motives were mixed, and differed widely. Some motives, in that rationally conscious age, were not conscious. The author of *The Castle of Otranto* knew at first that his story was a joke, but the success and manner of its reception led him to suggest, in the second edition, that it was not. Almost every piece of interior decoration that Horace Walpole added to Strawberry Hill was a scholarly copy of an original, but applied to different purposes and in a different spirit. An exact copy of the tomb of Archbishop Bourchier, for example, became a fireplace in the Long Gallery: so much more *amusing* than the original in Canterbury Cathedral! 'Gothick horrour' had reigned for three decades when Jane Austen's heroine in *Northanger Abbey* (finished in 1803) 'cared for no furniture of a more modern date than the fifteenth century'. By this date Joseph Ritson, the first professional editor of medieval romances, had attacked the freedom with which amateurs like Percy and Scott had felt able to handle and supplement medieval texts. George Ellis smiled at the romances he brought to public notice, and Thomas Love Peacock's enlightened smile at Gothic fantasy lasted all his life. In *Rebecca and Rowena* (1850), a humorous sequel to *Ivanhoe*, W.M. Thackeray allowed Ivanhoe to tire of his marriage to Rowena, whose death enables him to marry the more attractive Rebecca. Parody and pastiche are tributes to success. Millais commissioned lines from Sir Isumbras to mock-authenticate his painting, and it was in Middle English that Sandys mocked Ruskin. Mockery salutes eminence in George du Maurier's parody of Morris's *The Earthly Paradise*. A pinch of fake archaism added zest to Du Maurier's caricature, 'Ye Æsthetic Young Geniuses'. In W.S. Gilbert's *Princess Ida*, Gilbert treated Tennyson's experiment in feminism, *The Princess*, to what he called 'a Respectful Operatic Per-Version'.[17]

A style can last a long time, but when a change in consciousness comes, the prevailing idiom no longer sounds right. The successes of Victorian medievalist literature, as these parodies indicate, had been in verse rather than prose. W.M. Thackeray's later novels concerned gentlemen, and Trollope, too, was interested in the conduct of gentlemen and ladies. But the ideal of social hierarchy had been sufficiently celebrated by the followers of Young England to receive gentle parody in the Ullathorne rural games in *Barchester Towers* (1856), an Arcadian version of an ideal feudal hierarchy benignly maintained.[18]

We have seen late Victorian medievalism modulate into a general mythological aestheticism. Such a category fairly contains the later work of Burne-Jones and the art and craft of William Morris, whether decorative or symbolic. But in the work of Aubrey Beardsley, Burne-Jones's admirer, all the original impulses of medievalism are unrespectfully perverted. Beardsley's assumed urbanity and real wit do not conceal his divided mind, nor his contempt for the ideals that had once fascinated him. More generally, the avant-garde of the 1880s, having exhausted medievalism as a style, turned against its idealism. Aestheticism was only residually medieval, and the Decadence was not medievalist. The Decadents were so called after an article published in 1893 by Arthur Symons, 'The Decadent Movement in Literature'.[19] Those who turned from aestheticism to decadence often turned also from medievalism to Catholicism. A high proportion of this set of artistic dandies became Catholic converts and a similar proportion took up homosexual practices. It is just what Charles Kingsley would have predicted. The uniformity of this flight into the Catholic Church, and to forbidden forms of 'beauty', is remarkable. An obvious if partial explanation is that the Catholic Church, the Church for sinners, was exactly what such habitual sinners needed. They had an attraction to sins forbidden by social convention as well as by Christian ethics, pursuing social exclusion and self-destruction through alcohol or illicit forms of sex, or both. They needed the peace which the world cannot give, a forgiveness which the Catholic Church offers, though only to the penitent. Those who converted to Catholicism include Symons, Beardsley, Lionel Johnson, Ernest Dowson, Wilde, André Raffalovich,

Robert Ross and John Gray, the model for Wilde's Dorian Gray. Gray became a parish priest, dying in 1934. Wilde was received into the Catholic Church on his deathbed. (So, earlier in that year, was the man he chose to sue for describing him as homosexual, the Marquess of Queensberry.) The Catholic Church to which these converts turned was the post-Reformation Church, represented in London by the Jesuits at Farm Street, Mayfair, and by the Oratorians at Brompton. Dandy Catholicism was metropolitan, French-led, international.

The world regards deathbed repentance and conversion with reserve. Wilde, however, claimed that his interest in Catholicism preceded his homosexuality. He came close to conversion when young, approaching Father Sebastian Bowden of the Brompton Oratory in April 1878. Bowden told André Raffalovich that Wilde had failed to turn up for the crucial meeting, and had instead sent to the Oratory a large bunch of lilies. Joris-Karl Huysmans, whose *À Rebours* ('Against Nature') of 1884 had influenced Wilde, was eventually reconciled to the Catholic Church, as were Verlaine, Rimbaud and other French aesthetes. When in 1898 Wilde heard from Maeterlink that Huysmans had joined a monastery, he remarked: 'It must be delightful to see God through stained glass windows. I may even go into a monastery myself.' Wilde's Canon Chasuble would observe that this 'hardly points to any very serious state of mind at the last'. Yet Wilde knelt before priests, and sought a blessing from the Pope. Three weeks before his death he told a *Daily Chronicle* correspondent that 'much of my moral obliquity is due to the fact that my father would not allow me to become a Catholic. The artistic side of the Church and the fragrance of its teaching would have cured my degeneracies. I intend to be received before long.'[20]

CHAPTER 11

'I Have Seen . . . A White Horse'

CHESTERTON, YEATS, FORD, POUND

> For years almost my only relaxation had been reading
> Chaucer and Langland, visiting pre-Reformation churches,
> listening to plainsong and Gregorian chant or spending hours in
> the Victoria and Albert Museum studying the craftsmanship of
> the thirteenth and fourteenth centuries, revealed in gloriously
> illuminated books and, equally, in perfectly designed things for
> everyday use.
>
> Douglas Hyde[1]

Victorian medievalism had lost its vitality before the lives of its
remaining practitioners came to an end in the 1890s. Tennyson died
in 1892, Morris in 1896, Burne-Jones in 1898, and Ruskin in 1900.
Yet 1900 was the year in which medievalism once more became a
revival rather than a continuation: a minority movement, not going
with the flow of the times, but oppositional in a new way. The old
medievalism was fading into artistic wallpaper and stained glass,
urban Art Nouveau and vernacular Arts and Crafts. It was just a
style. In architecture, the tide of Gothic Revival building had ebbed,
leaving much behind it to be wondered at. Poetry and painting had
moved from medieval legend to mythology in general. Historical
novels set in the Middle Ages were usually boys' adventure stories.
On the other hand, knowledge about the Middle Ages had greatly
increased. 'Historian of the Middle Ages' is the first line on the
memorial tablet to Henry Hallam (1777–1859) in St Paul's Cathedral,
presumably on the strength of his *State of Europe During the Middle
Ages* (1818). Since then, archives and artefacts had been assembled,
and medieval texts had been published. At Queen Victoria's death,
James Murray's *New English Dictionary on Historical Principles* had
reached the end of the letter G. Standard Histories of England had

substantial medieval sections. University graduates in history, language and literature were now informed about the Middle Ages, and there was a popular awareness of the medieval past. This was one of the factors which made possible an Edwardian relaunch of medievalism, a second Medieval Revival. Another was a clearer prospect of what the Tractarians had called national apostasy.

'I have seen the forces of death with Mr Chesterton at their head upon a white horse.' T.S. Eliot was writing about modernism in poetry, at the height of the battle about style. His 'forces of death' are writers of an English which is stale in comparison with the 'living English' of 'Mr Pound, Mr Joyce and Mr Wyndham Lewis'.[2] Eliot takes a smack at Chesterton's popular poem *The Ballad of the White Horse* (1911). This ninety-seven-page verse romance celebrates King Alfred's heroic defence of Wessex, the last English kingdom left standing, against an invading army of heathen Danes. Inspired by a vision of the Blessed Virgin, Alfred is eventually victorious in 878 at Ethandune in the Vale of the White Horse – now Edington, Wiltshire. The popularity of this historical ballad romance lasted: it was quoted on public occasions between 1914 and 1918, and between 1939 and 1945. In 1976 H.P.R. Finberg's *The Formation of England 550–1042* quoted the following without feeling it necessary to name its source: ' "The high tide!" King Alfred cried, / "The high tide – and the turn." '[3] Graham Greene said, in 1978, that he was not sure that he did not prefer *The Ballad of the White Horse* to *The Waste Land*.[4]

Eliot's vision of G.K. Chesterton on a white horse at the head of the forces of death is a rhetorical stroke. It combines the *Ballad* with the Bible – 'And I saw heaven opened, and behold a white horse; and he that sat upon him was called Faithful and True' (Apocalypse, 19:11). This cocktail is from Chesterton's own cabinet of paradox, hyperbole, allusion and Christian fantasy. The joke is also personal, since Chesterton, who regularly made fun of his own obesity, was too spherical to mount a horse of any colour. Eliot's sally casts Chesterton as a king defending English against the Four Horsemen of Modernism, born in Idaho, Dublin, Canada and (his own birthplace) St Louis. Eliot was to begin *The Waste Land* with a salvo of epigraphs in foreign dead languages before reaching English. The man on the white horse had originated a new Medieval Revival in the first decade of the new century, a medievalism to which literary modernism seems entirely opposed, although neither side much liked the way the world was going. G.K. Chesterton, if less singular than Hopkins or Beardsley, was an original. A High Anglican, he united in his capacious person the purposes and some of the gifts of the medievalists of the 1840s. He combined intelligence, bounce and social idealism in a way reminiscent of Pugin, Carlyle, Ruskin and Kingsley, but with more agility, a better informed understanding of industrial society, and a better temper. His reputation as an entertaining controversialist has not helped him with intellectuals. The English like those who make them laugh, but do not take them seriously. Yet Chesterton was more than a clown. He had an independent mind, an original vision and a quick sense of how to relate ideas. In the opinion of some competent philosophers today, Chesterton's philosophical superiors, among the names mentioned so far in this story, would be Burke, Coleridge and possibly Newman.

Chesterton's medievalism profits from the knowledge built up in Victoria's reign. An Edwardian reader with curiosity or imagination could feel an informed continuity with Saxon England – could see white horses. Ford Madox Brown had imagined Wyclif and Chaucer as directly patronised by Edward III's family. But the late Victorians who put up statues to King Alfred were informed about how he had defended England and Christianity, established education for laymen, and translated Boethius and Augustine. They could read the *Anglo-Saxon Chronicle* in a good translation. In the 1880s, Tennyson had translated 'The Battle of Brunanburh', an Old English poem which appears in the *Chronicle* annals as the entry for the year 937. He claimed in a prefatory note that it was in this battle that 'England conquered'. England indeed survived as a united kingdom as a result of this victory of Christian Wessex and Mercia over pagan Vikings from Dublin and York, and their Christian allies from Scotland.[5] Tennyson also wrote a play about Harold and Hastings. In 1906 Kipling wrote about England's successive inhabitants in *Puck of Pook's Hill*, beginning with the Romans. The thread of the book is that a land lives not through its owners but through its workers, who don't change much. The theme of much of Tennyson and of Hardy is that the plough passes over the reaper's head. Chesterton was not the first

English writer to feel this thousand-year continuity with Saxon England – and for him, as for Tennyson, it was a Christian continuity. Chesterton's love of old England, in *The Ballad of the White Horse* and elsewhere, was combined with hatred of the imperialism which had led to the Boer War.

After St Paul's School, Chesterton went to art school, but gave up the pencil for the pen. Versatile and fluent, he wrote essays, columns, volumes of controversy, romances, short stories and poems. Early in his career came fantastic fiction, *The Napoleon of Notting Hill* (1904) and *The Man Who Was Thursday: a Nightmare* (1908) and much verse. Chesterton was naturally high-spirited and hopeful, but in *Heretics* (1905) mocked a social optimism based simply on technical advances. Challenged to state his own beliefs, he wrote *Orthodoxy* in 1908. He developed a Christian social ideal which combined broad sympathies with a relish for individuals, evident in his studies of Dickens and Browning. *The Innocence of Father Brown* came in 1911. Chesterton's democratic liberal instincts eventually combined with an economics informed by biblical standards of social justice. These principles had been applied to the oppression of industrial workers in Pope Leo XIII's encyclical letter of 1891, *Rerum novarum* – 'Of New Matters'. This Christian social teaching was neither capitalist nor socialist, criticising monopoly and plutocracy, but not private property. Property-ownership, Chesterton argued, should be spread as widely as possible, the central plank of a programme known as Distributism, often caricatured as 'three acres and a cow'.

It was through Chesterton that a medievalist vision was associated with Catholicism for the first time since Pugin. Pugin had transformed English design both by example and by proclaiming its moral relation to society. His 'true principles' affected architecture for generations. Chesterton was more consciously fantastic and addressed a general public. He was as versatile with a pen as Pugin was with a pencil, with a wealth of ideas, a nimble mind, a wide range and a critical faculty. He wrote several books on medieval subjects, including studies of Thomas Aquinas and Francis of Assisi, and a still valuable celebration of Chaucer's Christian comedy. He used his journalism to illuminate principles derived from Aquinas, moving from the Anglican into the Roman Catholic communion in 1922. 'G.K.C.' entertained the public on a range of topics, from a golden Edwardian decade until his death in 1936. In the world of journalistic controversy, at that time concerned with ends as well as means, George Bernard Shaw successfully confused Chesterton with Hilaire Belloc in the public mind by his invention, the Chesterbelloc. Chesterton became interested in Rome only after meeting Belloc. Sir James Gunn painted these two in conversation with their unpolemical friend, the writer Maurice Baring. G.K.C.'s comment on this triple portrait – 'Baring, overbearing and past bearing' – puts himself third.

The names with which Chesterton should be associated, in a discussion of medievalism, are not Baring and Belloc but his juniors, Ronald Knox, Christopher Dawson, Eric Gill, David Jones, Christopher Hollis and Evelyn Waugh. The sound of Belloc's trumpet stirred some readers, but was too brazen for others. Chesterton persuaded readers by fantasy, acuteness and laughter. He had the lighter touch, and a keener interest in the contemporary and in ideas.

Chesterton wrote, with Shaw, Arnold Bennett and H.G. Wells (who were among his 'heretics'), for a press in which literature enjoyed popularity and esteem. The brio of Chesterton's apologetics won him enemies as well as friends. On his deathbed, Thomas Hardy dictated a hostile epigram about G.K.C., who remained on jovial terms with most opponents, including Shaw. His intellectual influence reached far. To the names listed above could be added many more, including that of Graham Greene, who was deeply impressed by *The Everlasting Man* of 1935. Among Anglican admirers of this philosophical work were C.S. Lewis and Dorothy Sayers, who wrote in 1952: 'To the young people of my generation G.K.C. was a kind of Christian liberator. Like a beneficent bomb, he blew out of the Church a quantity of stained glass of a very poor period, and let in gusts of fresh air in which the dead leaves of doctrine danced with all the energy and indecorum of Our Lady's Tumbler' (the title of a Chesterton story). 'Wisdom his motley, Truth his loving jest' is a line from Walter de la Mare's commemorative verse on G.K.C.[6]

He was anthologised by two aficionados of light verse, Auden, and Kingsley Amis, who ends *Lucky Jim* with a farcical lecture on 'Merry England'. Hearsay prefers jokes to books, and Chesterton is remembered as an entertainer. Greater writers have been worse diminished, Chaucer for example. But the Edwardian baize on which Chesterton gambolled so gladly has faded badly. Its writers are now known for their lighter books: Kipling for *The Jungle Book*, Belloc for *Cautionary Verses*, and Chesterton for detective stories. The name of Arnold Bennett was until recently known to university students of the novel only because Virginia Woolf thought him material and external. The poetry of the reign of Edward the Caressor (as Ezra Pound called him) is hidden by modernism, and the reign itself lies in the shadow of the First World War. Subsequent generations look back at Edwardian affluence and confidence across an abyss. Pre-war assumptions went up in smoke, including the idea that material advances would improve human behaviour. These must be among the reasons why a G.K. Chesterton can still enjoy less literary favour than a Lytton Strachey.

English writing, it was once claimed, was permanently altered by the victories of modernism, and by the influence of Bloomsbury. Chesterton saw these movements as pretentious. His own pre-war banter and high spirits made him, for some who first read him post-war, too jolly and journalistic. After 1918, Chesterton wrote bitterly as well as blithely, but his style never lost the rhetoric of one who was twenty-one in 1895 – the love of paradox, large gesture and emotive swoop. 'We are all in the gutter, but some of us are looking at the stars' comes from Wilde's *The Importance of Being Earnest* (1895). 'We are all worms, but I believe that I am one of the glow-worms' is attributed to Winston Churchill. This kind of paradox is habitual with Chesterton. W.S.C. and G.K.C. were both born in 1874. Their journalism and their convivial lifestyles had something in common, their politics almost nothing.

Chesterton was a lifelong critic of imperialism, of laissez-faire capitalism, and of the millionaire as role-model. His brother Cecil had in 1912 exposed insider trading in Marconi shares; among those involved were Lloyd George, who was Chancellor of the Exchequer, and Godfrey Isaacs, the Managing Director of the British Marconi company, whose brother, Rufus Isaacs, was Attorney General. Their insider speculation had been in the shares of the American Marconi company, not the British company, a point which allowed Lloyd George and Isaacs successfully to mislead the House. Roy Jenkins confirms in his biography of Churchill that these ministers suppressed the truth.[7] After Cecil Chesterton died of wounds in France in 1918, G.K.C. was too ready to suspect financial conspiracy, and to blame it on Jews. Although there was corruption in public life, and though blaming it on Jews was common in Britain, this mental habit must now, in retrospect, fall under the fatal light of the Nazi attempt to exterminate European Jewry. An article Chesterton wrote for his last Christmas, in 1935, shows prescience:

> We live in a terrible time, of war and rumour of war ... International idealism in its effort to hold the world together ... is admittedly weakened and often disappointed. I should say simply that it does not go deep enough. ... If we really wish to make vivid the horrors of destruction and mere disciplined murder we must see them more simply as attacks on the hearth and the human family; and feel about Hitler as men felt about Herod.

A new massacre of innocents began in 1941, the 'mere disciplined murder' of millions of Jews, Slavs, gypsies, homosexuals and the mentally handicapped.[8]

Chesterton and Belloc, advocates of Catholic social teaching and the programme of Distributism, jousted regularly with Shaw and Wells, believers in progress and in the Soviet Union. In 1927, Belloc ended a public debate with Shaw by improvising a poem:

> Our civilisation
>   Is built upon coal,
> Let us chant in rotation
> Our civilisation
> That lump of damnation
>   Without any soul,
> Our civilisation
>   Is built upon coal.
>
>   In a very few years
>   It will float upon oil ...[9]

Chesterton ridiculed teetotal beverages, vegetarianism, vitamins – and, from early on, eugenics. The literary modernists disliked him; what they had in common emerged only later. Pound has an epigram comparing a cake of soap to the cheek of a Chesterton. Eliot found Chesterton's style 'exasperating to the last degree of endurance' – past bearing, indeed. But the obituary Eliot wrote for *The Tablet* in 1936 records a change of mind.[10] He still thought G.K.C.'s verse no more than 'first rate journalistic balladry'. But Chesterton had

> reached a high imaginative level with *The Napoleon of Notting Hill* and higher with *The Man Who Was Thursday*, romances in which he turned the Stevensonian fantasy to more serious purpose. His book on Dickens seems to me the best essay on that author that has ever been written. But it is not I think for any piece of writing in particular that Chesterton is of importance, but for the place that he occupied, the position that he represented, during the better part of a generation.

Eliot had committed himself to defending a humane Christian society in 1927, and did so for the next generation.

Eliot was moderate in praise of the poetry of most of his immediate predecessors. 'First rate journalistic balladry' was not something he tried in public, unless we count the burlesque of *Sweeney Agonistes*. The rollicking verse collected by Kingsley Amis in *The Popular Reciter* was finished off by the triumph of modernism. By the time Eliot wrote Chesterton's obituary, he was himself trying to reach a wider audience, through drama. 'Journalistic balladry' places G.K.C. below Kipling, and above 'The Ballad of Reading Jail' and Robert Service. It is not an unfair description of 'The Rolling English Road' (1914), 'Lepanto' (1915) and 'The Secret People' (1915). Journeyman balladry describes Walter Scott's mock minstrel romances; and a journalistic balladry was the right medium for a verse narrative based on the prose of the *Anglo-Saxon Chronicle*. *The Ballad of the White Horse* is a poem I have known twenty-first-century students to enjoy.

The democratic Chesterton of 'The Rolling English Road' and 'We are the people of England, who have not spoken yet' (the refrain of 'The Secret People') was not far from the Guild Socialism of Ruskin and Morris, and the community-minded Arts and Crafts movement. Later Catholic artists who kept the association of craft with natural materials on the one hand and with literature on the other, the ideal of Ruskin and Morris since the 1850s, include Eric Gill, the engraver, letterer and sculptor, who formed communities of craftsmen at Ditchling and at Capel-y-ffin.[11] Gill's Guild of St Dominic and St George drew some of its ideas from the thinking of St Thomas Aquinas. Members included the printer René Hague, and the painter and poet discussed in the next chapter, David Jones. Gill's work can be seen in the figures of Prospero and Ariel above the front door of BBC Broadcasting House, London. His models were simple, plain and pre-Gothic. Gill's Stations of the Cross can be seen in Westminster's neo-Byzantine Cathedral, built in 1903. Gill's lettering, both elegant and strong, is more consistently successful; he designed the typefaces Perpetua and Gill Sans. The Arts and Crafts movement, like the arts generally, is now less associated with churches.

What might be called Social Medievalism had sprung originally from outrage at the unjust treatment of industrial working families. It was variously expressed by Cobbett, Pugin, Disraeli, Carlyle, Ruskin, Morris, Maurice, Kingsley and Hopkins, not to mention Karl Marx and Cardinal Wiseman. Although this impulse often took the form of Christian Socialism, some forms of it were neither Christian nor egalitarian. Communitarian rather than individualist, it had begun with Chartism and went into Trade Unionism. It could go further left, as happened in Russia in 1917, or further right, as happened in Italy in the 1920s, where Mussolini began as a socialist; or both ways, as in Spain. In Germany in the 1930s, Hitler's party called itself National Socialist. A socialism influenced by medievalist thought came from R.H. Tawney (1880–1962), a member of the executive of the Workers' Educational Association of 1905, and author of *The Acquisitive Society* (1921) and *Religion and the Rise of Capitalism* (1926).

Parliamentary democracies failed to handle the economic collapse of the interwar period, and politics polarised. A curious history is that of Douglas Hyde, news editor of the *Daily Worker*, the Communist Party paper, who in 1948 famously resigned from both

his post and the Party to become a Catholic. He had accused the
Weekly Review, the journal of Distributism (previously *G.K.'s Weekly*),
of having 'fascist' links, a libel for which he was successfully sued. To
prepare for the case, he read everything in the *Weekly Review* for
evidence of 'fascism', and found himself warming to certain aspects
of the magazine:

> I found in it a quotation from William Morris. For such people to
> quote my Morris seemed blasphemy.
>
> Then I found that the parts of the paper I had been deliber-
> ately missing, because, being non-political, they had no bearing
> on my case, were very much in tune with Morris. It was almost
> humiliating to discover that these people were medievalists –
> and so was I.
>
> For years almost my only relaxation had been reading
> Chaucer and Langland, visiting pre-Reformation churches,
> listening to plainsong and Gregorian chant or spending hours in
> the Victoria and Albert Museum studying the craftsmanship of
> the thirteenth and fourteenth centuries, revealed in gloriously
> illuminated books and, equally, in perfectly designed things for
> everyday use.
>
> These were, it seemed, the *Weekly Review*'s interest too ... I
> resolved the problem by putting the medievalist attraction of the
> *Weekly Review* into one watertight compartment of my mind
> and its politics into another.[12]

Hyde's mental compartments correspond to the artistic and the
political sides of medievalist social concern, in tension since the
1840s. Tories such as Ruskin and Hopkins saw the noble side of
the communist ideal. Wilde wrote a book called *The Soul of Man
Under Socialism*, and there has even been a Liberal medievalism.
E.M. Forster wrote a 'medieval' morality play about how enclosures
had deprived the people of common land. Belloc and Chesterton
were Liberals until 1911, when they lost faith in the old two-party
system. Many British Liberals want employees to be granted rights of
share-ownership. Christian forms of communitarian thinking have
been found at every point of the political spectrum, from 'liberation'

theology and 'Worker Priests' to Methodist care for the exploited, to the Welfare State, to the Catholic anti-capitalism of Graham Greene, to the One Nation Conservatism of the Butler Education Act, to the *intégrisme* of T.S. Eliot's dream, to the Tory anarchism of Evelyn Waugh. More recently, the global advance of free trade has reduced old ideological polarities, including those within Christianity. Medieval values contribute to the economics of Schumacher and to stewardship-and-sustainability environmentalism.

* * *

In considering the Medieval Revival's contribution to the twentieth century, one can be more positive about poetry than about politics. The chief poets who continued the aesthetic tradition of the medievalist movement were W.B. Yeats and Ezra Pound, who during his twelve years in London, acted as Yeats's secretary for three successive winters. T.S. Eliot later declared that Pound was 'more responsible for the XXth century revolution in poetry than any other individual'. The year of Pound's arrival, 1908, was also the year of the founding of *The English Review*. Its editor, Ford Madox Ford, wrote of Pound that, 'In a very short time, he had taken charge of me, of the review, and finally of London.' London was also the residence, for much of his life, of W.B. Yeats, who was for fifty-seven years a British subject. Yeats went to school from an artists' colony in Bedford Park. He knew the writers and artists of the 1890s, and spoke of 'the great English poet William Morris'; his own early tales of Aengus bewitched, or of Cuchulain led by the nose by beauty, are in the tradition of Morris's verse romances in *The Earthly Paradise*. Yeats also admired D.G. Rossetti, and worshipped female beauty. He first put this into forms derived from medieval Irish legends, then briefly in Rosicrucian terms, and finally in the more intelligible terms of the Helen of Troy of Greek legend. Yeats was not as fixated as Rossetti, but the theme of love's fatal power stayed with him. Yeats's 'stunner', Maud Gonne, was not a barmaid but an English Colonel's daughter, and an icon of Irish nationalism. Yeats often proposed to her, but Maud married the nationalist John MacBride. After she was widowed, he proposed to her again, and when declined proposed (in vain) to her daughter, whose name was Yseult.[13] Helen's beauty is in Yeats's poetry the cause not only of the

Trojan War but of havoc to mankind in general. In his late poem 'The National Gallery Revisited', Yeats wrote of his need to 'worship images', adding 'My medieval knees lack health until they bend'. But in the work of Yeats that is most valued today, he was not a medievaliser but a serial maker and destroyer of myths.

Yeats had brought out his first *Collected Works* in 1908. Pound admired Yeats's mastery of his craft, and valued him also as a link to the Pre-Raphaelites. Both men revered Rossetti, and both married relatives of the Nineties poet Lionel Johnson. It is significant that both Yeats, in 'The Tragic Generation' (1922), and Pound, in *Hugh Selwyn Mauberley* (1920), recount the story of the Aesthetes and Decadents who lost public favour with the fall of Wilde. Their accounts are similar, for Pound had listened to Yeats. The more historically minded Pound takes the story further back, to Ruskin, and to Buchanan's attack upon 'the Fleshly School'.

Pound is the most medievalist of modernists. He began as an academic medievalist, took two degrees specialising in early romance languages and literatures, subjects which he taught for a year in an American college, and in London at the Regent Street Polytechnic, now the University of Westminster. He lived in London from 1908 to 1920. His first prose book, *The Spirit of Romance* (1910), shows him as a devotee and translator of Provençal troubadour poetry, of Dante and *El Cid. The Spirit of Romance* is his equivalent of Rossetti's *Dante and his Circle.* Many of Pound's London poems in *Personae, Riposte* and *Lustra* (1914) adopt the personae of Provençal troubadours, in the way of Robert Browning in *Sordello* (1840). Pound could refer to Scott simply as 'Sir Walter', and to the end of his days preferred Yeats's earlier poetry. He also liked to point out that for a thousand years all the thinking in Europe had taken place *inside* the Catholic Church. All this may surprise those who know of him as *the* modernist: the publisher of Joyce, the 'discoverer' of Eliot, the man who sawed *The Waste Land* in half, the iconoclast. 'You let ME throw the bricks through the front window', he told Eliot. 'You go in at the back door and take the swag.' He was all those things. But he was also a medievalist, and the two are connected. Early Victorian medievalism was not escapist but radical, an incitement to machine-breaking; and Pound's values were radical in an early Victorian way. His Christian poem 'The Ballad of the Goodly

Fere' appears in *The Oxford Book of Victorian Verse* of 1912, edited by Sir Arthur Quiller-Couch. The language of Pound's ballad is medievalist; 'fere' is an old word for companion. The goodly fellow-seafarer is Christ. Ezra was the only child of a Quaker family, but his poem's virile Christianity might have appealed to Charles Kingsley.

Modernism and medievalism are labels for academic parcels. Labels should be scrutinised, and parcels checked, before they are passed to the young. Pound's medieval admirations are manifest from his earliest poems, which are full of troubadours and of Villon. Headline literary history gives the impression that shortly after the accession of King George V in 1910, Georgian Poetry (hedgerows, tweed, cider, nostalgia) was overtaken by Modernist Poetry (experimental, intellectual, American) and in 1916 by War Poetry (short, moving, British). But poets do not live in boxes. Several who were later called modernists or war poets appeared in the annual *Georgian Poetry* volumes edited by Edward Marsh, a friend of Rupert Brooke and private secretary to Winston Churchill.

Ezra Pound had found that on his arrival in London he seemed, as a poet, to have been 'born in a half-savage country, out of date', as he reports in *Hugh Selwyn Mauberley*. He was not a man to be patronised, but he rapidly modernised himself. Pound's other mentor in London, younger than Yeats but born into a Pre-Raphaelite family, was Ford Madox Hueffer (1873–1939), the grandson of Ford Madox Brown and the nephew of W.M. Rossetti. His father was Dr Francis Hueffer, a German musicologist, author of *The Troubadours*, a study of medieval song. F.M. Hueffer was over forty when he joined up to fight the Kaiser, changing his German surname to Ford only *after* the war. Pound said that it was Ford who made him less provincial and out of date, and modernised the English of his poems.

Ford's writing career embodies the transition from Victorian to modernist writing. His memoirs, *Return to Yesterday* (1931) and *It Was the Nightingale* (1933), tell how as a child he was dandled on Pre-Raphaelite knees. His *The Fifth Queen*, of 1906–8, a picturesque Tudor trilogy about Henry VIII's Catholic queen, Catherine Howard, was described as 'the swan song of Historical Romance' by Joseph Conrad, who had collaborated with Ford on two early novels. Ford now founded *The English Review*. His contributors included Thomas Hardy, Henry

James, Yeats, Conrad, Wells, Bennett, Chesterton, Belloc and George Moore; but also Ezra Pound, Wyndham Lewis, Rupert Brooke, E.M. Forster and D.H. Lawrence. *The English Review* was a London bridge where the generations met. A century later the bridge is down: some names are 'modern', others not. The transition from medievalist to modernist was often a matter of style, not of subject or value.

Ezra Pound was famous as a moderniser of language, who blue-pencilled the poetic drafts of Yeats and of Eliot. But Pound says it was Ford who laughed him out of his early, Pre-Raphaelite, manner: Pound was declaiming a 'medieval' poem when Ford 'laughed until he rolled on the floor'. Ford now described his own *The Fifth Queen* as 'a fake more or less genuine in inspiration and workmanship, but none the less a fake'. The style of his writing changed. Yet adultery, the subject of *The Fifth Queen*, remains the subject of his best-known novel, *The Good Soldier* (1915). Thanks to Lancelot and Guenevere, adultery reached English writing in medieval costume. For much of Victoria's reign it was not easily a contemporary subject: marital infidelity was more tractable within the inherited Matter of Britain than in a realist novel. Adultery is again Ford's theme in *Parade's End* (1924–8), a quartet about England and the First World War, also known as the Tietjens tetralogy, after its hero Christopher Tietjens, a Yorkshire squire who embodies old England. At the war's end, this Anglican gentleman leaves his treacherous wife for a suffragette schoolteacher. Ford gave the title 'Provence' both to his best poem and to his best travel book. He wrote again about the origins of romance in the last work he published in his lifetime, a survey of world literature, *The March of Literature, from Confucius to Modern Times* (1938), which is both discerning and a delight to read. Ford's literary likings were catholic and mutually compatible. The only writers with whom *The March of Literature* shows impatience are Cervantes, who mocked romance, and Leo Tolstoy, who in his later moralism was against romantic love.

Critics acknowledge the tonic effect of Ezra Pound's criticism upon other poets, but the poems he wrote in England are not read widely enough, perhaps because they reflect modern problems only indirectly. The mirrors Pound holds up are taken from medieval Provence and Italy. He translated from poetry of the Roman and Chinese empires at war rather than writing poems on the British empire at war.

Cathay (1914) comes from Tang China; *Homage to Sextus Propertius* (1917) from the Rome of Augustus. A personal quality may be more obvious in Pound's version of the Anglo-Saxon poem 'The Seafarer'. His first line is: 'May I for my own self song's truth reckon.' Pound turns this Christian elegy into a monologue on the fate of the modern artist. 'The Seafarer' gave him a Saxon rhythm and idiom, which he made into a medium for the overture to his *Cantos*. Canto I is a 'Saxon' translation of Odysseus' descent to the underworld: 'And then went down to the ship, set keel to breakers'. Pound's recreation of the earliest English line is a radically native and primitive medievalism, anticipating Eric Gill's proto-Romanesque statues, or David Jones's Romano-British Arthurians in *The Anathemata*.

To purge himself finally of the style and trappings of his medievalist heritage, if not of its themes and values, Pound wrote *Hugh Selwyn Mauberley*, a 'farewell to London'. Put simply, this highly sophisticated work is a series of cameos of the treatment of art and poetry in Victorian, Edwardian and Georgian England, from the PRB onwards, as experienced by a young survivor of the English 1890s, the aesthete, Mauberley.

> The Burne-Jones cartons
> Have preserved her eyes;
> Still, at the Tate, they teach
> Cophetua to rhapsodise;
>
> Thin like brook-water,
> With a vacant gaze.
> The English Rubaiyat was still-born
> In those days.[14]
>
>   'Yeux Glauques', Poem VI of *Hugh Selwyn Mauberley*

Mauberley is an invented version of what the younger Ezra Pound might have been like had he been English. Arnold Bennett's advice to this sensitive lover of art is 'Accept opinion. The "Nineties" tried your game / And died, there's nothing in it' (IX). Pound took his epic poem, *The Cantos*, elsewhere. He described the poem as an attempt to solve the historical crime of the First World War. The early cantos served Eliot as a model for *The Waste Land*.[15]

CHAPTER 12

Modernist Medievalism

ELIOT, POUND, JONES

The publication of *The Waste Land* in 1922 announced that the Americans had landed, and with some unfamiliar equipment. Eliot's poem was attacked as pretentious, chaotic and incomprehensible, and defended on similar grounds. Some found it impressive, fascinating, intoxicating. *The Waste Land* was certainly modern, but modern poetry was often understood negatively, as lacking the decorums of regular verse and the continuity in sense usual in literary English. Some of Eliot's lines were not even in English. *The Waste Land* uses three languages before it reaches English, and later uses three more. Eliot was modern poetry, as Stravinsky and Picasso were modern music and modern art. Soon *The Waste Land* was neither new nor contemporary, but it stayed modern for a long time. Now it is 'modernist'.

At the time of the First World War verse still had a public role. It was not confined to poetry magazines. As poetic modernists raised their banner, the prophet Eliot had seen the forces of death with Mr Chesterton at their head on a white horse. The American champion of 'living English' caricatured the forces ranged against him as medievalist. In 1915 John Buchan wrote to Chesterton that 'the other day in the trenches we shouted your "Lepanto".' But after 1916, the happy Christian warriors of 'Lepanto' seemed to belong to a past more remote than the white horse and the rolling English road. Chesterton did not use archaic English, but his verse can celebrate an innocent England. There will be pastoral literature for as long as there are cities, but some forms of innocence had become painful by 1916. From about 1909, Yeats, Ford and Pound had been trying to give up archaism, though Rupert Brooke, Edward Thomas and Wilfred Owen did not do so. And A.E. Housman, writing in 1896 of the land of lost content, had shown how much could be done in 'timeless English'.

In 1911, Eliot had opened 'The Love Song of J. Alfred Prufrock' by sacrificing a sacred cow. Evening is a subject tenderly treated by poets from Sappho to Hardy. Eliot's 'evening is spread out against the sky / Like a patient etherised upon a table': ready for surgery.[1] A clinical naturalism is characteristic also of Pound's epigrams. 'I am not prepared to say that I appreciate epigrams,' wrote Eliot in 1928, introducing his selection of Pound, 'my own taste is possibly too romantic'.[2] But 'Old Possum' was anti-romantic about the modern city, where the human engine waits, the typist comes home at teatime, and 'Doris enters on broad feet / With sal volatile and brandy neat'. Pruning Victorian pieties, the modernists cut back to live tradition. If they tried to reclaim areas of modern life lost in the previous century to prose fiction and non-fiction, and to make poetry at least as intelligent as prose, they also wanted to preserve the sacred role of poetry in a desacralised world. Although medievalism was Victorian, and modernism loudly anti-Victorian, the modernist poetry of the 1910s found fresh value in medieval literature. If *The Waste Land* defines the modernist poem, its title comes from Malory's *Le Morte Darthur* and its dedication from Dante's *Purgatorio*. Its first line, too, takes a medieval trope familiar from the opening of Chaucer's *Canterbury Tales* and reverses its tenor.

Eliot's first title was 'He Do the Police in Different Voices', but the voices needed an arrangement. Although the Notes he later provided say that the 'title, the plan and much of the incidental symbolism' came from Jessie L. Weston's *From Ritual to Romance*, the title comes ultimately from a sentence in Malory: 'And so befell great pestilence and great harm to both Realms, for sithen [afterward] increased neither corn nor grass nor well nigh no fruit, nor in the water was no fish, wherefore men called this – the landes of the two marches – the waste land.'[3] These last words gave Eliot a title for a poem which employs the twelfth-century legend of the Holy Grail, the vessel used by Christ at the Last Supper. Joseph of Arimathea is said to have caught in this vessel the blood from the wound made in the side of the crucified Christ, and to have brought it to Glastonbury, where it became attached to the Arthurian legend. Eliot uses the wasted land to symbolise the condition of humanity in post-war Europe. It is not pedantry to notice that 'Waste' and 'Land' are separate words and receive equal stress: the theme is human desolation, not an urban wasteland. During the poem's composition its author was treated by a psychotherapist.[4]

The dedication, 'To Ezra Pound / *il miglior fabbro*', uses a medieval phrase from Dante's *Purgatorio* Canto XXVI, line 117: 'fu miglior fabbro del parlar materno' – '*He* was the better maker in the mother tongue'. Dante says here that his verse is not as good as that of Arnaut Daniel, a Provençal troubadour. Dante's 'miglior fabbro' has gained a definite article, perhaps because in English it seems to need one. If Eliot calls his friend and editor a better craftsman than himself, he pays him quite a compliment. But the article makes the comparative *miglior* into a superlative, so that Pound becomes not 'better' but 'the best'. In any case, Eliot had a further point, for this is Dante's reply to Virgil, who had called him the best poet in the romance languages. The Tuscan Dante says that Arnaut was the better poet in the '*parlar materno*' of romance poetry, Provençal. Arnaut Daniel was the virtuoso versifier whom Pound admired most among the troubadours whom he translated, impersonated and wrote about. The 'mother tongue' of the two modern poets was American. So Eliot's compliment, like his vision of G.K.C. on a white horse, works in several ways. At his friend's death, Pound repaid the compliment: 'His was the true Dantescan voice – not honoured enough, and deserving more than I ever gave him ... I can only repeat, but with the urgency of 50 years ago: READ HIM.'[5]

The Waste Land held its readers. The poem's apparent chaos and evident distress received, ordered and gave back all the outraged sense of what Europe's inhabitants had done to one another: it is a war poem, and more than a war poem. Rereading shows that the arrangement of the voices has a dramatist's skill. Eliot carefully holds a shattered modern world up against ancient philosophical and religious texts. The distance between them remains painful to the end, an end which points in the direction which Eliot was later to take. The first line, 'April is the cruellest month', reacts to the ancient tradition which Chaucer takes up in the first line of his *Canterbury Tales*.

Whan that Aprill with his shoures soote   *sweet showers*
The droghte of March hath perced to the roote ...

The spring *reverdie* is a standard medieval opening and a 'chrono-graphia': a rhetorical enumeration of the stages by which nature grows green again, and the sap rises. The tradition also had a negative variant: 'I see life and love flourishing around me but not in me'. This was Eliot's variant; his psychotherapist was trying to cure his 'emotional frigidity'.[6]

By invoking Malory in his title and Dante in his dedication, Eliot begins with resonant ancient chords against which modern life sounds out of tune. These opening chords are medieval. By rewriting Chaucer in his opening, he makes us hear this first discord as a modern discord. Eliot was a New Englander, not a Merry Englander. A devoted student of the Western tradition from its earliest beginnings, he was now an unhappy man in a broken Europe.

Despite the success of *The Waste Land*, and despite the modernist reform of poetic expression, the subsequent course of literature shows that the change in sensibility involved in Romanticism remains the ruling mode of the modern imagination. The modernists could not disown their ancestors and start again. The dose of Attic salt adminis-tered by the modernists gave Romantic subjectivity a severe purge, checking its course. A one-sentence history of English Romanticism might say that the subjectivity of Wordsworth and Coleridge was amplified by Byron, Shelley and Keats, displaced by Browning and Tennyson into third-person speakers, and aestheticised or sophisti-cated by their successors. Some English poets, Thomas Hardy for example, had begun to give the lush idiom of English Romanticism a plainer, more vernacular voice. But the American modernists wanted radical change. They tautened and multiplied the ways of saying the many things they had to say. Their ambition was to take poetry beyond mere self-expression into an art more intelligently compre-hensive of modern life. Eliot engaged with fundamental questions. Yet the mode of poetry in English has remained Romantic. When the smoke of battle cleared, the changes made by the modernists had not, after all, changed everything, though there was more succinctness, less lyricism, more irony, less idealism.

The Waste Land is a poem of unhappy modernity, its agonised tone coming from a sense that the values built up over millennia had been lost. The poem deliberately tries to recapitulate the history of

Western culture from the ancient Indic scriptures, which Eliot had studied at Harvard, to 1920s jazz – 'it's so elegant, so intelligent'. That is why he made the poem so inclusive and eclectic, 'doing' the ancient voices he had heard at Harvard, the Sorbonne, Marburg and Oxford, in counterpoint with contemporary voices.

The part played by the medieval in Eliot's work as a whole is not very large. Despite his love of Dante, he is a philosophic realist only in a qualified sense; he is more of a searcher for origins. Yet he chose a medieval keynote for the first of his two major poems. By finding his unifying myth in the story of a waste land whose king has to die so that new life can germinate, Eliot had to begin with spring (twisted, but still spring), and he began by twisting the famous line that begins the modern English tradition, 'Whan that Aprill with his shoures soote'.

Eliot continues to twist – or be twisted by – that tradition in the lines that follow. He acknowledges spring in order to deny that there is now any new growth. The synthesis of classical, medieval and humanist found in Chaucer embodies the European cultural tradition which Eliot and Pound so prized. Eliot made occasional medieval gestures before 1927. But after his conversion from the Unitarianism of his family and the scepticism of his youth to orthodox Anglican belief, medieval poems, prayers, rites and institutions became stations on his way in life. 'Because I do not hope to turn again', the opening line and theme of 'Ash-Wednesday, 1930', varies Guido Cavalcanti's 'Perch'i' non spero di tornar giammai'. The fourth section of this poem concerns a Marian vision in the garden of a convent. In the closing section, 'Our peace in His will' comes from Dante. Eliot's *Murder in the Cathedral* gave Becket's murder a medieval dramatic form. *Four Quartets* has many ingredients, and its medieval references make up one colour in a mosaic composed of (chiefly) Christian thought and moments of (chiefly) English and Christian history. Eliot's English history is not medieval, but is taken from the period between the execution of Mary Queen of Scots and those of Laud and Charles I. The Caroline spirituality ended by the Cromwellian reformation figures as a little Middle Age of Anglicanism. Eliot took the life of Nicholas Ferrar's household at Little Gidding as a model of the Anglican religious life. In his essay

'The Metaphysical Poets' of 1921, he proposed that 'In the seven-teenth century a dissociation of sensibility set in', a separation of thought and feeling. This famous simplification has been attacked, but there is something in it.

The medieval values Eliot prized are suggested in his Chorus of Women of Canterbury in *Murder in the Cathedral*, a revival of the ritual origins of medieval drama, in which the murder of the Archbishop at his altar re-enacts the Crucifixion which he himself re-enacted at Mass. Another medieval memory comes in 'East Coker, I', with the vision of the village's former inhabitants:

> In that open field,
> If you do not come too close, if you do not come too close,
> On a summer midnight, you can hear the music
> Of the weak pipe and the little drum
> And see them dancing around the bonfire
> The association of man and woman
> In daunsinge, signifying matrimonie.

Medievalism is mediated: the lines allude to Sir Thomas Elyot's *The Boke of the Governour*, to *A Midsummer Night's Dream* and to *Paradise Lost*. 'Little Gidding, I' begins 'Midwinter spring is its own season / Sempiternal though sodden towards sundown . . '. This, with the verse paragraph that follows, borrows form and content from Langland's *Piers Plowman*, in which the natural seasons carry a Christian symbolism. Such communal Anglo-Catholic thinking is a central feature of the mature Eliot. It took him from isolation into a community of shared belief and practice.

Pound's work after he left London is little read in Britain. As predicted in *Hugh Selwyn Mauberley*, he departed 'from [English] men's memory' in the thirty-first year of his age; that is, in 1916. The phrase is adapted from the fifteenth-century poet-outcast, François Villon, the subject of one of Pound's two short operas on medieval poetic exiles; the other is *Cavalcanti*. A canto regularly included in British anthologies was *XLV*, which defends medieval values against 'usura' – usury. Calvin permitted such taking of interest, but the universal Church did not:

With Usura hath no man a house of good stone
each block cut smooth and well fitting
that design might cover their face,
with usura
hath no man a painted paradise on his church wall . . .[7]

In this canto Pound honours the line, definition and translucence of a Quattrocento sculptor such as Pietro Lombardo, and a litany of painters such as Fra Angelico, Mantegna, Piero della Francesca and Botticelli, preferring them to 'the brown meat of Rembrandt'. He prefers these painters for aesthetic, spiritual, ethical and economic reasons – reasons which are very close to those of John Ruskin but far from those of Giorgio Vasari and further still from the 'tactile values' of Bernard Berenson.

The line, 'Came no church of cut stone signed: *Adamo me fecit*', singles out as an instance of the freedom of the medieval craftsman a carved and signed column in the church of San Zeno in Verona, the very column which Ruskin draws and comments on in *The Stones of Venice*.[8] The syntax and rhythmical form of this *Usura* canto imitate those of a medieval litany. Usury is against natural increase, for high interest rates keep young people poor, deferring marriage, the conception of children and new growth. The sterility entailed by separating sex from procreation is a theme of *The Waste Land*: 'What you get married for if you don't want children?' This question, overheard in a pub discussion of an abortion, is natural, like the Natural Law thinking of Aquinas.

Pound uses both medieval and medievalist touchstones in the *Pisan Cantos*. These cantos were written in a US Army Detention Training Center near Pisa in 1945, where the writer awaited the decision of the US Government, which eventually charged him with treason. The *Pisan Cantos* are a last testament. They contain political defiance and present experience, but a persistent theme is remembrance of old friends. Ford and Yeats had died in 1939, Joyce in 1941, and Pound had no reason to suppose he would live long himself. He begins with a line from his own translation of 'The Seafarer':

Lordly men are to earth o'ergiven
these the companions:

Fordie that wrote of giants
    and William who dreamed of nobility
        and Jim the comedian singing
           'Blarney castle me darlin'
      you're nothing now but a StOWne'
and Plarr talking of mathematics
    or Jepson lover of jade
Maurie who wrote historical novels
    and Newbolt who looked twice bathed
        are to earth o'ergiven.[9]

Maurice Hewlett's historical romances are medievalist. Pound remembers the gossip of the writers and artists he had known in London between 1908 and 1920, in the company of Ford and Yeats:

    ... the mass of preraphaelite reliques
        in a trunk in a walled-up cellar in Selsey
    "Tyke 'im up ter the bawth" (meaning Swinburne)
    "Even Tennyson tried to go out
    through the fire-place."

which is what I suppose he, Fordie, wanted me to be able to picture ...

Pound was an indefatigable scalp-hunter; Swinburne (d. 1909) was the only famous living poet whom he had failed to meet. Conversations are reported from the 1890s:

La beauté, "Beauty is difficult, Yeats" said Aubrey Beardsley
    when Yeats asked why he drew horrors
    or at least not Burne-Jones
    and Beardsley knew he was dying and had to
    make his hit quickly

Hence no more B-J in his product.

"I am the torch" wrote Arthur "she saith"[10]

This is Arthur Symons, the poet who gave the word Decadent to a decade, and survived until the year Pound wrote these lines. Pound mentions scores of Edwardian and Georgian figures; not only friends like Maurice Hewlett but others, such as Chesterton and Kipling. He recalls the lordly manners of the *ancien régime*, and smiles at its archaic locutions; the tone is elegiac and affectionate.

> "He stood" wrote Mr Newbolt, later Sir Henry,
> "the door behind" and now they complain of cummings.
> . . .
> "forloyn," said Mr Bridges (Robert)
> "we'll get 'em all back"
> meaning archaic words and there had been a fine old fellow
> named Furnivall . . .[11]

* * *

We have glanced at Eliot's medieval allusions, and seen Pound inspired by medieval and medievalist example. In both, the medieval stands for organic natural values, a standard by which modern life is often found wanting. What Eliot liked in the medieval is suggested on the one hand by his Women of Canterbury and his peasants dancing round in a ring, 'signifying matrimonie', and on the other hand by Becket and martyrdom, the theme of his later drama. Eliot shows an urban life pervaded by an occult dodginess: the 'Egyptian' Madame Sosostris (who is a man); and Mr Eugenides, whose proposal of 'a weekend at the Metropole' would have had tactile values. In Cantos XIV and XV, Pound put usurers and war-profiteers into an Inferno. Pound's hell, Eliot remarked, was 'for other people'. What Eliot valued most in the Middle Ages was the disciplined style and the ordered metaphysical vision of Dante, the pattern to which he aspired in his own later poetry: the order that he sought and which the (modern) world did not yield. Dante is the model for the encounter with the 'familiar compound ghost' in 'Little Gidding'.

Both Pound and Eliot set poems in Venice, the scene of modern/ medieval arguments about decadence ever since *The Merchant of Venice* and *Volpone*. The city is amphibious and ambiguous, good and bad: good, for Pound, up to 1510, the time of Titian.[12] 'Venice' in

English pronunciation is distinct from 'Venus', but for Pound they were both 'Vennus'. Medieval Venice is the home to a good Venus; a living forest of marble, with 'Stone trees, white and rose-white in the darkness' (Canto XVII), and a pleached arbour of stone, a sacred space for love's mysteries. Venice is born from the sea, the home to the Nereids, with nymphs playing around a 'Cave of Nerea, she like a great shell curved'. Pound's bad Venus, at the end of Canto XVII, is called Vanoka, a baroque goddess of lust:

> and at last, between gilded barocco,
> Two columns coiled and fluted,
> Vanoka, leaning half naked,
> waste hall behind her.

Here 'waste' again seems to signify barrenness, sexual emptiness. In his Venetian poem, Eliot also uses the baroque as a sign of oriental decadence, invoking Shakespeare's Cleopatra. In 'Burbank with a Baedeker: Bleistein with a Cigar', the Princess Volupine is a courtesan: 'Her shuttered barge / Burned on the water all the day'. Cleopatra appears also in *The Waste Land*: 'The Chair she sat in, like a burnished throne, / Glowed on the marble ...'. This also is an image of a luxurious sensuality, unnatural compared with the plainness of the pre-baroque.

Although Pound admired the intellectual clarity of Aquinas, Cavalcanti and Dante, the medieval for him includes the pre-modern, and especially the ancient Mediterranean. For Eliot, too, the medieval includes the pre-modern, but he goes from romance to ritual more seriously than Pound. Both follow the comparative anthropology of Sir James Frazer, who saw Christianity as an adaptation of older nature-religions. After his conversion in 1927, Eliot saw the old religions as fulfilled, rather than varnished over, by Catholicism. For both men, the medieval was natural and uncontaminated, and comprehended the pre-civilised. This is part of a general modernist return to 'savage' sources, seen in Picasso's interest in African masks and Stravinsky's *Rite of Spring* (1913), or in Henri Gaudier-Brzeska's 1914 bust of Ezra Pound, a primitive totem, phallic in form. But one study for this head is a profile not unlike those on the medals of Pound's admired Pisanello, a recourse to a Quattrocento style. A similar step back in order to leap forward was recommended by the Scot Hugh MacDiarmid in his slogan: 'Not Burns, Dunbar'. The model for modern Scots poetry, that is, should be not the popular heart-throb Robbie Burns, but the late fifteenth-century virtuoso of the aureate style, William Dunbar; not the Romantic poet warbling native wood-notes, but the conscious medieval artist.

In these instances, poets use medieval standards to criticise a modern trust in the technical and the utile. Their early propaganda was against the emotional effusiveness of the Victorians. In their iconoclastic prose, these Americans turned their backs on Whitman and Emerson, whose British Romantic ancestors they also ignored: Coleridge, Scott, Keats; Pugin, Carlyle, Tennyson, Ruskin; Rossetti and the Pre-Raphaelites; William Morris. Pound, and to some extent Eliot, shared the Romantic aversion to modern industrial clutter, as seen in Pugin's *Contrasts*, and they shared a transcendental orientation. Romantic poetry had found it a strain to maintain metaphysical vision in a world disenchanted by science. This is a theme of Blake's 'Single vision and Newton's sleep' and of Coleridge's 'Dejection: An Ode', and contributes to Hopkins's 'terrible sonnets'. Godforsakenness troubled Eliot but not Pound, who explicitly renounced any orthodox metaphysics, while retaining a guarded mystical theism, a gnostic neo-Platonic polytheism. His Chinese cantos offer a tough 'Confucian' critique of Chinese history from an Enlightenment perspective. Yet the final cantos are Taoist, visionary, open to supernatural intuitions. Pound was always paradoxical, as his title *Jefferson and/or Mussolini* admits. He did not reconcile his democratic economics with his Romantic history. His support for Mussolini after the Italian invasion of Abyssinia was political folly, and led him into the evil delusion of racial scapegoating.

Pound and Eliot, despite their recoil from Romantic gush, and despite their achievement of a poetry equal to the modern world, inherited a poetics which owed much to a Romantic movement which had itself begun in a revival of romance.

* * *

Later literary modernism took its most medieval bearings in the work of David Jones (1895–1974), although Basil Bunting's use of

Norse example in *Briggflatts* (1966) also deserves to be mentioned. Jones was a London Welshman, and may be better known for his work in the visual arts than for his writing. He was an artist in sign and word who tried in both media to maintain the old vocabulary of analogy and symbolism. In this his writing follows that of Hopkins, published in 1918, and of Eliot. Jones trained at art school in London, as had other medievalists. After war-service as a private in the Royal Welch Fusiliers, he was received into the Catholic Church by a Father O'Connor, who was Chesterton's model for Father Brown.[13] Jones joined Eric Gill's craft community at Ditchling to learn wood-engraving and lettering, traditional skills in traditional materials. For Jones, these materials spoke of the human, as buildings of steel and glass could not. In *A, a, a, Domine Deus*, a piece written in 1938 but not published until 1966, Jones sought for the presence of Christ in such buildings: 'I have said to the perfected steel, be my sister and for the glassy towers I thought I felt some beginnings of His creature, but *A, a, a, Domine Deus*, my hands found the glazed work unrefined and the terrible crystal a stage-paste ... *Eia, Domine Deus*.'[14]

His *Petra im Rosenhag* (1931) shows Gill's daughter, Petra, in the guise of the goddess Flora in Botticelli's *Primavera* though the subject also has a Marian meaning. Petra Gill had broken off her engagement to Jones, which caused him to stop painting for a while. After a nervous breakdown he began, for the first time, to write, producing, in 1937, *In Parenthesis*, a narrative in prose and verse of the 1914–18 War, to which its title alludes; it is a fiction, not a memoir. The frontispiece to *In Parenthesis* shows the soldier in the guise of the Crucified, a return to the central medieval tradition of analogy. The naked soldier puts on an army jacket. The broken trees and barbed wire suggest both Calvary and a waste land. In a letter, Jones links this with Langland's image in *Piers Plowman* of Christ putting on human nature to 'joust in Jerusalem'. Christ going to his crucifixion is presented as a knight entering the lists in the armour of human nature: 'This Jesus of his gentries wole juste in Piers armes, / In his helme and in his habergeoun, *humana natura*.'[15] 'This Jesus in his nobility wishes to joust in the arms of Piers, in his helmet and his coat of mail: human nature.'

The approved mini-canon of First World War poetry reports raw experience, finding in it more pain than sense. David Jones's *In*

Parenthesis sees the war against a perspective of previous conflicts. Its protagonist, Private John Ball, wounded in an attack on Mametz Wood, abandons his rifle in no man's land. (His name is that of a leader of the Peasants' Revolt of 1381, used also by William Morris in his *Dream of John Ball*.) *In Parenthesis* is more assimilated and digested than other books about the war, though Edmund Blunden's *Undertones of War* has some similar qualities. Jones's work, in its fragmented, accumulative style, and in its ambitious historical perspective, is clearly modernist, its allusiveness and word-play owing something to Joyce, though Jones has a modesty uncharacteristic of the first English-language modernists. In 1937 the popularity of war books had long passed but *In Parenthesis* won high praise. Eliot, its publisher, called it 'a work of genius'. Waugh wrote that it had 'a painter's realism which lifts [Jones's] work above any of Mr Eliot's followers and, in many places, above Mr Eliot himself'.[16] *In Parenthesis* tells one man's story, and is more straightforward than Jones's more ambitious *The Anathemata* (1954), a syncretic Christian account of the pre-history of Britain up to the time of King Arthur, and (more thinly) down to the present. W.H. Auden regularly recommended it as the finest long poem of the century.

The passage chosen to illustrate Jones is from *In Parenthesis*, the final part, and describes the scene as Ball's platoon advances:

Mr. Jenkins half inclined his head to them – he walked just
barely in advance of his platoon and immediately to the left of
Private Ball.
        He makes the conventional sign
and there is the deeply inward effort of spent men who would
make response for him,
and take it at the double.
He sinks on one knee
and now on the other,
his upper body tilts in rigid inclination
this way and back;
weighted lanyard runs out to full tether,
                swings like a pendulum
                and the clock run down.

Lurched over, jerked iron saucer over tilted brow,
clampt unkindly over lip and chin
nor no ventaille to this darkening
    and masked face lifts to grope the air
and so disconsolate;
enfeebled fingering at a paltry strap –
buckle holds,
holds him blind against the morning.
    Then stretch still where weeds pattern the chalk predella
– where it rises to his wire – and Sergeant T. Quilter takes over.

The death of Lt Jenkins is pitiable, but may not be pointless. It is given a Christian frame. The '(chalk) predella' onto which Mr Jenkins 'sinks on one knee' is the step in front of the altar in a Catholic church.[17] With the last word devoted to the lieutenant's death, we are reminded of the re-enactment of Christ's death at Mass. In retrospect, the lieutenant's 'conventional sign', the sign to advance, takes on meaning. Further, the words 'nor no ventaille to this darkening', alluding to the visor of a medieval helmet, recall the incorporation of the life of the *miles Christi* into the knightly code. The Victorian reappropriation of Arthurian chivalry to the code of the English Christian gentleman, by Tennyson and others, here finds one of its later incarnations, though the gentle Ball is not an officer. (A later one is Evelyn Waugh's *Officers and Gentlemen* (1955), the second of his *Sword of Honour* trilogy, in which the conduct of English officers in a later war is found wanting.)

The heroic dimension offered by Jones is not individual but collective and retrospective, applying to the most surprising people. Ball is protagonist, not hero. He is an Everyman, a Tommy Atkins, a centre of narrative consciousness, a follower not a leader: not the 'hero' of popular literature whom we simply admire. Insignificant, last on parade, he does his best in the battle, which is not much. Wounded in the leg in the attack on Mametz Wood, Ball crawls away, unheroically leaving his rifle. One of the things which made the war hard to assimilate to older patterns of heroic conduct is that the rifle, the 'last personal arm', played a small part in the destiny of its bearer, who was up against impersonal arms.

In a final pastoral sequel, a Queen of the Woods, a figure recalling Diana, the Blessed Virgin Mary and the Perdita of *The Winter's Tale*, awards flowers to the 'secret princes', reconciling the fallen in the 'undercrypt' of the wood. Some of her awards are surprising: 'That swine Lilywhite has daisies to his chain – you'd hardly credit it.'[18] The Welsh fall in the fratricidal blindness of English and German 'square-heads'. The secret princes are thus enrolled not only in a Christian litany of remembrance but also into an unglorified version of the chivalric legend of British history. This litany and legend do not deny the present misery, the suffering or the unintelligibility of the waste. Though the point may not have been evident to those who fell, their sacrifice is presented as not without meaning. The kind of heroism implied is not especially valorous, more a question of putting up with things – Milton's 'the better part of patience and heroic martyrdom', where 'martyr' means 'witness'. The cause is obscure, the motive is a sense of duty rather than the need to resist Prussian militarism; and the kind of Christianity implied is of the most inclusive sort. Jones's notion of the Catholic Church was that it included 'many chaps who did not know they were in it'.

The experience of the life of the ordinary soldier came to have a sustaining significance for Jones, in the light of the religion he adopted after the war, in which the necessity for accepting suffering, cheerfully if possible, was a tenet. The significance and incomplete order Jones eventually made out, with painful and continuing diffi-culty, was the product of years of patiently living with his experi-ences. It was hard to find any redeeming sense, any sacramental symbolic dimension or any metaphysical analogy for the apparently godforsaken life and death of the trenches. Yet this is what Jones seeks to lay the ground for. The broken texture of *In Parenthesis*, its relapse into prose, is related to the intense strain of finding any formal analogy in human and sacred history to the dire actuality of a subject matter which did not easily yield sense, still less grandeur. Yet the soldiers of the First World War were not the first soldiers, or men or women, to feel themselves godforsaken. On the cross, Jesus himself repeated the opening of Psalm 22, traditionally attributed to King David, of a thousand years earlier: 'My God, my God, why hast thou forsaken me?' Such continuities held David Jones, who often quoted a line from the *Dies irae* which allowed him to associate his Christian name with King David and with the Sybil of Virgil's Messianic Eclogue: TESTE DAVID CUM SIBYLLA: 'the Psalmist and the Sybil say the same'.

But *In Parenthesis* has not found favour with one school of critics, of whom Paul Fussell, in his *The Great War and Modern Memory* (1975), is representative.[19] Fussell refuses the analogy Jones offers with earlier wars, some of them heroic or chivalric, for to accept it would deny the traumatic claim of the literature which protested that the First World War was absolutely unprecedented, uniquely sense-less and an experience without the possibility of redeeming sense. Worse things have happened since. But for nearly all the victims of the war, the trauma was unprecedented, and although each new generation is innocent, innocence has perhaps never again been so general. For a Welshman like David Jones, however, who as a little boy spat on the tomb of the 'ruthless king' of page 1 of this book, King Edward I, in Westminster Abbey, the Great War was not unprece-dented. And for a Christian, the precedent is fundamental, for the career of the person whom Christians aspire to follow ended in abject failure, in torture and a degrading death before the world.

In a Penguin anthology of the prose of the war Jon Silkin quotes from Jones's Introduction to *In Parenthesis*: 'The wholesale slaughter of the later years ... knocked the bottom out of the intimate, contin-uing domestic life of small contingents of men, within whose struc-ture Roland could find, and, for a reasonable while, enjoy, his Oliver.' This sentence reduces Silkin to incoherence.[20] To him, the heroic friendship of Roland and Oliver is an impermissible analogy to the First World War, for the *Chanson de Roland* is a prototype of crusade-literature, with a sacred cause and self-sacrificing, chivalrous Christian heroes. Yet Owen did indeed, for a reasonable while, enjoy his Sassoon. As for whether the *Chanson* is relevant, supporters of both sides took copies to the Spanish Civil War. In his Introduction to *In Parenthesis*, Jones mentions other literary precedents, including Shakespeare's *Henry V*.[21]

David Jones believed that it had been necessary to resist Prussian aggression, a view common among combatants. But it is not a trav-esty to present the entrenched poetic history of that war as a boxing match. In the blue corner the pre-match favourite, Brooke's 'The Soldier' (with its patriotic words, 'there's some corner of a foreign field / That is forever England'). Brooke's death was lamented by such very different people as Winston Churchill, Henry James, D.H. Lawrence, T.S. Eliot and E. Nesbit. In the red corner, the protest poetry of Owen, Sassoon and Rosenberg. The result, in the opinion of many critics, though not of all, has been a knock-out. The ground for this judgement is hindsight, which shows Brooke's idealism as mistaken. The outraged protest of Owen and Sassoon at the trauma of the trenches has led to a cult of their work. In British school examinations, many English essays have been written saying that war is 'Futility', the title of one of Owen's poems. Many History essays have been written, perhaps by the same candidates, on the rightness of resistance to Nazism. The merit of the poetry of the trenches cannot easily be separated from the pathos of what it treats, but its canon is small. Owen, Sassoon and Rosenberg gave courageous and necessary witness to the traumatic experience of mechanised slaughter after a long age of liberal peace. Owen and Sassoon returned to the front and another form of heroism. Like Jones, Owen hopes in his Preface that the spirit of his poetry would 'survive Prussia'. 'The poetry is in the pity' is not the only thing Owen said.

The chivalric historical comparison published by David Jones in 1937 and denounced in 1975 by Fussell finds a parallel in the thoughts which at the beginning of the First World War came to the mind of Maurice Baring. Baring's sentiments can also be compared with those of Rupert Brooke. Baring had reported on the horrors of the Russo-Japanese war, and joined up with his eyes open. He was forty years of age when he wrote to a friend from Mauberge on 25 October 1914:

When the troops arrived, singing 'It's a long way to Tipperary' at Mauberge, after forced marches in the dark, it was one of the most tremendous moments I have ever experienced ... they looked so young, so elastic, and so invincibly cheerful, so unmixedly English, so tired and so fresh. And the thought of these men swinging on into horror undreamt of – the whole German Army – came to me like the stab of a sword, and I had to go and hide in a shop for the people not to see the tears rolling down my cheeks . . . .

I went to Mass this morning and it was nice to think I was listening to the same words said in the same way with the same gestures, that Henry V and his 'contemptible little army' heard before and after Agincourt, and I stood between a man in khaki and a French Poilu and history flashed past like a jewelled dream.[22]

CHAPTER 13

Twentieth-century Christendom

WAUGH, AUDEN, INKLINGS, HILL

> Alone in a room Pope Gregory whispered his name.
>
> W.H. Auden, 'Memorial for the City'

After 1918, the medieval no longer offered an all-purpose decorative style, or repertory of artistic motifs, to be used, as before the war, for railway stations, bank-buildings, fabrics and wallpaper. An often functionalist modernism broke with Victorian decorativeness, and consequently with the blanket application of medievalist decor. The criterion was appropriateness. There is a paradox here, for the growth of a sense of history had permitted the Medieval Revival, but a more informed historical sense now confined it to its proper subjects. Medieval styles were increasingly restricted to such things as the typography of a medieval book, period illustration, church art, stained glass, nurses' uniforms and war-memorials. The propriety is more often historical than ethical. Gothic churches continued to be built, completed or restored – as they had been since the Middle Ages. Writers and artists who came to maturity after 1918 obeyed the principle of medieval styles for medieval subjects. This chapter follows the fortunes of literary medievalism after the period of full-strength modernism, which in England ended in about 1927.

The belated case of David Jones largely confirms the rule of propriety, since in his art and his writing he was drawn to models from the Gothic period and before. After *In Parenthesis* he did not write on modern subjects. He also developed a philosophy of art deriving from the thought of Aquinas. Aquinas attracted much attention in the 1920s and 1930s, notably in France, from such scholars and thinkers as Etienne Gilson and Jacques Maritain. The scholarly recovery of Scholastic philosophy found echoes in the Anglo-Saxon world, a process which continues. One effect of the

gradual recovery of the Middle Ages was some increase in the awareness, in Protestant countries, not only of Catholic cathedrals and of
Catholic painting in Flanders and Italy, but of Catholic thought. This
was part of the general recovery of the historical past in all its aspects,
itself part of the *sciences humaines* project of the Enlightenment. As
the West lurched through the crises of the 1930s, there were advances
in science and improvements in technology, in transport, communi-
cation, mass entertainment and medicine. New methodologies, such
as psychology, gained ground in the social sciences, as did other
programmes, material, rational or otherwise; political programmes
included communism, Fascism and National Socialism.

It has been noticed that the modernist poets increasingly found
themselves on the political right. Yeats, Pound and Eliot saw little
future for an art such as theirs in a mass democracy. The Russian poet
Mandelstam, asked to define the modernist kind of poetry known
as Acmeism, replied: 'Nostalgia for world culture'. Politics divided
in the interwar decades: democracies suffered economic collapse,
unemployment, inflation; dictatorships arose, opinion polarised. The
English-language modernist writers, including Lawrence and Jones
(but not Joyce), mostly went to the right, Auden and his generation
(but not Waugh) mostly to the left. The 1930s saw many people
espouse political opinions which they later concealed. Words of
W.B. Yeats were often quoted: 'The best lack all conviction, while
the worst / Are full of passionate intensity'. Some modernists were
tempted by Fascism, briefly for the most part, though Pound, living in
Italy from 1924, persisted in admiring Mussolini, a position which
the British poet Thom Gunn has compared to William Hazlitt's
persistent hero-worship of Napoleon.[1] Louis MacNeice, who had
accompanied Auden on his trip to Iceland, afterwards wrote of the
early 1930s, 'Young men were swallowing Marx with the same naive
enthusiasm that made Shelley swallow Godwin'. Several of these
young men went to Spain to support the Republicans; sobered by the
Civil War, many of them returned social democrats.

When Auden arrived in Barcelona, he found that the Republicans
had closed the churches. 'To my astonishment', he wrote later, 'this
discovery left me profoundly shocked and disturbed. The feeling was
far too intense to be the result of a mere liberal dislike of intolerance,

the notion that it is wrong to stop people from doing what they like, even if it is something silly like going to church. I could not escape acknowledging that, however I had consciously ignored and rejected the Church for sixteen years, the existence of churches and what went on in them had all the time been very important to me.'[2] Trying to answer the question of how he was so sure that Hitler was evil led Auden back to the Christian belief in which he had been brought up.

Coming to adult consciousness in the 1920s, the generation of Waugh, Greene, Powell, Auden and MacNeice suffered the trauma of the Great War indirectly. They were not convinced, as some of their elders had been, that civilisation had suffered a fall or break of an irremediable kind. A love of the medieval is not central to the work of any of these writers, but it contributes to half of Evelyn Waugh's books and to parts of Auden's poetry. Waugh's case is the clearer, since the traditions to which he gave his own peculiar twist are familiar from the previous century: Victorian-Romantic, with no relation to medieval texts. Waugh attended Lancing, a Gothic Revival school with a prominent chapel. Like other revivalist writers, he at first wished to be an artist, and illustrated some of his own books. His first published works are as medievalist as those of Ezra Pound: an essay on the Pre-Raphaelites and a book on D.G. Rossetti. Like Rossetti, he collected odd friends and bric-à-brac, including grotesque Victoriana. His modernism began with the farce of *Decline and Fall* (1928), passed into an almost nihilist satire, and soon became consciously reactionary, though his scepticism protected an idealism which found no object. He pursued a modernist satire on modernity in novels apparently traditional in form, often with medieval motifs. Thus, in *A Handful of Dust* (1934), Tony Last inherits Hetton, a neo-Gothic stately home which is a monument to Victorian chivalry. He is an honourable but feeble anachronism, a hero-victim. His wife Brenda leaves him for Beaver, a drone. When Tony telephones Brenda in London, he is answered by Beaver. 'Oh dear,' says Brenda, 'I feel rather awful about him. But what *can* he expect, coming up suddenly like this. He's got to be taught not to make surprise visits.' Betrayed, Last leaves for South America. In a fantastic ending which piles Swift on Conrad, Last is enslaved in the jungle by a madman called Todd, who makes him read aloud the works of

Dickens in a continuous cycle. The names are significant. *Tod* is
German for 'death', and Mr Death compels the last of the Lasts to
read Dickens aloud to him for ever. This is Waugh's idea of Hell, one
of the Four Last Things in the Catechism of the Catholic Church.
The study of the Last Days is called eschatology.[3]

Not long before he wrote this novel, Waugh's wife of only a few
months had left him for another man, and he had afterwards become
a Catholic. Waugh was soon to write his own versions of another
medieval genre, hagiography: heroically in *Campion*, humbly in
Ronald Knox. His third Saint's Life, *Helena*, is a witty historical
romance about the Emperor Constantine's British mother, who found
the True Cross in Jerusalem. It is a sophisticated version of the saints'
lives of the 1850s, *Fabiola* and *Callista*. Waugh thus revived eschatology, romance and hagiography. Most of his other writing satirises
the emptiness of fashionable life. Like some Victorian revivalists,
Waugh admired courage, which he had, and sanctity, which he had
not, but his sense of humour was blackly his own.

A Handful of Dust takes its title from *The Waste Land* – 'I will
show you fear in a handful of dust' – and adopts some of its locations.
Waugh had not expected a revival of chivalry in the modern world,
but war against Hitler and Stalin seemed just. His *Brideshead
Revisited* (1945) is a nostalgic wartime romance about the operation
of divine grace in a Catholic family, reported by a painter who does
not believe in such things. But the war trilogy, collected as *Sword of
Honour* in 1965, has chivalry as its theme. Guy Crouchback, from an
old Catholic family, as his names suggest, is thirty-five, and has been
abandoned by his wife. On reading of the Nazi-Soviet non-aggression
pact, Guy volunteers: 'The enemy at last was plain in view, huge and
hateful, all disguise cast off. It was the Modern Age in arms. Whatever
the outcome there was a place for him in that battle.'[4] Waugh's family
was neither Catholic nor aristocratic, but a wife had abandoned him,
and he had enlisted for the same reasons as his protagonist, for a
place in that Last Battle. Life in the armed forces disillusions the
quixotic Crouchback in three volumes. There is farce, satire and a
serious undertow. When Guy finally sees action (in the failed defence
of Crete), he is ashamed of the conduct of officers he had previously
admired. The trilogy's title alludes to the Sword of Honour presented

to the cadet who passes out first in his year at the Royal Military Academy, Sandhurst, and to two swords associated with the British war effort: the Sword of the Spirit, a Catholic movement; and the Sword of Stalingrad, Churchill's tribute to the defence of the city named after Josef Stalin, Churchill's peacetime enemy and wartime ally. These allegiances are, for Guy, in dishonourable conflict.

In the third volume, Virginia, the wife who had left Crouchback, becomes pregnant by Trimmer, a hairdresser who adjusts his sails to catch every passing wind. Trimmer is made the hero of a propaganda campaign in praise of the ordinary soldier. After a posting to Yugoslavia, where British policy is to support Communist partisans against Catholic ones, Guy returns to London, where he remarries Virginia in order to give her unborn child a father. After the child is born, she is killed by a bomb. He brings up the boy and lives a quiet, conventional life. The epilogue is more cheerful than the end of *Middlemarch*. Even if the heroic age is dead, a defeated survivor can swim against the stream and lead, obscurely, a life of some worth. The book ends with a medievalist gesture, as Guy's sister's son goes into a monastery.[5]

Waugh and Jones continued Medieval Revival ideals as fundamentally opposed to the main currents of modern British life as those of John Ruskin. So, in another way, did J.R.R. Tolkien and C.S. Lewis, scholars of medieval language and literature at the University of Oxford: Tolkien was a Professor of Old English and Lewis an authority on late medieval romance. Lewis later became the first holder of a new chair of Medieval and Renaissance Literature at Cambridge. Each made major scholarly contributions to his field. Although there was no better British scholar of Old English poetry than Tolkien, he published little. Lewis, by contrast, had an incisive mind and a bullish personality. A classicist with an excellent memory for primary texts, he mastered large subjects quickly. His clarity and trenchancy (he was an Ulsterman) made him a good simplifier, lecturer and populariser. He was perhaps the most popular Christian apologist and controversialist of his day. A second literary reputation for Tolkien and Lewis was created by their fiction. Lewis's stories were fantastic or futuristic, while Tolkien's were set in an imagined northerly landscape populated by men, boys and ladies, by elves and trolls, and by the Orcs and Hobbits of his own invention. Tolkien's self-illustrated books were dreamed up for his children, not for the public. Lewis published briskly for other people's children. In both cases, the mode and materials of their fiction drew directly on their professional knowledge of medieval literature and of folk and fairy tale. They were romancers.

David Jones had been born in the 1890s, had served in the First World War, and had written medievalist romance. All this is also true of Tolkien and Lewis (and of Charles Williams, a fellow member of an Oxford group known as the Inklings). Jones's work is learned and modernist in style, but Tolkien and Lewis wrote in the tradition of the stories they had read as children. Their books are simple, moral, allegorical and Christian, like Charles Kingsley's *The Water Babies*. The immense and lasting popularity of the medievalist romances of Lewis and Tolkien, and their influence on a growing genre of fantasy literature, boosted by the cinema, has taken some academic medievalists by surprise. The scale of their success has also puzzled critics who stick to the Enlightenment view that probability is necessary in fiction, since realist fiction is adult, whereas romance, fantasy and fairy tale are puerile. Yet the popularity of these modern medieval romances is not hard to account for. Unlike modernist fiction, they tell simple, innocent and edifying stories clearly, in the 'timeless' archaic prose of the genre. Literary critics sometimes underrate things which defy explanation: humour is one example, and the power and pleasure of narrative are others. Written for children, these romances are good of their kind; and childhood reading is now the only attentive and imaginative reading which many people undertake.

As in their medieval originals, the fictional universe of these romances is polarised, and good triumphs over evil. Innocent questers meet the power-hungry and devious. Lewis and Tolkien draw on their professional reading. In an episode of Lewis's children's serial, *The Chronicles of Narnia*, an envious boy turns into a dragon, jealous of his possessions. This is the psychology of Spenser's *The Faerie Queene*: moral change produces physical change. A spiritual physiology also informs *Beowulf*, as when Grendel is said to descend from Cain. Tolkien's Orcs are evil spirits of the dead, a race seeded from a single word in *Beowulf*, 'orcneas', one of the three kinds of monsters descending from Cain. *Beowulf*'s verse is tightly wrought, but Tolkien's prose ambles on, including the odd poem, much as the Icelandic sagas do. The Inklingasaga (as the children's stories written by the Inklings might collectively be called) have, like *Sword of Honour* and the Bible, a Last Battle. Lewis's fables are short effective parables of moral improvement and Christian salvation. The mode of Tolkien's saga is more symbolic. It shadows a larger Christian mythology of good and evil, one more obviously affected by the war of 1914–18. The evil kingdom of Mordor, which takes its name from the Old English word for murder, is the home of industrial weaponry, like Milton's Hell. It has recently been suggested that an underlying theme of Tolkien's work, in which women play inspiring roles, is the return of England to the old faith. In Tolkien's day, English Catholics prayed for the conversion of England, using a prayer which speaks of England as Mary's Dowry.

Tolkien also wrote a sequel to *The Battle of Maldon* in Old English metre, rather as Scott had done for *Sir Tristrem*. It is a verse playlet recounting the homecoming of one of Byrhtnoth's followers. Tolkien's sequel points out the disastrous consequences for such a follower and his family of the rashness of the East-Saxon leader at Maldon. Tolkien's sequel is a comment not so much on Byrhtnoth at Maldon as on what the high command had asked of the British infantry with whom he had served in the war.[6] Rather, as with F.D. Maurice's comment on Chaucer's Friar, or with Ezra Pound's version of 'The Seafarer', the concerns of the present modify what is made of the past.

In the history of modern poetry in England, W.H. Auden occupies a crucial and contested position between the modernists and their successors. Independent of mind, he was also a serial admirer and absorber: of T.S. Eliot, for example, and of W.B. Yeats. The youngest son of a medical doctor father and an Anglo-Catholic mother, Wystan Hugh Auden went up to Christ Church, Oxford, to study biology. Switching a year later to English, he retained an appetite for knowledge, analysis and technique; a poem was 'a verbal contraption'. Auden was intellectually omnivorous. His early poetry is precocious, dazzling, puzzling. He shared with Eliot the desire 'sharply to inhibit the rehearsed response'. Obscure and unfamiliar features in his early manner were thought modern. Early commentators emphasised his interest in science and psychology and noted a Marxist glee in his hints that the social order was doomed. His inherited interests, however, were not at all modern.

Auden's father, an antiquarian, held that the family was descended from an Auden who was one of the first Norse settlers of Iceland. Wystan was born in Yorkshire at Bootham, a Viking settlement. He was brought up on Morris and Magnusson's *Icelandic Stories*.[7] His mother taught him the words of Wagner's *Tristan and Isolde* and they sang duets from it together. His Christian name is distinctive and Anglo-Saxon. Wystan is a saint from Repton, a Derbyshire village where the poet's father went to school. Wystan Auden was brought up to consider his Norse inheritance part of his identity, and later liked to derive his name from 'weoh-stan' meaning '(pagan) altar stone'. In the early English poems he studied at Oxford, Wystan would have found two Wistans. A historical Wistan was a faithful retainer of the Byrhtnoth who fell at Maldon. In *Beowulf*, Wihstan is the name of the father of Wiglaf, the sole retainer who dares to help Beowulf in his last fight against the Dragon. Beowulf, who has no son, makes this Wiglaf his heir and successor. What's in a name depends upon who's looking and upon their education.[8]

In 1926, the Honour School of English Language and Literature at Oxford was thirty years old. Oxford English was then very unlike what it is now, and quite unlike the degree courses offered today in most British universities. It included five compulsory papers in historical linguistics, and the standard was stiff. Auden was a botanist of words, but his philology was neither systematic nor scholarly; he gained a Third class degree. Yet this was his 'first introduction to the "barbaric" poetry of the North'. He wrote of Old English verse in *A Certain World: A Commonplace Book* that he was 'immediately fascinated both by its metric and its rhetorical devices, so different from the post-Chaucerian poetry with which I was familiar'.[9] Auden had a poet's professional interest in the possibilities of this metric and rhetoric. He recalls hearing Tolkien, an unmemorable lecturer, 'recite, and magnificently, a long passage from *Beowulf*. I was spellbound. This poetry, I knew, was going to be my dish'.[10] Not all literary undergraduates were attracted to Old English verse. 'Auden really admired the boring Anglo-Saxon poets like Beowulf whom we had read in the English school', as John Betjeman recalled. Since Beowulf is not a poet, Betjeman must have been very bored.[11] Auden became friendly with Tolkien, for whom he wrote 'A Short Ode to a Philologist'. Tolkien responded with a composition in Old English, 'To Wystan my friend', with facing translation. The Chaucer scholar Neville Coghill found that his very first tutorial student in Middle English was a Mr Auden. The student told the tutor that he intended to be a poet. Coghill was encouraging, but Auden replied: 'You don't understand: a great poet.' In 1962 he recorded that 'Anglo-Saxon and Middle English poetry have been one of my strongest, most lasting influences.' He included verse translations of the Old English poems 'Deor' and 'Wulf and Edwacer' in *A Certain World*. Later, with the help of the Old Norse scholar Paul Taylor, he produced an anthology of translations, *Norse Poems* (1983).[12]

Auden preferred old mine workings and industrial archaeology to brass rubbings and cathedrals. He admired not the Gothic thirteenth century, the golden age of Aquinas, Dante and Chartres, but the darker and more mysterious world of Anglo-Saxon verse and of Norse saga. He went in 1936 to Iceland, retracing the family legend, and following in the steps of William Morris, whose liking for democracy he shared. If the modernists felt that an old high culture had become degraded in modern industrial civilisation, Auden was more routinely conscious of human nature as fallen, a sense intensified for him by the guilt he felt about his homosexuality.

Auden's *Paid on Both Sides, A Charade* (1928) was drafted at Oxford and finished in Berlin. Its elliptical title comes from line 1305 of *Beowulf*. Grendel's mother has just taken vengeance for her dead son by killing a friend of Hrothgar the Dane. The poem comments 'Ne wæs thæt gewrixle til, / thæt hie on ba healfa bicgan scoldon / freonda feorum' – 'The bargain was not a good one: for both sides had to pay with the lives of friends' (1304–6). This comment on the ethos of the Germanic blood feud is expressed in the gnomic form dear to the Anglo-Saxons, who loved wisdom, preferably in verse. Auden's *Charade*, written in alternating verse and prose, concerns a feud between two families. It is not clear what the action is about (the allegory is both political and psychological). The sense is often locally obscure also, except that this Germanic feud relates both to the First World War and to contemporary Germany (one family has Jewish names). It has recently been realised that much of the text, though printed as prose, consists of imitations of Old English verse. (In Anglo-Saxon manuscripts, verse is written as prose.) A speech in *Paid on Both Sides* ends: 'They fought, exhausted ammunition, a brave defence, but fight no more.' This prose roughly observes the rules of Old English prosody and idiom, and the passage could be lineated as verse: 'They fought, / exh*au*sted *am*munition, / a *brave* de*fence*, but *fight* no more.' Stressed syllables (italicised) are pointed by alliteration; all vowels alliterate. Auden also imitates the effect upon speakers of an uninflected language such as modern English of reading verse in an inflected language such as Old English. In Old English, grammatical inflections do the job done in modern English by conjunctions, pronouns and prepositions, small relational words which Auden leaves out as much as he dares. The effect is elliptical, and also paratactical: the syntax works by addition rather than subordination. As the only previous English poet to have done similar things was Hopkins, commentators on Auden who know no Old English have attributed to the influence of Hopkins, who knew no Old English verse, characteristics which Auden had imitated directly from Old English verse.[13]

It has been shown that Auden, in his first two published collections, quotes, translates or alludes to a score of Old English poems: not only 'The Dream of the Rood', 'The Wanderer' and 'The Seafarer', *The Battle of Maldon* and *Beowulf*, but also 'Finnsburh', 'Brunanburh' and 'Genesis', and some little-known gnomic poems in the manuscript miscellany known as the Exeter Book. He seems to imitate the miscellaneousness of the Exeter Book, and its use of roman numerals rather than titles for poems. The effect on the instructed reader is one of pastiche; the uninstructed must have been quite lost. In the second edition of Auden's first *Poems* is a poem later entitled 'The Wanderer'. Several lines come from the Old English poem of that name, but the first line, 'Doom is dark and deeper than any sea-dingle' is taken from a Middle English prose text, *Sawles Warde* ('The Guardian of the Soul').

In *The Orators, An English Study* (1931), Auden also makes considerable use of Old English, often by a parodic updating of the gnomic style, as in 'One delivers buns in a van, halting at houses'. He reattributes the most famous lines of *The Battle of Maldon*:

Fear
That laconic war-bitten captain addressing them now
'Heart and head shall be keener, mood the more
As our might lessens.'[14]

In the original, these words are spoken after the death of Wistan, and near to the point at which the text breaks off. Auden translates the words faithfully but transmutes the effect by putting them in the mouth of Fear, that laconic captain. The speaker in *Maldon* is a fearless old companion who is not an officer. Auden hints a view akin to that of Tolkien's continuation of *Maldon*, 'The Homecoming of Byrthelm, Beorhtnoth's son': modern warfare is such that heroism of this kind may be misplaced.

If the motives for Auden's compulsive imitation of Old English metre and style were familial and formal, he was drawn also to the moral understatement of Anglo-Saxon verse: 'They fought . . . a brave defence, but fight no more'. But Auden does not endorse the heroic code of *Maldon*. He takes his critique of the duty of vengeance directly from *Beowulf*'s 'Ne wæs that gewrixle til' – 'That was not a good bargain'. Contrary to what is often supposed, *Beowulf* does not endorse the blood feud but shows its human cost. Old English gave Auden an ethical inflection, and a repertory of stylistic, syntactic and metrical patterns. These he plays with in various ways, including pastiche, parody and travesty.

The classical side of Auden's schooling had fostered an interest in prosody and in etymology; his philology was not linguistics but a love of individual words. Classical Philology in the European sense included Literature, and had been used for generations as *paideia* to form the ethos of rulers, soldiers and administrators. In England this was done at public schools, such as the one Auden attended, Gresham's, Holt. A recent biography of P.G. Wodehouse – whose work was one of Auden's later enthusiasms – says that in his last year at Dulwich College, 1899, this academically unexceptional member of the First Fifteen and First Eleven could write Latin and Greek as rapidly as he

wrote English.[15] A favourite improving instance in Greek came from
Herodotus' account of Thermopylae, where a mixed force led by the
Spartan Leonidas successfully held the pass for days against the far
larger Persian army of Xerxes. When the pass was sold, the three
hundred Spartans were killed to a man. Their epitaph is given in a
distich by Simonides: 'Stranger, go tell the Lacedaimonians that here
we lie obedient to their commands.' Spartans came from Lacedaimon,
and spoke Laconian. The brevity and understatement characteristic of
stiff-upper-lip Spartans are laconic. Auden could not, in such a context,
give Captain Fear the epithet 'laconic' without recalling Sparta. His
allusion links the fight at Maldon with the heroic defence of a narrow
place at Thermopylae. But it remains clear that he questions the virtue
of dying for one's country. Nicety in word-use can also be instanced in
a phrase from 1927: 'Spring's green / Preliminary shiver'.[16] Persephone,
the goddess of Spring, shivers as she crosses the *limen*, the threshold,
into a world chillier than Hades. Auden's medievalism, or Saxonism,
does not stop him using classical etymology. The sources of his
imagery, words and idea were as eclectic as those of John Donne.

Embarrassed by his role as 'court poet to the Left', Auden sailed with
Christopher Isherwood to New York in January 1939.[17] His departure
from the secular Left and from England went down badly, and his
reputation in England also went down. In America, his style relaxed
and his sense became clearer, but his English reputation rested on his
pre-war work, which was terse, elliptical, experimental. Although he
returned to Europe after the war, and eventually to Oxford, some still
regard the poet of the 1930s as the real Auden. The best early poems
are electrifying, mysterious, occluded; their sophistication can mask
their ethical simplicity. After 1939 Auden took his hand away from his
mouth, and the address of his poetry became more social and genial.
This opening out had personal origins, but its expression often drew
on Christian social thinking. Among Auden's new interests was medieval Christendom, when, according to him, in 'Memorial for the City',
dedicated to the memory of Charles Williams, and with an epigraph
from Juliana of Norwich concerning 'the City', the City of God,

Alone in a room Pope Gregory whispered his name
While the Emperor shone on a centreless world

From wherever he happened to be; the New City rose
   Upon their opposition, the yes and no
Of a rival allegiance; the sword, the local lord
   Were not all; there was Rome and home;
Fear of the stranger was lost on the way to the shrine.[18]

Of Auden's longer poems, *For the Time Being*, though an Oratorio, is modelled upon the late medieval Second Shepherds' Play, which he had read at Oxford. Likewise much of *The Age of Anxiety* is in the Anglo-Saxon verse-form first tried in *Paid on Both Sides*. *The Age of Anxiety* is subtitled 'A Baroque Eclogue' and dedicated to John Betjeman. Thus Auden regularly clashes his form and content. Alliteration is used for un-Anglo-Saxon things and attitudes:

Opera glasses on the ormolu table,
Frock-coated father framed on the wall
In a bath-chair facing a big bow-window,
With valley and village invitingly spread.[19]

As Professor of Poetry at Oxford from 1956, Auden expressed regret at the replacement of Latin by the vernaculars, and in answer to an invitation to speak to a college literary society, read a paper on usury in medieval social theory. From within his old college at Oxford, he continued 'sharply to inhibit the rehearsed response'.

It has been shown that major modernist poets drew on medieval things, and that the medieval centuries had become part of what the English can inherit. 'What thou lovest well is thy true heritage', as Pound put it. But what followed? The most widely appreciated English poet since the war is probably still Philip Larkin, whose public pose was 'Blessed are those who do not hope; for they shall not be disappointed'. Professing suspicion towards such large ideas as God or love, he was devoted to England, its older social institutions, and its landscapes. When he died (something he was not looking forward to), it was discovered that when young he had once considered ordination. This chimes with such churchy poems as 'Church Going' and 'An Arundel Tomb'. 'Going, Going', a poem written for the Society for the Preservation of Rural England, has as its penultimate stanza:

And that will be England gone,
The shadows, the meadows, the lanes,
The guildhalls, the carved choirs.
There'll be books; it will linger on
In galleries; but all that remains
For us will be concrete and tyres.[20]

A despairing later poem, 'Aubade', refers to religion as 'That vast moth-eaten musical brocade / Created to pretend we never die'. The religion that meant most to this determined sceptic is what is embodied in medieval English parish churches. The church he did not go to was Gothic: 'I would like to write a poem with such elaborate stanzas that one could wander round in them as in the aisles and side-chapels of some great cathedral.'[21] He preferred choirs to tyres.

'Great British poets begin with H', wrote the Australian Peter Porter, of the poets born in the 1930s: Ted Hughes, Geoffrey Hill, Tony Harrison and Seamus Heaney (British by birth). Though Hughes's primitivism occasionally takes medieval forms (the pool in 'Pike' is 'as deep as England'), only for Hill and Heaney does the medieval have much significance, and then as part of the whole human story. Hill has the keener sense of history. Heaney writes as a Catholic whose literal belief has faded, though much of his writing draws on the communal Catholicism of his home. In the 1990s Hill returned to the Church of England of his upbringing.

Each of these poets was, like Larkin, a scholarship boy, the first in his family to go to university. At Cambridge, Hughes switched from English to Archaeology and Anthropology. At Leeds, Harrison studied Classics. At the Queen's University, Belfast, Seamus Heaney took an English degree. So did Geoffrey Hill at Oxford, as had Larkin before him, and Auden. The English graduates all followed courses which took the form of a historical study of English verse, from medieval to the recent (but not the contemporary). All studied Old and Middle English. All read, or inhaled, T.S. Eliot's 'Tradition and the Individual Talent', an essay of 1919 which claims that the poet 'must be aware that the mind of Europe – the mind of his own country – a mind which he learns in time to be much more important than his own private mind – is a mind which changes, and that this change is a development which abandons nothing *en route*, which does not superannuate either Shakespeare, or Homer, or the rock drawing of the Magdalenian draughtsmen.'[22] Eliot's essay was almost canonical for students of English Literature for five decades. Its theory of tradition seemed to consecrate the historical approach which had already been adopted in English faculties, not always for reasons connected with the mind of Europe.

'Our language is Difficult,' Dickens's Mr Podsnap explains to a French visitor in *Our Mutual Friend*. 'Ours is a Copious Language, and Trying to Strangers.' Philip Larkin enjoyed playing Podsnap, who 'considered other countries ... a mistake, and of their manners and customs would conclusively observe, "Not English!"', clearing them away 'with a peculiar flourish of his right arm'. Larkin liked to boast that he had 'no belief in "tradition" or a common myth-kitty'. Another of his calculated blasphemies was, 'To me, the whole of the ancient world, the whole of classical and biblical mythology means very little.'[23] These negations were strategic. The know-nothing chauvinism professed in interviews by this university librarian is belied by the accuracy with which the titles of his poems mock poems of the past; as in 'He Hears that His Beloved has become Engaged', a parody of the kind of title once affected by Yeats, and by Aubrey Beardsley. Other allusive titles are 'I Remember, I Remember', 'Sad Steps' and 'Annus Mirabilis'. French titles are mocked in 'Femmes Damnées' and 'Poetry of Departures'. 'Sympathy in White Major' parodies both Théophile Gautier's 'Symphonie en blanc majeur' and Whistler's *Symphony in White*. If Larkin's allusiveness is more cautious than Eliot's, his irony is broader and more sardonic. He often echoes J. Alfred Prufrock's 'I have measured out my life with coffee spoons', drinking British Rail coffee – 'Until the next town, new and nondescript, / Approached with acres of dismantled cars.' Larkin loved tradition, mistrusting only the altitude and internationality of Eliot's notion of it, and the pretentiousness of *The Waste Land*'s Notes. The concluding line of Larkin's intimate 'Poem about Oxford' locates his arrival at the university 'In the depths of the Second World War'. Larkin came from Coventry, where these depths were deep. Before the war, the poet's father, who was City Treasurer of Coventry and admired efficiency, had kept on his mantelpiece a statue of Germany's new Chancellor, Mr Hitler, one which gave the Nazi salute. Hitler's air force dismantled acres of Coventry, a centre of motor manufacturing, with some efficiency. The Treasurer's son was at first impressed by Yeats, who dipped into various unorthodox religions. He later turned to Thomas Hardy, who had published collections entitled 'Life's Little Ironies' and 'Satires of Circumstance'.

Geoffrey Hill and Seamus Heaney have in comparison simpler attitudes to family, upbringing and inheritance. 'I began as a poet when my roots were crossed with my reading', wrote Heaney in *Preoccupations*. A Northern Irishman from a rural Catholic background, Heaney moved to Ireland but was at ease in the larger of the offshore islands conquered by Normans in the Middle Ages. History has given the words Catholic and Protestant different resonances in Ireland and England, and different bearings to the words medieval and modern. Never part of the Roman empire, medieval Ireland is less historical and more legendary than medieval England. For Heaney, medieval Ireland was not far from Dark Age Ireland or megalithic Ireland, nor from the Bog People of Denmark. Heaney, like Pound, Eliot, Waugh, Auden, Hill and Harrison, began as a teacher. He honoured teachers, including teachers of language, and his dead masters include those venerated by Eliot. The voice of tradition in Heaney, as in Eliot, comes from a 'familiar compound ghost, both intimate and unidentifiable'. His early poem 'Personal Helicon' ends 'I rhyme / To see myself, to set the darkness echoing'. The tributes to the spring of the Muses, and to the story of Narcissus and Echo, are less ostentatious than similar references in the early work of T.S. Eliot. Heaney's work became increasingly haunted by the voices of Virgil and of Dante. His translation of *Beowulf* brought Scandinavian feud home to Northern Ireland.

Geoffrey Hill, the last poet to be considered here, was born in 1932 near Bromsgrove, a Worcestershire market town not far from Birmingham. Hill went from its High School to Oxford in 1950, lectured at Leeds from 1954, moved to Cambridge in the 1980s and to Boston University in the 1990s, retiring finally to England. Critics admired his poems, and he found more readers with *Mercian Hymns* (1971). Hill's seriousness is so striking that his variety and his humour can be overlooked. He distilled his early poetry to a demanding strength, but in his later work he became more exuberant and viewy.

Mercian Hymns shows him growing up during the Second World War, when England's industrial West Midlands were bombed. An only child, he was the son of the village policeman and grandson of a more senior policeman. In the 1970s, a reorganisation of local government revived some ancient names, notably the West Mercia Constabulary. Boyhood and family impressions merge with the life of Offa, King of Mercia. The hymns are a sequence of thirty brief prose poems, set in the West Midlands/Mercia, the ancient midland kingdom of the Angles, whose king, Offa, was the most powerful ruler in eighth-century Britain. If Anglo-Saxon England is remote, Offa's Mercia is unknown. What little survives of Offa includes a coin with the legend *Rex Totius Anglorum Patriae*, 'King of the Whole Country of the English'. We have little writing from his very long reign. Hill's *Mercian Hymns* are fictional, but their title comes from 'Mercian Hymns' in Sweet's *Anglo-Saxon Reader* of 1876. Henry Sweet included them as 'Examples of Non-West-Saxon Dialects'. They are still there in my copy of the revised edition of the *Reader*, of 1959. The texts which Sweet called 'Hymns' are Anglian glosses written between the lines of Latin biblical texts: a Psalm and five Canticles. Like Auden, Hill took format, style and some content from Old English collections. Unlike Auden, he makes scrupulous acknowledgement. His models are in prose, but they translate liturgical chants. Hill's 'Mercian' models are part of a religious, not a literary, canon. Like Auden's models, they are part of the poet's family legend.

Mercian Hymns is a sequence, like Hill's *Péguy* and *The Triumph of Love*. Although the verbal texture of each hymn is closely woven, the sequence creates a larger field, inviting the reader to walk in and find his bearings. The hymns are a series of short 'versets in rhythmical prose', headed with Latin numerals, as in Auden's early collections. A List of Titles is at the *back* of the book, followed by Acknowledgements. The first of Sweet's 'Mercian Hymns' is the Psalm in which David says he was smaller than his brothers and younger in his father's house. Hill had no brothers.

XXII

At home the curtains were drawn. The wireless boomed
its commands. I loved the battle-anthems and the
gregarious news.

In the 'fantastic context' of *Mercian Hymns*, Offa, Father, Grandfather and Mr Churchill are not distinct from the boy's fantasies of warrior heroism. Ancient weapons and ruined insignia lie with toy aeroplanes in the soil. The hymns celebrate the home ground of Hill's childhood, of things hoarded and a boy's dreams, as does J.G. Ballard's *Empire of the Sun*. In texture, the sequence forms a palimpsest of old and new, the archaic and the anachronistic, 'Offa' with 'Special Offers' from Merovingian car-dealers. Despite the learned nature of some of its sources, it is not dry. It hymns outdoor sensations with exuberance, and can be as sticky as the grasses of *Tess of the d'Urbervilles*, as clinical as *A Portrait of the Artist as a Young Man*, as red in tooth and claw as Ted Hughes, and as boggy as Heaney. It is also fun. For all its seriousness about power and pain, its modernism and the depth of its history, it also has the comic schoolboy quality of *Just William* and Adrian Mole.

XIII

Trim the lamp; polish the lens; draw, one by one, rare
　　coins to the light. Ringed by its own lustre, the
　　masterful head emerges, kempt and jutting, out of
　　England's well. Far from his underkingdom of crin-
　　oid and crayfish, the rune-stone's province, *Rex*
　　Totius Anglorum Patriae, coiffured and ageless,
　　portrays the self-possession of his possession,
　　cushioned on a legend.[24]

'Legend' is a scholarly term for the lettering on a coin. Hill's phrasing clots into Anglo-Saxon doublets: 'kempt and jutting', 'crinoid and crayfish', 'coiffured and ageless'. Hill's tricks of the tongue are held in check by his reflectiveness. His language weighs history scrupulously. Words are distilled, a phrase has several aspects: vigilant precision; respect for due authority; horror of cruelty; knowledge of how the ear misunderstands the tongue; a playfulness under control. He has a Jacobean combination of dark moral concern and a theatrical sense of the absurd.

'Riding through the glen'

Robin Hood, Robin Hood,
Riding through the glen;
Robin Hood, Robin Hood,
With his band of men.
 Feared by the bad,
 Loved by the good,
  Robin Hood,
  Robin Hood,
  Robin Hood!

Theme song by Dick James for *The Adventures of
Robin Hood* (Granada TV series, 1955–9)

The chapters on twentieth-century medievalism have increasingly
focused on literature, the art in which English-speaking people have
since the Reformation expressed themselves more readily than in
painting or music. The medieval has contributed more to literature,
especially to poetry, than it has to other forms of cultural expression; or
so it seems to someone interested in poetry. Literature in English has a
long history, and it has for centuries been conscious of its history. The
syllabus of some older universities has long required the study of texts
in early forms of the language, which, thanks partly to the Norman
Conquest, are more remote from its modern forms than is the case in
other European vernaculars. The effect of the recovery of medieval literature is visible in writers from Gray to Hopkins, and the impress of the
academic study of Old and Middle English literature stamps the writing
of poets from Ezra Pound to Geoffrey Hill. Old English verse has been
translated by Edwin Morgan, Seamus Heaney and Paul Muldoon.

In the twentieth century, the Medieval Revival often took up
Christian themes. This may be because poets have come to feel they

are an endangered species with a need to defend ancient springs. This fear, which goes back as far as the myth of Orpheus, had visited a number of English poets in the eighteenth century. Language is a defining human gift, and in poetry the patterning and power of language appear fully. In some poetry, figures such as metaphor and symbol use language to point beyond itself, as religious language can. If transcendence is essential to religion, Christianity is also a religion of immanence and history, and historical awareness has vastly increased since the late eighteenth century. But the rise of history does not show a triumph of consensus. Narratives of English history have lost confidence in a single national perspective. The simpler assumptions of the Whig consensus are not made by conscientious professional historians, though such assumptions retain popular resonance. Academic history is both ideologically contested and fragmented by specialisation. Many modern historians know little medieval history, and the same goes for professional students of modern English literature. Sophisticated voices have suggested that true historical knowledge is unattainable, a position which robs enquiry of its point. For these and other reasons, the textbooks which gave outlines of a connected national history were discarded in the 1970s. But the abandonment of Our Island Story, like the dropping of Grammar, leaves a vacuum. BBC radio has run, and repeated, an updated, and politically corrected, version of Winston Churchill's super-Whig *History of the English-Speaking Peoples.* Television surveys of English history, such as that by Simon Schama, can succeed. Publishers exploit niche instances of both popular and professional history. But in the continuing absence of a connected national historiography, haziness has grown, especially regarding earlier periods. In popular legend, the only golden age which is reliable at the box office is the age of Elizabeth I, unspotted by the blood shed in enforcing religious uniformity and in colonising Ireland.

The period between the fifth and the fifteenth centuries, once almost uniformly obscure, has been studied in detail, so that scholars can now articulate this vast stretch of history. Since English medieval history involves reading in Latin and two vernaculars, medieval historians are never simply nationalist. Two generations ago, an inclusive survey of medieval Europe in its widest geographical sense, achieved in 1996 by Peter Brown in *The Rise of Western Christendom*, could scarcely have been attempted by a British historian.[1]

The narrative of events, and the publishing of medieval records, have long been supplemented by social history and a host of specialist studies. The part played by religion in history is now studied in its own terms, not explained in other terms. Two generations ago, the writings of David Knowles offered an overdue understanding of the monastic order in the Middle Ages. Academic medievalists have gone beyond events and politics to include, for example, medieval art-history, museum curatorship, manuscript studies, medieval Latin writing, linguistics, the social and economic history of cities and of agriculture, medicine, demography, the liturgy, medieval literary theory, the world of the female mystics, numismatics, place-name studies and medieval archaeology. Revived forms of medievalism have, with the exception of the revived religious orders, become more academic, as for example in the revivals of medieval drama and of medieval music. As Larkin the librarian said, of England, 'There'll be books; it will linger on / In galleries'.

At the beginning of the third millennium of the Christian era, although the English Church and state, landscape and language, have medieval roots, it seems that living influences from the Middle Ages are now less acknowledged in politics, social thinking and the visual arts than they were in the nineteenth century, when a newly rich Britain was interested in its origins. The present effort to identify and trace the leading developments in medievalism has concentrated chiefly on its manifestations in high culture: in literature, social thinking, the arts, political thought and religion. This study, like others, is limited by the author's interests and knowledge, and further limited by conscious decision. Different areas might well have been considered, and other instances might very well have been chosen. A list of what has not been considered might include the Jacobite tradition; the more Christian of the socialist utopias celebrated in Edmund Wilson's *To the Finland Station* (the English tradition owing more to the guild thinking of Ruskin and Morris); other experiments in communal Christian living and social theory; the Arts and Crafts movement, ecclesiastical history, the formation of library and museum collections, the development of palaeography and textual criticism, the history of History and of English and other academic disciplines, legal history, liturgical studies and musicology, the early music movement, the story of twentieth-century cathedral building, the architecture of Sir Ninian Comper, public ceremonials such as coronations and funerals, the study of typography and book illustration, the painting of Samuel Palmer at one end of this story, and of David Piper towards the other end, and the revival of medieval and mock-medieval music. Yet the author's expertise is in literature, medieval and modern, in English.

A criterion adopted at the outset of this essay in cultural history was that medievalism must have some historical reference to a set of medieval texts or facts. Gothic fiction was ruled out as fantasy. This decision was made in full consciousness that the border between history and fiction is a debatable land, and that the atmosphere through which it is viewed changes over time. Thus Scott's medievalist romances had a historical grounding, or clothing, and were welcomed as acceptable, if imaginary, pictures of medieval life; not unlike Shakespeare's History plays. With growing historical knowledge, however, the historical setting of romances such as *Ivanhoe* came to seem flimsy. The historical criterion applied only tangentially to the world which Tennyson created from Arthurian romance and legend, a domain to which Victorian painters so devoted themselves that medievalism remains a defining characteristic of Victorian culture. Gothic Revival architecture is so often Victorian that it seems a constitutive element of that cultural phase. It is said that we shape our buildings, and that they afterward shape us. An example of this is the monastic church which Edward the Confessor built to the west of London. This Minster has for nearly a millennium been the place of consecration of the English monarchy and around it have grown up the buildings which house the British government and Parliament.

Tracing the course of medievalism shows that the historical/ textual criterion initially adopted applies best to the work of Percy and Scott, and works well with the applied medievalism of the period 1840 to 1870, sometimes very well. But it does not apply well to late Victorian art and poetry, which are less medievalist than mythological. The Medieval Revival which began in about 1900 was consciously Christian, and has typically continued as (Anglo-)Catholic. In close parallel with this development, a historically informed medievalism, instituted in the educational syllabus, became a positive element in the poetic literature of modernism, beginning with Pound and Eliot, and continuing in David Jones, Auden and Geoffrey Hill. In prose fiction, the figure of Evelyn Waugh stands in as belated and isolated a position as he could have wished. *Après lui le déluge.*

But for more than a century, mass civilisation and minority culture have pulled apart. In a democracy increasingly dominated by popular media, the high culture of the past can be seen, and is now often represented, as too exclusive. Its contrary, an exclusive populism, now threatens the quality of education and therefore of democracy. For what is called popular culture is now very largely a commercial product, promoted by the media in order to make money for those who own the media. Rupert Murdoch is a worthy successor to the press barons of the Rothermere–Beaverbrook era and to the moguls of Hollywood. The discourse of British political, social and cultural life has firmly been taken in populist directions, often by educated people. Correction is not likely to come from any institutional source, for professional elites are under attack from government. Churches have become marginal, and universities have lost independence. The Chief Executive of the Higher Education Funding Council for England said that 'It was once the role of Governments to provide for the purposes of universities; it is now the role of universities to provide for the purposes of Governments.'[2] An Oxford-educated Conservative Prime Minister described the study of history as a luxury, and a Cambridge-educated New Labour Minister of Education did not want people to study medieval history. Degrees in History now often neglect earlier periods. The literary syllabus usually begins with Shakespeare. In the school syllabus, and in the syllabus of many universities, he is the only required pre-Romantic writer, which makes it difficult to study him historically.

It takes time for new knowledge to become a public possession, and the divide between high and popular culture is widening. Until now, the art of the elites has regularly drawn on the culture of the people, from Chaucer to Shakespeare to Percy to Scott to Dickens. Popular art has in its turn recycled high culture. Shakespeare, who recycled medieval history and romance, has been endlessly recycled.

Scott and Dickens have been staged, put to music and filmed. Chaucer's cruder tales have been put on the stage. Even *Beowulf* is translated, staged and filmed. But the transfer of cultural capital to global audiences is shaped by strong market forces, and popular culture is dominated by a media industry which treats history as a theme park or a source of violent fantasy, as in the American TV series *Game of Thrones*, based on a sexed-up version of formulas deriving from *Ivanhoe*, Alexandre Dumas and Norse saga. The future of high culture, outside its own elites, is precarious, and the elites become precarious. The names of Turner and Ruskin do not sit well in the same sentence as the Turner Prize. The future roles of history, tradition and cultural inheritance are obscure, though the medieval will hold its place among them.

The rise of the visual media, film, television, video, DVD and other forms of electronic transfer, has transformed the mediation of the stories which human beings need, stories previously transmitted through the spoken, the written and the printed word, or by words spoken in live theatres. The visual entertainment media of greater Anglo-Saxondom now have global audiences, and the Middle Ages, like other historical periods, are thereby mediated more by images than by words, though images derived from words. Scott's own romances were staged as soon as they came out. The popularity of historical costume drama transferred quickly into film. 'Medieval' costume dramas have, since *Ivanhoe*, been more romance than history. There are scores of films in the mould of *Ivanhoe*, and of the swashbuckling European romances which followed in the wake of Scott's *Quentin Durward*, such as Alexandre Dumas's *Le Comte de Monte Cristo* and *Les Trois Mousquetaires* of the 1840s. Scott's *Kenilworth*, which tells of the love of Elizabeth I and Leicester, and the murder of Leicester's mistress, Amy Robsart, is told too slowly to be popular today. Yet every year brings a new film on the supposed love life of the Virgin Queen, and, increasingly often, the heroine, like Keats's Madeline, 'loosens her fragrant bodice'.

The exaggerations of popular romance, when rehearsed by sophisticated writers, are often consciously playful; Byron rightly called Scott the Ariosto of the North. On stage, and in Hollywood, this turns into self-parody. Chaucer made fun of romance, and Shakespeare of wizardry. 'This prophecy Merlin shall make, for I live before his time,' jokes Lear's Fool. The words quoted at the head of this epilogue come from the theme song of a TV series descended from *Ivanhoe*. They show the tendency of burlesque is towards vacancy. Nottinghamshire being a county without a glen, Dick James here salutes Walter Scott.

Keats, as we saw, drastically revised Scott's idealised medievalism. Much later, the visit of Mark Twain's Connecticut Yankee to King Arthur's Court turned out very badly.[3] Thackeray wrote a comic sequel to *Ivanhoe* in *Rebecca and Rowena*, and T.H. White's *The Sword in the Stone* perfects a comic modern Arthurianism. In the cinema these revisionary impulses make very old jokes. *Monty Python and the Holy Grail* is a burlesque, in which John Cleese's ability to fight on after his legs have been cut off parodies a scene found in medieval popular romances. The *Grail* film is also a crusade against chivalry. In comparison, Rowan Atkinson's *Blackadder* TV series, though critical of some historical practices, was more a send-up of the cinematic conventions of historical costume drama.

Film, like fantasy, lies beyond the scope of this study. Yet it would be odd to close without mentioning the success with which moving pictures of various kinds have recently fed the appetite for medieval romance. We have noted the success of children's books by J.R.R. Tolkien and C.S. Lewis, members of the Oxford Inklings. Tolkien became a cult on American campuses in the 1960s: the slogan 'FRODO LIVES' decorated the New York subway in 1965. These children's stories, the Inklingasaga, share a social, ethical and metaphysical structure informed by scholarly reading in medieval epic and romance, though their form is mediated by the authors' childhood reading. Innocent, and without the complications of adult sexuality, they feature the brave young man of humble background, the grasping old lord in his castle, the lovely princess, the old dragon guarding gold in the ground, and good and bad magic. They are set in a legendary pre-history or in a fairyland reached through a wardrobe in the school holidays. They take for granted that courage, fidelity, self-sacrifice and love are virtues, and provide the satisfactions of poetic justice and providential endings. It is a boy's world, not of history but of romance: ultimately pre-medieval but clothed (especially by Tolkien) in medieval forms which descend from the romances of

Walter Scott, the verse tales of William Morris and the fantasy of George MacDonald. J.K. Rowling is old-fashioned enough to use her initials, like Tolkien and Lewis, but she is no medievalist.[4] Her school stories have access to a magic world, but have little more than that in common with the tales of C.S. Lewis. She crosses the formulas of the boarding school story (bullies, snobs, swots, games, tyrants and crushes) with the formulas of kiddie Gothic (the magic castle, the young hero, broomsticks, witches, forbidden knowledge). She has Good and Evil, but her morality is less Christian than that of the Inklings.

These phenomena of popular culture do not rely on historical knowledge; their debt is to romance. All are downstream from the meltdown of neo-classical canons and the recovery of pre-modern history and popular literature which began in the mid-eighteenth century. Their mode goes back to kinds of story readmitted at that time, and recreated by Scott. As for history itself, any history written for a general readership needs a story, and stories require prior simplifications. These simplifications have changed since 1760 and since 1860 and since 1960, and are changing now. Those who know any history are now more aware than they once were that the origins of England are medieval and European. Despite one reading of the result of the 'Brexit' referendum, the English are no longer bound to the story of a national independence gained for reasons of conscience at the Reformation, nor to the prospectus of the Enlightenment, nor to imperial projections of the Elizabethan age as simply glorious.[5] Thanks to historical researchers, visionaries, prose romancers and poets, England has since 1760 regained an awareness of and regard for her medieval past, which is now a permanent part of her identity and of her future.

Notes

INTRODUCTION

1. Government buildings in Washington, Paris and Berlin show democracies choosing classical models. Parliament's decision 'established the Gothic as the national style even for secular architecture'. Pevsner, Nikolaus, *London I: The Cities of London and Westminster*, The Buildings of England (Harmondsworth, 1957), 455.
2. Riding, C. and Riding, J., eds, *The Houses of Parliament* (London, 2000), 15.
3. 'Inigo Jones [had] put a renaissance shell on the West end, nave and transepts [of St Paul's] before the Civil War put an end to the work . . . When the chief Gothic monument of the land was to be given a new classical shell, men's vision must have been dominated by new forms.' Clark, Kenneth, *The Gothic Revival: An Essay in the History of Taste* (London, 1928), 4. Wren's St Paul's is smaller than Old St Paul's. For the rebuilt St Peter's in Rome a long nave had also been required.
4. Clark was twenty-five in 1928. Some of his assertions show how taste has changed: for instance, the Gothic Revival produced 'little on which our eyes can rest without pain'. Or, 'art historians have neglected the Gothic Revival. They write about works of art.' Clark records his changed attitudes in footnotes to the third edition (1962).
5. For a brief introduction which does justice to the European and American dimensions of the Revival, see Lewis, Michael J., *The Gothic Revival* (London, 2002).
6. The name 'Ivanhoe' is found in the area in 1839. Wamba Road appears in 1927; Ravenswood Avenue in 1942. *The Heidelberg Historian* 30 (Melbourne, 1972).
7. Acceptance of this subsidy marks the end of the Stuart claim. See Champ, Judith, *The English Pilgrimage to Rome* (Leominster, 2000), 121.
8. See Robinson, Fred, 'Medieval and the Middle Ages', in *The Tomb of Beowulf and Other Essays on Old English* (Oxford, 1993), 304–15.
9. See Lewis, C.S., *De Descriptione Temporum*, his inaugural lecture in the Cambridge Chair of Medieval and Renaissance Literature. *Essays in Criticism* VI (Oxford, 1956), 247.
10. Panofsky, Erwin, *Renaissance and Renascences in Western Art* (New York, 1969), 10, note 1.

CHAPTER 1: THE ADVENT OF THE GOTHS

1. Percy, Thomas, *Reliques of Ancient English Poetry* (London, 1765, 1767, 1794, 1812). Quoted from the essay on ballads in the edition of Edward Walford (London, 1880), 18. The maxim also appears as, 'If a man were permitted to make all the ballads, he need not care who should make the laws of a nation.' Fletcher of Saltoun was author of *An Account of a Conversation concerning a Right Regulation of Governments for the Common Good of Mankind . . .* (1703).
2. Fairer, D. and Gerrard, C., eds, *Eighteenth-Century Poetry* (Oxford, 1999), 'The Bard', 388.

3. Ibid., 'Fragment 8', 410.
4. Walpole, Horace, *The Castle of Otranto*, Lewis, W.S., ed., introduced by E.J. Clery (Oxford, 1998), x.
5. Walpole entitled his first publication, a catalogue of his father's paintings at Houghton Hall, *Aedes Walpolianae*, 'The House of Walpole'. William Marshall is the name of the man whom Thomas Cromwell commissioned to translate Marsilius of Padua's *Defensor Pacis* (1535), which maintains the superiority of the State to the Church. On Chatterton and Walpole, see Meyerstein, E.H.W., *A Life of Thomas Chatterton* (London, 1930), 262ff.
6. Fairer and Gerrard, *Eighteenth-Century Poetry*, 313.
7. Thus, the Earl of Surrey's epitaph on Sir Thomas Wyatt claims that his friend's verse had 'reft Chaucer the glory of his wit'. Jones, Emrys, ed., *The New Oxford Book of Sixteenth-Century Verse* (Oxford, 1992), 111, line 14.
8. Butt, J., ed., *The Poems of Alexander Pope, A One-Volume Edition of the Twickenham Pope*, rev. edn (London, 1968), *Essay on Criticism*, 295–6, 153.
9. Hayden, John O., ed., *William Wordsworth, The Poems*, 2 vols (Harmondsworth, 1977), II, 873.
10. Keegan, Paul, ed., *New Penguin Book of English Verse* (Harmondsworth, 2000), 398, lines 1–5, 11–12.
11. Butt, *The Poems of Alexander Pope*, 'Eloisa to Abelard', 1–3, 252.
12. Pope's slumbering abbot is picturesque but unhistorical. 'The Black Monks have rendered invaluable services to civilization, not only in preparing the social organization of the Middle Ages during the chaos of barbarian rule after the fall of the Roman empire, but also in preserving (for instance through the eighteenth century in France) the ideals and practice of true scholarship . . .'. Cross, F.L. and Livingstone, E.A., eds, *Oxford Dictionary of the Christian Church*, 2nd edn (Oxford, 1990). English Benedictines included Bishop Walmsley (1722–97), a mathematician who led Britain to accept in 1752 the Gregorian Calendar introduced by Pope Gregory XIII in 1582.
13. Butt, *The Poems of Alexander Pope, Essay on Criticism*, 166, 690–1. Thomas Hearne (Wurmius), though a layman, lost his Bodleian Library post for his Non-Juring principles. He had printed the text of *The Battle of Maldon* and much else. Anglican Non-Jurors declined to take the oaths of allegiance and supremacy to William and Mary, as breaking those they had sworn to James II. Non-Juror scholarship preserved many documents of the past, as in Bishop George Hickes's *Linguarum veterum Septentrionalium Thesaurus* of 1703–5.
14. Walpole, *Otranto*, Clery's introduction, xxxiii.
15. Johnston, Arthur, *Enchanted Ground: The Study of Medieval Romance in the Eighteenth Century* (London, 1964). Johnston's full exploration of this 'important byway in eighteenth-century studies' leaves out ballads, Chatterton, Ossian, Tyrwhitt, Gray's Old Norse, Horace Walpole, etc. Also 'architecture, art, sculpture, tapestries, wall-paintings, political institutions and social organisation. Before any adequate study of the Medieval Revival as a whole can be written, these separate topics need to be studied thoroughly.'
16. Spenser, Edmund, *The Faerie Queene*, ed. Roche, T.P. (Harmondsworth, 1978).
17. Percy, in Boswell's *Life of Johnson*, ed. Chapman, R.W. (Oxford, 1953), 36.
18. Crabbe, George, *The Library*, 1781; Johnston, *Enchanted Ground*, 28.
19. Mayhew, Henry, *London Labour and the London Poor* (London, 1864), I, 324. Johnston, *Enchanted Ground*, 40.
20. Pope, Alexander, *The Dunciad*, I, 128–30. Cf. Scott, Walter, *Marmion*, IV, 87–90: 'For Eustace much had por'd / Upon a huge romantic tome, / In the hall window of his home, / Imprinted at the antique dome / Of Caxton or De Worde.' *Poems by Sir Walter Scott* (Oxford, 1913), 174.

21. Duncan-Jones, Katherine, ed., *Sir Philip Sidney* (Oxford, 1989), 231. 'Chevy Chase' is a ballad on one of the many clashes between English Percys and Scottish Douglases in the hunting forest of the Cheviot Hills.

22. Gray added some Norse mythology to 'The Bard', arguing that a poet might be 'permitted (in that scarcity of Celtic ideas we labour under) to adopt some of these foreign whimsies, dropping however all mention of Woden and his Valkhyrian virgins'. Johnston, *Enchanted Ground*, 85. The scholarship of 'The Bard' is scrupulous yet unhistorically eclectic.

23. In a note, Percy quotes Sidney's praise for 'the old song of Percy and Douglas', and Joseph Addison's account of the ballad in *The Spectator*. Its first line is 'The Persé out of Northumberlonde'.

24. Cf. the comment of a civil servant on Charles Dickens: 'he seems ... to get his first notions of an abuse from the discussions which accompany its removal'. Sir Stephen James Fitzjames, 'The Licence of Modern Novelists', in Wall, Stephen, ed., *Charles Dickens: Penguin Critical Anthologies* (Harmondsworth, 1970), 106.

25. Hayden, *Wordsworth, The Poems*, II, 939–42. *Lyrical Ballads* (1798) begins with 'The Rime of the Ancyent Marinere', a ballad in form and spelling. Coleridge's 'Dejection: An Ode' begins 'Well! If the Bard was weather-wise, who made / The grand old ballad of Sir Patrick Spence'.

CHAPTER 2: CHIVALRY, ROMANCES AND REVIVAL

1. Johnston, Arthur, *Enchanted Ground: The Study of Medieval Romance in the Eighteenth Century* (London, 1964), 56.

2. Ibid., 50.

3. Burke, Edmund, *Reflections on the Revolution in France*, ed. Mitchell, L.G. (Oxford, 1993), 77.

4. Duncan-Jones, Katherine, ed., *Sir Philip Sidney* (Oxford, 1989), 169; see also the French Triumph, ibid., 299ff.

5. Johnston, *Enchanted Ground*, 22.

6. Anderson, W.E.K., ed., *The Journal of Sir Walter Scott*, rev. edn (Edinburgh, 1998), 286.

7. Hardy, F.E., *The Life of Thomas Hardy* (London, 1962), 49. Some Victorian classicists accepted *Marmion* as a true epic, John Conington using its metre for his 1867 translation of the *Aeneid*. See Gransden, K.W., ed., *Virgil in English* (Harmondsworth, 1996), xxvi.

8. Sutherland, John, *The Life of Walter Scott* (Oxford, 1995), 150.

9. Johnston, *Enchanted Ground*, 179.

10. Chaucer, Geoffrey, *The Canterbury Tales*, Fragment VII, lines 712–17, 778–91, 891–3. Benson, L.D., ed., *The Riverside Chaucer*, 3rd edn (Oxford, 1987).

11. Ibid., *Troilus and Criseyde*, III, 1090ff.

12. Carley, James, *Glastonbury Abbey: The Holy House at the Head of the Moors Adventurous*, rev. edn (Glastonbury, 1996), 36–7.

13. Biddle, Martin, *King Arthur's Round Table: An Archaeological Investigation* (Woodbridge, 2000).

14. Sisam, Kenneth, ed., *Fourteenth Century Verse and Prose*, 1921; corrected edn (Oxford, 1975), 14–15.

15. Buchan, John, *Life of Sir Walter Scott* (London, 1932), 50; Johnson, Edgar, *Sir Walter Scott: The Great Unknown* (London, 1970), 93.

16. Coleridge could have found 'Fair Cristabelle', the daughter of a 'bonnye kinge', in 'Sir Cauline', the fourth poem in Percy's *Reliques*. *Christabel*'s octosyllabic, four-stress couplet comes from Chatterton's 'Unknown Knight'.

17. *The Works of Sir Walter Scott* (London, 1995), 2.

18. *Poems by Sir Walter Scott* (Oxford, 1913), *The Lay of the Last Minstrel*, Canto I, iv, 4–5.

19. Ibid., 32–2.

20. Saintsbury, George, *A Short History of English Literature* (London, 1898, 1908), 664.

21. Scott, Walter, *Ivanhoe*, ed., Tulloch, Graham, Penguin rev. edn of the Edinburgh Edition of the Waverley Novels (Harmondsworth, 2000), 70.

22. The way Isaac of York pushes to the front at Ashby may be modelled on the way prominent Jews were accused of behaving at Richard's coronation, causing a riot. I thank Professor John Gillingham for confirming details of this incident.

23. See introduction and notes of *Ivanhoe*, ed. Duncan, Ian (Oxford, 1996).

CHAPTER 3: DIM RELIGIOUS LIGHTS

1. Percy, Thomas, *Reliques of Ancient English Poetry*, ed. Walford, Edward (London, 1880), 62.

2. The first of the 'Ballads that Illustrate Shakespeare', ibid., Book II, 95.

3. *Poems by Sir Walter Scott* (Oxford, 1913), *Marmion*, Introduction to Canto VI, 10–13.

4. Scott, Walter, *Ivanhoe*, ed. Duncan, Ian (Oxford, 1996), 16. Strutt's O.E. does not make sense: *Glig-Gamena* means 'Of the Glee-Games', but Angel—Deod joins 'Englan(d)' to 'Theod' ('Nation'), without making 'Angel' possessive. Strutt, an engraver, also wrote *A Complete View of the Dress and Habits of the People of England*, 1796–9. Scott's completion of Strutt's unfinished novel *Queen-Hoo Hall* in 1808 was a flop, but gave him the idea of *Waverley*.

5. Carey, J. and Fowler, A., eds, *Poems of John Milton* (London, 1968), 46, lines 155–60.

6. As in 'L'Allegro', 77–80. Ibid, 136: 'Towers and battlements it sees / Bosomed high in tufted trees / Where perhaps some beauty lies / The cynosure of neighbouring eyes.' The 'it' is 'mine eye'.

7. Colmer, J., ed., *Coleridge: Selected Poems* (Oxford, 1967), 119–20, lines 175ff.

8. Crawford, T., ed., *Sir Walter Scott: Selected Poems* (Oxford, 1972), *The Lay of the Last Minstrel*, V, xi, 176–8; V, xii, 199–202.

9. Ibid., V, xii, 218–24.

10. Ibid., II, xi, xv.

11. *Poems by Sir Walter Scott* (Oxford, 1913), *The Lady of the Lake*, III, stanza xxix; *Marmion* II, xix, xxv, xxxii.

12. A sectarian libel; originally, perhaps, a misunderstanding of the cells of the hermits known as anchoresses. Julian(a) of Norwich was a famous anchoress. Dame Julian, born *c.* 1343, was the most winning of the mystics of her era. At the window of her cell, in the wall of a church in the middle of Norwich, many came to consult her. Margery Kempe walked from King's Lynn to Norwich to do so.

13. In his 'Essay on Chivalry' in the *Encyclopaedia Britannica* Scott wrote of 'the Romish clergy, who have in all ages possessed the wisdom of serpents, if they sometimes have fallen short of the simplicity of doves . . .' Scott 'had little understanding of Catholicism. This man, for whom when he was dying John Henry Newman besought the prayers of the faithful, cherished a blunt Protestantism, to which he was never weary of testifying.' Buchan, John, *Life of Sir Walter Scott* (London, 1932), 227–8.

14. Matthew, 27:56. For the identification of the 'sinner' with Mary Magdalene, see Murray, Peter and Linda, eds, *The Oxford Companion to Christian Art and Architecture* (Oxford, 1996), 291–3.

15. Barnard, J., ed., *John Keats: The Complete Poems*, 2nd edn (Harmondsworth, 1977), 'The Eve of St Agnes', stanzas xxiv–vi.

16. Newman, J.H., *A Letter Addressed to the Duke of Norfolk* ... (London, 1875), section 5.

17. Letter of 3 February 1883. Gardner, W.H., ed., *Poems and Prose of Gerard Manley Hopkins* (Harmondsworth, 1953), 194–6.

18. Although his 'Jerusalem' employs the romance legend of Joseph of Arimathea having brought Jesus to Glastonbury, Blake was not a historical medievalist. See Carley, James, *Glastonbury Abbey* (Glastonbury, 1996).

CHAPTER 4: 'RESIDENCES FOR THE POOR'

1. Doyle, William, *The French Revolution* (Oxford, 2001), Ch. 1.

2. Beales, A.C.F., *Education under Penalty* (London, 1963), 272–3.

3. Scott, Walter, *The Monastery* (London, 1878), 28.

4. Anderson, W.E.K., ed., *The Journal of Sir Walter Scott*, rev. edn (Edinburgh, 1998), 249. Jeffrey Wyatt was the nephew of James Wyatt, Beckford's architect at Fonthill Abbey, drastic restorer at Salisbury Cathedral and elsewhere and Pugin's 'Wyatt the Destroyer'. In 1824 Jeffrey Wyatt had his name chivalricly augumented to Wyattville.

5. Girouard, Mark, *Return to Camelot: Chivalry and the English Gentleman* (New Haven and London, 1981).

6. Lewis, Michael J., *The Gothic Revival* (London, 2002), 52; Anderson, *Journal of Sir Walter Scott*, 66; Sutherland, John, *The Life of Walter Scott: A Critical Biography* (Oxford, 1995), 134 and 27.

7. Lewis, *Gothic Revival*, 81.

8. Ibid., 84.

9. Milner's scholarship was not confined to architecture. See Couve de Murville, Archbishop M.N.L., *John Milner*, Archdiocese of Birmingham Historical Commission 2, 1986.

10. Lewis, *Gothic Revival*, 84.

11. See Atterbury, Paul and Wainwright, Clive, eds, *Pugin: A Gothic Passion* (London, 1994).

12. Pugin's fervour can be seen in this comment upon the demand for his church designs in Australia: 'England is, indeed, awakened to a sense of her ancient glory, and the reverence for things speedily passes on to the men and principles which produced them. But why do I say England, – Europe, Christendom is aroused; wherever I travel, I meet pious and learned ecclesiastics and laymen all breathing the same sentiments regarding mediaeval art, and more than one Bishop has departed across the ocean to the antipodes, carrying the seeds of Christian design to grow and flourish in the New World, and soon the solemn chancels and cross-crowned spires will arise, the last object which the mariner will behold on the shores of the Pacific till their venerable originals greet his glad view on England's shores.' Andrews, Brian, *Australian Gothic* (Melbourne, 2001), 69.

13. Hewison, Robert et al., *Ruskin, Turner and the Pre-Raphaelites* (London, 2000), 18.

14. Wainwright, in Atterbury and Wainwright, *Pugin*, 19.

15. Wainwright, quoted in Parry, Linda, *William Morris* (London, 1996), 355.

16. In 1842 the Home Secretary put the number receiving poor relief in England and Wales at nearly 1,500,000. See Disraeli, Benjamin, *Sybil*, ed. Smith, Sheila (Oxford, 1988), viii. As for Irish immigration, the 1841 census showed 289,404 Britons born in Ireland living in England; and in 1851, nearly 520,000. See Winder, Robert, 'Bloody Foreigners', *The Tablet* (London, 5 June 2004).

17. The idea that Gothic is natural and classical artificial is ancient. 'In 1510, in the report of the so-called Pseudo Raphael ... the theory is first advanced that

the Gothic style had its origins in the forests, because the Germans could not cut down trees, but bound together the branches of living trees, thus creating the pointed arch. This theory that the Gothic style was born in the forests of Germany lived on in various forms with unbelievable tenacity, sometimes in a literal form, and sometimes in the form of metaphors.' Frankl, Paul, *Gothic Architecture*, rev. Crossley, Paul (London and New Haven, 1962, 2000), 263.

18. Most of Pugin's commissions were ecclesiastical, but some Catholic authorities objected to rood-screens as preventing sight of the elevation of the consecrated host. Some of his screens were later removed. Among buildings he designed are the Catholic cathedrals of Birmingham, Newcastle, Southwark and Killarney; St Giles, Cheadle; also Taymouth Castle, Alton Towers and Maynooth seminary. His sons carried on his work.

19. An interesting exception is the (Nonconformist) chapel of the Countess of Huntingdon's Connexion, Bath, 1765: 'purely Gothick of the most playful kind'. Pevsner, Nikolaus, *North Somerset and Bristol* (Harmondsworth, 1958; London, 2000), 68.

20. 'The invisible structure – foundations, construction, ventilation, heating, fireproof construction and the iron framing of its towers – was a triumph of industrial technology, making it the world's first large modern building, where the architect was forced to consider the mechanical systems as a central part of his task.' Lewis, *Gothic Revival*, 83.

21. Ibid., 82.

22. James Harrington's *The Commonwealth of Oceana*, 1656, posits the existence of an ancient or Gothic constitution. For the influence of this idea see Pocock, J.G.A., *The Ancient Constitution and the Feudal Law* (London, 1987). Also Smith, R.J., *The Gothic Bequest: Medieval Institutions in British Thought 1688–1863* (London, 2002).

23. 'Cwaeth hwaethre that he wolde mid his freondum and mid his ealdormannum and mid his witum spraece habban and getheaht.... Tha haefde he spraece and getheaht mid his witum, and synderlice was fram him eallum frignende hwelc him thuhte and gesewen waere...' Davis, N., ed., *Sweet's Anglo-Saxon Primer*, 9th edn (Oxford, 1970), 90.

24. Onions, C.T., *Sweet's Anglo-Saxon Reader* (Oxford, 1959), 6.

25. See Jones, Edwin, *The English Nation: The Great Myth* (Stroud, 1998).

26. Henry Hoare the Second wrote to his daughter in 1762, 'As I was reading Voltaire's *L'Histoire Générale* lately, in his character of Alfred the Great he says, *Je ne sais s'il y a jamais eu sur la terre un homme plus digne des respects de la postérité qu'Alfred-le-Grand, qui rendit ses services à sa patrie.*' At Stourhead, Wiltshire, Hoare built Alfred's Tower (160 feet), completed in 1772. The inscription reads 'ALFRED THE GREAT / A.D. 879 on this summit / Erected his standard against the Danish Invaders / To Him we owe / The origin of Juries / The Establishment of a Militia / the Creation of a Naval Force / Alfred the light of a benighted age / was a Philosopher and a Christian / The Father of his People / The Founder of the English / MONARCHY AND LIBERTY.' Hoare also acquired Bristol High Cross in 1764. This medieval monument originally stood at a crossroads in the city, but was removed by petition of the citizens, who described it as '... a ruinous and superstitious Relick, which is at present a public nuisance ...' Alfred had appeared in the Temple of British Worthies at Stowe in the early 1740s. Woodbridge, Keith, *The Stourhead Landscape* (London, 1986, 2002), 26. See also Lewis, *Gothic Revival*, 19–20; Bevington, Michael, *Stowe House* (London, 2002).

27. Macaulay, Thomas, 'Sir James Mackintosh', *Essays contributed to the Edinburgh Review*, Vol. 2 (Edinburgh, 1843).

CHAPTER 5: BACK TO THE FUTURE IN THE 1840s

1. Riding, C. and Riding, J., eds, *The Houses of Parliament* (London, 2000), 15.
2. Carlyle, Thomas, *Past and Present* (London, 1843); edn of 1872, 19.
3. Ibid., 57.
4. Ibid.,182.
5. Ibid., 238.
6. Ibid., 221.
7. Blake's 'On Virgil', engraved in 1820, Keynes, Geoffrey, ed. *The Complete Writings of William Blake*, 2nd edn (Oxford, 1966), 778.
8. Disraeli, Benjamin, *Sybil or, The Two Nations*, ed. Smith, Sheila (Oxford, 1998), Ch. 3, 9.
9. Ibid., 10.
10. Ibid., Ch. 5, 65–6.
11. The editor of *Sybil* (ibid., 434) quotes Carlyle's 'this once merry England of ours' (*Chartism*, Ch. 10), and Pugin's 'Catholic England was merry England, at least for the humbler classes', from *The True Principles of Pointed or Christian Architecture* (1841).
12. Disraeli, *Sybil*, 78.
13. Ibid., 273.
14. Cf. 'The Crimes & Cruelties of this Prince, were too numerous to be mentioned & nothing can be said in his Vindication, but that his abolishing Religious Houses & leaving them to the ruinous depredations of Time has been of infinite use to the Landscape of England in general, which probably was a principal motive for his doing it, since otherwise why should a Man who was of no Religion himself be at so much trouble to abolish one which had for Ages been established in the Kingdom?' Jane Austen, *The History of England by a partial, prejudiced & ignorant Historian* (1791).
15. Disraeli, *Sybil*, 434 and 323.
16. Blake, Robert, *Disraeli* (London, 1966), 172.
17. Ibid., 581–7.
18. Ibid., 273.
19. Ibid., 171–2.
20. Riding and Riding, *Houses of Parliament*, 15.
21. See this volume, Ch. 11.
22. Wheeler, Michael, *Ruskin's God* (Cambridge, 1999), 125–52.
23. Blake, *Disraeli*, 504.
24. Disraeli, *Sybil*, Ch. 12, 111.
25. General Preface to 8th edn of *Lothair*, 1870; quoted in Vernon Bogdanor's introduction to his edition (Oxford, 1975), xiii. See Hunter Blair, Right Rev. Sir David, *John Patrick, Third Marquess of Bute, K.T.* (London, 1921); Macrides, R.J., 'The Scottish Connexion in Byzantine and Modern Greek Studies', St John's House Papers No. 4 (St Andrews, 1992); and Mordaunt Crook, J., *William Burges and the High Victorian Dream* (London, 1981).
26. Newman, J.H., *Apologia pro Vita Sua*, ed. Ker, Ian (Harmondsworth, 1994), 99. Compare the wording of this comment on Sir Kenelm Digby's conversion, which took place in 1825: 'his boyish mind, like that of so many others, was turned in a Catholic direction by the chivalrous poems of Sir Walter Scott'. Holland, Bernard, *Memoir of Sir Kenelm Digby* (1919; Sevenoaks, 1992), 37.
27. Newman, *Apologia*, 99–100.
28. Everett, Barbara, review article on Coleridge, *London Review of Books* (London, 7 August 2003).
29. Ker, Ian, *John Henry Newman: A Biography* (London, 1988), 323. See also Kemp, Martin, *The Chapel of Trinity College Oxford* (London, 2014).

CHAPTER 6: 'THE DEATH OF ARTHUR WAS THE FAVOURITE VOLUME'

1. Ellis, George, ed., *Specimens of Early English Metrical Romances*, 3 vols (London, 1805).
2. Scott, Walter, *Ivanhoe*, ed. Duncan, Ian (Oxford, 1996), viii.
3. Jones, George, 'The Coronation Banquet of George IV', in Riding, C. and Riding, J., eds, *The Houses of Parliament* (London, 2000), 79.
4. Mancoff, Debra N., *The Return of King Arthur: The Legend through Victorian Eyes* (New York and London, 1995), 35.
5. Keegan, Paul, ed., *New Penguin Book of English Verse* (Harmondsworth, 2000), 675; Priestley, J.B., ed., *The Novels of Thomas Love Peacock* (London, 1967), 222.
6. Malory, Sir Thomas, *Le Morte Darthur*, ed. Shepherd, Stephen H.A. (New York and London, 2004), xxxix.
7. Cited in ibid., xxix.
8. The 1634 edition, 'still quite widely available' in the 1790s, was on sale in 1798 at £2.10s, and in 1814 at 12 guineas. Cooper, Helen, 'Malory and the Early Prose Romances', in Saunders, Corinne, ed., *A Companion to Romance: Classical to Contemporary* (Oxford, 2004), 104–20.
9. Digby, Sir Kenelm, *The Broad Stone of Honour* (1822). *The First Book: Godefredus* (London, 1829), 3. Digby's conversion to Catholicism in 1825 informs the third edition of his book.
10. Ibid., 5. 'If the inspiring conception of Kenelm Digby's first book took place in pastoral dauphiny, its title flashed upon him, he says, when he saw the ruined castle of Ehrenbreitstein, on the opposite bank of the Rhine to the ancient city of Coblenz. Ehrenbreitstein means, in English, Broadstone of Honour.' Ibid., 62.
11. Ricks, Christopher, ed., *The Poems of Tennyson* (London, 1969), 1755–6, lines 33–41.
12. Abbott, C.C., ed., *The Correspondence of G.M. Hopkins and R.W. Dixon*, 2nd edn (Oxford, 1955), 24.
13. Ricks, *Poems of Tennyson*, 595, lines 239–41.
14. The Duke of Argyll wrote to Tennyson on 22 February 1862: 'It will touch you, I think, that she [Victoria] had substituted "widow" for "widower" and "her" for "his" in the lines "Tears of the Widower" [XIII].' See Dyson, Hope and Tennyson, Charles, *Dear and Honoured Lady* (London, 1969), 67. I am obliged to Professor Michael Wheeler for this point and to Sir Christopher Ricks for the reference.
15. Ricks, *Poems of Tennyson*, 354. The lines quoted below, 46–50, 55–9, 69–72, 73–7, 93–4 and 109–7, are from the 1842 revised text. Only 46–50 has substantial differences from 1832.
16. Pope, *Epistle to Arbuthnot*, lines 43–4, Butt, J., ed., *The Poems of Alexander Pope* (London, 1968).
17. Tillotson, Kathleen, in Ricks, *Poems of Tennyson*, 164.
18. Ibid., 1461.
19. Malory, Sir Thomas, *Le Morte Darthur: The Winchester Manuscript*, ed. Cooper, Helen (Oxford, 1998).
20. Cooper, in Saunders, ed., *A Companion to Romance*, 112.
21. Cooper glosses: 'wan] darken'. This is modelled on Malory's source in the Stanzaic Morte: 'waters deep and waves wan'. But 'wan' could be an adjective. See Cooper edition (note 154), 562.
22. Ricks, *Poems of Tennyson*, 591–2, lines 136–42. The numbers of the lines quoted next are 1–2, 9–10, 182–3, 226–7 and 269–72.

CHAPTER 7: HISTORY, THE REVIVAL AND THE PRB

1. Wedgwood, Alexandra, 'The Mediæval Court', in Atterbury, Paul and Wainwright, Clive, eds, *Pugin: A Gothic Passion* (London, 1994), Ch. 18.
2. Brown, Peter, *The Rise of Western Christendom*, 2nd edn (Oxford, 2003).

3. See for example 'An Octangular Umbrello to Terminate a View', in Batty Langley's Preface to his *Gothic Architecture Improved* (1742); Pl. III in Clark, Kenneth, *Gothic Revival: An Essay in the History of Taste* (London, 1928), 51.

4. See Mordaunt Crook, J., *The Problem of Style* (Chicago, 1987).

5. Geats would become Yeats in modern English. (Ancestors of W.B. Yeats came from Yorkshire.)

6. Scott knew Sharon Turner's *The History of the Manners, Landed Property, Government, Laws, Poetry, Literature, Religion and Language of the Anglo-Saxons* (London, 1805). Turner translates passages from *Beowulf.* Liuzza, R.M., *Beowulf, A New Verse Translation* (Broadview, Ontario, 2000), prints an extract from Turner's version, and from the partial versions made by Conybeare (1826), Kemble (1837) and Longfellow (1838).

7. *The Anglo-Saxon Poems of Beowulf, The Traveller's Song, and the Battle of Finnesburh* (London, 1833); 2nd edn, I (1835), II (Translation, Introduction, Notes, Glossary) (1837). See Hall, J.R., 'The First Two Editions of Beowulf: Thorkelin's (1815) and Kemble's (1833)', in Scragg, D.G. and Szarmach, Paul E., eds, *The Editing of Old English: Papers from the 1990 Manchester Conference* (Woodbridge, 1994), 239–50.

8. Samuel Palmer and his Shoreham 'Ancients' of the 1820s had no magazine, no manifesto.

9. Hilton, Timothy, *The Pre-Raphaelites* (London, 1970), 23.

10. Ibid., 20.

11. Ibid., 11.

12. Clark, *The Gothic Revival*, 14; Hewison, Robert et al., *Ruskin, Turner and the Pre-Raphaelites* (London, 2000), 30.

13. In a sermon of 10 March 1849, 'Sacramental and Anti-sacramental Systems'. Wheeler, Michael, *The Old Enemies: Catholic and Protestant in Nineteenth-Century English Culture* (Cambridge, 2006), 190. Holman Hunt put John the Baptist in his *A Converted British Family Sheltering a Christian Priest from the Druids*; Hilton, *Pre-Raphaelites*, pl. 26; Whiteley, Jon, *Oxford and the Pre-Raphaelites* (Oxford, 1969), 9.

14. 'Depend upon it, Sir, were it not for the Academy we should all be treated as carpenters' (William Collins, father of Charles Collins, a Pre-Raphaelite influenced by the Oxford Movement, to Haydon). Hilton, *Pre-Raphaelites*, 66.

15. Ibid., 52; Hewison, *Ruskin, Turner and the Pre-Raphaelites*, 30.

16. Ibid., 30.

17. Dante Gabriel Rossetti's comment: Abrams, M.H. and Greenblatt, S., eds, *The Norton Anthology of English Literature*, 7th edn (New York, 2000), 1574. The poem is quoted in the 'seriously revised' form in which 'it appeared in the volume of 1870'. Rossetti, W.M., ed., *The Works of Dante Gabriel Rossetti* (London, 1911), 617.

18. Hilton, *Pre-Raphaelites*, 164.

19. Crump, R.W., ed., *Christina Rossetti: The Complete Poems* (Harmondsworth, 2001), 796.

20. Wedgwood, in Atterbury and Wainwright, eds, *Pugin*, Ch. 18.

CHAPTER 8: HISTORY AND LEGEND

1. Hewison, Robert et al., *Ruskin, Turner and the Pre-Raphaelites* (London, 2000), 31.

2. Wheeler, Michael, *The Old Enemies: Catholic and Protestant in Nineteenth-Century English Culture* (Cambridge, 2006), Ch. 1.

3. Belcher, Margaret, 'Pugin Writing', in Atterbury, Paul and Wainwright, Clive, eds, *Pugin: A Gothic Passion* (London, 1994), 115. Wheeler, *Old Enemies*, 78.

4. See Lewis, Michael J., *The Gothic Revival* (London, 2002). Mordaunt Crook, J., *The Problem of Style* (Chicago, 1987).

5. Cf. 'Four thousand winter thought he not too long', in 'Adam Lay Ibounden', a lyric in Gray, Douglas, ed., *The Oxford Book of Late Medieval Verse and Prose* (Oxford, 1985), 161.

6. Cook, E.T. and Wedderburn, A., eds, *The Works of John Ruskin*, 39 vols (London and New York, 1903–12), XXXVI, 115.

7. Trevor, Meriol, *Newman's Journey* (London, 1962), 111.

8. Burne-Jones's *King Cophetua and the Beggar Maid* borrows iconography and many details from Tennyson's poem 'The Beggar Maid' (1833): 'Bare-footed came the beggar maid / Before the king Cophetua. / In robe and crown the king stepped down …' Ezra Pound refers to Burne-Jones's drawings for this painting in his *Hugh Selwyn Mauberley* (see page 202). The painting is now in Birmingham.

9. Martin, R.B., *Tennyson: The Unquiet Heart* (London, 1983), 392.

10. Whiteley, Jon, *Oxford and the Pre-Raphaelites* (Oxford, 1969), 10.

11. Ibid., 46.

12. Hewison, *Ruskin, Turner and the Pre-Raphaelites*, 31 (Pl. 6).

13. Ibid., 216.

14. Dr Rhiannon Purdie of St Andrews summarises the incident: 'Sir Isumbras carries two young children across a ford. He, his wife and three children have been banished from their land. The extract below may serve as a sample of popular romance. In it he loses the two elder children while crossing a river; he goes on to lose his wife to pirates and the youngest son to a unicorn.' Dr Purdie also provides the following extract from Mills, Maldwyn, ed., *Six Middle English Romances* (London and Melbourne, 1973):

Sex deyes were come and gone	
Mete ne drynke hadde they none,	
For hongur they wepte sore.	
They kome by a watur kene,	*arrived at*
Therovur they wold fayn have bene,	
Thenne was her kare the more.	*their*
His eldeste sone he toke there	
And ovur the water he hym bere,	
And sette him by a brome.	*broom-plant*
He seyde, 'Leve sone, sytte her styll,	*Dear*
Whyle I fette thy brodur the tyll	*to thee*
And pley de with a blome.'	*do you play with a flower*
The knyghte was both good and hende	
And ovur the watur he ganne wende;	*began to go, went*
His othur sone he nome.	*took*
He bare hym ovur the wature wylde;	
A lyon fette his eldeste chylde	*took*
Or he to londe come.	*before*
With carefull herte and sykynge sore,	
His myddleste sone he lafte thore,	*there*
And wente wepynge aweye.	
Ther come a lybarte and fette that other,	*leopard*
And bare hym to the wode to his brother,	
As I you seye in faye.	*truth*
The knyghte seyde his lady tyll,	
'Take we gladly Goddes wyll,	*Let us accept*
Hertyly I yow praye.'	
The lady wepte and hadde grette care;	
She hadde almoste herself forfare,	*died*
On londe ther she ley.	

(lines 163–92)

15. In Sandys's *A Nightmare* (Plate 18) a PRB paste pot with stick and peacock feather swings from the saddle. Huddling together on the far shore are the diminished idols of the Royal Academy, Michelangelo, Raphael and Titian. The horse in Millais's original painting had been criticised as being too big. Sandys makes his ass even bigger. The riddling lines, again provided by Tom Taylor, could be translated: 'He used to bray for Turner; Millais called him Russet-skin; but women, and men of understanding, called him Great Humbug.'

CHAPTER 9: THE WORKING MEN AND THE COMMON GOOD

1. Gilmour, David, *The Long Recessional* (London, 2003), 9–10; Hilton, *The Pre-Raphaelites* (London, 1970), 204.
2. Hilton, *Pre-Raphaelites*, 148.
3. Ibid., 158.
4. Ibid., 133.
5. See Murray, K.M. Elizabeth, *Caught in the Web of Words: James A.H. Murray and the Oxford English Dictionary* (London, 1977).
6. In Ellis, Steve, *Geoffrey Chaucer, Writers and their Work* (London, 1996), 62.
7. Malory, Sir Thomas, *Le Morte Darthur: The Winchester Manuscript*, ed. Cooper, Helen (Oxford, 1998), 480. Rossetti takes as his subject the critical moment of Malory's narrative in *Sir Lancelot in the Queen's Chamber*, 1857 (Plate 20). Lancelot is denounced to Arthur as a traitor by Agravain and Mordred. Ambushed in Guenevere's chamber, Lancelot kills most of his accusers, but the Round Table is broken up. In defeating Mordred, King Arthur will die.
8. Benson, L.D., ed., *The Riverside Chaucer*, 3rd edn (Oxford, 1987), *The Nun's Priest's Tale*, lines 3212–13, 3163–5.
9. The line means 'Swollen with anger, he destroyed the doomed creature'. See Crawford, R., ed., *Launch-Site for English Studies* (St Andrews, 1997), 146.
10. Morris's translation of the *Aeneid* makes it 'sound more like an Anglo-Saxon poem than a translation of Virgil'. Gransden, K.W., ed., *Virgil in English* (Harmondsworth, 1996), xxix.
11. Mendelson, Edward, ed., *The English Auden: Poems, Essays, and Dramatic Writings 1927–1939* (London, 1977), 243.
12. *The Cantos of Ezra Pound* (London, 1975), Canto LXXXIII, 528, line 5.
13. Morris: 'If a chap can't compose an epic poem while he's weaving tapestry he had better shut up.' MacCarthy, Fiona, *William Morris* (London, 1994), 262.
14. *The Cantos of Ezra Pound*, Canto LXXIV, 426.
15. Gardner, W.H., ed., *Poems and Prose of Gerard Manley Hopkins* (Harmondsworth, 1953), 171.
16. Ibid., 245.
17. Gladstone wrote on the half-title of his copy of Cobbett, in 1837: 'A "rollicking", impudent, mendacious book; most readable; with great art and felicity of narration ... Here truly is a man master of his work, not servant of it.' In a letter of 1885, Ruskin called Cobbett's 'little *History of the Reformation*, the only true one ever written as far as it reaches', adding 'the sum of my 44 years of thinking on the matter ... has led me to agree with Cobbett in all his main ideas, and there is no question whatever, that Protestant writers are, as a rule, ignorant and false in what they say of Catholics – while Catholic writers are as a rule both well-informed and fair'. Wheeler, Michael, *The Old Enemies: Catholic and Protestant in Nineteenth-Century English Culture* (Cambridge, 2006), 142.
18. Gardner, *Poems and Prose of Gerard Manley Hopkins*, 234.
19. Abbott, C.C., ed., *The Correspondence of G.M. Hopkins and R.W. Dixon*, 2nd edn (Oxford, 1955), 98.
20. Ibid., 99.

21. Letter of 7 September 1888. Abbott, C.C., ed., *Letters of G.M. Hopkins to Robert Bridges* (Oxford, 1935), 284.
22. Gardner, *Poems and Prose of Gerard Manley Hopkins*, 11.
23. Ibid., 184.
24. 'Attempting to convince the sceptical Robert Bridges of the pedigree of sprung rhythm, Hopkins writes in a letter dated 18 October 1882: "So far as I know – I am enquiring and presently I shall be able to speak more decidedly – it existed in full force in Anglo saxon verse and in great beauty; in a degraded and doggerel shape in *Piers Ploughman* (I am reading that famous poem and coming to the conclusion that it is not worth reading)." From this it is clear that by 1882 Hopkins had not read much, if any, Anglo-Saxon poetry in the original. A few weeks later he wrote: "in fact I am learning Anglosaxon and it is a vastly superior thing to what we have now." Tantalisingly (and perhaps tellingly), that reference is the last he makes in any of the surviving correspondence to his study of Anglo-Saxon. We are left to guess at which texts he read, in which editions, how long he continued his study, and indeed whether the poetry lived up to his high expectations.' Jones, Chris, *A Deeper 'Well of English Undefyled': The Role and Influence of Anglo-Saxon in Nineteenth- and Twentieth-Century Poetry, with Particular Reference to Hopkins, Pound and Auden* (Ph.D., St Andrews, 2001), 57–8.
25. Ibid.
26. Colmer, J., ed., *Coleridge: Selected Poems* (Oxford, 1967), 141, lines 58–64.

CHAPTER 10: AMONG THE LILIES AND THE WEEDS

1. Vinaver, Eugène, ed., *Malory: Works*, 2nd edn (Oxford, 1971), 618. Spelling modernised.
2. Gardner, W.H., ed., *Poems and Prose of Gerard Manley Hopkins* (Harmondsworth, 1953), 174.
3. Prettejohn, Elizabeth, *Rossetti and his Circle* (London, 1997), 12.
4. *On The Death of Chatterton*, see Hilton, Timothy, *The Pre-Raphaelites* (London, 1970), 122.
5. Gardner, *Poems and Prose of Gerard Manley Hopkins*, 196.
6. Prettejohn, *Rossetti and his Circle*, 52.
7. Ibid., 59.
8. Hewison, Robert et al., *Ruskin, Turner and the Pre-Raphaelites* (London, 2000), 243.
9. Ricks, Christopher, ed., *The Poems of Tennyson* (London, 1969), 1593, published as *Vivien* in 1859 (later 'Vivien and Merlin'); Prettejohn, *Rossetti and his Circle*, 62.
10. Prettejohn, *Rossetti and his Circle*, 45.
11. Ibid., 62.
12. Ibid., 35.
13. See the Malory epigraph to this chapter. Crane's Knight is too pale and slender for Lancelot, and has little in common with Spenser's Red-Crosse Knight, mentioned in Wilton, A. and Upstone, R., eds, *The Age of Rossetti, Burne-Jones and Watts: Symbolism in Britain 1860–1910* (London, 1998), 133.
14. Bradley, Ian, ed., *The Complete Annotated Gilbert and Sullivan* (Oxford, 1996), 269.
15. Ibid., *Patience*, Act I, 412–20.
16. Wilton and Upstone, eds, *The Age of Rossetti, Burne-Jones and Watts*, 222.
17. Bradley, *The Complete Annotated Gilbert and Sullivan*, 451.
18. Ullathorne was the name of the first Bishop of Birmingham (1850–88). See Champ, Judith, *William Bernard Ullathorne 1806–1889: A Different Kind of Monk* (Leominster, 2006).

19. Bristow, J., ed., *The Cambridge Companion to Victorian Poetry* (Cambridge, 2002), 229. For the effect on T.S. Eliot of reading Symons's *The Symbolist Movement in French Poetry* (1899) in 1908, see Press, John, *A Map of Modern English Verse* (Oxford, 1977), 71.

20. See Pearce, Joseph, *Literary Converts* (San Francisco, 1999), 3, an account based on Ellmann's biography of Wilde.

CHAPTER 11: 'I HAVE SEEN . . . A WHITE HORSE'

1. Pearce, Joseph, *Literary Converts* (San Francisco, 1999), 244ff.

2. Bergonzi, B., *T.S. Eliot* (London, 1972), 39.

3. Finberg, H.P.R., *The Formation of England 550–1042* (London, 1976). 'The Turn of the Tide' is the title of Vol. X of Churchill's *History of the Second World War*.

4. Pearce, *Literary Converts*, 420.

5. Alexander, M., 'Tennyson's "Battle of Brunanburh"', *Tennyson Research Bulletin* 4.4 (1985), 151–62.

6. Pearce, *Literary Converts*, 51. Chesterton, G.K., *Autobiography* (London, 1937; Sevenoaks, 1992), 10.

7. Jenkins, Roy, *Churchill* (London, 2001), 224.

8. Pearce, *Literary Converts*, 199.

9. Ibid., 69.

10. Ibid., 192.

11. See MacCarthy, Fiona, *Eric Gill* (London, 1989); Miles, Jonathan, *Eric Gill and David Jones at Capel-y-ffin* (Bridgend, 1992).

12. Hyde, who later involved himself in liberation theology in South America, left the Catholic Church, believing it had drawn back from radical action against social injustice. Pearce, *Literary Converts*, 244ff.

13. See MacBride White, Anna and Norman Jeffares, A., eds, *The Gonne–Yeats Letters, 1893–1938* (London and New York, 1992), 391.

14. *Hugh Selwyn Mauberley*, in *Personae of Ezra Pound* (New York, 1926). Fitzgerald's *Rubaiyat* (1859) was 'discovered' in 1861 by D.G. Rossetti. See also note 8 to Ch. 8.

15. Alexander, Michael, *The Poetic Achievement of Ezra Pound* (London, 1978; Edinburgh, 1998).

CHAPTER 12: MODERNIST MEDIEVALISM

1. Eliot quotations from *Complete Poems and Plays of T.S. Eliot* (London, 1969).

2. Eliot, T.S., ed., *Selected Poems of Ezra Pound* (London, 1928), 17.

3. Modernised from Caxton's text: 'And so bifelle grete pestylence and grete harme to both Realmes for sythen encrecyd neyther corne ne grasse nor wel nyghe no fruyte, ne in the water was no fysshe werfor men callen this the landes of the two marches the waste land.' Southam, B.C., *A Student's Guide to the Selected Poems of T.S. Eliot*, 6th edn (London, 1994), 135, is convenient for such references.

4. Ibid., 166.

5. Cookson, William, ed., *Ezra Pound: Selected Prose* (London, 1973), 434.

6. See 'Foules in the frith', Duncan, T.G., ed., *Medieval English Lyrics 1200–1400* (Harmondsworth, 1995), 16; Southam, *A Student's Guide to the Selected Poems of T.S. Eliot*, 138.

7. Pound, Ezra, *The Cantos of Ezra Pound* (London, 1975). Eliot's 'Mr Eliot's Sunday Morning Service' makes comparable use of Piero della Francesca's *Baptism of Christ*.

8. The signed column is inscribed: 'Adaminus de S(an)c(t)o Georgio me fecit' – 'Little Adam of St George made me'. See the discussion in Ruskin, John, *The Stones of Venice*, 3 volume popular edition (London, 1908), Vol. 1, 320–1, and Pl.

17, facing 318. Hugh Kenner's *The Pound Era* (London, 1971), 323–4, has a photograph of this column on 232.

9. Pound, *The Cantos* (1975), LXXV, 432–3.

10. Ibid., LXXX, 511.

11. Ibid., 507; for Furnivall, see ibid., note 193.

12. See Alexander, M., 'Images of Venice in the Poetry of Ezra Pound', in Zorzi, R. Mamoli, ed., *Ezra Pound a Venezia* (Florence, 1985).

13. Pearce, Joseph, *Literary Converts* (San Francisco, 1999), 188.

14. Jones, David, *The Sleeping Lord and Other Fragments* (London, 1974), 9.

15. Langland, William, *The Vision of Piers Plowman, A Complete Edition of the B-Text*, ed. Schmidt, A.V.C. (London, 1984), Passus xvii, 22–3.

16. Pearce, *Literary Converts*, 209.

17. Jones, David, *In Parenthesis* (London, 1937, 1963), 165.

18. Ibid., 185.

19. Fussell, Paul, *The Great War and Modern Memory* (Oxford, 1975).

20. Glover, Jon and Silkin, Jon, eds, *The Penguin Book of First World War Prose* (Harmondsworth, 1988), 8–9. Corcoran, Neil, 'Spilled Bitterness: *In Parenthesis* in History', in Matthias, J., ed., *David Jones: Man and Poet* (Orono, Maine, 1995), 209–26.

21. A Christian heroism is to be found in the Anglo-Saxon poem 'The Dream of the Rood', where the Redeemer himself is presented as a young hero eager to meet death. See Plate 26.

22. Pearce, *Literary Converts*, 102.

CHAPTER 13: TWENTIETH-CENTURY CHRISTENDOM

1. Thom Gunn wrote of Ezra Pound, 'His politics were abhorrent, but if we forgive Hazlitt for his admiration of Napoleon then we should be prepared to do likewise to Pound for his delusions about Mussolini. And at least he apologized for his anti-Semitism at the last minute, which is more than his genteeler contemporaries did. In any case, he is demonstrably a poet of the highest order.' Gunn was introducing his *Ezra Pound: Poems selected by Thom Gunn* (London, 2000).

2. Mendelson, Edward, ed., *The English Auden: Poems, Essays, and Dramatic Writings 1927–1939* (London, 1977), xviii.

3. Dickens was published by Chapman and Hall, whose chairman was Arthur Waugh, the father of Evelyn; who liked to kill two birds with one stone.

4. Waugh, Evelyn, *Sword of Honour*, 'a final version of the novels *Men at Arms* (1952), *Officers and Gentlemen* (1955) and *Unconditional Surrender* (1961)' (London, 1965), 15.

5. Ibid. The trilogy has other medievalist moments: 'Childermas', 695; 'Guy, you're being *chivalrous*', 698; 'The Last Battle', 700; *'facilius loqui latine'*, 749. The (fictional) regiment Guy joins is the Halbardiers, called after a medieval weapon still carried by the Swiss Guard at the Vatican.

6. Tolkien, J.R.R., 'The Homecoming of Beorhtnoth Beorhthelm's Son', *Essays and Studies by Members of the English Association*, New Series Volume VI (London, 1953), 1–18.

7. Osborne, Charles, *W.H. Auden: The Life of a Poet* (London, 1980), 12.

8. Jones, Chris, 'W.H. Auden and "the 'Barbaric' poetry of the North": Unchaining one's Daimon', *Review of English Studies* 53, 210 (2002).

9. Auden, W.H., *A Certain World: A Commonplace Book* (London, 1971), 22–4.

10. Auden, W.H., *The Dyer's Hand* (London, 1963), 41.

11. Spender, Stephen, ed., *W.H. Auden: A Tribute* (New York, 1975), 44.

12. Jones, Chris, *Strange Likeness: The Use of Old English in Twentieth-Century Poetry* (Oxford, 2006), Ch. 2.

13. Ibid.

14. Auden, W.H., *The Orators: An English Study* (London, 1932), III, 5; Mendelson, Edward, ed. *The English Auden: Poems, Essays, and Dramatic Writings 1927–1939* (London, 1977), 108.

15. McCrum, Robert, *Wodehouse: A Life* (London, 2004), 31.

16. 'From the very first coming down', Mendelson, *The English Auden*, poem vii.

17. Ibid., *Introduction*, xviii.

18. Auden, W.H., *Collected Shorter Poems 1927–1957* (London, 1966), 200.

19. Jones, Chris, *A Deeper 'Well of English Undefyled': The Role and Influence of Anglo-Saxon in Nineteenth- and Twentieth-Century Poetry, with Particular Reference to Hopkins, Pound and Auden* (Ph.D., St Andrews, 2001), 57–8.

20. Thwaite, A., ed., *Philip Larkin: Collected Poems* (London, 1988).

21. Motion, Andrew, *Philip Larkin* (London, 1982), 37.

22. Eliot, T.S., *Selected Essays* (London, 1951), 16.

23. Press, John, *A Map of Modern English Verse* (Oxford, 1977), 258–9. On sabbatical at All Souls' College, Oxford, Larkin was 'falling over backward to be thought philistine'. Bennett, Alan, *Writing Home* (London, 1998), 571.

24. Hill, Geoffrey, *Mercian Hymns* (London, 1971).

EPILOGUE

1. For Peter Brown, see above Ch. 7, note 2.

2. Sir Howard Newby, quoted in *The Oxford Magazine* 239 (Oxford, Fourth Week, Trinity Term, 2005), 1.

3. See Bowden, Betsy, 'Gloom and Doom in Mark Twain's *Connecticut Yankee*, from Thomas Malory's *Morte Darthur*', *Studies in American Fiction*, 28, 2 (Autumn 2000), 179–202.

4. J.K. Rowling is said to have retained her initials in order not to alienate boys unlikely to open a story by a female author.

5. There has been so much revision of the received versions of English history that it is invidious to mention names, but among those which should be mentioned are Eamon Duffy, Norman Davies and Linda Colley. See also Jones, Edwin, *The English Nation: The Great Myth* (Stroud, 1998).

Bibliography

Abbott, C.C., ed., *The Correspondence of G.M. Hopkins and R.W. Dixon*, 2nd edn (Oxford, 1955).

Abbott, C.C., ed., *Letters of G.M. Hopkins to Robert Bridges* (Oxford, 1935).

Abrams, M.H. and Greenblatt, S., eds, *The Norton Anthology of English Literature*, 7th edn (New York, 2000).

Alexander, Michael, *The Poetic Achievement of Ezra Pound* (London, 1978; Edinburgh, 1998).

Anderson, W.E.K., ed., *The Journal of Sir Walter Scott*, rev. edn (Edinburgh, 1998).

Andrews, Brian, *Australian Gothic* (Melbourne, 2001).

Atterbury, Paul and Wainwright, Clive, eds, *Pugin: A Gothic Passion* (London, 1994).

Auden, W.H., *A Certain World: A Commonplace Book* (London, 1971).

Auden, W.H., *Collected Shorter Poems 1927–1957* (London, 1966).

Auden, W.H., *The Dyer's Hand* (London, 1963).

Auden, W.H., *The Orators: An English Study* (London, 1932).

Auden, W.H. and Taylor, P., trans, *Norse Poems* (London, 1983).

Austen, Jane, *The History of England by a partial, prejudiced & ignorant Historian, 1791* (Harmondsworth, 1995).

Barnard, J., ed., *John Keats: The Complete Poems*, 2nd edn (Harmondsworth, 1977).

Barringer, Tim, *The Pre-Raphaelites* (London, 1998).

Beerbohm, Sir Max, *The Poets' Corner*, with introduction by John Rothenstein (Harmondsworth, 1943).

Bennett, Alan, *Writing Home* (London, 1998).

Benson, L.D., ed., *The Riverside Chaucer*, 3rd edn (Oxford, 1987).

Bergonzi, B., *T.S. Eliot* (London, 1972).

Blake, Robert, *Disraeli* (London, 1966).

Blake, William, 'On Virgil', *The Complete Writings of William Blake*, ed. Keynes, Geoffrey, 2nd edn (Oxford, 1966).

Bradley, Ian, ed., *The Complete Annotated Gilbert and Sullivan* (Oxford, 1996).

Bristow, J., ed., *The Cambridge Companion to Victorian Poetry* (Cambridge, 2002).

Brittain-Catlin, Timothy, Maeyer, Jan de and Bressani, Martin, eds, *Gothic Revival Worldwide: A.W.N. Pugin's Global Influence* (Leuven, 2017).

Brown, Peter, *The Rise of Western Christendom*, 2nd edn (Oxford, 2003).

Buchan, John, *Life of Sir Walter Scott* (London, 1932).

Burke, Edmund, *Reflections on the Revolution in France*, ed. Mitchell, L.G. (Oxford, 1993).

Butt, J., ed., *The Poems of Alexander Pope, A One-Volume Edition of the Twickenham Pope*, rev. edn (London, 1968).

Carey, J. and Fowler, A., eds, *Poems of John Milton* (London, 1968).

Carley, James, *Glastonbury Abbey: The Holy House at the Head of the Moors Adventurous*, rev. edn (Glastonbury, 1996).

Carlyle, Thomas, *Past and Present* (London, 1843, 1872).

Champ, Judith, *The English Pilgrimage to Rome* (Leominster, 2000).

Champ, Judith, *William Bernard Ullathorne 1806–1889: A Different Kind of Monk* (Leominster, 2006).

Chesterton, G.K., *Collected Poems*, 8th edn (London, 1941).

Clark, Kenneth, *The Gothic Revival: An Essay in the History of Taste* (London, 1928).

Colmer, J., ed., *Coleridge: Selected Poems* (Oxford, 1967).

Cookson, William, ed., *Ezra Pound: Selected Prose* (London, 1973).

Crawford, T., ed., *Sir Walter Scott: Selected Poems* (Oxford, 1972).

Crump, R.W., ed., *Christina Rossetti: The Complete Poems* (Harmondsworth, 2001).

Davis, N., *Sweet's Anglo-Saxon Primer*, 9th edn (Oxford, 1970).

Digby, Sir Kenelm, *The Broad Stone of Honour*, 1822. *The First Book: Godefredus* (London, 1829).

Disraeli, Benjamin, *Lothair*, ed. Bogdanor, Vernon (Oxford, 1975).

Disraeli, Benjamin, *Sybil; or, The Two Nations*, ed. Smith, Sheila (Oxford, 1998).

Doyle, William, *The French Revolution* (Oxford, 2001).

Duncan, T.G., ed., *Medieval English Lyrics 1200–1400* (Harmondsworth, 1995).

Duncan-Jones, Katherine, ed., *Sir Philip Sidney* (Oxford, 1989).

Eliot, T.S., *The Complete Poems and Plays* (London, 1969).

Eliot, T.S., *Selected Essays* (London, 1951).

Eliot, T.S., *The Waste Land, a facsimile and transcript*, ed. Eliot, Valerie (London, 1971).

Eliot, T.S., ed., *Selected Poems of Ezra Pound* (London, 1928).

Ellis, George, ed., *Specimens of Early English Metrical Romances*, 3 vols (London, 1805).

Ellis, Steve, *Geoffrey Chaucer*, Writers and their Work, British Council (London, 1996).

Everett, Barbara, review article on Coleridge, *London Review of Books*, 7 August 2003.

Fairer, D. and Gerrard, C., eds, *Eighteenth-Century Poetry* (Oxford, 1999).

Finberg, H.P.R., *The Formation of England 550–1042* (London, 1976).

Fussell, Paul, *The Great War and Modern Memory* (Oxford, 1975).

Gardner, W.H., ed., *Poems and Prose of Gerard Manley Hopkins* (Harmondsworth, 1953).

Gilmour, David, *The Long Recessional* (London, 2003).

Girouard, Mark, *Return to Camelot: Chivalry and the English Gentleman* (London, 1981).

Glover, Jon and Silkin, Jon, eds, *The Penguin Book of First World War Prose* (Harmondsworth, 1988).

Goebel, Stefan, *The Great War and Medieval Memory: War, Remembrance and Medievalism in Britain and Germany, 1914–1940* (New York, 2007).

Gransden, K.W., ed., *Virgil in English* (Harmondsworth, 1996).

Gray, Douglas, ed., *The Oxford Book of Late Medieval Verse and Prose* (Oxford, 1985).

Gunn, Thom, ed., *Ezra Pound: Poems selected by Thom Gunn* (London, 2000).

Hall, J.R., 'The First Two Editions of Beowulf: Thorkelin's (1815) and Kemble's (1833)', *The Editing of Old English: Papers from the 1990 Manchester Conference*, ed. Scragg, D.G. and Szarmach, Paul E. (Woodbridge, 1994).

Hardy, F.E., *The Life of Thomas Hardy* (London, 1962).

Hayden, John O., ed., *William Wordsworth, The Poems*, 2 vols (Harmondsworth, 1977).

Hewison, Robert et al., *Ruskin, Turner and the Pre-Raphaelites* (London, 2000).

Hill, Geoffrey, *Mercian Hymns* (London, 1971).

Hill, Rosemary, *God's Architect: Pugin and the Building of Romantic Britain* (Harmondsworth, 2007).

Hilton, Timothy, *The Pre-Raphaelites* (London, 1970).

Hunter Blair, Right Rev. Sir David, *John Patrick, Third Marquess of Bute, K.T.* (London, 1921).

Jacobi, Carol and Kingsley, Hope, *Painting with Light* (London, 2016).

Jenkins, Roy, *Churchill* (London, 2001).

Johnson, Edgar, *Sir Walter Scott: The Great Unknown* (London, 1970).

Johnston, Arthur, *Enchanted Ground: The Study of Medieval Romance in the Eighteenth Century* (London, 1964).

Jones, Chris, *A Deeper 'Well of English Undefyled': The Role and Influence of Anglo-Saxon in Nineteenth- and Twentieth-Century Poetry, with Particular Reference to Hopkins, Pound and Auden* (Ph.D., St Andrews, 2001).

Jones, Chris, *Strange Likeness: The Use of Old English in Twentieth-Century Poetry* (Oxford, 2006).

Jones, Chris, 'W.H. Auden and "the 'Barbaric' poetry of the North"': Unchaining one's Daimon', *Review of English Studies* 53, 210 (2002).

Jones, David, *In Parenthesis* (London, 1937, 1963).

Jones, David, *The Sleeping Lord and Other Fragments* (London, 1974).

Jones, Edwin, *The English Nation: The Great Myth* (Stroud, 1998).

Jones, Emrys, ed., *The New Oxford Book of Sixteenth-Century Verse* (Oxford, 1992).

Keegan, Paul, ed., *New Penguin Book of English Verse* (Harmondsworth, 2000).

Kemble, John M., ed., *The Anglo-Saxon Poems of Beowulf, The Traveller's Song, and the Battle of Finnesburh* (London, 1833); 2nd edn, I (1835), II, Translation, Introduction, Notes, Glossary (London, 1837).

Kenner, Hugh, *The Pound Era* (London, 1971).

Ker, Ian, *The Catholic Revival in English Literature, 1845–1961: Newman, Hopkins, Belloc, Chesterton, Greene, Waugh* (Notre Dame, Indiana, 2003).

Ker, Ian, *John Henry Newman: A Biography* (Oxford, 1988).

Langland, William, *The Vision of Piers Plowman, A Complete Edition of the BText*, ed. Schmidt, A.V.C. (London, 1984).

Lewis, C.S., *'De Descriptione Temporum', Essays in Criticism* (1956), VI, 247.

Lewis, Michael J., *The Gothic Revival* (London, 2002).

Liuzza, R.M., *Beowulf, A New Verse Translation* (Ontario, 2000).

MacCarthy, Fiona, *Eric Gill* (London, 1989).

MacCarthy, Fiona, *William Morris* (London, 1994).

Macrides, R.J., 'The Scottish Connexion in Byzantine and Modern Greek Studies', St John's House Papers No. 4 (St Andrews, 1992).

Malory, Sir Thomas, *Le Morte Darthur*, ed. Shepherd, Stephen H.A. (New York and London, 2004).

Malory, Sir Thomas, *Le Morte Darthur: The Winchester Manuscript*, ed. Cooper, Helen (Oxford, 1998).

Mancoff, Debra N., *The Return of King Arthur: The Legend through Victorian Eyes* (New York and London, 1995).

Martin, R.B., *Tennyson: The Unquiet Heart* (London, 1980).

Matthews, David, *Medievalism, A Critical History* (Martlesham, 2015) – a key volume in the Medievalism series published by Boydell and Brewer, a series which is bringing out a number of specialised scholarly studies.

Matthias, J., ed., *David Jones: Man and Poet* (Orono, Maine, 1995).

Mendelson, Edward, ed., *The English Auden: Poems, Essays, and Dramatic Writings 1927–1939* (London, 1977).

Meyerstein, E.H.W., *A Life of Thomas Chatterton* (London, 1930).

Miles, Jonathan, *Eric Gill and David Jones at Capel-y-ffin* (Bridgend, 1992).

Mordaunt Crook, J., *The Problem of Style* (Chicago, 1987).

Mordaunt Crook, J., *William Burges and the High Victorian Dream* (London, 1981).

Motion, Andrew, *Philip Larkin* (London, 1982).

Murray, K.M. Elizabeth, *Caught in the Web of Words: James A.H. Murray and the Oxford English Dictionary* (London, 1977).

Murray, Peter and Linda, eds, *The Oxford Companion to Christian Art and Architecture* (Oxford, 1996).

Newman, J.H., *Apologia pro Vita Sua*, ed. Ker, Ian (Harmondsworth, 1994).

Onions, C.T., *Sweet's Anglo-Saxon Reader* (Oxford, 1959).

Osborne, Charles, *W.H. Auden: The Life of a Poet* (London, 1980).

Panofsky, Erwin, *Renaissance and Renascences in Western Art* (New York, 1969).

Parry, Linda, *William Morris* (London, 1996).

Pearce, Joseph, *Literary Converts* (San Francisco, 1999).

Pearsall, Derek, *The Life of Geoffrey Chaucer* (Oxford, 1992).

Percy, Thomas, *Reliques of Ancient English Poetry*, ed. Walford, Edward (London, 1880).

Pevsner, Nikolaus, *London I: The Cities of London and Westminster*, The Buildings of England (Harmondsworth, 1957).

Pound, Ezra, *The Cantos* (London, 1975).

Press, John, *A Map of Modern English Verse* (Oxford, 1977).

Prettejohn, Elizabeth, *Art for Art's Sake: Aestheticism in Victorian Painting* (London, 2007).

Prettejohn, Elizabeth, *Rossetti and his Circle* (London, 1997).

Priestley, J.B., ed., *The Novels of Thomas Love Peacock* (London, 1967).

Ricks, Christopher, ed., *The Poems of Tennyson* (London, 1969).

Riding, C. and Riding, J., eds, *The Houses of Parliament: History, Art, Architecture* (London, 2000).

Robinson, Fred, *The Tomb of Beowulf and Other Essays on Old English* (Oxford, 1993).

Rossetti, W.M., ed., *The Works of Dante Gabriel Rossetti* (London, 1911).

Ruskin, John, *The Stones of Venice*, 3 vols popular edition (London, 1908).

Saintsbury, George, *A Short History of English Literature* (London, 1898, 1908).

Saunders, Corinne, ed., *A Companion to Romance: Classical to Contemporary* (Oxford, 2004).

Scott, Walter, *Ivanhoe*, ed. Duncan, Ian (Oxford, 1996).

Scott, Walter, *Ivanhoe*, ed. Tulloch, Graham, Penguin rev. edn of the Edinburgh Edition of the Waverley Novels (Harmondsworth, 2000).

Scott, Walter, *The Monastery* (London, 1878).

Scott, Walter, *Poems by Sir Walter Scott* (Oxford, 1913).

Scott, Sir Walter, *Works*, Wordsworth Poetry Library (London, 1995).

Sisam, Kenneth, ed., *Fourteenth Century Verse and Prose* (Oxford, 1921, 1975).

Southam, B.C., *A Student's Guide to the Selected Poems of T.S. Eliot*, 6th edn (London, 1994).

Spenser, Edmund, *The Faerie Queene*, ed. Roche, T.P. (Harmondsworth, 1978).

Sutherland, John, *The Life of Walter Scott: A Critical Biography* (Oxford, 1995).

Thorkelin, G.J., ed., *De Danorum rebus gestis secul. III & IV, poema danicum dialecto anglosaxonica* (Copenhagen, 1815).

Thwaite, A., ed., *Philip Larkin: Collected Poems* (London, 1988).

Tolkien, J.R.R., 'The Homecoming of Beorhtnoth Beorhthelm's Son', *Essays and Studies by Members of the English Association*, New Series Volume VI (London, 1953).

Trevor, Meriol, *Newman's Journey* (London, 1962).

Turner, Sharon, *The History of the Manners, Landed Property, Government, Laws, Poetry, Literature, Religion and Language of the Anglo-Saxons* (London, 1805).

Vinaver, Eugène, ed., *Malory: Works*, 2nd edn (Oxford, 1971).

Walpole, Horace, *The Castle of Otranto*, ed. Lewis, W.S., introduced by E.J. Clery (Oxford, 1998).

Waugh, Evelyn, *Sword of Honour*, 'a final version of the novels *Men at Arms* (1952), *Officers and Gentlemen* (1955) and *Unconditional Surrender* (1961)' (London, 1965).

Wheeler, Michael, *The Old Enemies: Catholic and Protestant in Nineteenth-Century English Culture* (Cambridge, 2006).

Wheeler, Michael, *Ruskin's God* (Cambridge, 1999).

Whiteley, Jon, *Oxford and the Pre-Raphaelites* (Oxford, 1969).

Wilton, A. and Upstone, R., eds, *The Age of Rossetti, Burne-Jones and Watts: Symbolism in Britain 1860–1910* (London, 1998).

Woodbridge, Keith, *The Stourhead Landscape* (London, 1986, 2002).

Zorzi, R. Mamoli, ed., *Ezra Pound a Venezia* (Florence, 1985).

Index